Do It Yourself
Networking with LANtastic®

Do It Yourself

Networking with LANtastic®

Mark Gibbs

A Division of Prentice Hall Computer Publishing
11711 North College, Carmel, Indiana 46032 USA

 *To my wife, Arianne, and my family on both sides of the Atlantic.*

©1992 by Sams Publishing

All rights reserved. No part of this book shall be reproduced, stored in a retrieval system, or transmitted by any means, electronic, mechanical, photocopying, recording, or otherwise, without written permission from the publisher. No patent liability is assumed with respect to the use of the information contained herein. Although every precaution has been taken in the preparation of this book, the publisher and author assume no responsibility for errors or omissions. Neither is any liability assumed for damages resulting from the use of the information contained herein. For information, address Sams Publishing, 11711 N. College Ave., Carmel, IN 46032.

International Standard Book Number: 0-672-30026-5

Library of Congress Catalog Card Number: 92-60386

95 94 93 92   8 7 6 5 4 3 2 1

Interpretation of the printing code: the rightmost number of the first series of numbers is the year of the book's printing; the rightmost number of the second series of numbers is the number of the book's printing. For example, a printing code of 92-1 shows that the first printing of the book occurred in 1992.

Screen reproductions in this book were created by means of the program Collage Plus from Inner Media, Inc., Hollis, NH.

Printed in the United States of America

Publisher
Richard K. Swadley

Associate Publisher
Marie Butler-Knight

Managing Editor
Elizabeth Keaffaber

Product Development Manager
Lisa A. Bucki

Acquisitions Editor
Stephen Poland

Development Editor
Wayne Blankenbeckler

Senior Production Editor
Linda Hawkins

Copy Editor
Howard Peirce

Editorial Assistant
Hilary Adams

Cover Designer
Tim Amrhein

Designer
Michele Laseau

Indexer
Johnna L. VanHoose

Production Team
Paula Carroll
Keith Davenport
Terri Edwards
Tim Groeling
Carla Hall-Batton
Carrie Keesling
Phil Kitchel
Betty Kish
Linda Quigley
Linda Seifert
Kelli Widdifield
Allan Wimmer

Special thanks to Rick Roth for ensuring the technical accuracy of this book

About the author

Mark Gibbs was cofounder of Novell's UK operation, where he was responsible for the management of all technical services. He was with Novell five years and, since leaving, has pursued a successful career as an independent consultant.

Prior to Novell, Gibbs created and managed the technical support and consulting services for Digital Microsystems, Ltd. and managed software development and technical support for Oberon International, an OCR company. He has also had a career as a scientific programmer.

He recently completed a special research report for Patricia Seybold's Office Computing Group on corporate strategies for dealing with computer viruses. Also for Seybold, he developed the recently released research report *PC LAN E-mail Architectures.* He is coauthor of *Networking Personal Computers,* Third Edition (Que, 1989) and holds a degree in architecture from Plymouth School of Architecture, Plymouth, England.

Contents

Acknowledgments	xvii
Introduction	xix

1 Introduction: Why Network? — 1

What Is a Network for?	3
Sharing Data and Documents	3
Sharing Peripherals	6
Office Communications	8
Managing Your PCs	9
So, What Will Networks Give Your Organization?	10
Summary	11

2 The Basics of Networking — 13

Networking Hardware	15
Networking Software	18
Summary	21

3 The LANtastic Networking System — 23

LANtastic Network Hardware	24
Personal Computers	24
Peripherals	24
Standard Communications	26
Add-in Communications Boards	26
A View from the Top	27
Local Services	29
DOS Support	29
File-Sharing Services	29
The Network Interface Subsystem	30
Network Interface Card Drivers	30
The NETBIOS	32

The Network Operating System	32
The Redirector	34
The Server	35
The LANCACHE.EXE Utility	37
The ALONE Utility	37
Memory Matters	37
Remote Booting	39
Performance Considerations	40
LANtastic Network Utilities	40
Installation Utilities	41
Management Applications	41
Operations Utilities	41
Network Security	42
LANtastic Disk Organization	42
Applications in the LANtastic Environment	43
Summary	45

4 Planning Your Network   47

Needs Analysis	49
Problems	49
Identifying Your Problems	52
Goals	53
Identifying Your Goals	53
Site Analysis	55
Premises and Services	55
The Basic Plan	58
Selecting Equipment	61
Cost	61
Performance	61
Compatibility	62
Configuration Plans	64
The Detailed Configuration	64
The General Configuration	67
Naming Machines on the Network	70
Workstation, Workstation/Server, or Server Only?	70
What Functions Will Each Server Have?	71
Configuring the Servers	71
General Setup	71
Server Resources	76

The Timetable	76
Getting Sign-Off	83
Management	85

5 Selecting a Network Technology — 87

Cost and Performance Issues	88
Network Layout	90
Star	90
Bus	91
Ring	92
Daisy Chain	92
Tree	93
Appearances Can Be Deceiving	94
Network Adapter Design	94
Adapter Card Data Width	95
Bus Design	96
How Network Technologies Work	97
ARCnet	97
EtherNet	98
Token Ring	98
Making a Decision	99
Network Design Rules	100
ARCnet Design Rules	101
ARCnet Hardware	102
EtherNet Design Rules	103
EtherNet Hardware	104
Token Ring Design Rules	105
Token Ring Hardware	106
Repeaters, Bridges, and Routers	107
Making Decisions	108
Summary	110

6 Installing LANtastic — 113

Preparing for Installation	114
Advance Preparations	114
Day-of-Installation Preparations	115
Checklist: Installation Preparation	116
Hardware Installation	117

LANtastic Network Software Installation	121
Beginning the Installation	121
General Options	124
Machine Name:	124
Machine Type:	124
Installation Directory:	125
Network Startup Batch File:	125
Network Adapter Installed:	126
Adapter Drivers to Install:	126
Modify CONFIG.SYS:	127
Special Options	129
Printer Connections: (new installations only)	129
Disk Drive Connections: (new installations only)	133
Install Default Resources: (new server installations only)	136
Control Directory: (server installations only)	137
Perform Installation: Select to Install	137
Testing the PC's Network Hardware	139
Server Configuration	142
The STARTNET.BAT File	144
Starting the Network	147
Solutions to Common Problems	147
Reconfiguring Applications and Utilities	148
Summary	153

7 Shared Resources — 155

Disk Resources	156
Alternative Disk Resource Definitions	157
Rights	158
Shared Printers	159
Printer Resources	161
General Printer Configuration	162
Serial Printer Configuration	165
Mail Resource	166
Summary	168

8 Protecting Your Network — 169

The Concept of Security	169
Who and What Are You Protecting Your Network from?	170
Physical Threats	170
Flood	171
Fire	171
Theft	171
General Hardware Failures	171
Cable Failures	172
Hard Disk Failures	172
Nonphysical Threats	172
Users	173
Vandals	173
Software-related Problems	174
Login Security	175
User Names	176
Group Accounts	177
Passwords	178
Protecting Passwords	180
Controlling Access to the Server	181
Guest Accounts	182
Access Rights	183
How Access Control Lists Work	188
Account Privileges	190
Audit Trails	192
Summary	194

9 Avoiding and Solving Problems — 197

The Site Log	198
The Site	199
Physical Site	199
Power and Services	199
Network Layout	199
Equipment	199
Personal Computers	199
Printers	200
Other	200
Configuration	200
Server Configurations	200
Workstation Configurations	200

Printer Configurations	200
Miscellaneous Configurations	201
Procedures and Standards	201
Password Management	201
Backup and Restore Plan	201
Rules and Policies	201
Documentation	202
Receipts and Invoices	202
Warranties	202
Hardware and Software Manuals	202
History	202
Problems	203
Backup and Recovery	203
Network Backups	203
When to Back Up	204
Backing Up the Minimum	205
Backup Systems	205
Server Backup Devices	208
Creating a Backup Schedule	209
Archiving Files	211
System Managers, Supervisors, and Network Management	212
System Managers	212
System Supervisors	214
Diagnostic Disks	214
PC Diagnostics	215
Training	216
Background—Why You Have a Network	216
Services—What the Network Does	217
Use—What You Need to Know to Use the Network	217
Rules—What You Must, and Must Not, Do	217
The B.E.A.R. Approach to Solving Problems	218
Basics	219
Extend and Test	219
Analyze	220
Repair	220
The Problem Log	221
Basic System Diagnostic Procedure	221
Using Vendor Technical Support	226
Summary	230

10 Advanced Topics — 231

Working with Windows	232
WNET.EXE	233
WNET_MGR.EXE	236
Dynamic Data Exchange (DDE)	237
DR DOS	239
Batch Files for Networking	241
Central Station	242
Mixing LANtastic and NetWare	244
Multiple Network Adapters	245
Remote Control and Monitoring	246
Sharing Modems	248
Voice Mail	249
LANtastic Z	250
Expanding Your Disk Space	252
Summary	253

A Resources — 255

Artisoft	255
CompuServe	256
Microsoft Corporation	256
Uninterruptable Power Supplies	256
Magazines	257

B Forms — 259

C Utilities Reference — 277

Parameters	285
Switch Files	286
The REMOVE Switch	287
AILANBIO.EXE	289
AIMOVE.EXE	307
ALONE.EXE	309
LANCACHE.EXE	311
LANCHECK.EXE	325
LANPUP.EXE	327
NBSETUP.EXE	339

Networking with LANtastic

NET.EXE	345
NET_MGR.EXE	383
REDIR.EXE	393
SERVER.EXE	403
UPS.EXE	423
LANtastic Special Strings	435
Audio Warnings	440
The Menu Interfaces	441
LANCHECK	443
NET.EXE	451
NET_MGR.EXE	469

Glossary   499

Index   507

Foreword

When we launched the LANtastic network in 1987, we wanted to take the mystery and confusion out of connecting computers, while making it affordable and usable for everyone. We had high hopes back then. We wanted our network to do for computing what Volkswagen had done for cars: take what had been a product for the elite and bring it down to a workable level.

Our concept of an inexpensive, easy-to-use network has grown through several generations of software. The LANtastic system remains true to our original vision of a network "for the rest of us."

Do-It-Yourself Networking with Lantastic reflects the hands-on, user-friendly approach that has been the hallmark of our product. We wanted to make networking accessible to smaller businesses and nontechnical people, and easier for network technicians. But we could only have guessed how LANtastic networks would take the computing world by storm, first as a cult product, and more recently as a no-nonsense network for businesses interested in getting the most from their computers. We are delighted to see this guide to help you implement your network. Whether you use this book for a hands-on installation or to help you understand the issues your installer needs to consider, it will further your network education.

The challenge of doing more with less and simplifying the complex is what has made the computer industry more exciting from the beginning. It's been our privilege to help people use their machines to communicate with each other. We hope that using LANtastic makes you more productive and ultimately makes your work more rewarding. LANtastic networks are expanding to portable PCs, whether in the home office or on the road. We're adapting the system to accommodate Macintosh and other computing platforms.

Artisoft's success has made us more dedicated to our corporate mission to create innovative connectivity solutions that improve the productivity of the business community. While our product base grows, we remain committed to providing the means for people to communicate, to producing results, and to building a world that works for the twenty-first century.

C. John Schoof II
President and CEO
Artisoft, Inc.

Acknowledgments

I'd like to thank all of the following people:

At Artisoft: Scott Ehrsam, Paul Hubbard, Ken Johnson, Herb MacBride, Rick Roth, Neil Stevens, Joe Stunkard, Nora Tangemen, Joe Waldygo.

At Sams Publishing: Steve Poland, Wayne Blankenbeckler, Linda Hawkins, and Howard Peirce.

This book was developed using the following products: AE2 Network Adapters, LANtastic 4.1, LANtastic for Windows 4.10, Central Station, ArtiCom, Voice Adapters, The Network Eye, LANtastic for NetWare, NetWare Printer Server StationWare, LANtastic Printer Server StationWare, and LANtastic Z from Artisoft; DOS 5.0 from Microsoft; DR DOS 6.0 from Digital Research; Windows 3.1 from Microsoft; Designer v1.00 from Micrografx; Scanman 256 and Ansel from Logitech; Word for Windows v2.0a from Microsoft; Still River Shell from Bill White; cc:Mail from Lotus Development Corporation; OzCIS from Steve Sneed; Collage from Inner Media; Stacker v2.0 from Stac Electronics; SHEZ from Jim Derr; PKZIP and PKUNZIP from PKWARE; OnTarget from Symantec; Excel from Microsoft; Builder 2.0 from hyperkinetix; Scrapbook+ from Eikon; Packrat from Polaris Software; ZED from Zortech. Thanks, guys.

Trademark Acknowledgments

All terms mentioned in this book that are known to be trademarks or service marks are listed below. In addition, terms suspected of being trademarks or service marks have been appropriately capitalized. Sams Publishing cannot attest to the accuracy of this information. Use of a term in this book should not be regarded as affecting the validity of any trademark or service mark.

ARCnet is a registered trademark of Datapoint Corporation.

CompuServe Information Service is a registered trademark of CompuServe Incorporated and H&R Block, Inc.

 *Networking with LANtastic*

DR DOS is a trademark of Digital Research Inc.

IBM is a registered trademark of International Business Machines Corporation.

LANtastic, LANtastic Z, LANtastic for Windows, LANtastic for NetWare, LANtastic Central Station, ArtiCom, Sounding Board, Network Eye, Voice Adapter, AE/2, and 2Mbps are trademarks of Artisoft, Inc.

NetWare is a registered trademark of Novell, Inc.

Stacker is a trademark of Stac Electronics.

Windows is a trademark and MS-DOS is a registered trademark of Microsoft Corporation.

Introduction

You can become involved with networking in much the same way that you can become involved with cars. For a car, you can read the owner's manual, starting with the section that tells you how to start it and find the air-conditioning controls.

Since you can get someone else to put fuel in it, change the tires, and top off the coolant, you don't have to bother to read any further. This means that you have to rely on others to keep the thing running.

If you want to attain the next level of involvement, you can read the whole owner's manual from cover to cover so that you can do a lot more maintenance, including changing the tires and so on. You have now gained several benefits:

- You'll save money.
- You'll know exactly what's going on, which will save you money when you run into problems.
- You won't have to trust someone else to do the work correctly, which could save you even more money.

Consider this book a LANtastic network owner's manual. As a do-it-yourself networker, you want to be able to handle all the basics of getting your LANtastic system up and keeping it running — this book will give you all the information you need.

This book is designed for PC users who have a basic level of familiarity with MS-DOS and are comfortable with taking a PC apart and following instructions on how to enhance and modify the hardware.

You don't have to be a PC or a networking expert to install a LANtastic network system. All you need is a basic understanding of PCs, a working knowledge of MS-DOS at the command-line level, and the ability to follow instructions.

Right up front, I'll state the golden rule of managing computer systems:

Plan and document.

 *Networking with LANtastic*

Throughout this book, this will be a recurrent theme: it can make the difference between a networking nightmare and a straightforward, cost-effective service.

What You Should Know

You should have a basic understanding of:

- *Disk drives* — how they are named (that is, A, B, C, and so on), how they should be used, and how to make backups.
- *Files* — types of files, how they are named, and how to specify where files are.
- *Peripherals* — types of printers, what modems are for.
- *Communications* — the difference between serial and parallel connections (not an in-depth technical knowledge, just the fact that different devices use serial ports, others use parallel ports, and that they use different cables).
- *MS-DOS utilities* — how to list files and directories, how to copy, delete, and set the attributes of files, how to set environment strings, how to create and delete directories, and so on.
- *Batch files* — the basics of creating batch files and their uses.
- *Basic PC technology* — a basic appreciation of the PC system (again, not an in-depth, technical one).

Introduction: Why Network?

Open any computer magazine or trade paper that deals with *personal computers (PCs)* and the one word that you see almost as much as PC is *network*. Until a few years ago, no one took networking seriously — it was too expensive, too technical, too leading-edge, and too far from the mainstream of "real" computing. But now, networking has become not just a useful tool, but a fundamental way of organizing people and their work.

Many companies that have realized the value that networks might have to their business have been put off by the potential complexity and cost. This is because, until recently, the major market offerings were very elaborate, requiring considerable expertise and time to plan and implement.

The network revolution was started back in the early 1980s. The issue of having isolated PCs scattered around organizations was the driving force and the problem was how to connect them. The solution was what has come to be called a *network file server*. File servers are PCs that run software that allows other PCs (the server's clients) to share files, printers, and other resources. See Figure 1.1.

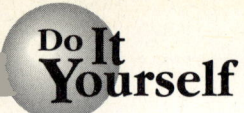

Networking with LANtastic

With the appearance of *peer-to-peer* networking systems such as Artisoft's LANtastic, complexity and cost are no longer problems. These networks, which we'll call simply "peer networks," are designed to be simple to install, configure, use, and manage. Instead of having one central PC that supplies services for clients as in the file-server systems, peer networks allow any PC to be a client, a server, or a client and server at the same time. This allows you to make the best use of the resources you have without having to become a networking expert.

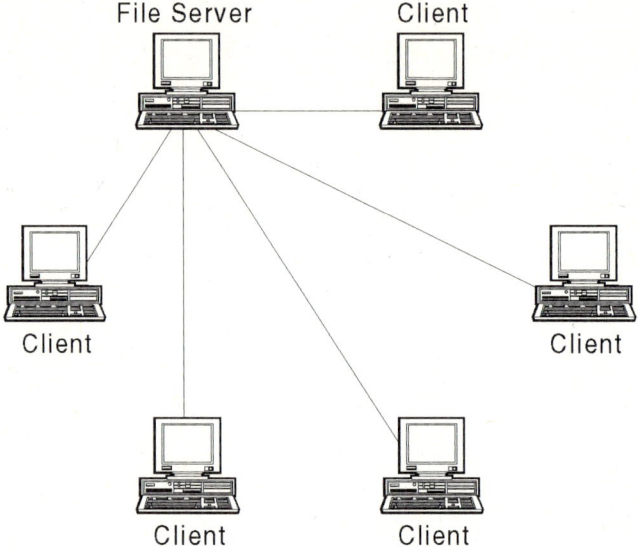

Figure 1.1 *The organization of a file-server system.*

If you are planning to network your company or department and you want to "Do-It-Yourself" without investing in extensive training and costly file-server systems, this book will show you how to use Artisoft's LANtastic networking products to achieve your goals. I'll cover:

- What a network is.
- How to design a network.
- How to implement a network.
- How to make your network support your company.
- How to keep your network running.
- How to solve problems.

Introduction: Why Network?

What Is a Network for?

Before I discuss what the components of a network are, you need to understand what benefits you can get from using one.

The most important thing that a network can do is organize people's work and the PCs that support their activities. Networks provide the means for people to:

- Share data (name and address lists, stock records).
- Share documents (reports, templates, letters).
- Share peripherals (hard disks, printers, plotters, modems).
- Communicate with each other.
- Improve the management of their PC resources.

As an example, look at the peer network at Acme Secretarial Services, Inc., shown in Figure 1.2. Jean has access to Pat's hard disk and Pat can use Jean's laser printer.

Sharing Data and Documents

When you have an organization with more than two or three PCs, you will often find that you need to share data (such as name and address information) or documents (such as word processing files). You could copy files from a PC's hard disk to one or more floppy disks and give them to another person, but there are problems with this approach:

Data integrity Floppy disks are pretty reliable, but they occasionally fail (this is signaled by messages such as `Data error on drive x`). They are also accidentally used as coffee mug coasters, or misplaced. While this can be easily cured using a new disk and recopying the data, it can be time consuming. With networks, file transfers are "reliable." That is, the network system guarantees that a file will be moved from one PC to another without errors.

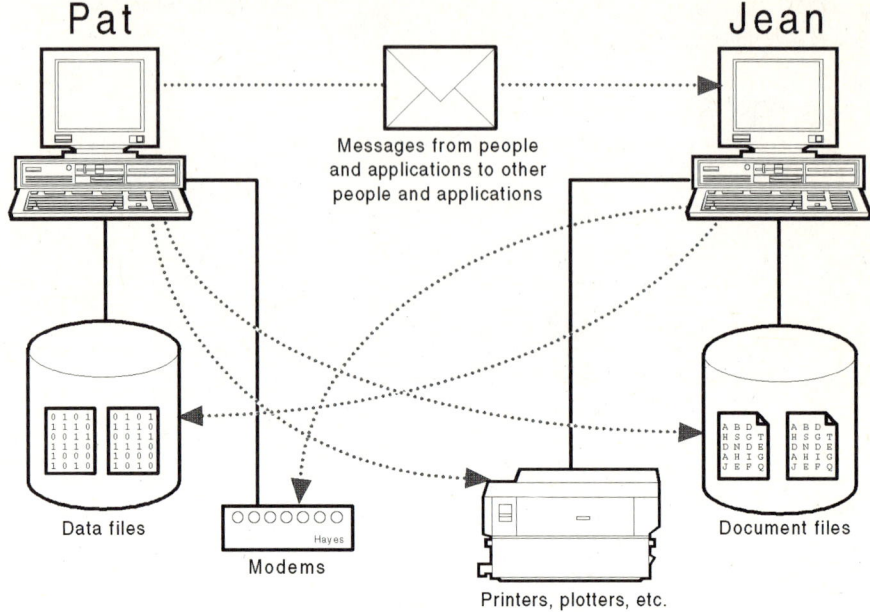

Figure 1.2 *A peer network, its resources, and some of the connections users can make to those resources.*

Speed   Even when reliability problems don't slow down the transfer process, floppy disks are very slow in comparison with hard disks. Networks are fast, running at anything from 10 to 100 times faster than a floppy disk.

Slow updates of information   In situations where one PC is used for data entry, for example, taking customer orders, and another is used to maintain account information, data will have to be transferred between the machines on some schedule, perhaps once or twice each day. Under these circumstances, the order taking system could show that a customer has exceeded their credit limit because the updated information from the accounting machine hasn't been transferred. Networking can make data and documents available when they are needed, and problems of information being old and out of date can be completely overcome.

Data loss and theft   If the data on the floppy disks has any degree of confidentiality, the disks either have to be carefully controlled or protected. In any case, if there are more than a few disks, ample opportunity will arise for the disks to be lost or stolen. Because networks have security systems that can limit individuals from accessing and using files, the problems of theft, unauthorized modification, and loss can be effectively controlled.

Wasted disk space   The need to keep multiple copies of data and documents will require each PC to allocate the same space for the same data. If each PC needs to have, say, a megabyte of common documents and there are 10 PCs, a total of 10 megabytes is needed, of which 90% is redundant. With networks, only one copy of the data or document is needed, so hard disk space isn't wasted.

Cost   The process of transferring the data will take someone a lot of time. If that person is an employee, there will be a definite cost involved in their labor. In addition, the redundant disk space has an associated cost, as well as the networking. But when all the factors are taken into account, it is often much less than manual transfers.

Taking all of these issues into consideration, transferring data between PCs that use floppy disks is only practical if it is rarely needed. Networking is an effective and efficient solution where transfers:

- Occur regularly.
- Involve a large volume of data.
- Need to be done on demand.

The ability to share data between several PCs and for users to see the results of each other's changes virtually instantaneously is something that isn't possible without a network. LANtastic allows you to build networks that will make sharing data efficient and cost-effective.

LANtastic can support the important industry networking standards such as EtherNet, and Artisoft offers versions of LANtastic that allow it to coexist with the top-end networking products such as Novell's NetWare. This means that you use an off-the-shelf product to create systems that can improve, if not revolutionize, the way that you do business.

Networking with LANtastic

Sharing Peripherals

When an organization has a number of PCs, giving users access to the hard disks, printers, plotters, and other output devices they need can be a problem — one that's hard to solve without networking. If the PCs are *standalone* (that is, not networked), then decisions must be made as to who gets which devices.

For example, many users will only need infrequent use of a peripheral like a plotter. Requiring them to copy files to a floppy and then go to another PC to generate their output is, at best, inconvenient and, at worst, time-consuming. For devices like modems, going to another PC to use a high-speed modem can be very awkward if there are files to be transferred which are several megabytes in size. The user would have to copy the files to several floppy disks, go to the PC with the modem, copy the contents of the floppies to the hard disk, and then use the modem.

Some people have used data switches that allow several computers to share a printer or plotter, but these are poor solutions because they are expensive and offer no other services than sharing a peripheral. Another problem with data switches is that they can't effectively solve the problem if more than a dozen computers want to share a peripheral.

Networks can support multiple users sharing printers that are at different locations on the system. A user who outputs to a plotter frequently might have that device directly attached to his or her PC. Another user who requires only occasional access can send his or her data across the network for output on that plotter. Figure 1.3 shows an example of how four users might share a printer and a plotter.

Sharing devices like modems can also be very effective. An effective strategy is to *pool* modems; that is, to have several modems attached to one machine, and allow users to access whichever modem is free. Artisoft offers software to make a modem-sharing system that will work with any NETBIOS system.

When there are 20 users on a network who require, for example, infrequent use of a modem, three or four modems can be pooled and, depending on the users' usage patterns, can provide a free modem whenever needed. Another advantage to being able to access modems across a network is the situation where there is a need for a specialized and expensive modem. For example, a high-speed, error-correcting modem can be made available to all potential users.

Introduction: Why Network?

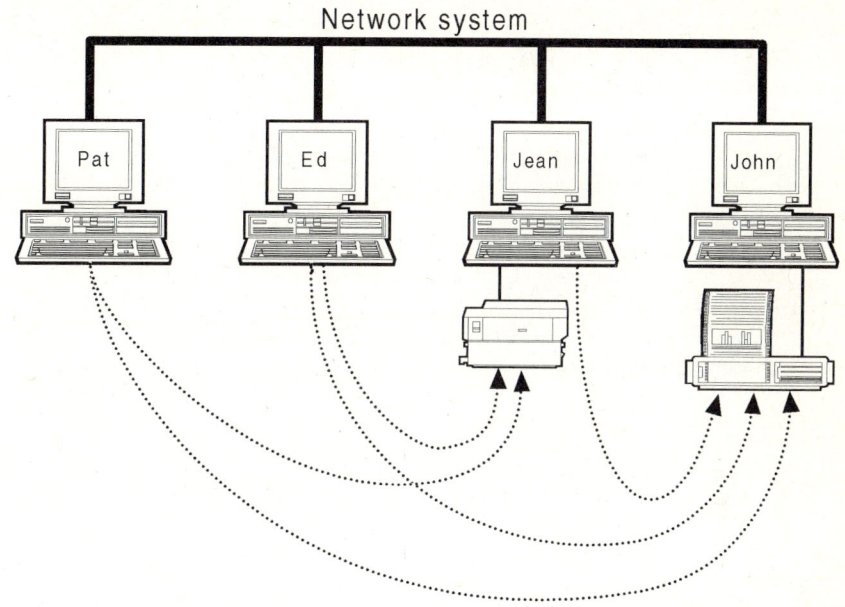

Figure 1.3 *Sharing printers and plotters.*

Another aspect of sharing devices on networks is the ability to control who uses them and who has physical access to them. If the hard disk that holds the company's accounting data has controlled network access and the PC that it is kept in is in a controlled room (locked, or simply near to the person who is responsible for the PC), the chances of preventing unauthorized access or removal are far greater. This can also be used to control the use of modems by only allowing access to authorized users.

LANtastic supports the sharing of data and devices across a network with sophisticated access controls to ensure that resources are properly controlled. This allows users to be controlled at various levels that range from what days and even hours access is permitted, to what level of access is available. For example, the ability to only read files ensures that unauthorized changes to text documents can't happen.

Networking with LANtastic

Office Communications

In many offices, one of the most frequently played games is telephone tag. Trying to schedule a meeting or discuss a problem can be a frustrating series of near misses and lost messages. With a network, messages can be handled in a variety of ways, all providing greater efficiency and reliability than traditional methods.

There are many types of messages that can be found on networks:

- Messages where people exchange files and messages with other people (often called *interpersonal messaging*).
- Messages between programs and people or vice versa.
- Diary and schedule exchanges for project management, managing meetings, and recording events.

A network makes it possible to exchange certain types of data that would be very difficult without a network. For example, scheduling three or more people for a meeting requires a large number of exchanges of data to find a commonly available time.

Without a network, trying to arrange a meeting for five or six people can be very difficult to nearly impossible to coordinate. For ten or more people, anything but a computerized scheduling system based on a network may be impractical unless the meeting is very far in the future.

There are two kinds of messaging:

- Real-time.
- Store-and-forward.

Real-time messages are messages that are received with the minimal amount of delay after transmission. The connection between the sender and receiver is usually direct, that is, there is no intermediate storage of the message data.

Store-and-forward messaging relies on intermediate storage to hold the message between transmission and delivery. This means that when you send a message, it is stored in a message database, and forwarded at a later time to the person for whom it is intended. This allows the sender to "post" messages even though the intended recipient isn't using their computer at that time.

When store-and-forward messaging is used for inter-personal messages (either between people or people and programs, as distinct from between programs), it is usually called *electronic mail*, or *E-mail*.

LANtastic includes both types of messaging; real-time chat services that allow you to type a message that is immediately seen on another user's terminal, and E-mail that supports store-and-forward messaging between users.

An advanced feature of LANtastic E-mail is support for Artisoft's Voice Board. This product allows you to send and receive spoken messages that are transferred across the network as electronic mail.

Managing Your PCs

There is another area where networks can make PCs more productive and reliable. That area is the management of the PCs themselves.

When you have more than a couple of PCs, it is difficult to ensure that regular backups are done. There are two options: you have to rely on the users to do their own backups, or someone has to be given the responsibility to do it for them.

Either way, it is a time-consuming task. And how time-consuming it is depends on whether the backup is to floppies (which are slow and sometimes unreliable) or to tape or a similar kind of device. If it is to tape, then either every PC must have a tape unit, or the person doing the backups must have a portable unit. A tape unit at every PC would be expensive. Using a portable tape device is cheaper as each PC only needs whatever connection device the tape requires.

With a network, however, users can back up critical files on their local drives to other PCs on the network. Sometimes a specific machine is used for backups; this machine is, in turn, backed up to tape. Even more useful, peer networks can allow for one person to back up PCs from across the network. This means that the reliability of data on PCs is centralized and can be managed without having to take a tour around the building to back up each machine.

Networks also allow other PC management responsibilities to be distributed. Tasks such as caring for printers and plotters can be handled

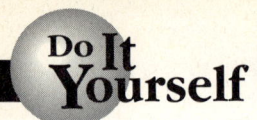

Networking with LANtastic

by the person to whose machine the peripheral is attached. This covers tasks such as putting paper in, distributing output, fixing paper jams, and so on.

When a company needs vast amounts of storage for commonly used data or a large number of staff need access to expensive peripherals like CD-ROM drives, networks can spread the cost among all of the users. For example, instead of buying a larger hard disk for each PC as the user's needs grow, one or more networked PCs can be upgraded with bigger disks that can be shared.

LANtastic makes it easy to build these kinds of systems because it is a peer network. This means that any PC can be set up to access any other. This allows for the greatest possible flexibility. LANtastic also includes specific support for CD-ROM drives.

So, What Will Networks Give Your Organization?

You can probably see from the topics discussed that a network can help your company:

- Communicate better internally.
- Share information more effectively.
- Manage your PC more efficiently.
- Enable ways of doing things that can't be done with traditional methods.

Because you are planning to implement a network using LANtastic, you may need to develop an argument to justify your needs. This justification may be required to get a budget from the company to allow you to get a network or simply to show that there is a need for one. We will cover building a case for a network in Chapter 4, "Planning Your Network."

Summary

Networking is a strategy for organizing PC-based computer resources to maximize their benefit to the company. Networks allow you to:

- Manage and distribute information and data.
- Share resources.
- Improve and enable communications.
- Improve resources management.

Peer-to-peer networks offer a low-cost and flexible approach to networking. They allow the organization to use existing resources (PCs, hard disks, printers, etc.) without installing complex and expensive centralized file-server systems.

2

The Basics of Networking

Before we can look at the LANtastic system in detail, we need to outline what a network is and, in particular, what a peer network is.

The broadest description of a network is a communications system for computers, a way of allowing two or more computers to communicate with each other; and the purpose of this communication is to allow data to be exchanged between computers. With local area networks, this data exchange is the foundation of the system.

The most important aspects of local area networks lie in supporting existing DOS applications as well as programs designed for the network environment. This means that the network must be an extension of the PC environment that is compatible with applications, utilities, and existing hardware. The fact that data is located somewhere other than on local drives or that a printer is actually attached to another PC are issues that networks are designed to hide.

One way to look at networking is as a layer cake with data exchange as the bottom layer (see Figure 2.1). The layer on top of that is the service that controls the connections between computers. The next layer integrates the network services with the applications. The icing on the cake is in two "flavors" — the utilities that are used to define the connections, and the user applications that are what the whole system is there to support.

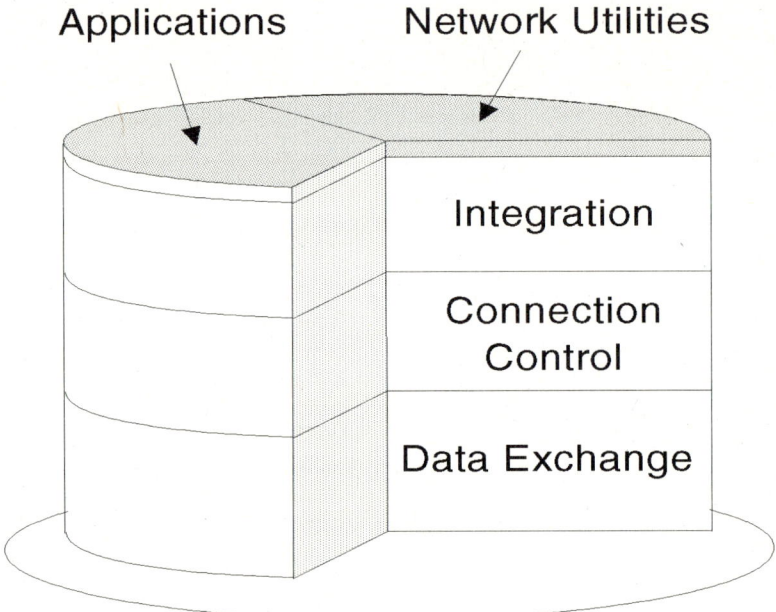

Figure 2.1   *The networking layer cake.*

This kind of layering of functions is what gives LANtastic its flexibility. By including different "flavors" (components) in each layer, the characteristics of the overall "cake" (configuration) can be changed. And because they are layered, changes are easy to make.

The lowest layer of this model, data exchange, has both hardware and software components. The other layers are purely software. We'll look at the hardware and software components in turn.

Networking Hardware

To network PCs, you need to have special hardware. This hardware provides the means by which the PCs are interconnected and can transfer data. The hardware consists of add-in boards that support different networking technologies such as EtherNet or ARCNET, which are discussed in detail in Chapter 5, "Selecting a Network Technology."

These boards are often referred to as *network interface cards*, or *network adapters* (throughout the rest of this book, we'll refer to them simply as adapters). Figure 2.2 shows a common type of EtherNet adapter.

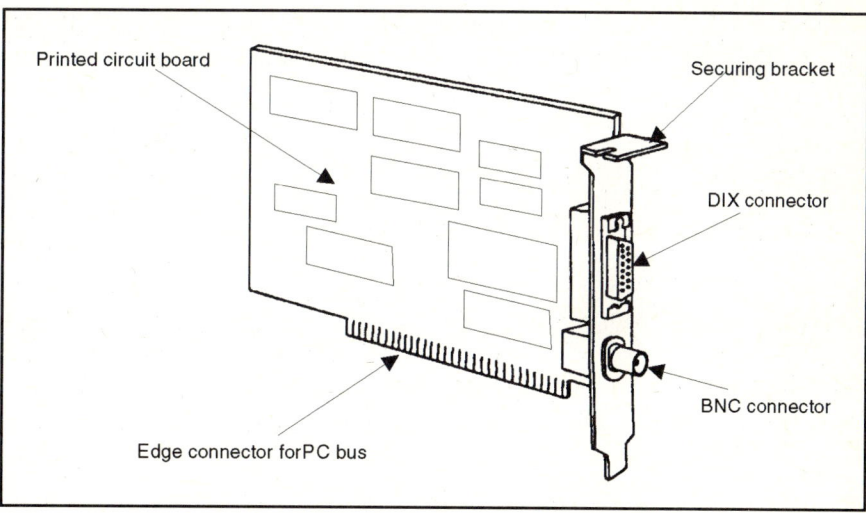

Figure 2.2   *A typical network interface card.*

There is one basic reason why we need to use special communications hardware — performance. PCs come equipped with a variety of communications facilities, which may include:

- Serial ports that can transfer data at rates as high as 40,000 characters per second.

- Parallel ports that can send and receive data at up to 150,000 characters per second.

Networking with LANtastic

These ports have been used to build network systems, but they are simply too slow to support any serious use. Network technologies that support data rates of 310,000 characters per second are at the low end of today's LANs. Without going to leading-edge products, well-priced network adapters will deliver data transfer rates of 1,250,000 characters per second.

Some adapters can have different aspects of the operation or configuration changed by switches or jumpers on the adapter. Some of the latest adapter designs can be configured using software; this means that you don't have to physically mess around with the board to change settings. The reason that you might want to change the adapter's configuration is to prevent conflict with other components in the PC system.

> **Note:** Although most manufacturers claim, and usually manage, to ship hardware preconfigured, it is always wise to check that the board's configuration is what you expect it to be. This can save you literally hours of work if you have problems.

Network adapters are much like any other add-in cards and come in different configurations depending on the type of bus used by the PC. This means that there are different adapters for PCs that use the various bus standards:

- ISA (Industry Standard Architecture)
- EISA (Extended ISA)
- MCA (MicroChannel Architecture)

Network adapters communicate with each other by cable. These cables can range from standard telephone cable to very heavy coaxial cable. The actual network wiring scheme will depend on the network technology, the options that are available within that standard, and the constraints imposed by a particular site. This book will concentrate on the three most commonly used networking technologies:

- EtherNet
- ARCnet
- IBM Token Ring

Figure 2.3 shows a generalized view of the hardware components of a network.

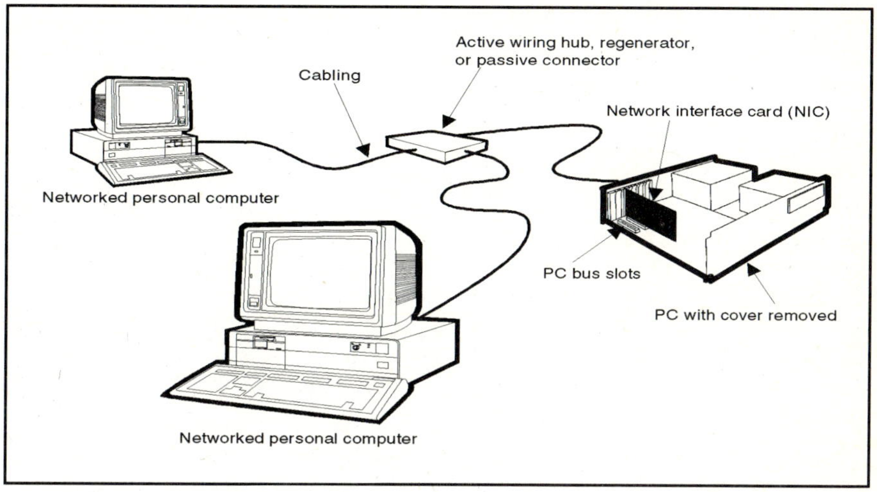

The Basics of Networking

Figure 2.3 *The major components of network hardware.*

Different networking technologies rely on various cabling systems.

A cabling system consists of:

- The cable itself.
- Connectors and junction boxes, etc.
- Any other active or passive components required.

Active components are units that regenerate or modify signals to ensure that the network transmissions maintain the highest possible quality. They do this by amplifying or duplicating the signal. *Passive components* simply condition connections to the network cabling to ensure electrical compatibility. These active and passive units are called *wiring hubs* or *concentrators* and may be used to connect PCs or cable sections.

Passive network wiring components also include terminators and grounding straps. The use of these in networks should always be done according "to the book." If you don't follow the recommendations, you will almost certainly have problems.

Each networking technology uses different cabling systems because each technology sends signals across the network at a different rate. I'll discuss the issues of selecting adapters and cabling systems more thoroughly in Chapter 4, "Planning Your Network."

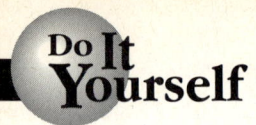

Networking with LANtastic

Networking Software

If interconnection and the ability to transfer data between computers was all you wanted to do, then the network hardware (the adapters) would be all that was required. Each application that needed to do data transfer would have to know how to "talk" to the network adapter.

Further, the program at the other end would have to know all about the way that the first program was going to use the connection — they would have to have a common protocol or "language" with which to communicate. This would also mean that every program that needed access to remote data or services would have to be specially written. Although this kind of setup would work, it would obviously be very limiting and inefficient.

By having software that sits between the networking hardware and the applications, and integrates the network services with the local services, the network can be made invisible to programs that are not network aware.

The network software extends the Disk Operating System (DOS) so that network resources and facilities are effectively part of the PC's resources. LANtastic does just that — it makes network resources look as if they were local. This means that most off-the-shelf applications that are not network-aware will operate perfectly on a LANtastic network.

The network software in peer systems allows a PC to be configured in any of three ways:

- As a server.
- As a workstation.
- As both a server and a workstation at the same time.

In networking, a *server* is a PC that makes its resources available for use by other machines on the network. The machines that use the resources are the *workstations* (clients). Thus, in the network shown in Figure 2.4, Pat's PC (a workstation) sees the hard disk on Jean's PC (the server) as drive D:. In addition, Pat sees Jean's laser printer as if it were on her local printer port called LPT2:.

The Basics of Networking

To Jean, her hard disk is drive C: and her printer is on LPT1:. Because Jean's PC is a server only, it can't provide Jean with access to any other servers on the network (such as Lucy's PC). Lucy's hard disk appears to Pat as drive E:, and Jean's hard disk and printer are Lucy's D: drive and LPT1:, respectively.

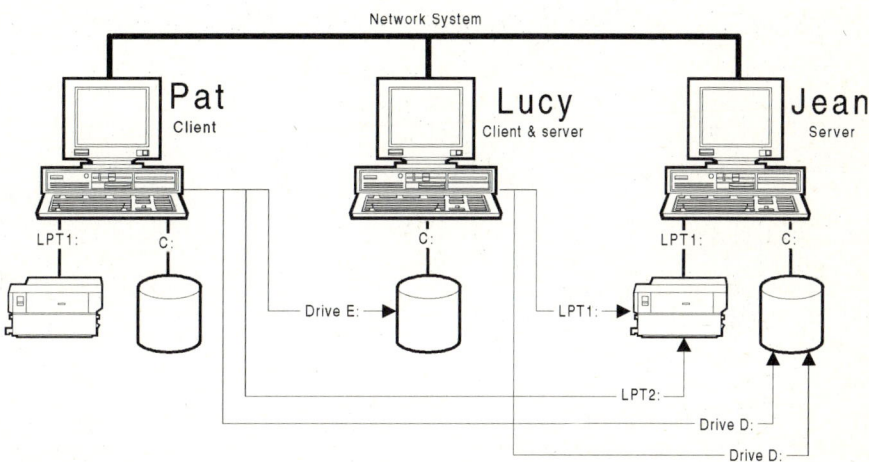

Figure 2.4 *How PCs configured as workstations, servers, and workstation/servers see the network resources and their own local resources.*

Although the diagram may seem complex, from each user's point of view, her environment is straightforward. Table 2.1 shows the resources that each of these users will "see."

Table 2.1 The resources and the devices that users access for the network shown in Figure 2.4.

User	Local Device	Remote Resource
Pat	Drive C	Local hard disk
	Drive D	Jean's hard disk
	Drive E	Lucy's hard disk
	Printer on LPT1	Local printer
	Printer on LPT2	Jean's printer on LPT1

continues

Networking with LANtastic

Table 2.1 Continued.

User	Local Device	Remote Resource
Jean	Drive C	Local hard disk
	Drive D	Lucy's hard disk
	Printer on LPT1	Local printer
Lucy	Drive C	Local hard disk
	Printer on LPT1	Local printer

The networking software not only makes the remote resources available, but it also:

- Controls who is allowed to access the resources (access control).
- Controls the way they are allowed to access them (access rights).
- Prevents and resolves any conflicts if two users try to share a resource at the same time (contention management).

Access control and *access rights* are two of the most important aspects of network management. Without access control anyone could use any resource in any way. This would make it possible for users to connect to and use services, whether you want them to or not. Without access rights, once users access the network, they can do whatever they please with the data or resources. This could include deleting files, making alterations, or monopolizing services.

Network security, which covers both access control and access rights, is vital to the network's robustness, reliability, and integrity. LANtastic has extensive network security that we will discuss in detail in Chapter 8, "Protecting Your Network."

Contention management, that is, resolving multiple users trying to access the same peripheral, is one of the basic functions of a network server. For example, if both users are trying to output to the same printer, the network must resolve who goes first and how it will handle the user who must wait.

The way that sophisticated network software manages several people all trying to use the same printer is through a *spooler system*. This means that the printer output from an application that will go to a shared printer is first diverted to a file. The file is then queued as a print job and is output to the printer when it reaches the head of the queue. The spooler system sends the print data to the printer if the printer is available. If the printer is busy outputting another document, the spooler system will put the *print job* (the data to be output) on hold.

This means that a printer fed by a spooler can be kept busy. An expensive device like a postscript laser printer or a color printer is much more cost-effective when used in this way as its cost is shared among many users.

Summary

When an organization has more than one or two PCs, the problems of sharing data between them can be a serious hindrance to business efficiency. The critical benefit of networking is to enable people to share data, documents, and peripherals in an organized and controlled way. LANtastic, a peer network, is a networking system that supports resource sharing services in a sophisticated and cost-effective manner.

The LANtastic Networking System

LANtastic, while simple to install, configure, manage, and run, is very comprehensive in its facilities and features. To get the most out of a LANtastic network, you need to:

- Plan your installation.
- Understand the process of installation and configuration.
- Know how to manage a running network.
- Understand how to use the various LANtastic network utilities.

Although you could jump into building a LANtastic system right away, to really get the best out of a LANtastic network you should understand how the Artisoft network products are structured. In this chapter, we'll look at the hardware and software components that make up the nuts and bolts of the LANtastic networking system.

 *Networking with LANtastic*

LANtastic Network Hardware

LANtastic can support four groups of network hardware (see Figure 3.1):

- The PC itself, which is the reason for needing a network.
- The PC's peripherals, which are to be shared resources across the network.
- The PC's standard communications (serial and parallel), to which some of the peripherals (printers and modems) are attached.
- Add-in communications boards, which support the actual data exchanges across the network.

Each of these types of hardware require different controls, configuration, and management.

Personal Computers

Any PC that is broadly IBM PC-compatible can run LANtastic. This includes PCs based on the Intel 8086, 8088, 80286, 80386, and 80486 microprocessors. LANtastic requires only a small amount of memory for each configuration:

- 13KB for a workstation-only PC using Artisoft's 2 Mbps network adapter cards (around 25KB using EtherNet adapters).
- Just under 41KB for a server running on Artisoft's 2Mbps network cards (about 51KB using EtherNet).

Peripherals

LANtastic can make many types of peripherals available as network resources:

- Floppy drives.
- Hard disk drives.

The LANtastic Networking System

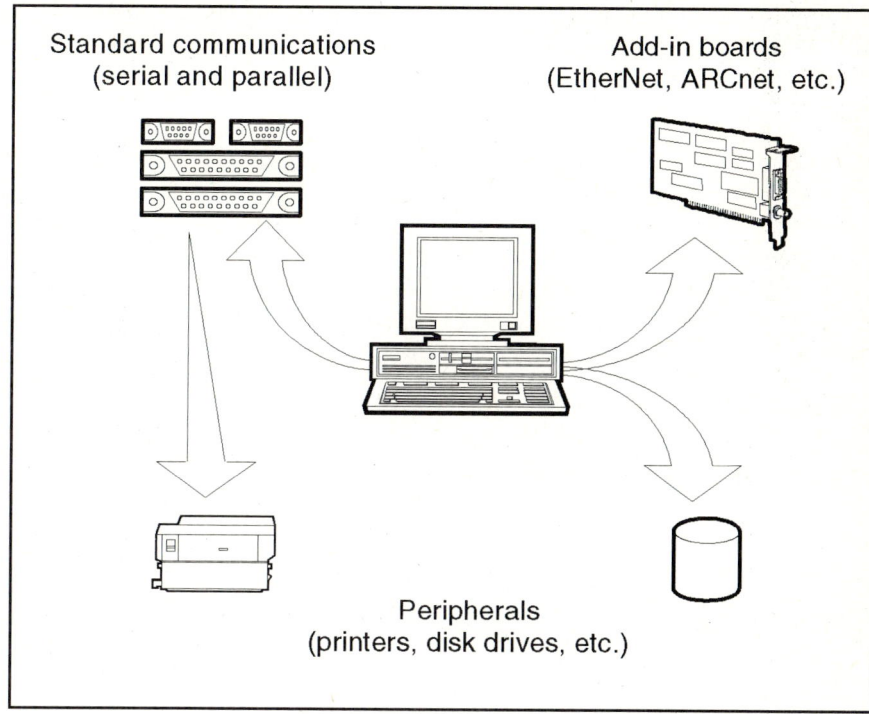

Figure 3.1 *The LANtastic hardware environment.*

- Printers.
- Plotters.
- CD-ROMs.
- WORM (Write Once, Read Many) drives.
- Any other peripheral that is a DOS-type device (that is, can be used like a printer or floppy disk drive).

Some devices, such as CD-ROMs, may be shared by several users only on a one-at-a-time, first-come/first-served basis, rather than several users at the same time.

LANtastic is particularly flexible in its approach to networked device support. You can communicate with a resource through *spooling* (queuing batches of data to be output to the device when it is available) or *directly* (data is sent to or received from the device, and there is no queuing or delay other than the small amount of time it takes to transfer the data across the

Networking with LANtastic

network). This means that you can use devices that must "talk" to the software as shared resources. For example, you might need this kind of interaction to use a plotter that must have a dialog with the application to report status and progress.

In general, almost any input or output device can be supported across a LANtastic network.

Standard Communications

PCs usually come with a selection of serial and parallel ports. LANtastic can use these ports to allow PCs to network with each other without using additional hardware. This allows you to make a connection from one PC's parallel port to another PC's parallel port, from serial to serial, or through modems attached to serial ports.

Using modems allows LANtastic to support remote PCs and mobile PCs. Even with modems running at low speeds like 2400 baud, transferring small files and sending and receiving mail are practical operations, if more time-consuming than over a LAN connection. High-performance networks use technologies such as EtherNet. Using an EtherNet network system with LANtastic is over 400 times faster than a modem connection at 2400 baud.

An outstanding feature of LANtastic is the low impact it makes on a PC's resources in terms of performance and memory use. This makes network connections through serial or parallel ports a limited but simple way to enhance the connectivity of low-powered notebook and laptop PCs.

Offices can make serial or parallel connections available either directly to people's desks or pooled at some central location for people who require casual or light network access.

Add-in Communications Boards

Add-in communications boards are available to support a huge variety of network technologies. The common name for these boards is *adapters*. They plug into the bus of the PC along with other adapters, such as video controllers, RAM expansion cards, and modem boards.

The LANtastic Networking System

When these adapters support networks, they are also called *network interface cards*. LANtastic can work with any network interface card that comes with a LANtastic-compatible NETBIOS interface, as well as the network interface adapters and supporting software sold by Artisoft. (NETBIOS is part of the network operating software. See "The NETBIOS" later in this chapter.)

> **Note:** All PCs on a network must use the same type of NETBIOS. Small implementation differences between manufacturers or between different releases by the same manufacturer often will not "understand" each other.

For PCs that don't have any capability to support add-in boards (such as laptops), there is another solution. This solution is to use add-on units like the Xircom EtherNet Adapter, which plugs into the parallel port of a PC and provides an EtherNet connection using a special driver in the PC.

Another consideration for sites that need very flexible network connections and that will be putting only a light load on the network is *wireless networks*. These systems rely on infrared and radio links to support networking. While they have performance limitations and are fairly pricey, they make the cabling of networks very simple (as there is little actual cable in these systems other than connections from the antennas or transceivers to the PCs), and they offer the ultimate in flexibility.

A View from the Top

The LANtastic peer-to-peer networking system extends the *DOS operating system* — either IBM's PC DOS, Microsoft's MS-DOS, or Digital Research's DR DOS. In Chapter 1, I discussed the three configurations for PCs running LANtastic:

- Workstation only.
- Workstation/server.
- Server only.

Different components of the networking software must be loaded in a PC for each configuration. These components fall into three groups:

- The local services.
- The network operating system.
- The network interface subsystem.

Figure 3.2 shows a high-level view of the component groups and their relationship to applications and the networking hardware.

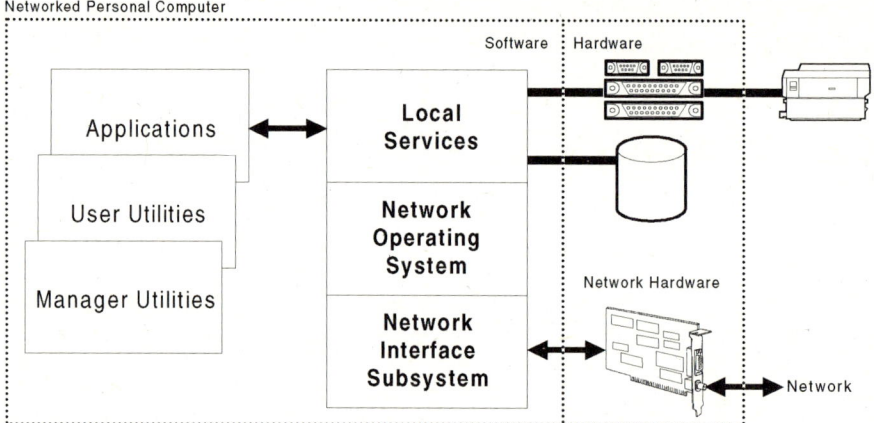

Figure 3.2 *The overall organization of a networked PC in a LANtastic network system.*

The local services are the route to the resource that can be shared across the network. They manage the hard disk drives, serial and parallel communications ports, and their attached printers and modems.

The network operating system supports and manages the access by local programs to remote resources, and by remote programs to local resources.

At the bottom of the model is the network interface subsystem. This is the software that talks directly to the network hardware and through which the network operating system gets access to the network.

Local Services

LANtastic is an *extension* of MS-DOS. Because it adds to MS-DOS by building on standard interfaces rather than replacing or bypassing the system, it offers full compatibility with the vast majority of stand-alone and networking MS-DOS applications.

The DOS services fall into two groups: DOS support and file-sharing services.

DOS Support

LANtastic will work with all versions of MS-DOS above 3.1 and with versions of Digital Research's DR DOS above 6.0. It is also compatible with Microsoft Windows 3.0 and the recently released version 3.1. Artisoft also offers specific support for Windows that includes Windows-compatible network utilities. The LANtastic for Windows package also provides advanced facilities that extend the Windows environment across the network (see Chapter 10, "Advanced Topics").

File-Sharing Services

If a PC is to be a server, MS-DOS needs support for the control of two or more users attempting to simultaneously use the same files before networking software is added.

The MS-DOS component that allows multiuser access control is a memory-resident utility called SHARE.EXE. The purpose of SHARE.EXE is to support the *sharing* and *locking* of files. Sharing a file is when two or more users access a file to read from it or write to it at the same time. Locking a file is an operation used by programs to resolve the problems of multiuser access.

There are three ways that two or more users (programs) can access files: reading from the file, writing to the file, or both. Without a control

mechanism, there are three basic conflicts that can happen: data can be out-of-date, corrupted, or lost.

> **Note:** The problems of multiuser data access are more complex than can be covered here. Network-aware applications that share data files are designed to resolve access issues; to do so, the SHARE utility must be loaded on the server.

It is possible to run a server without loading SHARE, but you must ensure that nobody can write to files on that server. Because clients don't usually need to manage shared files, you don't need to load SHARE.EXE.

There is one other reason to use SHARE that applies to both servers and clients. For MS-DOS versions 4.00 and 4.01 with a drive larger than 32 megabytes, SHARE must be run. If you fail to do so in the CONFIG.SYS configuration file, MS-DOS will attempt to load it automatically.

The Network Interface Subsystem

At the lowest level in the system is the network interface subsystem (see Figure 3.3). This consists of two components:

- A network adapter card driver.
- NETBIOS.

Network Interface Card Drivers

Because each networking technology has different ways of transferring data and operates at different speeds, the system requires a piece of software called a *driver* to control access to the network interface card. A driver is different from other software (such as an application), because of its intimate relationship with the operating system. This intimacy is required because network hardware usually requires a very high priority when it is active. With some technologies, if the microprocessor doesn't respond to the network interface card when a data block is being received, data can be lost or corrupted.

The LANtastic Networking System

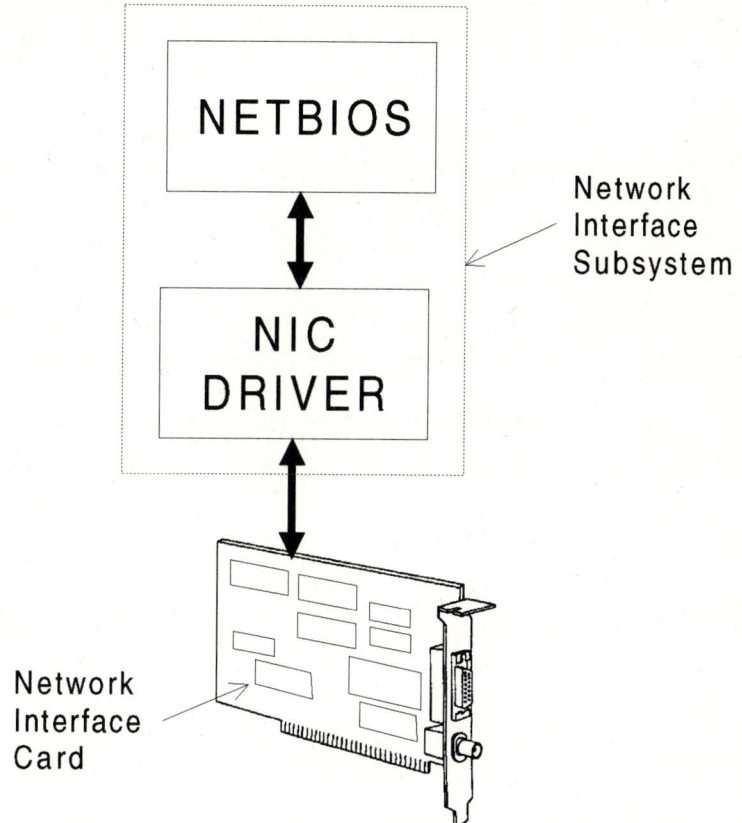

Figure 3.3 *The components of the network interface subsystem.*

With the Artisoft-supported products, the network interface card drivers are shipped with the network interface cards. For the Artisoft AE-2 network interface card, for example, the driver is called AEX.COM.

LANtastic can also support networking over serial, parallel, and modem connections. This allows direct communication only from one computer to another, so any servers connected to one of the computers will be invisible to the other.

Networking with LANtastic

The NETBIOS

LANtastic uses an industry standard called *NETBIOS*, which stands for *Network Basic Input/Output System*. The NETBIOS standard has a long history, is well understood, and is supported by many manufacturers. This means that you can use any network interface card with LANtastic that supports the NETBIOS standard.

Artisoft's networking software extends the NETBIOS services, which support a very basic set of data transfer services, to allow applications such as word processors to use files located on other machines across the network.

The NETBIOS standard defines a way of controlling and using a network interface card. The functions of a NETBIOS are:

- To establish, wait for, or terminate a connection (called a session) with a NETBIOS on another computer.
- To send and receive blocks of data.
- To add and remove names that identify each NETBIOS on the network.

Some manufacturers combine the NETBIOS and the network interface card driver in one piece of software. Artisoft's NETBIOS is a separate module from the network interface card driver. This piece of software is called the AILANBIOS, for Adapter (that is, network interface card) Independent Local Area Network Basic Input/Output System.

The Network Operating System

The LANtastic *network operating system* (*NOS*) comes in two modules: the redirector, REDIR.EXE, and the server, SERVER.EXE. In addition, there are two utilities that enhance performance. The first is a program that improves disk performance called LANCACHE.EXE. The other, called ALONE.EXE, puts a PC running as a client/server into the server-only mode. Table 3.1 shows which MS-DOS and NOS components are required for each configuration.

Table 3.1 LANtastic PC configurations and components.

	Client only	Server only	Client and server	Notes
DOS services				
MS-DOS	✔	✔	✔	Must be MS-DOS 3.01 or higher.
SHARE.EXE*	✘	✔	✔	May be automatically loaded for MS-DOS 4.0x.
Network interface subsystem				
NIC Driver*	✔	✔	✔	The name of this component will depend on the NIC.
NETBIOS*	✔	✔	✔	The name of this component will depend on the NIC.
Network operating system				
REDIR.EXE†	✔	✔	✔	
LANCACHE.EXE†	Optional	Optional	Optional	
SERVER.EXE†	✘	✔	✔	
ALONE.EXE	✘	✔	✘	For server only, ALONE program disables client services.

*   These are Terminate-and-stay-resident (TSR) modules.

†   These are TSRs and can be unloaded.

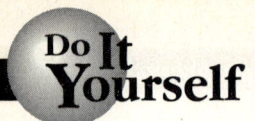

Networking with LANtastic

The Redirector

The *redirector*, called REDIR.EXE (a terminate-and-stay-resident utility), sits "in front" of DOS (see Figure 3.4). If an application makes a request for a local resource, the redirector just hands it to DOS, which, in turn, handles the request as normal.

But when an application wants to access a resource that is remote (whether or not the application is aware of the fact), the redirector intercepts the request and passes it to the network interface subsystem. It is then sent to the appropriate remote server, which then acts on the request. The server also returns the status of the operation, and any related data, through the network interface subsystem and back through the redirector.

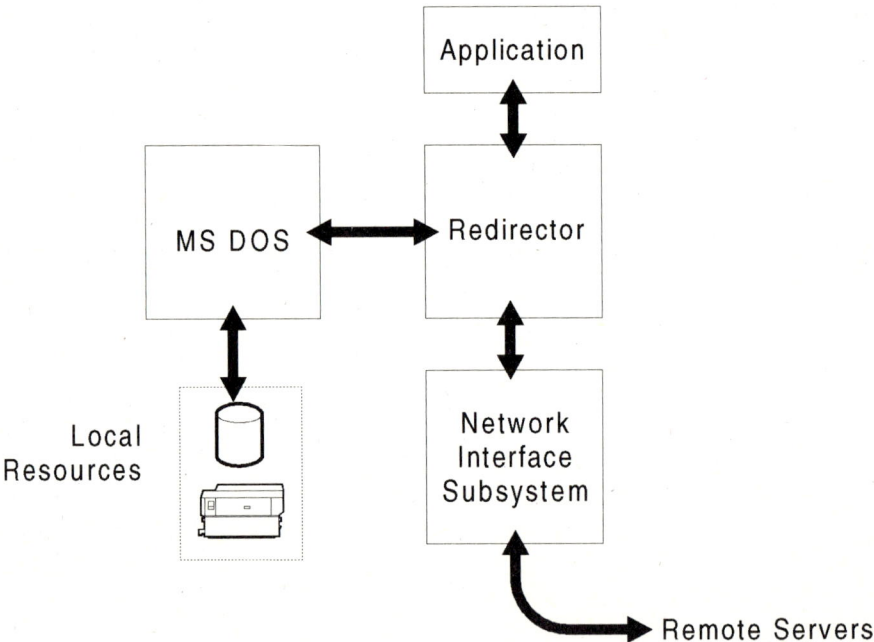

Figure 3.4 *The LANtastic redirector.*

For both local and remote requests, the existence of the network is invisible to the application. This invisibility (often called *transparency*) is vital if the network is used with application software that isn't written to work specifically on a LAN.

The LANtastic Networking System

In the LANtastic system, the redirector is always loaded, whether the PC is a client, a client/server, or a dedicated server. The LANtastic redirector is a well-engineered piece of software. Not only is it sophisticated and fast, but it also uses a relatively small amount of memory. In PC systems that run only MS-DOS (that is, without Windows), efficient use of memory can be vital to running memory-hungry applications. If necessary, the redirector can be removed (after the server component, if loaded, is removed) to allow large applications to run. In this case, the network services are, of course, not available.

The Server

The component that handles requests from clients is the *server*. This utility, SERVER.EXE, is another terminate-and-stay-resident program. Like the redirector, the server module is a sophisticated and highly optimized piece of software. This module is the crucial piece of the system, as it is not only in charge of making resources available to clients, but also responsible for access control and security (see Figure 3.5).

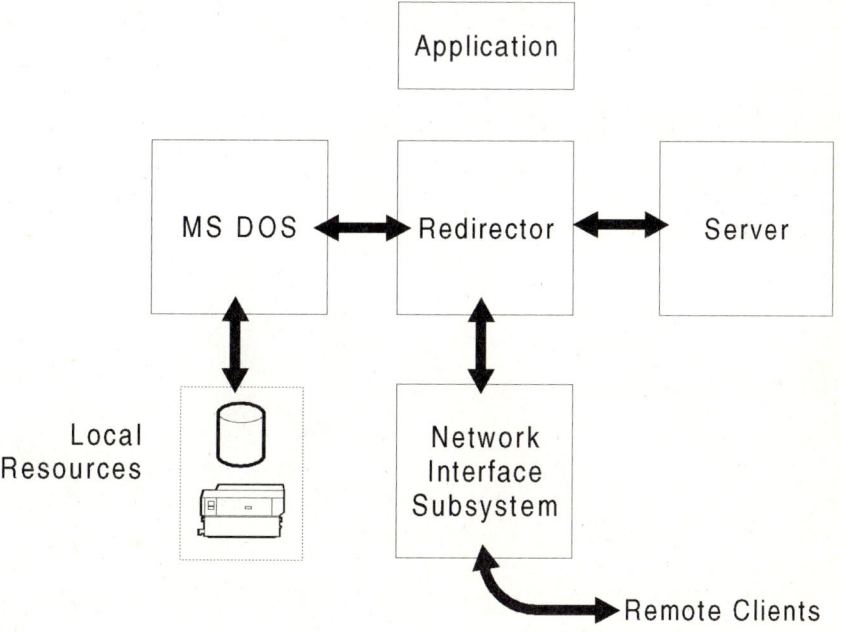

Figure 3.5 *The LANtastic server handling remote requests.*

Networking with LANtastic

Remote requests are received by the network interface subsystem and passed to the server. The server uses DOS to access the resources and returns the result of the operation and any data requested. It is also possible for the local user to log into the server. Requests from the local user (see Figure 3.6) are rerouted by the redirector to the server and then handled identically to remote requests.

One reason that a local user would log into the server running on their PC is to gain access to LANtastic network services such as local printing services or electronic mail.

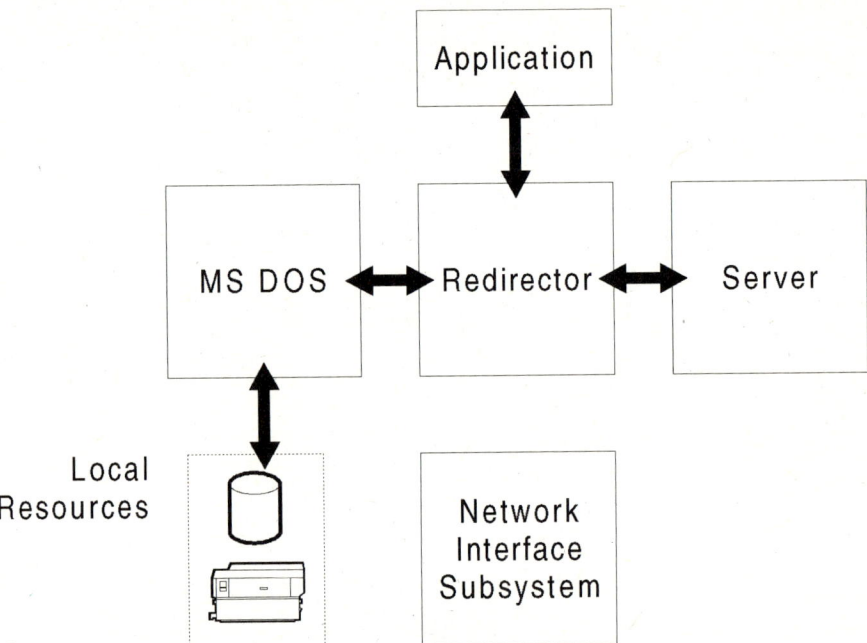

Figure 3.6 *The LANtastic server handling local requests.*

If necessary the server component, like the redirector, may be removed from memory to increase the RAM available to run applications. In this case, network access to other servers isn't lost, but the supply of services to other clients is.

The LANCACHE.EXE Utility

The LANCACHE.EXE program is a terminate-and-stay-resident utility that accelerates performance by acting as a "front end" to the hard disk. When you run LANCACHE.EXE, it provides a *buffer* or *cache* (a storage area in the computer's memory) to hold data from the hard disk. All reading and writing to disk that occurs through LANCACHE.EXE makes the disk appear to respond much faster. Because as much as possible of the PC's memory is used to cache the disk data and the LANCACHE.EXE program runs in the background (using up processor power), the utility can only be used on PCs with an 80286 processor or better. (See Appendix C, "Utilities Reference," for more details.)

The ALONE Utility

If you set up a network server to handle a large number of remote clients, performance may become a problem. To improve the throughput of a server, the LANtastic system comes with a program called ALONE.EXE. This utility tells the server software that nothing but the server functions will be supported. Because there is no other load from the local client side, all the processing capability is focused on servicing the remote clients.

ALONE can be stopped at any time without interfering with the work of remote users so that the PC can be used by a client/server again. (See Appendix C, "Utilities Reference," for more details.)

Memory Matters

In DOS systems, if there isn't enough memory available, certain applications will not run or have limited performance or functions. Table 3.2 shows the memory used by each component in the client-only and client/server LANtastic configurations.

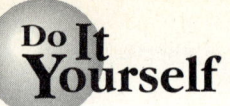

Networking with LANtastic

Table 3.2 LANtastic PC configurations and memory usage for LANtastic 4.00 with MS-DOS 5.0. (All numbers are shown in bytes.)

	Client only	Client and server	Notes
MS-DOS	24880	24880	Version 5.0. Configuration: no drivers, FILES=50, BUFFERS=32, FCBS=16,8.
SHARE.EXE	13344	13344	Configuration: All defaults.
NIC Driver	3248	3248	Artisoft's AEX.EXE driver, version 2.04.
NETBIOS	13536	13536	Artisoft's AILANBIOS, version 2.03.
REDIR.EXE	13200	13200	Version 4.00. Configuration: LOGINS=8, all other defaults.
SERVER.EXE	—	27632	Version 4.00. Configuration: All defaults.
Total used	68208	95840	
Free memory	**587152**	**559520**	Total RAM: 640KB

As you can see, LANtastic is extremely frugal in its use of memory. For the given configurations in a 640KB system, the client-only configuration leaves just over 573KB of RAM and the client/server leaves almost 546.5KB of free memory.

38

Remote Booting

An important service supported by LANtastic is *remote booting*. Remote booting allows a PC to get a copy of DOS and all the required network software from a server on the network. This requires that each PC that is to boot remotely must have a special *ROM* (a read-only memory chip) installed on the network interface card. Artisoft supplies Remote Boot ROMs for most types of network interface cards which they manufacture.

The reasons for using remote booting are to either limit network access or to support diskless workstations. A PC set up to remote boot loads its entire operating environment (the *boot image*) from the *boot server* (a server that is set up to supply the boot image file — see Figure 3.7). Once loaded, only the facilities enabled by the system manager when the remote boot was defined will be available to the user. This allows for very effective restrictions to be placed on the user's ability to interact with network resources and services.

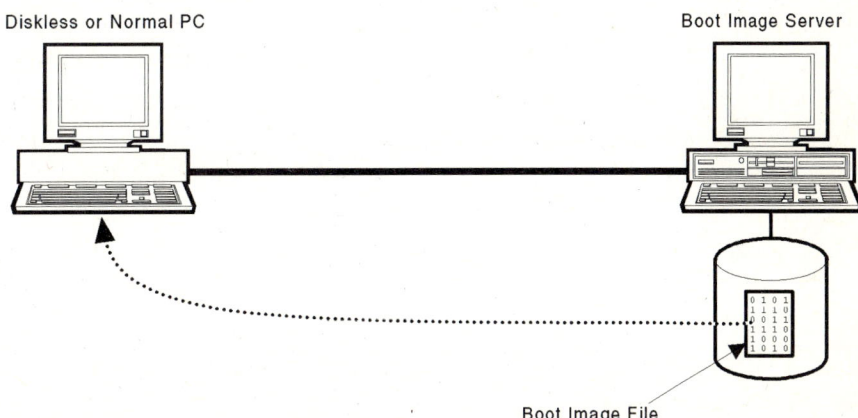

Figure 3.7   Remote booting.

A diskless PC is, as its name implies, without local storage facilities. This means that software and data can't be copied from the network at that PC, nor can they be introduced. This not only improves the security of the contents of the system, but also reduces the opportunities for the introduction of computer viruses through unauthorized software (see Chapter 8, "Protecting Your Network").

Networking with LANtastic

Performance Considerations

Estimating the potential performance of network systems is extremely difficult. Although the capabilities of each hardware and software component are measurable, the results for each component in combination with others may be different. Considering the number of possible component combinations, a general formula for performance prediction isn't practical. Worse still, when the actual patterns of use by real users on real networks is considered, each complete configuration will have different performance characteristics.

Performance may be a problem if you are planning to build a large network (more than, say, 50 users) or run programs that will do a lot of file input and output across the network, run huge printing jobs, or run programs that will heavily load network servers (operations like intensive database work or compiling programs). On the other hand, if you are using EtherNet or another equally fast network technology, and if you spend some time planning how to structure the network (in terms of who will access what, where, and when) and put that plan into practice, you should have adequate performance in most office environments.

The LANCACHE.EXE and ALONE.EXE programs can make a big difference to performance. LANCACHE.EXE, in particular, is an excellent accelerator for network servers that handle a lot of disk input and output.

LANtastic Network Utilities

While a network is being installed, configured, and is finally running, it must be controlled and managed. LANtastic comes with a suite of utilities to control all aspects of the network. These utilities fall into three main groups:

- Installation.
- Management.
- Operations.

Installation Utilities

Installation utilities include the software installation program, a utility to check the network hardware's operation, a program to modify non-Artisoft NETBIOS implementations, and a program to provide a *disk cache* facility. For PCs equipped with *Uninterruptable Power Supplies* (*UPS*s), there is a program that handles the various power supply indications that a "smart" UPS can provide. This allows for an orderly system shutdown if the power fails.

Management Applications

Management applications allow the control of the network environment. Most LANtastic network management functions are built into one utility called NET_MGR.EXE. This program allows you to set up user and group accounts, manage shared resources, define the server's startup and configuration, control security features, and configure remote booting. There are also two network management functions that are handled through the NET.EXE utility. These are server status reports and, provided you have the right privileges, the management of print queues.

Operations Utilities

Operations utilities allow users to control their own network environments. When the network is running, you need to be able to attach to servers and their resources, manage printer queues, "chat" with other users, and send and receive mail. These functions are supported by the NET.EXE and LANPUP.EXE (a pop-up TSR program that supports many of the functions of NET.EXE).

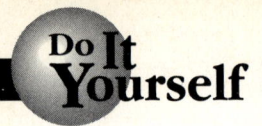

Network Security

LANtastic offers extensive security features that control access to servers and their resources. For simple LANtastic installations you can virtually ignore security. The network would then allow any user to access any resource that he or she wanted.

This expedient tactic is often used even in large networks and usually results in problems. With unrestricted access, a user making a mistake can cause as much damage to a network as a user who intends to cause damage. LANtastic's security features and facilities are covered in depth in Chapter 8, "Protecting Your Network."

LANtastic Disk Organization

The LANtastic network system uses a simple structure of subdirectories and files for control. During installation (covered fully in Chapter 6), a directory is created for the LANtastic files called (by default) LANTASTI. You can also specify that the files should be installed in another directory, which will be created automatically if it doesn't exist.

The files that are put into the LANTASTI directory are:

- Network interface card drivers.
- NETBIOS.
- The redirector program.
- The server program (if the PC is to be a server).
- Various user, management, and utility programs.
- Program help files.
- Any documents that Artisoft includes to explain last-minute changes to the release.

When the PC is configured as a server, LANtastic also needs a directory for its control files. By default, this directory is called LANTASTI.NET (although it looks like a file name, this is a valid name for a subdirectory), and, like the directory that contains the files (LANTASTI), can be called anything you like.

> **Note:** Using other names for the LANTASTI and LANTASTI.NET directories is not recommended, as it requires specifying the directories in many commands that expect to use the standard names as defaults. If you feel you have a *very* good reason to use other names, try to make that use consistent on all network PCs and document what you do.

This directory contains:

- Subdirectories that are named for each disk resource defined on the server.
- Files for mail queues (always called @MAIL).
- Printer queues.

The default setup is shown in Figure 3.8.

Applications in the LANtastic Environment

The LANtastic networking system provides a sound platform to create multiuser information systems, data stores, and electronic mail. Because the LANtastic environment is based on industry standards, there are many software packages that allow full multiuser operation or data file sharing with LANtastic. These include accounting, time-management, and database applications.

LANtastic also supports some very sophisticated features that can help you maximize the performance of the network. For example, LANtastic allows you to start a program running on another PC that is configured to be a client/server from another client. This is called *remote execution*.

Remote execution can be used, for example, in a programming environment when programs are to be compiled. Compiling puts a very heavy load on a computer, so a powerful PC — say, a 486-based system — might be made available for programmers to run their compilations on. This would allow the programmers to use much less powerful, and therefore cheaper, systems.

Remote execution is also a practical solution for searching a large database. If you try to search it with a program running on your PC, the data must first be transferred to your PC. By running the search on the remote PC where the database actually is, a much higher performance can be achieved.

With the Windows environment, LANtastic supports the system called *Dynamic Data Exchange*, or *DDE*. This allows programs such as Word for Windows or Excel to use LANtastic to directly output to network printers or send mail.

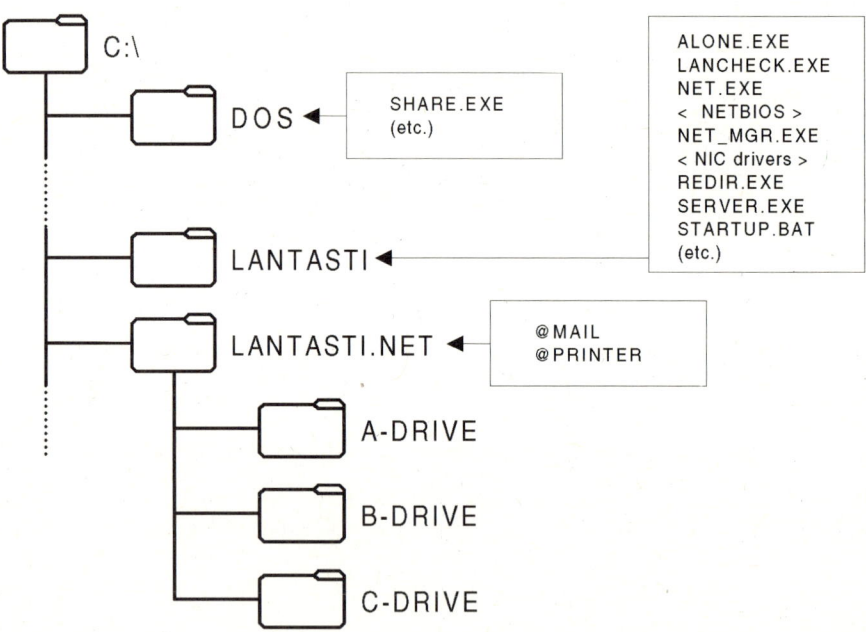

Figure 3.8 *The default directory structure of a PC set up as a LANtastic server.*

Summary

As you can see from this chapter, LANtastic is an extensive and sophisticated networking system. However, don't be put off by what may seem to be a complex system — LANtastic is reasonably simple to install, configure, operate, and manage. As the LANtastic system is built on MS-DOS, it offers complete compatibility with the huge range of professional DOS programs and is a lot easier to install than many applications.

LANtastic can be used on any PC that is broadly PC compatible (it will even tolerate some PCs that are marginal in this respect). For networking hardware, any network interface card that has NETBIOS support can be used.

The LANtastic networking system supports PCs as clients, as clients and servers at the same time, or as servers only (by using the ALONE.EXE utility). LANtastic also includes a caching utility to enhance disk performance.

Access is managed through an extensive system of security controls. For situations where greater access control or diskless PCs are needed, LANtastic supports remote booting.

4

Planning Your Network

In networking, planning and organization are fundamental to getting the most "bang for your buck." Organization is vitally important if you are to avoid problems and get the system you want. Planning in the early stages of bringing a network into your company will save your company time and money.

Following the strategies proposed in this chapter will help to make your network efficient and successful.

The secret to building and running a successful network of any size is planning. The basic steps that get you ready to network are:

1. Analyze your needs in terms of problems as well as goals.

2. Do a site analysis — determine what facilities and resources already exist.

3. Come up with a basic design.

4. Select the equipment.

5. Create a detailed configuration plan.

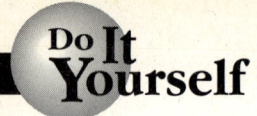 *Networking with LANtastic*

6. Create a timetable.
7. Get sign-offs (if required).
8. Plan the management tasks for the network.

While these steps may seem to involve a lot of work, they are what you'd still be doing in a disorganized way if you didn't follow the process! Moreover, unless you're planning just to join two PCs together, chances are you'll make mistakes and run into problems. A solid plan will help you avoid mistakes, and therefore save time and money. Even the briefest and simplest of plans will help you to dodge problems.

The planning process starts with focusing on what you want to achieve. This is done by writing down your problems, the needs that they point out, and the goals that the solution must achieve. The process of writing these items down encourages you to analyze what is to be done. People who don't use this method often find that what they thought were their goals were not realistic. Some reasons for this might be:

- They chose the wrong goals.
- They failed to buy the right equipment or systems.
- The goals they selected were simply impossible to achieve.

To illustrate how the planning process works, I'll use the example of Acme Secretarial Services, Inc., a small (and hypothetical) secretarial services business with a staff of six in Ventura, California. This business was started by an accounting firm, and all day-to-day control and operations are left to Acme's manager, Lucy Smith. This means that all decisions that are made need to be justified to the owners and signed off by them.

Lucy looked into the costs of networking and was initially put off, not only by the expense, but also by the complexity of installation and operation of systems such as Banyan VINES and NetWare. After reading *Do-It-Yourself Networking with LANtastic,* she realized that Acme could install their own LANtastic network — for a reasonable cost and without being networking experts.

Because the owners would make the final decision whether to go ahead with a network, Lucy decided to build a case for a network solution first, rather than just to start discussing the issue with them. Even if Lucy had known that the owners trusted her and would agree to whatever she wanted to do, the decision to build a case for the project was a wise one. By building a case, she had to analyze her current situation and demonstrate to at least her own satisfaction that the proposal was feasible.

Needs Analysis

The first step in determining your needs is to figure out what your problems are. The stimulus for networking will usually be one or more organizational or operational issues that can't be solved easily without using some method of intercommunication between your PCs. Once you've decided to look at networking as a solution, you need to make sure that you know what your problems are.

Problems

In the case of Acme Secretarial, Lucy summarized its problems using form DIY-001, "Needs Analysis: Problems" (see Figures 4.1 and 4.2). You'll find a blank copy of this form, and all other forms, in Appendix B, "Forms."

Analyzing problems in this way also allows you to build an argument to support your premise that money needs to be spent. In Acme's case, Lucy began building the argument by including loss-of-revenue issues in the problem summaries.

Even if you don't have to build a case, developing a rational justification for spending time and money to buy and install a network will show you whether you really need one. You may well find that you need to network only a few of the PCs instead of all of them or that you can phase in the network installation over several months. The cost/benefit justification process is so simple and its benefits so great that it is unwise to skip this step.

For Acme, the potential financial loss, assuming a projected gross revenue of $200,000, could have been around $52,000 (losing one client at an average value of $2,041 and being less competitive valued at $50,000). The cost of upgrading facilities (buying new printers and hard disks drives) to stay competitive and efficient would have been $4,100. The backup and update routines were expensive ($4,500 per year) and it was desirable to reduce this. Thus, if they carried on as they were, their problems would have cost them over $60,500. Even assuming that they wouldn't have lost a client, the need for upgrades and the cost of the backup and maintenance operations was going to cost $8,600!

© Mark Gibbs, 1992

Form: DIY-001

Needs Analysis: Problems

Acme Secretarial Services, Inc.

#	Description
1	Title: Access to laser printers. To stay competitive and efficient, all staff should have access to a laser printer. To give each PC its own laser printer would involve a minimum total cost of around $2000 for the simplest model and at least $3000 for the preferred type of laser printers. Cost: If this problem is not solved, Acme will become much less efficient and therefore less competitive in the next twelve months. This could reduce revenue by around 25%.
2	Title: Losing messages. Acme act as an answering service as well as having a lot of personal clients, so there is a large volume of notes and memos. Messages are occasionally misplaced or not delivered and once we lost a client because of this. Cost: Client loss reduced income for 1991 by just over $5,000. Assuming that we have another occurrence of lost messages, the average loss would be $200,000 / 98 = $2,041. (gross revenue / number of clients).

Prepared by: L.R. Smith
Date: 3/16/1992
Page: 1 of 1

This form is taken from "Do-It-Yourself Networking With LANtastic"
Published by SAMS (1992)

Figure 4.1   Acme's analysis of their problems, page 1.

Planning Your Network

```
© Mark Gibbs, 1992                                    Form: DIY-001
                    Needs Analysis: Problems
                      Acme Secretarial, Inc.
```

#	Description
3	Title: Lack of disk space. Acme do bulk mailings for local companies and handle quotations for a glazing firm. The mailings require a custom database that takes up 10 megabytes on each PC. The quotations use a large number of standard paragraphs that take up 5 megabytes on each PC. As all but one of the PCs have 20 MB drives, we are very tight on disk space. Cost: We'll need to upgrade all of the PC's to 40 megabyte drives in the next six months at an approximate cost of $350 * 6 = $2100.
4	Title: Time to update and backup systems. At present, it takes about 5 hours every month to update the mailing lists and document files, and about 20 hours each month to do backups for all of the PCs. Cost: This costs about $375 in staff time per month (that's $4,500 per year!).

```
Prepared by:              Date:               Page:
         L.R. Smith              3/16/1992            1    of    1
       This form is taken from "Do-It-Yourself Networking With LANtastic"
                         Published by SAMS (1992)
```

Figure 4.2   Acme's analysis of their problems, page 2.

This gave Acme a basis on which expenditure decisions could be rationally made. The bottom line is that if you can show that the proposed solution costs less than the problems, cures them, and has additional benefits, it becomes an easy and logical decision to buy into the project.

Identifying Your Problems

The key areas covered by Acme's network that may apply in your company are:

- Sharing the cost of expensive peripherals (printers and disk drives).
- Centralizing facilities to improve their manageability (again, printers and disk drives).
- Simplifying tasks by automation (backups).
- Improving reliability by automation (again, backups).
- Making better use of existing facilities (printers and disk drives).

There are other areas where you might look into how your PCs are costing you money. You can then see how a network could save money. Some of these areas are:

- Can you use the network to make work easier? For example, sharing files of boiler-plate text from one central source is less error prone than everyone having their own copies, and the files are much easier to update.
- Can you use the network to automate the flow of work? The progress of some tasks can be automated by sending files around a network. This can make the process faster and less error prone.
- Can you make your data more secure? Using the network to back up local files onto network servers as part of regular office routine can ensure that work isn't lost if a disk fails or files are deleted.

Goals

Once you've established what the problems and their financial implications are, you can identify what the *goals* — the desired results of the solution — should be. The objective is to itemize what you want the network to actually do *for the organization* rather than what you want it to do technically. In other words, consider your needs in terms of what you want to achieve rather than how you'll get there. This means that you should make statements like, "We need to share standard documents for word processing," rather than "The server called WALRUS will have a read-only directory where we'll store Word document files." This distinction is important as the latter description is a case of "putting the cart before the horse" — it defines a detailed solution rather than what the solution is to accomplish.

In the case of Acme, Lucy outlined their needs using the form "Needs Analysis: Goals," DIY-002 (see Figure 4.3).

Identifying Your Goals

To help you identify goals, use the following steps for each problem you identify:

1. Write down the problem.

2. Is the problem clearly stated? If you give it to others in your company, will they understand it? If they don't, you've either expressed it badly, or you're describing something that isn't relevant to the company.

3. Can you split the problem into two or more unrelated problems? If you can, write down each of the problems and start again at step 2 with each one.

4. Write down what solving the problem will achieve (the goal or goals).

5. If the results of step 4 involve any explanations of "how to," such as "keep records of 876 bytes in a Paradox database," you've jumped ahead to solutions. Go back to step 4 and try again.

6. Compare the problem and goal statements. Are they talking about the same issues? Are they real problems and goals? Are they actually needed? If the answer to any of these questions is "no," you need to carefully consider if the problem is worth addressing.

53

© Mark Gibbs, 1992	**Needs Analysis: Goals**	Form: DIY-002
	Acme Secretarial Services, Inc.	

#	Description
1	Existing and new printers must be sharable by all staff.
2	A centralized mailing database is needed that is accessible to all staff.
3	Message handling facilities are needed for all staff.
4	A central store of word processing templates and clause documents is required.
5	A simpler system to do backups and updates is required that involves less staff time to manage.

Prepared by: L.R. Smith	Date: 3/16/1992	Page: 1 of 1

This form is taken from "Do-It-Yourself Networking With LANtastic"
Published by SAMS (1992)

Figure 4.3 Acme's needs analysis.

Planning Your Network

Site Analysis

Now that you know what the goals are, you need to establish what you have to work with, that is, what the current assets are. There are two main areas to look at:

- Premises and services.
- Equipment.

Premises and Services

This first area requires a floor plan to be drawn up with all relevant equipment and electrical outlets shown. The use of electrical outlets can be very important, as many offices often overload their outlets with potentially disastrous results. If a circuit is overloaded, switching on a device (a fax, fluorescent lights, coffee machine, etc.) can cause *spikes* (fast peaks in the supplied voltage) or *brownouts* (short reductions in power). Either of these conditions can wreak havoc with network systems and need to be guarded against. Another problem is the danger that an overloaded outlet will create a fire hazard.

The Acme site is a shop on a commercial street and consists of two rooms. The front room is the main office and occupies a total floor space of 25 feet by 20 feet. All of the office equipment is connected to a 60-ampere circuit with no known problems such as spikes or brownouts. The back room is a storage area and leads to the restrooms and other services.

Acme's floor plan for the main office is shown in Figure 4.4, and their use of electrical outlets at that time is detailed in Figure 4.5, using forms DIY-003, "Site Analysis: Layout" and DIY-004, "Site Analysis: Power," respectively.

The power analysis showed that Acme had a total electrical current demand of around 40.4 amperes on the circuit that serves the PCs. This is well within the 60-ampere capability of the circuit.

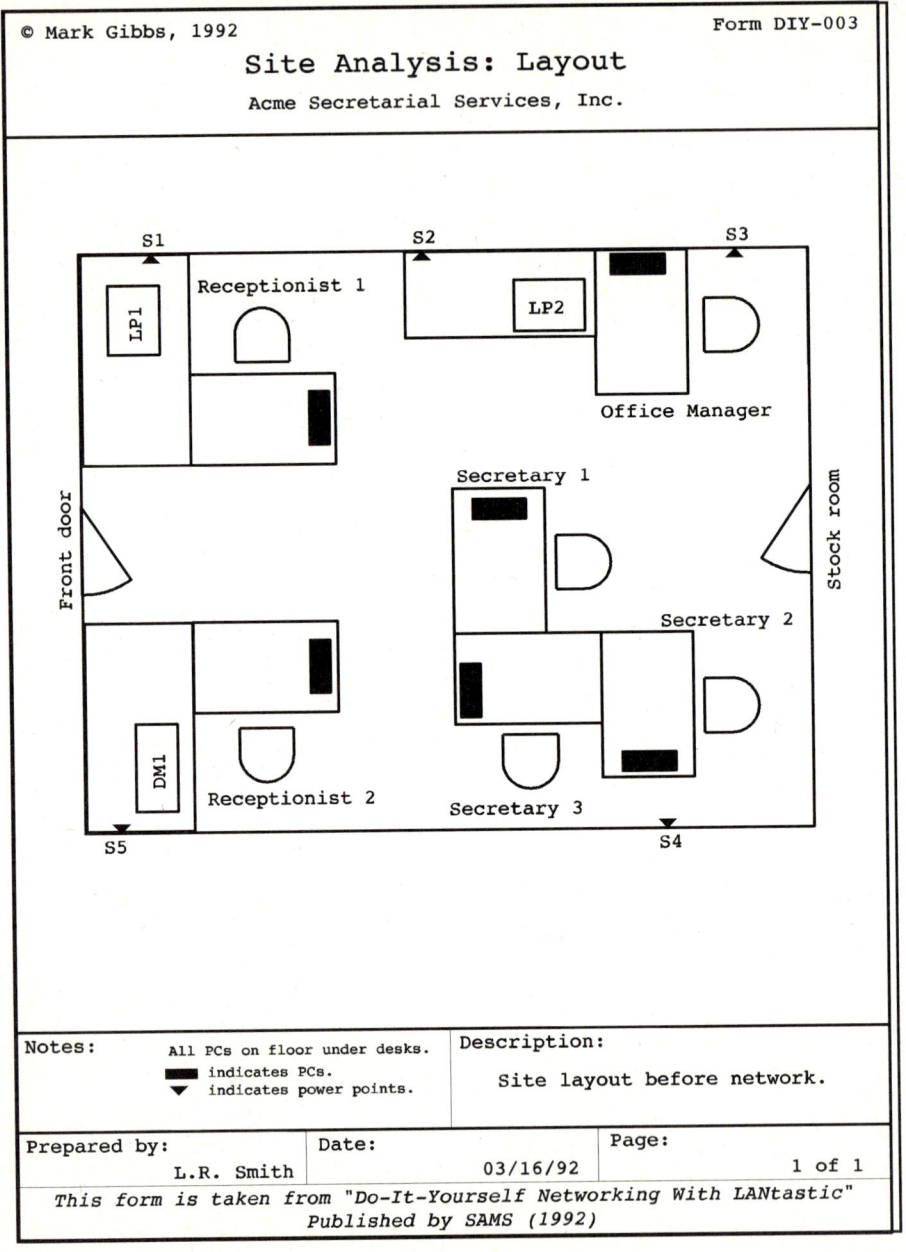

Figure 4.4 *Acme's floor plan.*

Planning Your Network

```
© Mark Gibbs, 1992                                         Form: DIY-004
                        Site Analysis: Power
                    Acme Secretarial Services, Inc.
```

ID	Type	Devices	Circuit ID:	Baseboard 60 amp
			Load	Skt. total
S1	Single	PC & screen (Recep.1)	4.5A	
		Laser Printer (LP1)	4.0A	
		Answering machines	0.9A	
		Desk lamp	0.3A	9.7A
S2	Double	Laser Printer (LP2)	4.0A	
		Desk lamp	0.3A	
		Dictation machine	0.3A	4.6A
S3	Double	PC & screen (Manager)	5.5A	
		Desk lamp	0.6A	
		Dictation machine	0.3A	6.4A
S4	Double	PC & screen (Sec. 1)	4.5A	
		PC & screen (Sec. 2)	4.5A	
		PC & screen (Sec. 3)	4.5A	
		Desk lamps (3)	0.9A	14.4A
S5	Single	PC & screen (Recep.1)	4.0A	
		Dot matrix printer (DM1)	1.0A	
		Desk lamp	0.3A	5.3A
			Circuit total:	40.4A

```
Prepared by:              Date:                Page:
          L.R. Smith              3/16/1992        1 of 1
      This form is taken from "Do-It-Yourself Networking With LANtastic"
                        Published by SAMS (1992)
```

Figure 4.5   *Acme's site analysis of power use.*

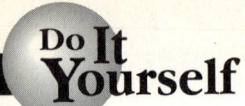 *Networking with LANtastic*

 **Caution:** If you're in doubt about the capability or safety of the power supply in your office, call a qualified electrician to check it out. It could save you a lot of problems — ranging from intermittent PC failures to fire.

Your company's equipment needs to be listed so that you know what you have and what is to be included in the network system. Figure 4.6 shows Lucy's listing of Acme's equipment. In Acme's case, all of the PCs and printers were to be put on the network.

The Basic Plan

At this point, you have analyzed your problems, defined your needs, recorded the site, and inventoried the equipment. Now you can begin planning the network itself.

At Acme, Lucy took her needs analysis and made some practical decisions about how to solve each problem. For this step, she used Form DIY-006, "Solutions" (see Figure 4.7).

In your planning, you should always look for simple solutions. If your solution sounds complex, it probably is. Some of the issues you should consider are:

- Is this a more costly solution than its benefit can justify?
- Will this solution be expensive or time consuming to keep running?
- Will this solution make other problems or solutions more difficult or complex?
- Will this solution be difficult to set up?

Planning Your Network

```
© Mark Gibbs, 1992                                          Form: DIY-005
                    Site Analysis: Equipment
                   Acme Secretarial Services, Inc.
```

Title & name	PC configuration	Printer & port	Notes
Office Manager Lucy Smith	80386 MCA 2 MB RAM 40 MB HD 3.5 & 5.25 FD	LaserWriter on COM1:	Also has modem card on COM2:
Secretary 1 Jean Gibbs	80386 ISA 640 KB RAM 20 MB HD 3.5 & 5.25 FD		
Secretary 2 Pat Lay	80386 ISA 640 KB RAM 20 MB HD 3.5 & 5.25 FD		
Secretary 3 Glaen Redeker	80386 ISA 640 KB RAM 20 MB HD 3.5 & 5.25 FD		
Receptionist 1 Ed Lay	80386 ISA 640 KB RAM 20 MB HD 3.5 & 5.25 FD	HP Laserjet II on LPT1:	
Receptionist 2 Brennen Redeker	80386 ISA 640 KB RAM 20 MB HD 3.5 & 5.25 FD	Epson FX-100 on LPT1:	

Prepared by: L.R. Smith	Date: 3/16/1992	Page: 1 of 1

```
    This form is taken from "Do-It-Yourself Networking With LANtastic"
                      Published by SAMS (1992)
```

Figure 4.6 *Acme's current equipment ("HD" stands for hard disk and "FD" stands for floppy disk).*

Do It Yourself — *Networking with LANtastic*

© Mark Gibbs, 1992
Form: DIY-006

Solutions
Acme Secretarial Services, Inc.

#	Description
1	Centralize all printers by having a PC act as a print server.
2	Use LANtastic electronic mail to give all staff messaging facilities.
3	Have the mailing database centralized (and removed from user PCs) and accessible to all staff. The PC acting as the print server will be used.
4	The central store of word processing templates and clause documents will also be kept on the print and database server.
5	Every machine on the network will do daily backups of working documents to the print and database server. Weekly backups will be taken from this server. Maximum staff time will be 1 hour per week (that is, $780/year).
6	All template documents and clauses will be held on the manager's PC and copied into documents as needed.
7	Buy a new PC for Secretary 3 and use her existing machine as the print/database/backup server.

Prepared by: L.R. Smith
Date: 3/16/1992
Page: 1 of 1

This form is taken from "Do-It-Yourself Networking With LANtastic" Published by SAMS (1992)

Figure 4.7 *Lucy's solutions to the problems identified at Acme.*

Selecting Equipment

One of the first decisions about the actual installation that needs to be made is which networking hardware to use. For organizations that have existing cabling installed, network hardware in place, or corporate standards to meet, the choice may be constrained by the need to be compatible with what's there. For completely new installations ("green field" sites), the choice of network hardware will depend on several factors, including cost, performance, and compatibility.

In this chapter, we'll discuss the general issues of selecting network hardware. See Chapter 5, "Selecting a Network Technology," for a more detailed discussion of network hardware.

Cost

Often the biggest factor, cost is directly related to performance — in general, the more you pay, the faster the network will go. The exception to this rule is that you can get high-performance adapters at very low prices, but the tradeoff may be that you have to use more expensive cabling or that the vendor's product and/or support quality is low.

Performance

The higher the *raw* data rate (the rate at which signals are transmitted across the network), the better the performance you'll see when you access network resources. Keep in mind, however, that very fast networking technologies are sometimes faster than PCs, so the PC itself becomes the limiting factor.

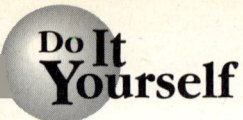

> **Note:** The raw data rate doesn't take into account the overheads of communications (the information that travels with data that specifies destination and sender, controls errors, and so on), and therefore the actual data rate is always lower by 4% to 50%, depending on the technology used by the hardware.

Compatibility

Some network adapters may not be compatible with LANtastic. You should make sure that any adapter you consider is certified by the manufacturer and, ideally, by Artisoft to be LANtastic compatible.

Acme, then, was a green field site — no existing networks, cabling, or company standards to comply with — and it definitely had a tight budget. To look at the choices, Lucy drew up a comparison table to compare the choices available and the prices she was quoted by various dealers.

From this analysis, Lucy concluded that Artisoft's AE/2 EtherNet system would be the best choice for Acme. The reasons for Lucy's decision were that the AE/2 system:

- Is fully supported by Artisoft.
- Has more than adequate performance for Acme's needs.
- Introduces nothing that might make diagnosing a problem difficult.
- Is priced well for their budget, and is an industry standard.

Armed with these decisions, it was easy for Lucy to draw up a shopping list so that specific products could be priced (see Figure 4.8).

At this point, however, the list is incomplete. You'll notice that the shopping list doesn't include any cabling or any of the odds and ends necessary for installation, such as cable clips.

Planning Your Network

```
© Mark Gibbs, 1992                                    Form: DIY-007
                       Purchase List
                 Acme Secretarial Services, Inc.
```

#	Description	Quantity
1	PC: 80386 ISA w. 640 KB RAM and 3.5 FD (n.b. no HD)	1
2	Artisoft 2mbps ISA Starter Kit (includes 2 network adapters, 2 terminators, one 15' cable).	1
3	Artisoft 2mbps ISA network adapters	4
4	Artisoft 2mbps MCA network adapters	1

```
Prepared by:              Date:               Page:
         L.R. Smith            3/16/1992            1   of   1
         This form is taken from "Do-It-Yourself Networking With LANtastic"
                          Published by SAMS (1992)
```

Figure 4.8 *Lucy's partial shopping list for Acme's network.*

 *Networking with LANtastic*

Configuration Plans

Once a basic design has been created, it needs to be "fleshed out." The specifics of the network need to be developed and detailed to the point where you know exactly what is going to be set up when the installation is done.

The Detailed Configuration

The next step is to do a detailed configuration of the physical layout of the network. This requires the Site Analysis Layout that has already been created and the planned additions and changes, such as:

- New and relocated PCs.
- New and relocated printers, plotters, etc.
- New and relocated modems.

By referring to the rules for cabling to support a particular network type (see Chapter 5, "Selecting a Network Technology"), you will be able to determine how long cable runs will be and what cabling components will be needed.

In the Acme case, the final site plan using Artisoft's AE/2 EtherNet system is shown in Figure 4.9.

Notice that Lucy switched the two receptionists' positions so that Receptionist 2 could still access the dot-matrix printer, even though it will be directly attached to the print/database server. Also notice that Lucy planned to run cables across open floor in two places and noted that cable cover strips would be needed. This is very important — network cabling can be a real hazard not only to people (injuries caused by tripping over cables have led to many lawsuits), but also to the integrity of the network (exposed cables can be easily damaged, PCs pulled off tables, and so on).

Now that the proposed floor plan is finished, the shopping list can be completed (see Figure 4.10 for Acme's list) and the final cost of the network determined.

Planning Your Network

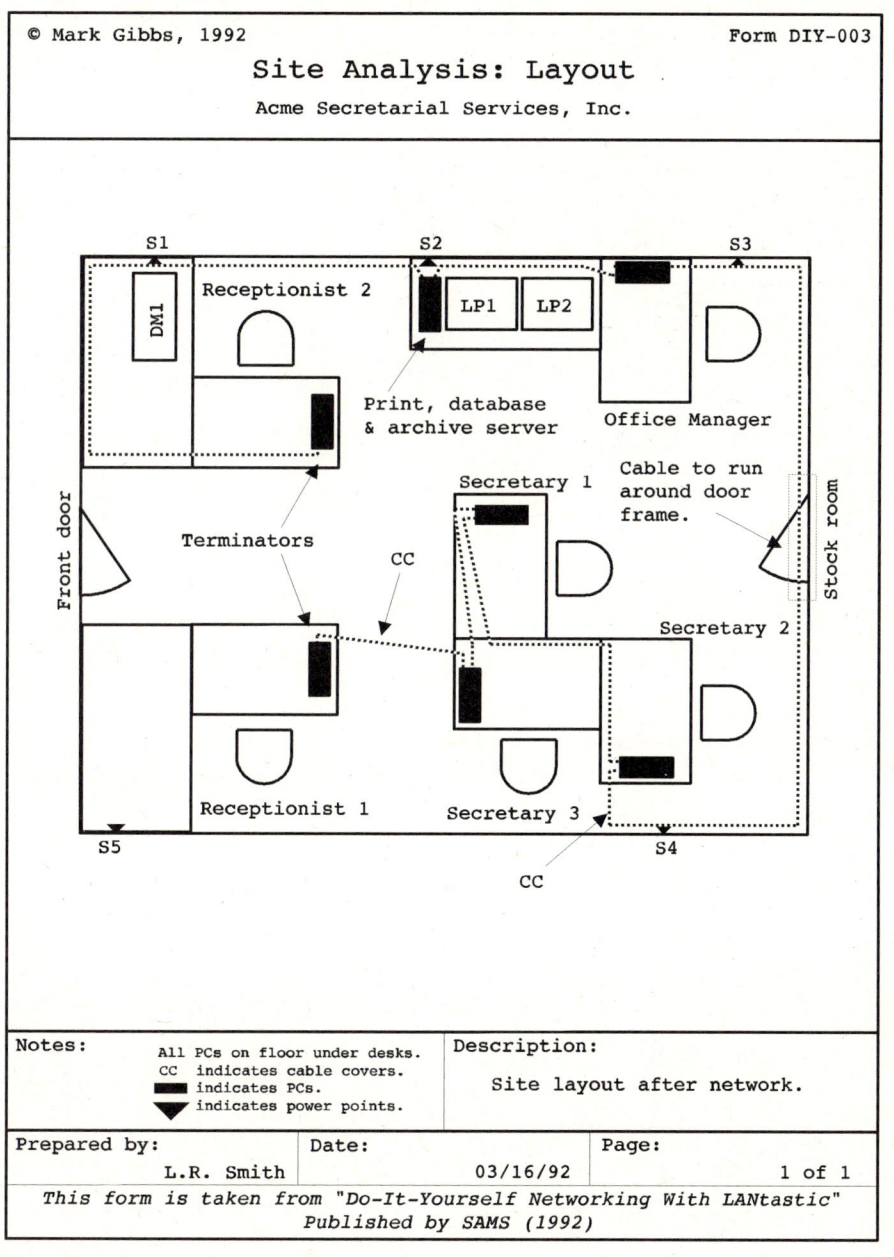

Figure 4.9 *The proposed layout for the Acme network.*

Networking with LANtastic

```
© Mark Gibbs, 1992                                    Form: DIY-007
                      Purchase List
                Acme Secretarial Services, Inc.
```

#	Description	Quantity
1	PC: 80386 ISA w. 640 KB RAM and 3.5 FD (n.b. no HD)	1
2	Artisoft 2mbps ISA Starter Kit (includes 2 network adapters, 2 terminators, one 15' cable).	1
3	Artisoft 2mbps ISA network adapters	4
4	Artisoft 2mbps MCA network adapters	1
5	50' cables (includes one spare).	6
6	Nailed cable clips (boxes, 25 per box)	8
7	Adhesive cable clips (boxes, 20 per box)	2
8	Cable cover strips .... 6' .... 3'	1 1

```
Prepared by:              Date:                 Page:
       L.R. Smith              3/16/1992              1   of   1
```

This form is taken from "Do-It-Yourself Networking With LANtastic"
Published by SAMS (1992)

Figure 4.10 Lucy's final shopping list for Acme's network.

Planning Your Network

Some of the items to be considered in finalizing the shopping list are:

- New major equipment items, such as PCs and printers.
- Cabling components, such as connectors, terminators, and so on (see Chapter 5, "Selecting a Network Technology").
- Cable clips and ties.
- Cable covers (to keep people from tripping on exposed cables).
- Extra power cords.

The new use of electrical outlets can now be checked and recorded. Acme's plan is shown in Figure 4.11. This analysis shows that the power consumption is still within the capability of the circuit.

Caution: If you find that your new system will exceed the power capacity of an electrical circuit, you will need to call in an electrician. Overloading power circuits is a real fire hazard, and if you are an employer, you could find yourself liable for violating building or safety codes.

The General Configuration

The next planning issue is to design the general configuration. This consists of:

- What each machine will be named on the network.
- What type of machine it will be (workstation, workstation/server, server only).
- What function each server will have.

Figure 4.12 shows the plan Lucy generated for Acme's general configuration.

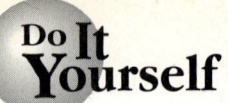
Networking with LANtastic

© Mark Gibbs, 1992   Form: DIY-004

Site Analysis: Power
Acme Secretarial Services, Inc.

Circuit ID: Baseboard 60 amp

ID	Type	Devices	Load	Skt. total
S1	Single	PC & screen (Recep.1)	4.0A	
		Dot matrix printer (DM1)	1.0A	
		Desk lamp	0.3A	5.3A
S2	Double	Laser Printer (LP1)	4.0A	
		Laser Printer (LP2)	4.0A	
		Desk lamp	0.3A	
		Dictation machine	0.3A	
		Print/Arch./Database server	4.5A	13.1A
S3	Double	PC & screen (Manager)	5.5A	
		Desk lamp	0.6A	
		Dictation machine	0.3A	6.4A
S4	Double	PC & screen (Sec. 1)	4.5A	
		PC & screen (Sec. 2)	4.5A	
		PC & screen (Sec. 3)	4.5A	
		Desk lamps (3)	0.9A	14.4A
S5	Single	PC & screen (Recep.1)	4.5A	
		Desk lamp	0.3A	
		Answering machines	0.9A	5.7A

Circuit total: 44.9A

Prepared by: L.R. Smith   Date: 3/16/1992   Page: 1 of 1

This form is taken from "Do-It-Yourself Networking With LANtastic"
Published by SAMS (1992)

Figure 4.11   Acme's new electrical outlet usage.

Planning Your Network

```
© Mark Gibbs, 1992                                    Form: DIY-008
                      Network Configuration
                     Acme Secretarial Services, Inc.
```

Location	Type	Function	Machine name
Manager	C/S	Document database	LUCY
Sec. 1	C		JEAN
Sec. 2	C		PAT
Sec. 3	C		GLAEN
Recep. 1	C		ED
Recep. 2	C		BRENNEN
Print/archive	SO	Mail, mailing database print, and archives	GRYPHON

Prepared by: L.R. Smith	Date: 3/16/1992	Page: 1 of 1

This form is taken from "Do-It-Yourself Networking With LANtastic"
Published by SAMS (1992)

Figure 4.12 *Acme's general network configuration.*

Networking with LANtastic

Naming Machines on the Network

How you name the PCs on your network is pretty much up to you. You can choose names based on the name of the normal user of that PC, or you can also make the name of the machine identical to the normal user's network login name.

In general, you should name the machines as is appropriate for your organization's needs. If your company is very formal, it may be inappropriate to call a server SNOOPY or BIGBOY. And unless you want to make casual network access difficult, names should also be reasonably easy to remember and relate to their function. For example, a server called T$R_PP would not be easy to identify.

Workstation, Workstation/Server, or Server Only?

If you want to have the greatest degree of access to all network resources, you may decide to make every user machine a workstation/server. While this makes access always available, it increases the number of servers that need to be managed. By the time you have 10 or 20 servers running, you may regret such a decision.

> **Note:** If you configure PCs with users on them as workstations only, you will increase the available memory, which can be a crucial issue with many of today's applications.

To increase performance, you can make a PC a dedicated server by running the ALONE.EXE program. This is also a wise idea when there is any chance of a casual user interfering or, even worse, disrupting the service supplied by the server. ALONE can be "locked" to prevent unauthorized access (although nothing beats locking servers away to ensure that they are secure).

What Functions Will Each Server Have?

Many people tend to load as many functions as possible on each server system. The usual result is a decrease in performance and an increase in complexity, both of which are probably not what was wanted in the first place.

In general, try to spread out the work required among all of the servers. Don't use one server for all of the databases, archiving, and printing if you have other servers that can share the load.

If a server is, in fact, a workstation/server and has a user on it, try to avoid making that system a focus for many users; otherwise, they will all see a drop in performance.

Configuring the Servers

Once you've established the general layout and configuration of the network, you need to do a detailed configuration for each server. This should cover:

- General setup.
- Server's resources.
- Server's users.

Figures 4.13 and 4.14 show the configurations of Acme's two server systems: GRYPHON (the print, database, and archive server) and LUCY (the office manager's PC that will hold the document templates).

General Setup

You'll notice that the mail system has been disabled on LUCY, as Lucy wanted all users to access just the one mail system on GRYPHON. Once the servers were planned in outline, Acme could start developing a user configuration plan for both servers (see Figures 4.15 and 4.16).

Do It Yourself
Networking with LANtastic

```
© Mark Gibbs, 1992                                    Form: DIY-009
                    Network Server Configuration #1
                      Acme Secretarial Services, Inc.
```

Server name	GRYPHON	Location	Main office
Control dir.	c:\LANTASTI.NET	Install dir.	C:\LANTASTI
Mail system	Enabled	Server user	None (dedicated)
Startup file	C:\LANTASTI\STARTNET.BAT merged into AUTOEXEC.BAT		

```
Directory structure:

    C:\
            LANTASTI
            LANTASTI.NET     - etc.
            DOS
            APPS
            BACKUP
                    JEAN
                    PAT
                    GLAEN
                    ED
                    BRENNEN
                    LUCY
            ARCHIVES
                    QUOTES
                    REPORTS
            ACCOUNTS
```

Prepared by:	Date:	Page:
L.R. Smith	3/16/1992	1 of 1

This form is taken from "Do-It-Yourself Networking With LANtastic"
Published by SAMS (1992)

Figure 4.13 *The planned configuration for Acme's server GRYPHON.*

Planning Your Network

```
© Mark Gibbs, 1992                                    Form: DIY-009
                  Network Server Configuration #1
                    Acme Secretarial Services, Inc.
```

Server name	LUCY	Location	Main office
Control dir.	c:\LANTASTI.NET	Install dir.	C:\LANTASTI
Mail system	~~Enabled~~	Server user	None (dedicated)
Startup file	C:\LANTASTI\STARTNET.BAT merged into AUTOEXEC.BAT		

```
Directory structure:

     C:\
             LANTASTI
             LANTASTI.NET        - etc.
             DOS
             APPS
             ARCHIVES
                     QUOTES
                     REPORTS
             ACCOUNTS
             WORK
             WP
                     DOCUMENT    - shared templates and files
```

Prepared by:	Date:	Page:
L.R. Smith	3/16/1992	1 of 1

This form is taken from "Do-It-Yourself Networking With LANtastic"
Published by SAMS (1992)

Figure 4.14 *The planned configuration for Acme's server LUCY.*

Networking with LANtastic

```
© Mark Gibbs, 1992                                    Form: DIY-010
              Network Server Configuration #2: Users
                   Acme Secretarial Services, Inc.
```

Server name		GRYPHON	

Real name		User name	* ("everyone")
Status	Group	Privileges	(none)
Acc. expiration	Never	Login days	M T W T F
Renew password	0 days	Login times	08:00 to 18:00
Real name	Lucy Smith	User name	LRSMITH
Status	System manger	Privileges	Q M U S
Acc. expiration	Never	Login days	S M T W T F S
Renew password	7 days	Login times	00:00 to 24:00
Real name	Jean Gibbs	User name	AJGIBBS
Status		Privileges	U
Acc. expiration	Never	Login days	M T W T F
Renew password	30 days	Login times	08:00 to 18:00
Real name	Pat Lay	User name	PLAY
Status		Privileges	U
Acc. expiration	Never	Login days	M T W T F
Renew password	30 days	Login times	08:00 to 18:00
Real name	Glaen Redeker	User name	GREDEKER
Status		Privileges	U
Acc. expiration	Never	Login days	M T W T F
Renew password	30 days	Login times	08:00 to 18:00
Real name	Ed Lay	User name	ELAY
Status	System manager	Privileges	Q M U S
Acc. expiration	Never	Login days	S M T W T F S
Renew password	7 days	Login times	00:00 to 24:00
Real name	Brennen Redeker	User name	BREDEKER
Status		Privileges	U
Acc. expiration	Never	Login days	M T W T F
Renew password	30 days	Login times	08:00 to 18:00
Prepared by: L.R. Smith	Date: 3/16/1992	Page: 1 of 1	

```
     This form is taken from "Do-It-Yourself Networking With LANtastic"
                      Published by SAMS (1992)
```

Figure 4.15 *The planned users and their configuration for Acme's server GRYPHON.*

© Mark Gibbs, 1992
Form: DIY-010

Network Server Configuration #2: Users

Acme Secretarial Services, Inc.

Server name	LUCY

Real name		User name	* ("everyone")
Status	Group	Privileges	(none)
Acc. expiration	Never	Login days	M T W T F
Renew password	0 days	Login times	08:00 to 18:00
Real name	Lucy Smith	User name	LRSMITH
Status	System manger	Privileges	Q M U S
Acc. expiration	Never	Login days	S M T W T F S
Renew password	7 days	Login times	00:00 to 24:00
Real name	Jean Gibbs	User name	AJGIBBS
Status		Privileges	U
Acc. expiration	Never	Login days	M T W T F
Renew password	30 days	Login times	08:00 to 18:00
Real name	Pat Lay	User name	PLAY
Status		Privileges	U
Acc. expiration	Never	Login days	M T W T F
Renew password	30 days	Login times	08:00 to 18:00
Real name	Glaen Redeker	User name	GREDEKER
Status		Privileges	U
Acc. expiration	Never	Login days	M T W T F
Renew password	30 days	Login times	08:00 to 18:00
Real name	Ed Lay	User name	ELAY
Status	System manager	Privileges	Q M U S
Acc. expiration	Never	Login days	S M T W T F S
Renew password	7 days	Login times	00:00 to 24:00
Real name	Brennen Redeker	User name	BREDEKER
Status		Privileges	U
Acc. expiration	Never	Login days	M T W T F
Renew password	30 days	Login times	08:00 to 18:00

Prepared by: L.R. Smith	Date: 3/16/1992	Page: 1 of 1

This form is taken from "Do-It-Yourself Networking With LANtastic"
Published by SAMS (1992)

Figure 4.16 *The planned users and their configuration for Acme's server LUCY.*

Networking with LANtastic

Server Resources

Next, each server's shared resources had to be planned. For GRYPHON, Acme's plan for shared disk resources is shown in Figure 4.17 and their plan for shared printers in Figures 4.18, 4.19, and 4.20. The shared disk resources for LUCY are shown in Figure 4.21 (as LUCY wasn't intended to have any printers attached, there is no shared printer resource plan).

The Timetable

Now that you've planned your network, what you'll need to purchase, and how it will be organized, you can start to build a *timetable*. This is simply a schedule of what will be done, when it will be done, and who'll do it.

It is vitally important that you don't rush any stage of the installation process. Haste does indeed make waste, as well as mistakes. When you don't allow adequate time for installing the network adapters, for example, a small problem such as having trouble fitting a card into a slot or trying to retrieve a screw that has fallen into the PC can delay you so that you're still rushing around like a lunatic at midnight.

> **Note:** Murphy's law of time states, "The time required to complete a task is at least twice the time allocated if you're in a hurry."

A strategy that can pay off if you're not in a tearing hurry to get the network running (which, according to Murphy, will not work properly under that constraint) is to allocate time (say, after work on a series of days) and upgrade one PC each session. It is important to ensure that when the network goes into active service, it works properly. If it doesn't, the users may not take the network seriously or may avoid using it because of the potential consequences of its failures. This lack of user confidence will not help integrate the network into the organization and will certainly delay your company seeing the benefits of the system.

Planning Your Network

```
© Mark Gibbs, 1992                                           Form: DIY-011
                    Network Server Shared Disk Resources
                       Acme Secretarial Services, Inc.
```

Server name	GRYPHON						Res. name		BACKUP			
Local definition	C:\BACKUP											
Order	User						Access rights					
8	*	~~R~~	~~W~~	~~C~~	~~M~~	~~L~~	~~D~~	~~K~~	~~N~~	~~E~~	~~A~~	~~I~~	~~P~~
1	GUEST	~~R~~	~~W~~	~~C~~	~~M~~	~~L~~	~~D~~	~~K~~	~~N~~	~~E~~	~~A~~	~~I~~	~~P~~
2	LRSMITH	R	W	C	~~M~~	L	D	~~K~~	N	E	A	~~I~~	~~P~~
3	AJGIBBS	R	W	C	~~M~~	L	D	~~K~~	N	E	A	~~I~~	~~P~~
4	PLAY	R	W	C	~~M~~	L	D	~~K~~	N	E	A	~~I~~	~~P~~
5	GREDEKER	R	W	C	~~M~~	L	D	~~K~~	N	E	A	~~I~~	~~P~~
6	ELAY	R	W	C	~~M~~	L	D	~~K~~	N	E	A	~~I~~	~~P~~
7	BREDEKER	R	W	C	~~M~~	L	D	~~K~~	N	E	A	~~I~~	~~P~~
		R	W	C	M	L	D	K	N	E	A	I	P
		R	W	C	M	L	D	K	N	E	A	I	P
		R	W	C	M	L	D	K	N	E	A	I	P
		R	W	C	M	L	D	K	N	E	A	I	P
		R	W	C	M	L	D	K	N	E	A	I	P
		R	W	C	M	L	D	K	N	E	A	I	P
		R	W	C	M	L	D	K	N	E	A	I	P
		R	W	C	M	L	D	K	N	E	A	I	P
		R	W	C	M	L	D	K	N	E	A	I	P
		R	W	C	M	L	D	K	N	E	A	I	P
		R	W	C	M	L	D	K	N	E	A	I	P
		R	W	C	M	L	D	K	N	E	A	I	P
		R	W	C	M	L	D	K	N	E	A	I	P
		R	W	C	M	L	D	K	N	E	A	I	P
		R	W	C	M	L	D	K	N	E	A	I	P
		R	W	C	M	L	D	K	N	E	A	I	P
		R	W	C	M	L	D	K	N	E	A	I	P
		R	W	C	M	L	D	K	N	E	A	I	P

Prepared by: L.R. Smith	Date: 3/16/1992	Page: 1 of 1

```
This form is taken from "Do-It-Yourself Networking With LANtastic"
                    Published by SAMS (1992)
```

Figure 4.17 *The configuration of shared disk resources on Acme's server GRYPHON.*

Networking with LANtastic

```
© Mark Gibbs, 1992                                    Form: DIY-012
```

Network Server Shared Printer Resources
Acme Secretarial Services, Inc.

Server name	GRYPHON				Resource name		@LASER1			
Printer	Apple LaserWriter II NT									
Port	COM1:	~~COM2:~~		~~LPT1:~~		~~LPT2:~~		~~LPT3:~~		
Baud rate	9600				Banner		ENABLED			
Form feeds	DISABLED				Lines/page		DISABLED			
Immed. despool	ENABLED				Despool timeout		60		seconds	
Tab width	0				Paper width		80			
Chars/second	0				Handshake		H/W S/W ~~None~~			
Setup delay	0				Cleanup delay		0			

Order	User	Access rights (R W C L are standard)										
8	*	R	W	C	~~M~~	L	~~D~~	~~K~~	~~N~~	~~E~~	~~A~~	~~I~~	~~P~~
1	GUEST	R	W	C	~~M~~	L	~~D~~	~~K~~	~~N~~	~~E~~	~~A~~	~~I~~	~~P~~
2	LRSMITH	R	W	C	~~M~~	L	~~D~~	~~K~~	~~N~~	~~E~~	~~A~~	~~I~~	~~P~~
3	AJGIBBS	R	W	C	~~M~~	L	~~D~~	~~K~~	~~N~~	~~E~~	~~A~~	~~I~~	~~P~~
4	PLAY	R	W	C	~~M~~	L	~~D~~	~~K~~	~~N~~	~~E~~	~~A~~	~~I~~	~~P~~
5	GREDEKER	R	W	C	~~M~~	L	~~D~~	~~K~~	~~N~~	~~E~~	~~A~~	~~I~~	~~P~~
6	ELAY	R	W	C	~~M~~	L	~~D~~	~~K~~	~~N~~	~~E~~	~~A~~	~~I~~	~~P~~
7	BREDEKER	R	W	C	~~M~~	L	~~D~~	~~K~~	~~N~~	~~E~~	~~A~~	~~I~~	~~P~~
		R	W	C	M	L	D	K	N	E	A	I	P
		R	W	C	M	L	D	K	N	E	A	I	P
		R	W	C	M	L	D	K	N	E	A	I	P
		R	W	C	M	L	D	K	N	E	A	I	P
		R	W	C	M	L	D	K	N	E	A	I	P
		R	W	C	M	L	D	K	N	E	A	I	P
		R	W	C	M	L	D	K	N	E	A	I	P
		R	W	C	M	L	D	K	N	E	A	I	P
		R	W	C	M	L	D	K	N	E	A	I	P
		R	W	C	M	L	D	K	N	E	A	I	P
		R	W	C	M	L	D	K	N	E	A	I	P

Prepared by:	Date:	Page:
L.R. Smith	3/16/1992	1 of 1

This form is taken from "Do-It-Yourself Networking With LANtastic"
Published by SAMS (1992)

Figure 4.18 *The configuration of shared printer resource @LASER1 on Acme's server GRYPHON.*

Planning Your Network

```
© Mark Gibbs, 1992                                          Form: DIY-012
              Network Server Shared Printer Resources
                   Acme Secretarial Services, Inc.
```

Server name	GRYPHON				Resource name			@LASER2			
Printer	HP Laserjet II										
Port		~~COM1~~		~~COM2~~		LPT1:		~~LPT2~~		~~LPT3~~	
Baud rate					Banner			ENABLED			
Form feeds	ENABLED				Lines/page			DISABLED			
Immed. despool	ENABLED				Despool timeout			60		seconds	
Tab width	0				Paper width			80			
Chars/second	0				Handshake			H/W	S/W	None	
Setup delay	0				Cleanup delay			0			
Order	User	Access rights (R WCL are standard)									
8	*	R	W	C	~~M~~	L	~~D~~	~~K~~	~~N~~	~~E~~	~~A~~	~~I~~	~~P~~
1	GUEST	R	W	C	~~M~~	L	~~D~~	~~K~~	~~N~~	~~E~~	~~A~~	~~I~~	~~P~~
2	LRSMITH	R	W	C	~~M~~	L	~~D~~	~~K~~	~~N~~	~~E~~	~~A~~	~~I~~	~~P~~
3	AJGIBBS	R	W	C	~~M~~	L	~~D~~	~~K~~	~~N~~	~~E~~	~~A~~	~~I~~	~~P~~
4	PLAY	R	W	C	~~M~~	L	~~D~~	~~K~~	~~N~~	~~E~~	~~A~~	~~I~~	~~P~~
5	GREDEKER	R	W	C	~~M~~	L	~~D~~	~~K~~	~~N~~	~~E~~	~~A~~	~~I~~	~~P~~
6	ELAY	R	W	C	~~M~~	L	~~D~~	~~K~~	~~N~~	~~E~~	~~A~~	~~I~~	~~P~~
7	BREDEKER	R	W	C	~~M~~	L	~~D~~	~~K~~	~~N~~	~~E~~	~~A~~	~~I~~	~~P~~
		R	W	C	M	L	D	K	N	E	A	I	P
		R	W	C	M	L	D	K	N	E	A	I	P
		R	W	C	M	L	D	K	N	E	A	I	P
		R	W	C	M	L	D	K	N	E	A	I	P
		R	W	C	M	L	D	K	N	E	A	I	P
		R	W	C	M	L	D	K	N	E	A	I	P
		R	W	C	M	L	D	K	N	E	A	I	P
		R	W	C	M	L	D	K	N	E	A	I	P
		R	W	C	M	L	D	K	N	E	A	I	P
		R	W	C	M	L	D	K	N	E	A	I	P
		R	W	C	M	L	D	K	N	E	A	I	P
		R	W	C	M	L	D	K	N	E	A	I	P
		R	W	C	M	L	D	K	N	E	A	I	P
Prepared by: L.R. Smith			Date: 3/16/1992						Page: 1 of 1			

```
This form is taken from "Do-It-Yourself Networking With LANtastic"
                    Published by SAMS (1992)
```

Figure 4.19 *The configuration of shared printer resource @LASER2 on Acme's server GRYPHON.*

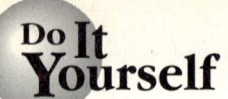

Networking with LANtastic

© Mark Gibbs, 1992								Form: DIY-012			
Network Server Shared Printer Resources											
Acme Secretarial Services, Inc.											

Server name	GRYPHON			Resource name			@DOTMATRIX				
Printer	EPSON FX-100										
Port		~~COM1~~	~~COM2~~	~~LPT1~~		LPT2:	~~LPT3~~				
Baud rate				Banner			ENABLED				
Form feeds	ENABLED			Lines/page			60				
Immed. despool	ENABLED			Despool timeout			60		seconds		
Tab width	0			Paper width			80				
Chars/second	0			Handshake			H/W	S/W	None		
Setup delay	0			Cleanup delay			0				
Order	User	Access rights (R WCL are standard)									
8	*	R	W	C	~~M~~	L	~~D~~	~~K~~	~~N~~	~~E~~	~~A~~	~~I~~	~~P~~
1	GUEST	R	W	C	~~M~~	L	~~D~~	~~K~~	~~N~~	~~E~~	~~A~~	~~I~~	~~P~~
2	LRSMITH	R	W	C	~~M~~	L	~~D~~	~~K~~	~~N~~	~~E~~	~~A~~	~~I~~	~~P~~
3	AJGIBBS	R	W	C	~~M~~	L	~~D~~	~~K~~	~~N~~	~~E~~	~~A~~	~~I~~	~~P~~
4	PLAY	R	W	C	~~M~~	L	~~D~~	~~K~~	~~N~~	~~E~~	~~A~~	~~I~~	~~P~~
5	GREDEKER	R	W	C	~~M~~	L	~~D~~	~~K~~	~~N~~	~~E~~	~~A~~	~~I~~	~~P~~
6	ELAY	R	W	C	~~M~~	L	~~D~~	~~K~~	~~N~~	~~E~~	~~A~~	~~I~~	~~P~~
7	BREDEKER	R	W	C	~~M~~	L	~~D~~	~~K~~	~~N~~	~~E~~	~~A~~	~~I~~	~~P~~
		R	W	C	M	L	D	K	N	E	A	I	P
		R	W	C	M	L	D	K	N	E	A	I	P
		R	W	C	M	L	D	K	N	E	A	I	P
		R	W	C	M	L	D	K	N	E	A	I	P
		R	W	C	M	L	D	K	N	E	A	I	P
		R	W	C	M	L	D	K	N	E	A	I	P
		R	W	C	M	L	D	K	N	E	A	I	P
		R	W	C	M	L	D	K	N	E	A	I	P
		R	W	C	M	L	D	K	N	E	A	I	P
		R	W	C	M	L	D	K	N	E	A	I	P
		R	W	C	M	L	D	K	N	E	A	I	P
		R	W	C	M	L	D	K	N	E	A	I	P

Prepared by: L.R. Smith	Date: 3/16/1992	Page: 1 of 1

This form is taken from "Do-It-Yourself Networking With LANtastic" Published by SAMS (1992)

Figure 4.20 *The configuration of shared printer resource @DOTMATRIX on Acme's server GRYPHON.*

Planning Your Network

```
© Mark Gibbs, 1992                                    Form: DIY-011
            Network Server Shared Disk Resources
               Acme Secretarial Services, Inc.
```

Server name	LUCY				Res. name			DOCUMENT			
Local definition	C:\WP\DOCUMENT										
Order	User					Access rights						
8	*	~~R~~	~~W~~	~~C~~	~~M~~	~~L~~	~~D~~	~~K~~	~~N~~	~~E~~	~~A~~	~~I~~	~~P~~
1	GUEST	~~R~~	~~W~~	~~C~~	~~M~~	~~L~~	~~D~~	~~K~~	~~N~~	~~E~~	~~A~~	~~I~~	~~P~~
2	LRSMITH	R	~~W~~	~~C~~	~~M~~	L	~~D~~	~~K~~	~~N~~	~~E~~	~~A~~	~~I~~	~~P~~
3	AJGIBBS	R	~~W~~	~~C~~	~~M~~	L	~~D~~	~~K~~	~~N~~	~~E~~	~~A~~	~~I~~	~~P~~
4	PLAY	R	~~W~~	~~C~~	~~M~~	L	~~D~~	~~K~~	~~N~~	~~E~~	~~A~~	~~I~~	~~P~~
5	GREDEKER	R	~~W~~	~~C~~	~~M~~	L	~~D~~	~~K~~	~~N~~	~~E~~	~~A~~	~~I~~	~~P~~
6	ELAY	R	~~W~~	~~C~~	~~M~~	L	~~D~~	~~K~~	~~N~~	~~E~~	~~A~~	~~I~~	~~P~~
7	BREDEKER	R	~~W~~	~~C~~	~~M~~	L	~~D~~	~~K~~	~~N~~	~~E~~	~~A~~	~~I~~	~~P~~
		R	W	C	M	L	D	K	N	E	A	I	P
		R	W	C	M	L	D	K	N	E	A	I	P
		R	W	C	M	L	D	K	N	E	A	I	P
		R	W	C	M	L	D	K	N	E	A	I	P
		R	W	C	M	L	D	K	N	E	A	I	P
		R	W	C	M	L	D	K	N	E	A	I	P
		R	W	C	M	L	D	K	N	E	A	I	P
		R	W	C	M	L	D	K	N	E	A	I	P
		R	W	C	M	L	D	K	N	E	A	I	P
		R	W	C	M	L	D	K	N	E	A	I	P
		R	W	C	M	L	D	K	N	E	A	I	P
		R	W	C	M	L	D	K	N	E	A	I	P
		R	W	C	M	L	D	K	N	E	A	I	P
		R	W	C	M	L	D	K	N	E	A	I	P
		R	W	C	M	L	D	K	N	E	A	I	P
		R	W	C	M	L	D	K	N	E	A	I	P
		R	W	C	M	L	D	K	N	E	A	I	P
		R	W	C	M	L	D	K	N	E	A	I	P

Prepared by: L.R. Smith	Date: 3/16/1992	Page: 1 of 1

```
This form is taken from "Do-It-Yourself Networking With LANtastic"
                    Published by SAMS (1992)
```

Figure 4.21 *The configuration of shared disk resources on Acme's server LUCY.*

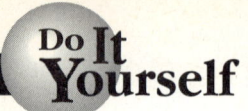

Networking with LANtastic

A timetable should cover the following events:

- *Ordering equipment.* This includes getting quotes and placing the order.

- *Receiving and checking equipment.* When the equipment arrives, you need to make sure that the packages aren't damaged and what the supplier says has been sent on the packing note is, in fact, there. Checking equipment becomes more important the larger the network is.

- *Reading manuals and checking plans.* Although you may have made detailed plans, you may find upon reading the manuals that come with the products that there are changes to software configuration or hardware settings. Allowing time to validate your plans can save a lot of time in the actual installation.

- *Site preparation.* In addition to installing cabling, it is likely that you'll have to move furniture, check or upgrade power supplies, and so on.

- *Hardware installation.* As has already been said, there are two ways to schedule installing hardware: all at once or spread over a few days or weeks. For larger networks, installation over a period of time is often the only choice. For smaller networks, and if you're new to doing things to PCs, make sure that you take your time.

- *Software installation.* As with the other phases, give yourself adequate time. If you're going to make major changes such as moving data from one PC to another, make backups first in case you have a problem or make a mistake.

- *Configuring and testing.* Configuring and testing can be a long process. With the kind of planning that I've discussed, this process will be shorter, but, again, you must not rush it. Testing, in particular, must be thorough. Trying to correct problems that occur when users are trying to do their jobs is always frustrating and stressful for all concerned.

- *Going "live."* A date should be set as a target for the network becoming operational. At this time, all planned facilities should have been tested and working correctly. For larger networks, you might phase the introduction of services over a period of time. This allows users to become familiar with facilities one at a time and reduces the time that the system needs to be out of commission to allow for configuration.

- *Training.* Although the network should be *transparent* (that is, it should not interfere with or be obvious to users), users will need instruction for the services that they are allowed to control. At the very minimum, users should be aware of the network and what it does for the company. This is good for building confidence in the system as well as making it more likely that any problems will be reported.

The timetable that Lucy Smith drew up for Acme is shown in Figure 4.22.

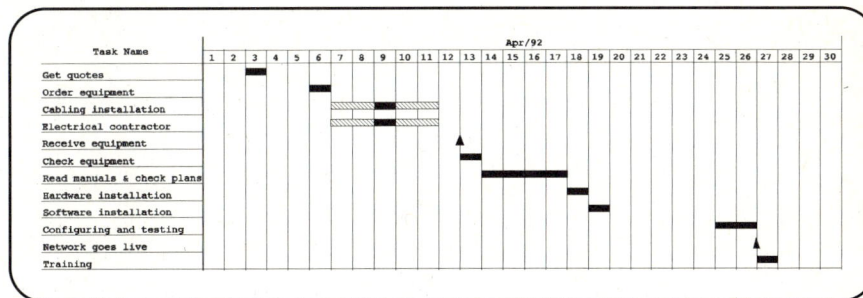

Figure 4.22 *Acme's network installation timetable.*

Getting Sign-Off

This is the point at which you should have developed a case for the proposed network that either stands up or doesn't. The viability of the plan will almost certainly be based on your financial argument — does the plan make financial sense to the company? The proposal that Lucy Smith took to the owners was based on the analysis of the problems, their monetary consequences, and the projected savings that solving those problems would give.

While the approach you take to building a cost-justification argument for a network may vary from the Acme example, there is a common set of rules to follow. The six rules to remember when you are seeking approval to introduce networking into your organization are:

Networking with LANtastic

- *Avoid issues that have unquantifiable benefits.* Just to say that a network will make business more efficient doesn't provide a basis for a yes-or-no decision. The alternative is to say that, for example, turnaround on jobs will be 50% faster and increase job profitability by 25%. That kind of argument, provided your figures are justifiable, will be very easy to agree to.

- *Avoid technical discussions.* Very few people are interested in, or can understand, the technical issues of networking. Keep your proposal grounded in business issues.

- *Make sure that time frames are realistic — preferably pessimistic.* Don't tie yourself to an implementation schedule that will be difficult to achieve. Err on the side of caution. (And remember Murphy's law of contingent failure — "If something can go wrong, it will.")

- *Keep it relevant.* Adding features or facilities that aren't relevant to business will not only be of no interest to those who can sign off the proposal but may detract from the perceived value of the system.

- *Address reliability and security.* Most decision makers will look for problems that are implicit in a proposal. The possibility and consequences of network failure or unauthorized access need to be considered and covered adequately for your company. For smaller, less critical networks, this will probably not be a big issue, but it is still worth addressing in order to ensure that you have a plan for dealing with problems.

- *Assess risks.* Again, decision makers are usually not keen on taking risks if they'll have to ultimately "take responsibility." As you develop your plans, you'll see areas of risk. For example, if you hit a major obstacle on installation, what will the consequences be? How would you recover from problems? These issues are easily handled if you keep them in mind as you plan and address them in your proposal.

Management

The final planning that you need to do is to define the management activities that you'll be doing. An invaluable tool to developing a management strategy is to establish and maintain a *system log*.

Where and how you keep the system log information is up to you, but if you do keep it on a computer, make sure that you have at least one easily accessible backup copy. An additional paper copy is also a good idea, as it is possible you'll be in a position where you cannot access a computer-based copy.

The table of contents might look like this:

- *Section 1: Plans.* All of the plans, notes, and design work should be kept here for future reference.

- *Section 2: Equipment.* It is important to record the equipment that makes up your network. You should log the details of each PC (make, purchase information, configuration), network adapter cards (supplier, serial number, configuration, PC installed in), printers (supplier, serial number, configuration, PC attached to), and so on.

- *Section 3: Current configuration.* This section should contain all of your notes and any forms dealing with the current configuration of the network.

- *Section 4: Activities.* Because of the importance of your networked resources, maintaining them is vital to ensuring continued service. This section should contain your backup plan (what gets backed-up and when and to what device), restore plan (how backed-up data will be restored), how names will be generated, how passwords will be generated, and where they'll be kept in case they're lost (preferably under lock and key and in someone's charge). Do not keep the passwords in the system log!

- *Section 5: Logs.* If you do have a backup plan, you should keep track of when backups are done, who does them, and what storage system those backups are on. Similarly, restores should be recorded.

While this may seem to be overkill — particularly for small networks — it is likely that your network will grow either in size (attaching

more PCs) or in importance to the organization (becoming critical to the efficient business operation).

You'll find that the forms in Appendix B, "Forms," will make your task of planning and documenting your network much easier. And by creating and maintaining a system log, you'll be on track to handle any eventuality — from handling problems and failures to coping with expansion.

A lot of planning before you get into the nuts and bolts of building a network will save you wasted time and make your system much more cost-effective. LANtastic is fairly simple in its configuration and the implementation of services. Even so, with the kind of extensive and exhaustive planning we've discussed, you can make the whole process of networking your organization as painless as possible.

5

Selecting a Network Technology

The choice of products that you can use to connect PCs has come a long way since the invention of the PC. The first networks crawled along at speeds up to a maximum of about 250,000 bits per second (just over 16 screens of data a second). This sounds fast, but compared to the rate that you can read data from a hard disk (about 60 screens of data a second), it's pretty slow.

Worse still, to manage the data transfer, you need information in the data that specifies who sent it, who is to receive it, error-checking information, and so on. This added data is called *overhead*. Overhead can be a significant percentage of the total data transferred, so in reality a rate of 16 screens per second might have been as low as 8 to 10 screens per second.

Today, there's a wide range of methods used to build networks; these methods are generically called *network technologies*. You can still buy systems that run at 250,000 bits per second, but they're now at the low end of the range.

Networking with LANtastic

At the top end are technologies such as *FDDI* (Fiber Distributed Data Interface), which runs at 100 megabits per second (that's 100,000,000 bits per second, or over 6,500 screens per second) and uses fiber-optic cabling. And the next generation of networking is targeted at speeds measured in gigabits per second (a gigabit is 1,000 megabits).

Today, the bulk of the market is in the middle range of performance between 2.5 megabits per second and 16 megabits per second. These are the mass-market products such as ARCnet, EtherNet, and Token Ring. All of these are mature networking solutions, and when you compare their cost to their performance, they are all realistic choices.

As you'll see later in this chapter, as a do-it-yourself networker, it's probable that you'll choose EtherNet or ARCnet rather than Token Ring, as the latter is generally more complex and, for large systems, more expensive.

To make sound decisions about your network, you should have an appreciation of:

- Cost and performance issues.
- Network layout.
- Network adapter design.
- How network technologies work.
- Network design rules.
- Repeaters, bridges, and routers.

Cost and Performance Issues

Since the early 1980s, the network market has seen increasing competition and more sophisticated manufacturing techniques push prices down by a factor of ten or more. The number of technologies which support networking has remained roughly the same, with a few of the old, slower systems dropping out and several new, high-performance solutions becoming available.

When selecting a network technology, you need to consider several issues. From a business point of view, the choice will be based on a compromise of cost against utility.

Selecting a Network Technology

Cost can be divided into several issues:

- The cost of the network adapters.
- The cost of cabling components.
- The cost of installing, configuring, and testing.
- The cost of maintenance.
- The cost of expansion.

The utility of a networking system is measured by performance:

- The real data rate — the actual rate at which data is transferred (rather than the raw, or "theoretical," data rate).
- The ease of management and reconfiguration.
- The system's reliability. (How often does the transport system fail?)
- The system's availability. (How much of the time is the network actually available for use?)

> **Note:** There is very little useful information available on the performance of local area networks. This may require you to run tests with real networks to determine whether a network will deliver the performance that you need. With LANtastic, you'll find that for most common applications for networks under about 20 users, the system's performance will be adequate. The time to start looking in depth at performance is when you plan to run large database applications or develop software.

There are also other less easily answered questions to consider when selecting a network technology. Whether the manufacturer will stay in business or the technology will be superseded are two important issues you need to evaluate.

Networking with LANtastic

Network Layout

An important aspect of a network is its *layout,* sometimes referred to as *topology.* This can be described in terms of physical layout (the actual shape of the system) and logical layout (the layout of connections on the network). Each view can be quite different for a single network, and both are defined by the technology that the network uses.

There are five basic ways to lay out a physical or logical network:

- Star.
- Bus.
- Ring.
- Daisy chain.
- Tree.

The physical layout is the actual layout that you can see when the various network components are linked together; the logical layout is the way the network looks from the viewpoint of the computers attached and how they see the packets of data flowing around the network. In pragmatic terms, the logical layout isn't that important.

Star

A star layout requires that an element of the network (a computer or a cabling component) is at the center of a group of computers that are networked together (see Figure 5.1).

This configuration requires that the central node routes all data that is to go between any computers on the points of the star. A star system requires more cable than other configurations. If the central node fails, the network will fail completely. On the other hand, failure of any network component other than the central node doesn't affect the network. Another problem with the star configuration is that the central node can become overloaded with data to be routed. This can limit the overall system performance.

Selecting a Network Technology

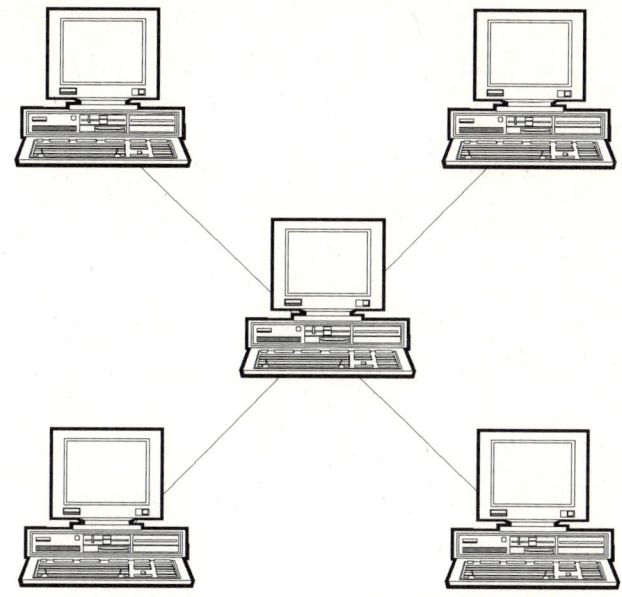

Figure 5.1   A star network layout.

Bus

A bus structured system uses about the same amount of cable as a daisy chain or ring system. All computers on the network connect to a common cable. This is the physical layout used by EtherNet and one of the configurations for ARCnet. Figure 5.2 shows an example of this type of layout.

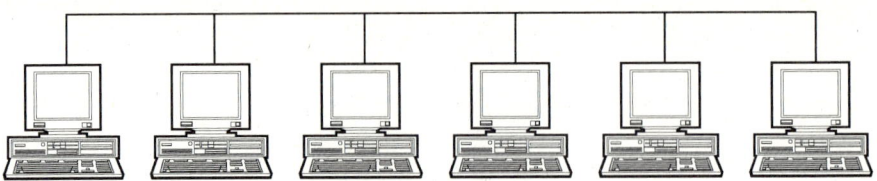

Figure 5.2 *A bus network layout.*

Ring

Ring-structured systems connect each computer to the next by a link that is dedicated to communication only between those two machines (see Figure 5.3). If a link fails, the ring is disabled.

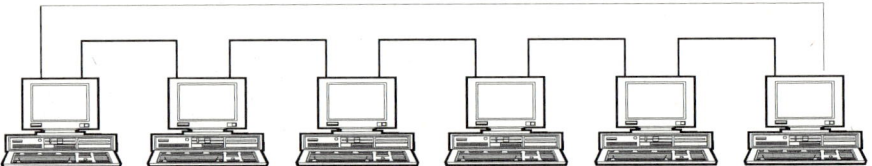

Figure 5.3 *A ring network layout.*

Some ring-structured systems have parallel rings to act as a fail-safe. If one ring fails, traffic is carried on the alternate ring. This, without the redundant ring, is the layout of Token Ring.

Daisy Chain

The daisy-chain layout is like a ring-structured system that is broken at one point (see Figure 5.4). Failure of any link will cause the system to split into two separate networks.

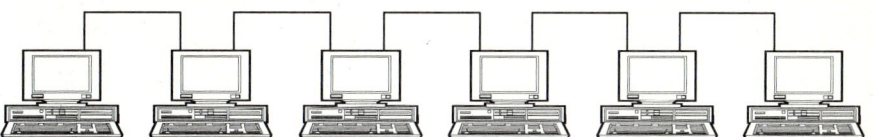

Figure 5.4. *A daisy chain network layout.*

Tree

A tree layout allows for a structure that has branches and branches on branches (see Figure 5.5). A computer is located at the end of each sequence of branches.

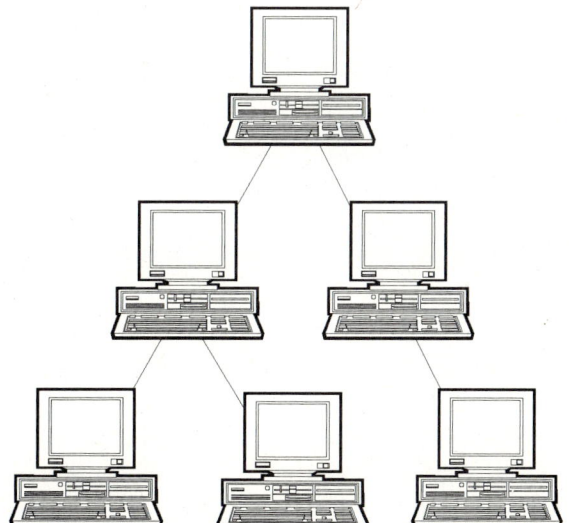

Figure 5.5 *A tree network layout.*

Networking with LANtastic

A network technology that allows a tree structure can be a very flexible solution in real situations. Providing that the connection rules are flexible enough, you can easily construct a layout that meets the needs of a fairly complex floor plan. ARCnet can be built as a tree structure.

Appearances Can Be Deceiving

When looking at the layout of a network, an issue that can be confusing is the additional cabling components: wiring hubs, repeaters, bridges and routers, concentrators, and wiring centers. These devices are either part of the cabling technology or are added to improve manageability or enable service. When these devices are involved, a bus-structured system can look like a string of stars.

Token Ring, for example, uses wiring centers called Media Access Units, or MAUs, to which PCs are connected. This makes a Token Ring system look physically like a ring of stars although it is logically a ring.

Although the five types are the basic layouts for networks, some systems, such as ARCnet, allow for mixtures of layouts within the same network. The various wiring devices that are part of the ARCnet system allow you to create these layouts. When you build real networks and interconnect them through bridges and repeaters, you will create all sorts of hybrid layouts.

In general, the K.I.S.S. principle ("Keep It Simple, Supervisor") should be applied — the more complex the final system, the harder it will be to find and solve problems.

Most of the aspects of building a network don't require you to pay much attention to the logical layout of the system. But in troubleshooting an existing network, an appreciation of the logical structure of the network can be useful.

Network Adapter Design

Network adapters come in a variety of configurations. There are two major types of architecture: those with coprocessors and those without. A coprocessor can be a major performance booster — it off-loads the work required to interface with the network from the host computer.

> **Note:** The coprocessor used to enhance the performance of a network adapter is not the same thing as a coprocessor that you add to your PC to improve the performance of mathematical operations. The numerical coprocessors, such as the 80287 and 80387, are designed to make calculation faster, not to deal with the problem of moving data around. A network adapter coprocessor can be a relatively low-powered device, such as an 8088 or 80186, or, for the really high-performance systems, it might be an 80286 or 80386 processor.

The trade-off for having a network adapter with a coprocessor is cost. As each network adapter is a computer in its own right, it has more components and therefore costs more. Network adapters without coprocessors are slower, of course, but cheaper.

Adapter Card Data Width

The original IBM PC had the ability to transfer data around its system in one-byte chunks (8 bits) at a time. This was due to the design of the processors used — the 8088 and 8086. The size of the "chunk" of data transferred is the *data width*. Adapter cards for these systems were also designed to this standard and are generically referred to as 8-bit cards.

The successor to the IBM PC, the AT, used a different processor, the 80286. This could handle data in 16-bit-wide chunks. This was one of the features that made the IBM AT run faster — it could handle more data at one time.

Now machines based on the 80386 and 80486 processors allow data to be handled in 32-bit chunks. These allow even greater levels of performance. And to capitalize on this, adapter cards are now designed to work in the 16- and 32-bit modes. With network adapters, the greater the data width, the faster that data can be moved from the PC to the network.

For most network workstation purposes, 8-bit network adapter cards are more than adequate to achieve acceptable performance. Once a

workstation starts accessing databases or moving large files around, a 16-bit card may be needed to maintain the desired performance.

For servers in small networks (supporting up to around 10 users) 8-bit network adapters will usually be adequate. If the server is supporting more users or the users are providing a heavy loading, a 16-bit network adapter may be needed.

32-bit adapters are more costly and will usually be needed only for servers that support many users or that are particularly heavily loaded.

> **Note:** In many cases, the system *bottleneck* (the system component that restricts performance) will not be the network adapter card. The most common component that limits performance is the disk subsystem. If the disk controller can be upgraded with additional cache memory or you can afford to upgrade the hard disk drives, you may find that server performance can be dramatically increased.

Bus Design

The next network adapter configuration issue is the bus interface. There are three major PC bus interfaces:

- The industry standard architecture (ISA).
- The extended industry standard architecture (EISA).
- The MicroChannel Architecture (MCA).

ISA network adapters can be used in EISA systems, but EISA cards will only work in EISA-based PCs. MCA cards can only be used in MCA machines (the IBM PS/1 and PS/2 product lines and a selection of other vendors).

Again, these different bus architectures have different performance characteristics: ISA is the slowest, EISA the next fastest, and MCA the fastest. However, different network adapters from different manufacturers may not support these broad descriptions when LAN performance tests are carried out.

The discrepancy is due to the way each manufacturer chooses to implement the network adapter technology and the components they select. With MCA, there is the potential for truly phenomenal performance using a technique called *bus mastering*.

Unfortunately, for various technical and marketing reasons, most network adapter manufacturers haven't yet implemented hardware or low-level drivers that can take advantage of this facility.

How Network Technologies Work

There are several networking technologies that form the mainstream of network adapter products:

- ARCnet.
- EtherNet.
- Token Ring.

ARCnet

The most venerable of these is ARCnet, an acronym for Attached Resource Computer NETwork. Designed and produced by the Datapoint Corporation in the 1970s, ARCnet is what is called a *token passing* network. The system uses a method based on passing control between the stations to give each an equal opportunity to access the network.

The token is a data packet that is sent from node to node in turn. The network has good error-recovery characteristics, is robust, and is easy to install. Unfortunately, it runs at only 2.5Mbps, making it one of the slowest networks.

For small systems, this may not be much of a problem, since ARCnet adapters are fairly cheap. Faster versions of ARCnet have been produced, but they have, of course, higher price tags.

Networking with LANtastic

EtherNet

EtherNet was developed in the 1970s by Xerox and completed by Digital Equipment Company (DEC), Intel, and Xerox (known collectively as DIX) in 1980. EtherNet uses coaxial cable that connects to all nodes on the network and uses a carrier-sense multiple-access with collision-detection network, or CSMA/CD, access scheme.

This method allows any node that wants to access the network to do so, first listening for traffic before transmitting (listening for a carrier). If there is no traffic, transmission begins and the node must immediately check to see if there is a collision due to another node sending data at the same time. If there is a collision, both nodes stop, wait a random time, and then retry their transmissions.

Although this sounds complex, it is all handled by the network adapter itself, and there is no impact on the computer. EtherNet systems run at 10Mbps, and since there is a large, highly competitive marketplace, network adapters are reasonably priced. Artisoft produces its own EtherNet network adapter called the LANtastic AE/2 EtherNet Adapter. This is an ISA card that can be used in almost all PC-compatible computers.

EtherNet can be used with several types of cabling. The thick and thin EtherNet kinds are coaxial cable while the Unshielded Twisted Pair (usually shortened to UTP) is much like telephone cabling. I won't discuss the details of systems based on thick EtherNet or UTP cabling, as they are more complex and costly to install than thin EtherNet.

Token Ring

The Token Ring system was introduced by IBM in 1985. This technology uses the logical configuration of a closed loop or ring. A token circulates around the ring that is grabbed by each station in turn. Once the token is in the possession of a node, it can begin to transmit data.

The benefits of the Token Ring are that it is well engineered, is fairly easy to install, is robust in service, and offers good performance. It carries a higher price tag than EtherNet and comes in either 4 or 16Mbps versions, the latter carrying the higher price tag.

Note: In the following descriptions, I will focus mainly on the "small" type of Token Ring installation that can be easily moved and reconfigured. Large Token Ring systems are complex beasts that require various wiring devices and considerations that make them unsuitable for do-it-yourself installations.

Making a Decision

Choosing the correct network type for you will depend primarily on your selection criteria and the depth of your pocket. The network technologies and their technical characteristics are summarized in Table 5.1.

Table 5.1   Comparing the three main networking technologies.

	ARCnet	*Thin EtherNet*	*Small Token Ring*
Market share	40%	50%	10%
Maximum number of stations per network	255	142	96
Maximum raw data rate	2.5Mbps	10Mbps	4 or 16Mbps
Cost per node	$300–$350	$350–$450	$900–$1200
Cabling type	Coax	Coax	IBM Type 1 or 3
Maximum length of network	20,000 ft.	3035 ft.*	500 ft.
Design complexity	Low	Low to Medium	Medium to High
Installation complexity	Low to Medium	Low to Medium	Medium to High

* Note: This can be greater, but you'll be dealing with a much more complex installation.

Networking with LANtastic

> **Note:** For all the systems discussed here, you can actually extend your network to cover miles rather than feet. To do this you need to use fiber-optic repeaters that connect two sections of normal cable using a fiber-optic link. These devices should be totally invisible to the network and are usually "plug-and-play." They are not cheap, but when you have a large distance to cover, they may be the only solution if you want a high-performance connection.

Network Design Rules

Every network technology has design rules. These rules define the limits of the number of connections, the length and types of cables, and other aspects of the network's physical layout.

Most of these rules can be broken, although not without a degree of risk. For example, a cable between a PC and a network connection might be defined as being a maximum of 10 feet. When you design your network, you may find that you have a 20-foot run so you decide to take a small risk.

Suppose you build your network, and — lo and behold — it does indeed work normally. Then, six months later, you add another machine to the network, and your PCs are suddenly losing connections, and chaos sets in. Disobeying design rules will often cause problems that can be difficult to diagnose.

> **Note:** If you do disobey design rules and your network is running satisfactorily, ensure that you do make a note in your site log of what you've done. This may save time, money, and your sanity when it comes to fault finding.

The design rules discussed in the following sections are generalized. You may find that the rules for a specific manufacturer may vary in either minor or major ways. You should read their manuals very carefully before producing a detailed design.

Selecting a Network Technology

The general rules for all technologies are:

- Do not crimp, fold, or create sharp bends in cables (easily done when you're pulling cable through ceiling or floor crawl spaces).

- Do not pierce or crush cables (particularly important if you're using cable clips).

- Do not stretch or twist cables (also easily done when you're pulling cable through ceiling or floor crawl spaces).

- Do not place unprotected cables in hostile environments (water, high humidity, heat, electrical interference, radiation, and so on).

- Do not use incorrect cable types.

- Do not buy low-quality cable and/or connectors. This can cause you endless and sometimes unsolvable problems (at least, problems that are unsolvable without recabling).

- Avoid using barrel connections to connect two lengths of cable, as they weaken and distort signals. They are, however, the only methods for splicing cables—use them sparingly if you must.

ARCnet Design Rules

The rules for designing ARCnet networks are simple even though ARCnet systems allow for more exotic layouts than either EtherNet or Token Ring. Here are the design rules for ARCnet (see Figure 5.6):

- The total cable length from one end of the network to the other must not exceed 20,000 feet.

- A network can support a maximum of 255 stations.

- Active hubs may be no more than 2,000 feet apart.

- The maximum distance between an active hub and a station must not exceed 2,000 feet. (This restriction also applies if you want to directly connect two stations to make a two-node network.)

- The maximum distance between an active hub and a passive hub must be no more than 100 feet.

- The maximum distance between a passive hub and a network adapter must not exceed 100 feet.

- Active hubs may be directly connected to other active hubs, passive hubs, or stations.

- Passive hubs may not be directly connected to other passive hubs.

- Loops must not exist (that is, circular connections between any active or passive hubs).

- Terminate all unused connections on passive hubs. Although not strictly necessary, the same should be done for unused connections on active hubs.

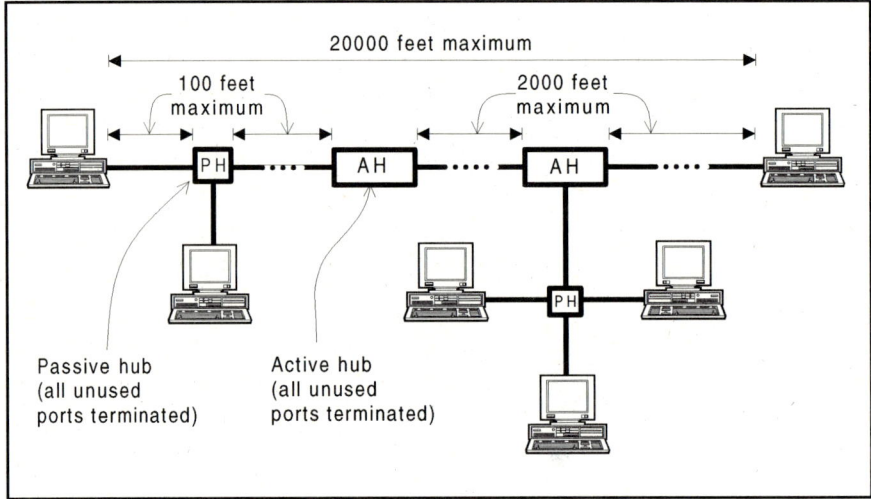

Figure 5.6   Design rules for ARCnet networks.

ARCnet Hardware

ARCnet consists of the following hardware:

- *Network adapter cards.*

- *Cabling.* Coaxial cable (actually, the type is RG-62/U, 93 ohm) with BNC connectors at either end.

- *BNC T-connectors.* T-connectors connect two cables with a third cable that attaches to a computer.

- *BNC barrel connectors.* To join two cables, use a BNC barrel connector.

- *BNC terminators (93 ohm).* Terminators are devices that must be attached to all unused hub connections to prevent signals "reflecting" from the cable ends (yes, it really does happen).

- *Passive hubs.* These devices are wiring centers at which four network cables meet. They relay the signal from one cable to the other cable but, being passive, degrade the signal slightly. For this reason, don't attach passive hubs directly to each other.

- *Active hubs.* Active hubs are connecting points for up to eight cables. They relay signals like passive hubs, but they also amplify and recondition them, so active hubs may be connected together.

EtherNet Design Rules

The rules for designing thin EtherNet networks are even simpler than those for ARCnet systems. Here are the design rules for a thin EtherNet installation (see Figure 5.7):

- The maximum number of segments (parts of the network joined by repeaters) between any pair of computers that need to intercommunicate is five. Although you can build networks with more than five segments, you will find all sorts of complexities that, as a do-it-youself networker, you might prefer to avoid.

- The maximum length of a segment is 607 feet.

- The maximum total length of cable (that is, the total length of all segments) is 3,035 feet.

- The maximum number of connected stations is 30 per segment or 142 in total. Note that each repeater counts as if it were a station for both of the segments that it connects to.

- The minimum distance between T-connectors is 1.6 feet. If the PCs are nearer than that, just loop the cable so that the distance limit is maintained.

- A terminator must be used at both ends of a segment, and one of the ends should also be grounded.

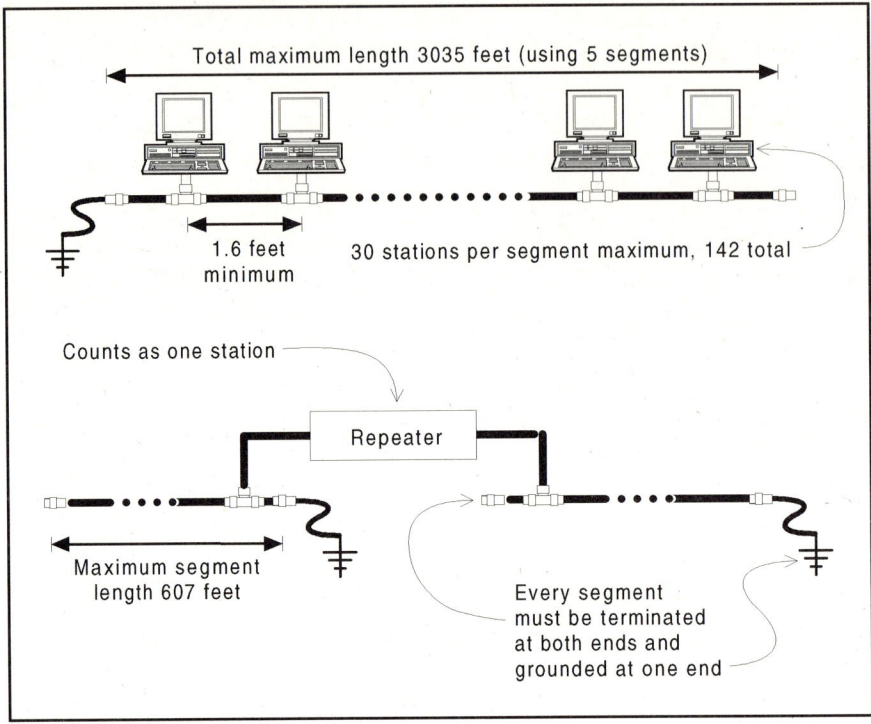

Figure 5.7 *Design rules for EtherNet networks.*

EtherNet Hardware

EtherNet consists of the following units:

- *Network adapter cards.*
- *Cabling.* Coaxial cable (RG-58A/U, or C/U 50 ohm for thin EtherNet) with BNC connectors at either end.

Note: Never mix cable types in an installation. It's a recipe for problems — usually those of the hard-to-solve and intermittent type.

- *BNC T-connectors.* T-connectors connect two cables with a third cable that attaches to a computer.

- *BNC terminators (50 ohm)*. As with ARCnet, terminators are used to prevent the ends of the cable causing signal problems. For any cable segment, one of the terminators must be grounded.
- *BNC barrel connectors*. To join two cables, use a BNC barrel connector.
- *Repeaters*. Where you exceed the limitations of an EtherNet segment, you can use a repeater to attach that segment to another segment.

Token Ring Design Rules

Token Ring networks are more complex to cable for than either ARCnet or EtherNet, even though you have fewer components to deal with. The rules below apply to small Token Ring systems only. A large Token Ring network should be installed and planned by professionals, as they are complex and expensive.

Here are the design rules for a small, movable Token Ring system (see Figure 5.8):

- The maximum number of stations is 96.
- The maximum number of MAUs is 12.
- The maximum length of a patch cable between an MAU and a station is 150 feet.
- The maximum distance between two MAUs is 150 feet.
- The maximum total length of cable connecting all MAUs must not exceed 400 feet.
- The MAUs must be wired as a ring using the Ring In and Ring Out connections. A single MAU doesn't need any connections to Ring In or Ring Out.
- Ring In connections must be attached only to Ring Out connections.

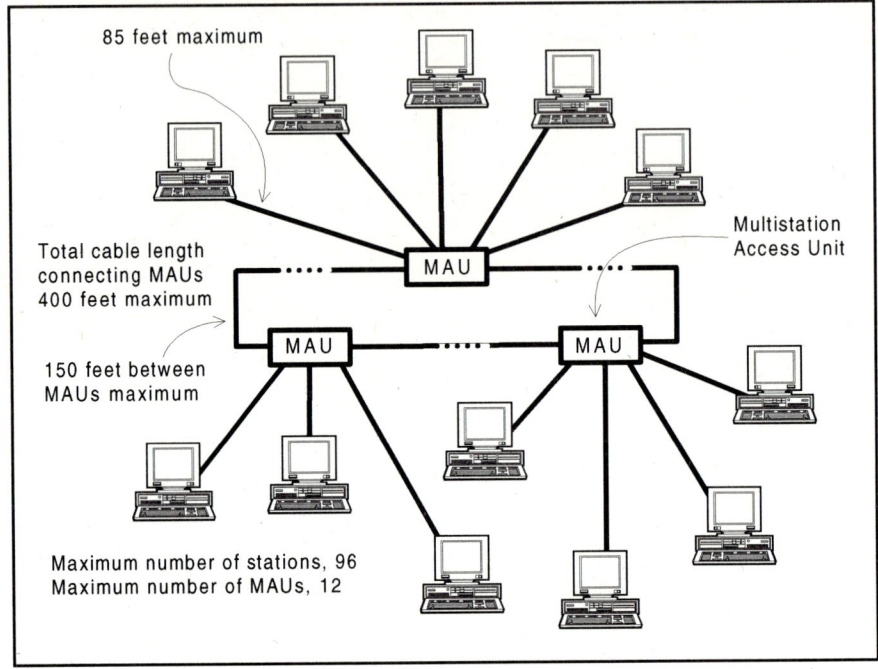

Figure 5.8   Design Rules for Token Ring Networks.

Token Ring Hardware

Token Ring consists of the following components:

- *Network adapter cards.*
- *Cabling.* Small Token Ring systems use IBM type 6 cabling in two forms: *adapter cables* and *patch cables.*
- *Multistation access units, or MAUs.* MAUs are wiring hubs that connect computers to the network and connect to other MAUs. They are available in four- or eight-connection versions. Each MAU also has two other connectors called Ring In and Ring Out. These are used to link MAUs together.

Repeaters, Bridges, and Routers

When you reach a limit to the number of computers that can be attached to your networks, either because the maximum addressing capability of that segment has been reached or some electronic constraint prevents further connections, you need a way to extend the system. The way to do this is to use a repeater, a bridge, or a router.

> **Note:** For the do-it-yourself networker, it is unlikely that you'll need to consider using any of these devices. But as your network grows and you start to think about expansion, these are topics that may give you the key to the next phase of your system. This section is just a brief overview so you will have somewhere to start. You'll need to ask vendors to find out what can be achieved and how.

A *repeater* is a signal regenerator. Its function is to recondition and relay signals from one piece of cable to another. When a signal travels from one end of a piece of wire to the other, it experiences various effects that distort its shape and weaken its strength.

Repeaters take a signal from one cable and repeat it in a cleaned-up form to the other cable. There may be limits on the number of repeaters that a particular network technology allows. The reason for this is that a chain of repeaters can introduce delays and problems with signal timing that can reduce the performance of the system significantly.

A *bridge* is a more sophisticated device than a repeater, as it is designed to support intercommunication between different networking technologies. For example, you might use a bridge to connect an ARCnet network to an EtherNet system.

A *router* is a more sophisticated connectivity system still. It can act as a bridge (in which case it is sometimes called a *brouter*) but is intended to perform a much more complex role. When connecting two networks, whether of the same type or not, a bridge will pass all traffic it sees from one side to the other.

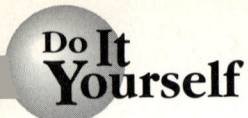
Networking with LANtastic

A router, on the other hand, builds a table showing which addresses are on which side of the router, and forwards only those packets that are destined for an address that is on the other side of the bridge. The benefit of this filtering process is that it keeps traffic on each interconnected network to a minimum — the router does not pass local traffic on one network to another network.

Making Decisions

For the do-it-yourself networker, the main choices are ARCnet or EtherNet. If you're in a department of a company and you're planning a network, you may have to cope with existing corporate standards such as EtherNet or Token Ring.

In general, most people find that ARCnet is an excellent solution for small networks or larger networks which won't be heavily loaded. If your network has to cover long distances, for example, covering a warehouse or factory, ARCnet is a very cost-effective and relatively trouble-free choice.

On the other hand, if your planned network is going to support many users or tremendous traffic, EtherNet is probably going to be the best choice. Of the three network technologies, EtherNet, at present, has the best pricing in relation to its performance.

Token Ring is intended for large-scale installations, and its cost and complexity make it less cost-effective for smaller networks.

You should also consider two very important aspects of whatever technology you'll use for your network — the price you'll actually pay for the hardware and whether you'll install it yourself.

The price you'll pay for your network hardware can vary considerably. If you buy from a local dealer, you probably pay more for products than if you mail-order from one of the big warehouse companies.

On the other hand, you may get a great deal of support from a local dealer that makes his higher prices more cost-effective. Keep in mind that many dealers simply don't understand networking. You may find that after reading this book, you have a much more practical approach to the subject than they do, but they "talk a good game."

Table 5.2 presents a comparison of the issues for and against using ARCnet, EtherNet, and Token Ring.

Table 5.2 A comparison of the issues for and against using ARCnet, EtherNet, and Token Ring.

For	Against
ARCnet	
Low cost and robust	Max. 20,000 feet network
Easy to expand	Low speed
	Few vendors
EtherNet	
High speed	Problem-solving can be difficult
Easy to expand	
Many vendors	
Token Ring	
Medium or high speed	High cost
Robust	Complex to expand
Can build very large nets	Few vendors

If your network is of more than, say, 15 computers, and your budget is large enough, having a cabling contractor install and test the cable can actually save you time and money. You should ensure that you have done your homework before even opening discussions with a cabling company. You should have developed your site plan, your cabling plan, and have a solid idea of how your network will be put together.

Some dealers offer cabling services or can recommend a cabling company. You should be very cautious about whom you employ for this job. Network cabling is still pretty novel stuff to many service companies. The best plan is to find another network manager and see whom that manager recommends.

Note: Whether you install the cabling yourself or use a cabling company, make sure that only quality components are used. Cheap cabling and connectors will cost you more in the long run, as they cause endless problems and faults.

Caution: If you are going to install cabling yourself, check with your local fire department and health and safety agency to ensure that your installation will be done "to code." This is particularly important if you plan to put cables in walls or through fire hazard areas.

The very organized and careful do-it-yourself networker might consider checking with these departments anyway rather than relying on contractors to get it right. After all, you'll be the one who is prosecuted if there's a fire due to a subcode installation or if an employee breaks a leg by tripping over a cable.

Summary

The main choices in network technologies for the do-it-yourself networker are ARCnet and EtherNet. There is a huge range of options (cards with or without coprocessors, on-board RAM expansion, and so on), and unless you know that you have special needs (you may have to cover great distances or need blinding performance, for example), the standard market products will solve your problems more than adequately.

Note: In terms of a do-it-yourself approach, the EtherNet and 2Mbps products from Artisoft are completely supported by Artisoft, so in the event of problems in either installation or operation, your network will present a "known" environment to their support staff.

Selecting a Network Technology

Here are some other issues to consider:

- Be careful on pricing. Mail order may be much cheaper.
- Consider dealers with regard to their support capability.
- Consider cabling companies carefully.
- Look for recommendations from other companies to select both dealers and cabling companies.

6

Installing LANtastic

Installing LANtastic is a fairly straightforward job. You should have your network configuration plan in hand (see Chapter 4), and you should have allowed yourself adequate time to complete the job.

There are five major steps involved in installing a LANtastic network:

1. Preparing for installation.
2. Installing hardware.
3. Installing network software.
4. Configuring the system.
5. Reconfiguring applications and utilities.

For many steps, I have created forms to help you document each step of the installation of your system. Even for small systems, this kind of thoroughness will pay off if you run into problems with damaged or faulty goods or need to make insurance claims (say, in the case of fire damage or theft). See Appendix B, "Forms," for blank forms you can copy and use.

 *Networking with LANtastic*

Within this chapter, go from one step to the next unless the instructions tell you otherwise.

Preparing for Installation

Preparing for installation will avoid problems due to wrong tools or missing components. Preparation falls into two sections:

- Advance preparations.
- Preparations on the day of installation.

Advance Preparations

The purpose of advance preparation is twofold. First, it gives you less to do on the actual installation day. Second, when installation day arrives, you'll have the right equipment, and you'll know that it's all available.

1. When the network products arrive, which should not be on the day of installation, log each item on form DIY-013, "Equipment Received Log" (see Appendix B), check all packaging for damage, and note any damage you find. This can be important if you need to resolve any problems caused by shipping damage.

2. Open each box or package in turn and check that the contents match what you ordered and include what the equipment's packing list says should be included. The user's manual for each Artisoft product has a section called "Package Contents," which details everything that should be in the box. If there are any omissions, check with whoever sold you the equipment before going any further. Log the contents of each package and note the numbers of any serialized components (also on the "Equipment Received Log").

3. Examine all hardware for damage. This includes looking for any bent metalwork, cracks in printed circuit boards, kinks in cables, and so on. Again, note any problems or queries.

4. Separate the manuals from the various product registration cards. Fill out the registration cards and return them to the manufacturers.

Note: Returning registration cards is always in your interest. Some manufacturers require a registration card before you can get technical support, and many of them will send you information about updates or technical information once you have been registered. Even if there are no obvious benefits, getting on the manufacturer's mailing list usually means that you'll be notified of upgrades and bug fixes.

Day-of-Installation Preparations

If you're building a network of any size, this may be "*Days*-of-Installation Preparations." Even for a few PCs, you'll be putting in a few hours of work.

1. Ensure that you will have adequate time to install the network. If necessary, you may have to install the network in phases so you don't disrupt your organization's normal work. If this is the case, you should set clear goals for each phase to ensure that there are no surprises that delay you or leave any PCs inoperable.

Note: If you can ensure that a spare PC is available and that the PC you're working on has been backed up and can be restored onto that spare, any really big problems won't leave someone without a machine. If this is a crucial issue for you and you don't have a spare PC in-house, talk to your local PC dealers about renting a PC on short notice.

2. Make sure that you have the right tools for the job. If you'll be installing the system on more than two or three PCs, a power screwdriver is fundamental to avoiding "engineer's wrist" (a severe tiredness of the wrist due to excessive use of a screwdriver). Some tools worth having on hand are:

Networking with LANtastic

- A selection of screwdrivers (power, flat-blade, and Phillips).
- Pliers (regular and needle-nosed).
- Wire strippers.
- Side cutters.
- A rubber mallet.
- Hammers (claw and ball peen).
- Tweezers (very useful for extracting screws that fall into cracks).
- A knife.

3. Wear the right clothes and expect to get dirty. Installations involve a lot of crawling on hands and knees. Also, the inside of a PC that's been in service for a while is very dusty. And if your plan requires that cabling go through ceilings or service ducts, you'll discover just how dusty the average building really is!

4. If you find that you are dealing with any sizable amount of equipment, make sure you have a clean work area and enough space to lay everything out. If the installation is in a large building, a wheeled cart to carry tools and give you a clear working space will make life much easier unless you can clear desktops or really like working on the floor.

Checklist: Installation Preparation

To help you get as well-prepared as possible, you should use the following checklist. If you can't check all items, then you're likely to run into problems.

☐ Do you understand the basics of LANtastic as covered in Chapters 1 to 4?

☐ Have you developed configuration plans as recommended in Chapter 4, "Planning Your Network"?

☐ Do you have adequate time to do the work you have planned?

☐ Do you have a supply of form DIY-014 for the installation?

☐ Do you have the right tools for the job?

Installing LANtastic

Hardware Installation

Hardware installation is more time-consuming than it is difficult. The golden rules are:

- Know what needs to be done.
- Don't rush.
- Document what you do.
- Test.

1. First the network cable needs to be installed. This is usually an easy step and, if you've planned your installation, a quick one. Follow the vendor's recommendations for cable-handling carefully (see Chapter 5, "Selecting a Network Technology"). For bigger networks — say, 20 or more PCs — you might want to get a professional cabling company to do this part if you can afford it.

2. Start the PC hardware installation by filling out a new "PC Hardware Configuration" form (form DIY-014; see Appendix B). You should list all the network-related items (marked with an asterisk).

3. At the first (or next) PC, disconnect all power cords and all cables (monitor, keyboard, and so on) from the PC.

> **Caution:** It is very important to remove all power cords from the PC to prevent electrical shocks. The power supply unit in the PC should be easily identifiable, and you must not, for any reason, attempt to open its casing. Some power supplies retain dangerous charges for a considerable period after the power is switched off.

4. Remove the PC's cover.

> **Caution:** Different PCs have cover screws in different positions. *Do not* remove any external screws without checking the PC manufacturer's instructions — you might detach the power supply, the motherboard, or something else that you'd probably rather not mess with.

 *Networking with LANtastic*

5. Locate an empty slot for the network adapter card and remove the blanking plate. The slot should be of the correct length for the card (see Figure 6.1). If your adapter card is a "short" one, it can go in any slot. If it is a "long" one, it can only go in a long slot.

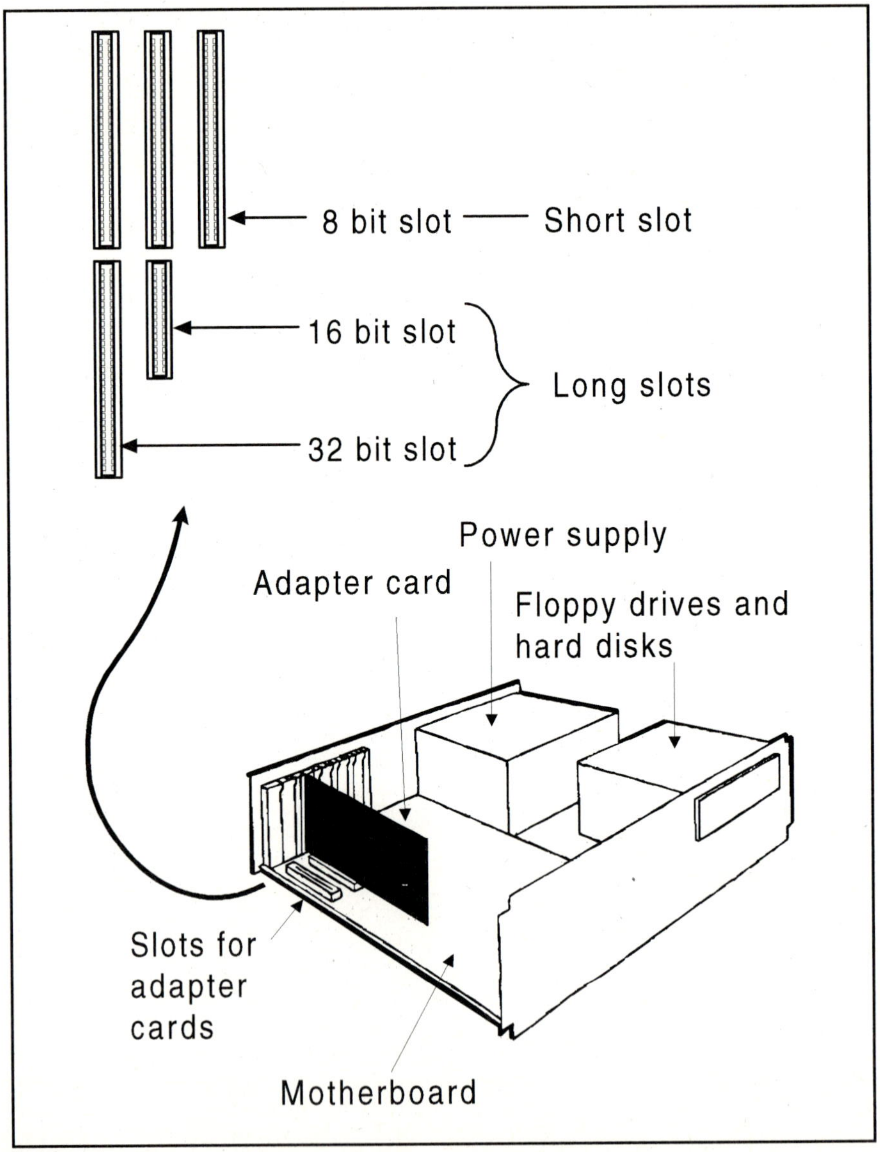

Figure 6.1 Locating a slot for the network interface card.

Installing LANtastic

6. Remove the network adapter from its plastic bag; remember to handle the card carefully and avoid touching the edge connector.

Caution: All adapters, including network adapters, are sensitive to static electricity. If you have a static charge, say, from walking across a carpet, touching the edge connector could damage components. This risk is small but common enough to warrant care. If you know that your site tends to have a static problem, take extra care, possibly buying a grounding clip from your local PC store to use when handling boards and PCs.

Note: Before you touch the adapter card, be sure you first touch the metal casing of the PC. That way, any static you've accumulated will be removed.

7. Set the switches and/or jumpers on the network adapter card as required. The adapter's manual will detail where these are and what settings should be used in which circumstances. If you don't know what setting should be used even after reading the manual, try the default settings. If these settings aren't compatible with your PC, you'll find out later either when you try to start your machine and you get an error report, or when you run the network test utility.

Note: Even if you select the wrong settings, rest assured that you can't easily damage the PC.

8. Insert the network adapter in the PC without using too much pressure. The securing bracket may have to be bent forward or backward very slightly to make the board fit. Be *very careful* not to break the board at the points where the bracket attaches. The network adapter should sit in the motherboard connector and be parallel with the motherboard. The retaining screw should be used to hold the board in place.

 *Networking with LANtastic*

> **Note:** Using the retaining screw is very important, as failure to do so may allow the network adapter to become unseated at a later time. This will probably prevent it from working properly, but, if the PC has been in service, the problem may not be obvious. The retaining screw also ensures that the adapter card is properly grounded to prevent damage to the card from electrical problems.

9. Replace the PC cover and replace the screws. Reconnect the power cord, monitor, keyboard, and other cables.

10. Power up the PC and check that everything is operating normally. If everything seems okay, skip to the next section ("LANtastic Network Software Installation").

If you have a problem — such as a machine that doesn't start or an error report — switch the PC off, remove the PC's cover, and take the network adapter out. Replace the cover.

Power up the PC again. If the PC still doesn't work, the problem lies in the PC. Check the cables, connectors, and other cards to make sure nothing is loose or damaged. If it still refuses to work, you should get support from the PC's vendor or your dealer.

If the PC doesn't work, the adapter card is the most probable culprit. Change the adapter card's I/O port setting and try again. When you have tried all the settings for that option without success, reset the option to its default and try another option (such as the interrupt setting). If you can't get the PC to start with the network adapter card in any reasonable configuration, try asking the adapter vendor's support for assistance.

> **Note:** First, the good news: It is unusual for you to have problems of any real magnitude at this stage. The bad news is that if there is going to be a conflict between the adapter and any other devices, it probably won't show up until you try to run the network software.

Installing LANtastic

LANtastic Network Software Installation

In this section, we'll cover the process of installing the LANtastic network software.

Beginning the Installation

At this point, you've gone through the steps in the previous section, and the PC is apparently working properly. You're now ready to install the LANtastic software. Begin by ensuring that you are at the DOS command prompt.

1. Put the LANtastic installation disk in a floppy disk drive and make that drive your default. Type INSTALL and press Enter. The screen will now look like Figure 6.2.

Tip: If you're using a monochrome monitor or an LCD display (on a portable, for example), you should enter INSTALL MONO to improve the readability of the screens.

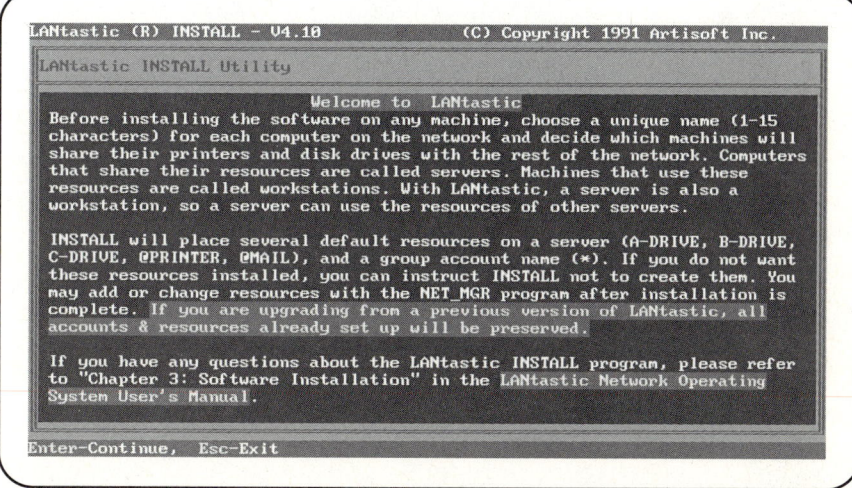

Figure 6.2 *The opening screen of the LANtastic installation program.*

121

Networking with LANtastic

2. The interface for this utility uses the up arrow and down arrow keys to move the highlight bar to each line in turn. Having the highlight on a line is called *selecting* the line. Pressing Enter will either change the selection to another option or bring up a window of options that you can select from. In an options window, you again move the highlight bar using the up arrow and down arrow keys to get to the item you want. Pressing Enter will select the highlighted item and return you to the previous screen.

The Esc key will allow you to abandon whatever you're doing. At the main screen, Esc will bring up a window offering you the choice of abandoning the installation or continuing. Pressing F1 at any time will bring up help information.

3. The next screen is shown in Figure 6.3. Type the network name for the PC and press Enter. This name, which can be up to 15 characters, should have already been decided in your configuration plan. In the figure, the PC's name will be GRYPHON.

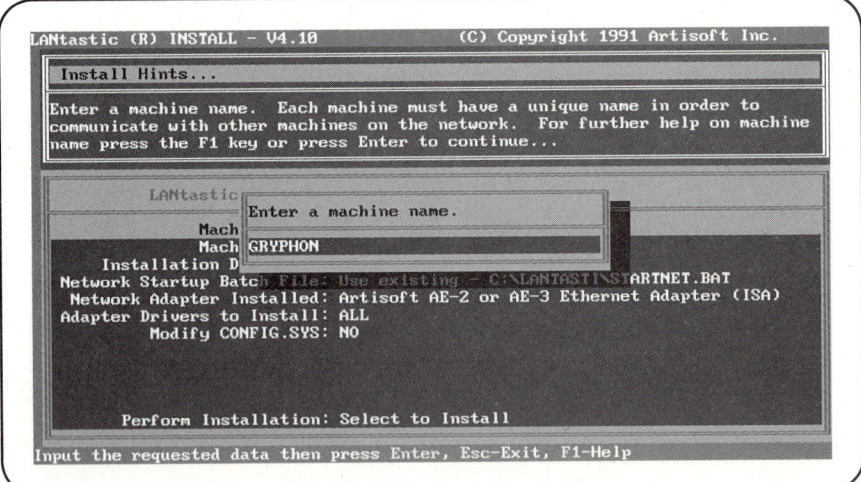

Figure 6.3 *The machine name entry screen of the LANtastic installation program.*

Note: You can change this name at any time before or after installation with very little effort. The consequences of changing it may require changes to other networked PCs, as they all need to know each other's names to establish connections.

4. The screen now shows the main installation screen. The options available on the main screen are determined by whether the installation is new or modifying/upgrading an existing one.

The steps in the sections "General Options" and "Special Options" cover each item on the main screen in turn. Some apply to workstations or servers only, some to new installations or existing installations only.

The screen for workstation installation is shown in Figure 6.4 and for a server in Figure 6.5. By selecting the item "Machine type" and pressing ENTER, you can move between the two screens.

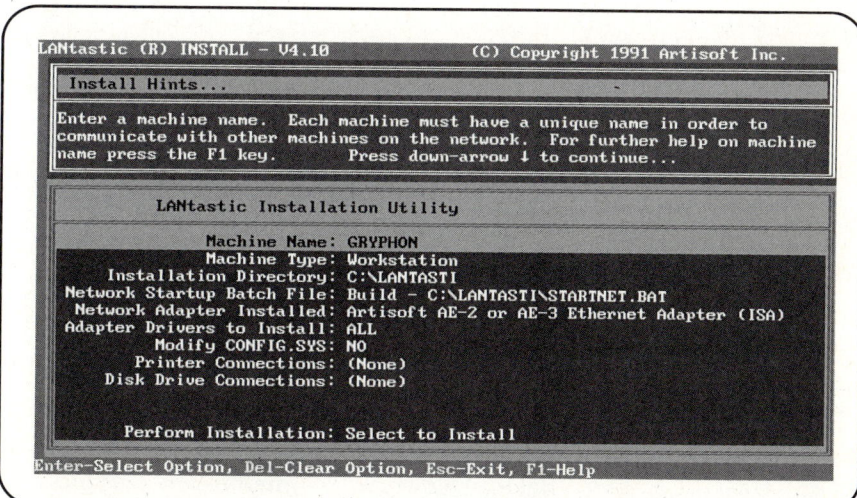

Figure 6.4 *The main installation screen for LANtastic workstations.*

 *Networking with LANtastic*

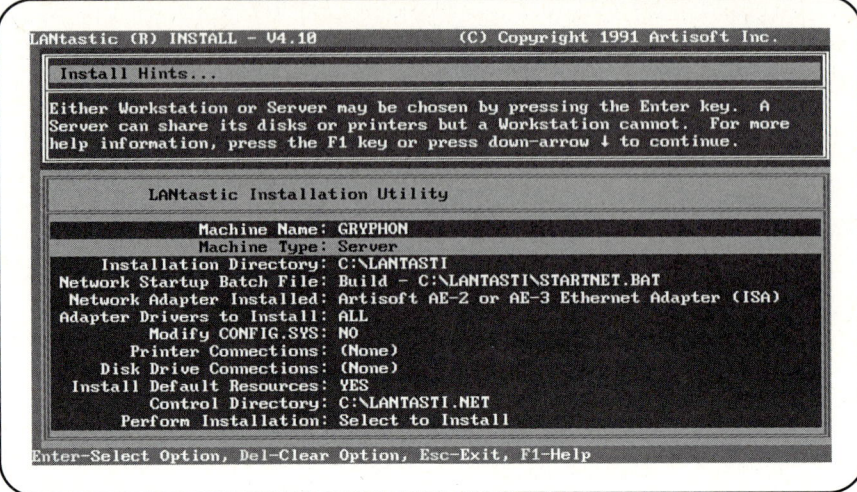

Figure 6.5 *The main installation screen for LANtastic servers.*

General Options

The items covered in this section are always available on the screen, whether the PC will be a workstation or server, or whether it's a new or modified installation.

Machine Name:

This is the name by which the PC will be addressed by other machines on the network. Select the "Machine name" item and press Enter to edit the machine name. The name is limited to 15 characters and cannot include commas, colons, semicolons, tabs, or spaces.

Machine Type:

This option can be toggled between Workstation (the default) and Server by selecting and repeatedly pressing Enter.

Installing LANtastic

> **Tip:** If you install LANtastic as a server on all machines that have hard disks, you can then create simple batch files that allow you to start up as either a server only, a workstation, or a server/workstation. This will make your installation much more flexible.

Installation Directory:

The installation directory defaults to C:\LANTASTI. This is the directory that the LANtastic utilities will be copied into. Selecting the line and pressing Enter will bring up an editing window. If you want to change the name of the installation directory, type the full path name and press Enter.

Pressing Delete will change the specification to (None Selected), but when you start the actual installation, the installation program will not continue without a valid entry.

> **Note:** You might want to put the LANtastic software in, say, your DOS utilities subdirectory. In general, *don't do it*. Using another subdirectory name will make it more complex to use and administer the network. If this warning doesn't dissuade you from using different directories, you should try to ensure that the same directory name is used on each PC. This will make support and troubleshooting much easier.

Network Startup Batch File:

This is the name for the batch file that will load each of the components of the configuration. The specification must contain the full path to where you want the file to be. The specification defaults to C:\LANTASTI\STARTNET.BAT.

- If this is to be a new start-up batch file, the specification will be preceded with Build -.

- If the start-up batch file exists, the specification will be preceded with Use existing -.

125

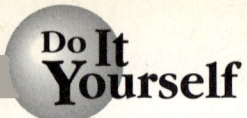

The specification can be changed by selecting this option and pressing Enter.

If you change the specification to an existing file when the option says `Build -`, a warning message will tell you that an existing file can't be overwritten. When you press Esc and return to the main screen, `Use existing -` will preface the specification. You can press Del to clear the specification to `(None)`. When you do this, a start-up batch file won't be created, and any existing one won't be modified.

> **Tip:** You can use different names for different start-up batch files so that you can have several configurations on the same PC. This could be useful if you want to start a PC sometimes as a workstation and at other times as a combined workstation/server.

Network Adapter Installed:

This option defaults to whichever adapter driver is first in the list of those supplied with the particular version of LANtastic you're using. Selecting this option and pressing Enter will bring up a list of the adapters available. Select the correct adapter type and press Enter.

> **Note:** If you're going to use an adapter from another manufacturer that has its own NETBIOS, see the "NBSETUP" in Appendix C, "Utilities Reference," for details of configuration and setup.

Adapter Drivers to Install:

This selection offers you three possible options:

- Install all of the drivers on the installation disk (the specification will say `ALL`).
- Install just the driver for the adapter you selected under `Network Adapter Installed`.
- Install no driver (`NONE`).

Note: The only reason to install all of the drivers would be if you were going to use multiple adapters of different types on that machine.

Select this line and repeatedly press Enter to set the specification to each option in turn.

Note: If you're going to use an adapter with its own NETBIOS program, set this option to "NONE" and refer to the vendor's manual for setup information.

Modify CONFIG.SYS:

This option defaults to NO. This allows you to choose whether the installation program will change certain settings in the PC's configuration setup file. Select this line and press Enter to bring up Figure 6.6.

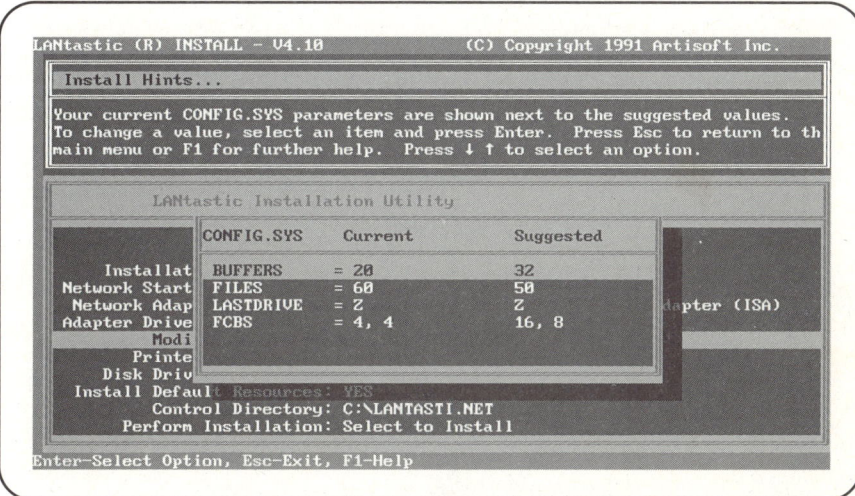
Figure 6.6 *Current and suggested CONFIG.SYS settings window.*

Select any option line and press Enter to bring up an editing window to allow you to set the value of the parameter (see Figure 6.7).

127

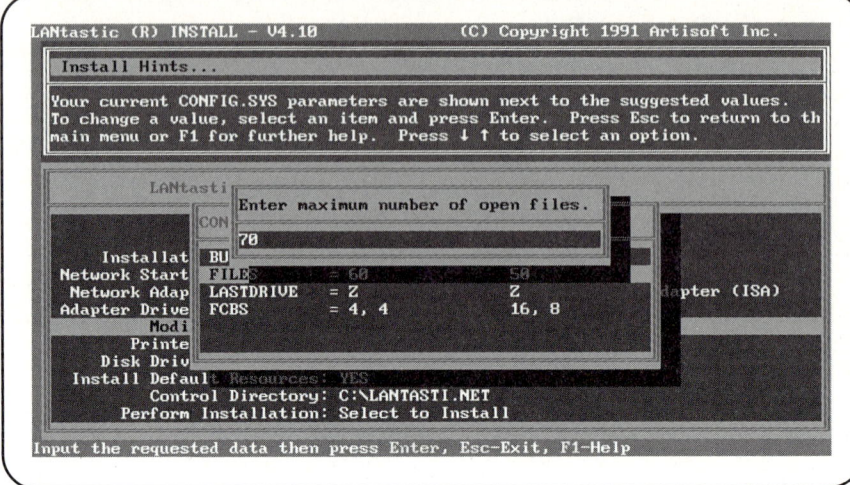

Figure 6.7   Changing the specification for the FILES parameter in CONFIG.SYS.

For basic installations, you have three options:

- If the current settings in CONFIG.SYS are *lower* than those suggested, you should let the installation program make the changes.

- If the current settings are *higher* than the proposed settings, CONFIG.SYS should not be changed.

- If only *some* of the current settings are higher, you can change the values as required.

For example, if you already have your system set for 50 files and you want to let the installation program make other changes, you would move the highlight to the FILES line and press Enter. A window will open and the required value can be entered.

When you return to the screen with the current and suggested values (Figure 6.6), press Esc. You will be asked if CONFIG.SYS should be updated with the suggested values.

If you enter Y and press Enter, the specification on the main screen will change to YES. If you enter N or press Esc again, the main screen specification will be set to NO.

Installing LANtastic

Special Options

Some of the options in this section are available only for certain configurations: for a new workstation, an existing server, and so on.

A new installation is one in which:

- A completely new installation is being done.

  Or

- A new installation directory has been specified.

  Or

- A new network start-up file has been specified.

Printer Connections: (new installations only)

This option allows you to specify which of five printer devices are attached to remote resources. The possible printer devices are:

- LPT1
- LPT2
- LPT3
- COM1
- COM2

Select the required device and press Enter to bring up the window shown in Figure 6.8.

> **Tip:** It's most common that you'll have local printers attached to LPT1 and serial devices (such as mice or modems) on COM1 and COM2, so you may want to set up remote printers on LPT2 and LPT3.

129

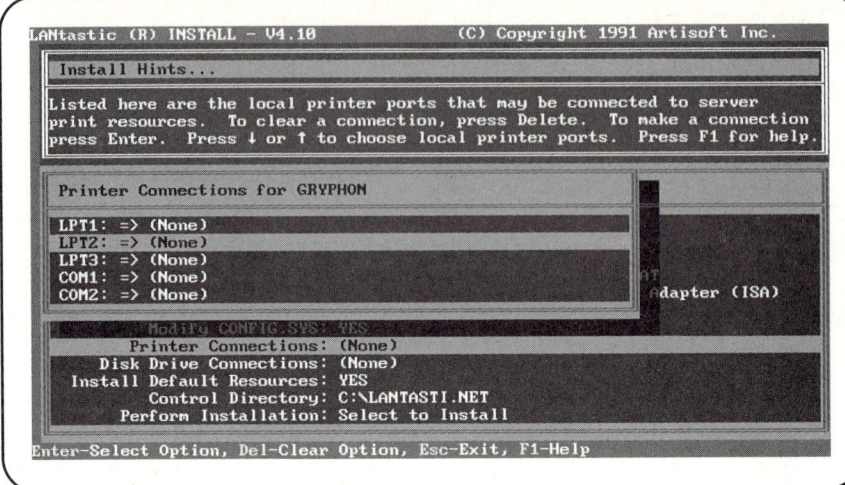

Figure 6.8 Changing the specification of local devices and their connection to remote printers.

1. Select each device you want to route to a remote resource and press Enter. A window (see Figure 6.9) will be opened allowing you to enter the name of the server that the remote printer is on.

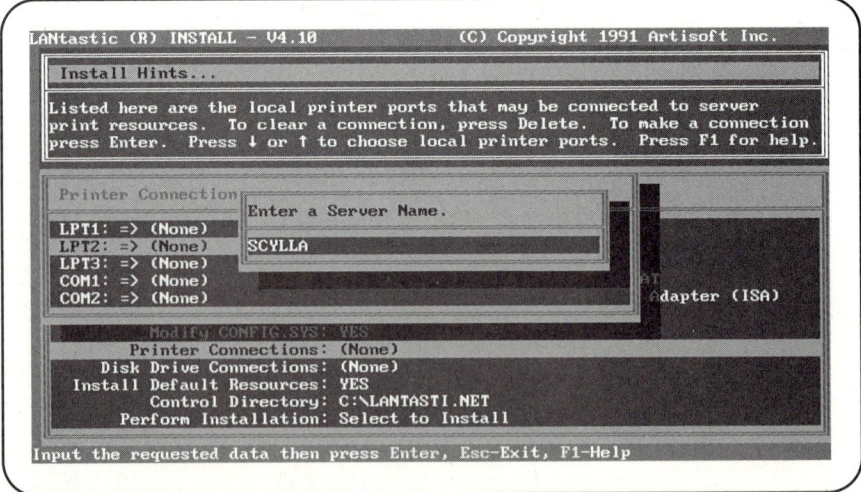

Figure 6.9 Entering the name of the server that has a resource that a local printer device is to use.

Installing LANtastic

2. When you press Enter, a window listing the remote resources is presented (see Figure 6.10). Two types of resources are listed, <<CUSTOM>> and @PRINTER. The resource @PRINTER is a default name for a remote printer.

Tip: A real network may have several printers attached to a server. Try to use descriptive names for the printers, like @LASER or @DOTMATRIX.

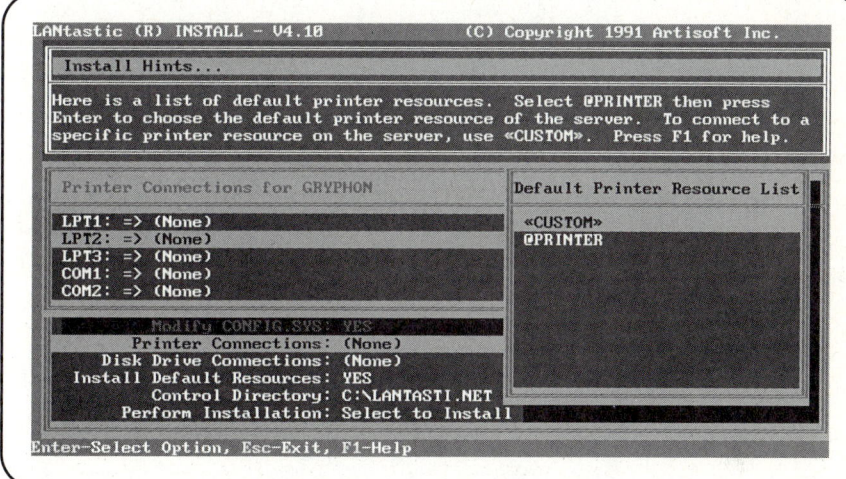

Figure 6.10 *The default printer resource list.*

Note: You'll have to finish the setup of the custom resource by using NET_MGR (see Appendix C, "Utilities Reference"). Although you've defined the custom resource, the rest of the setup is not automatic.

3. To specify a printer other than the default, select <<CUSTOM>> and press Enter. The screen shown in Figure 6.11 will appear.

Networking with LANtastic

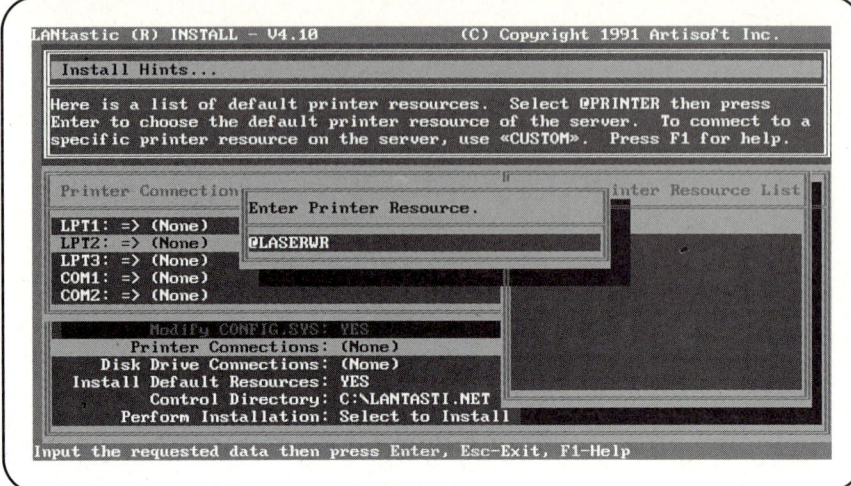

Figure 6.11 *Entering the name of specific remote printers.*

4. Enter the printer's name (@LASERWRITER in the example) and press Enter. You'll now be returned to the previous screen (as in Figure 6.12).

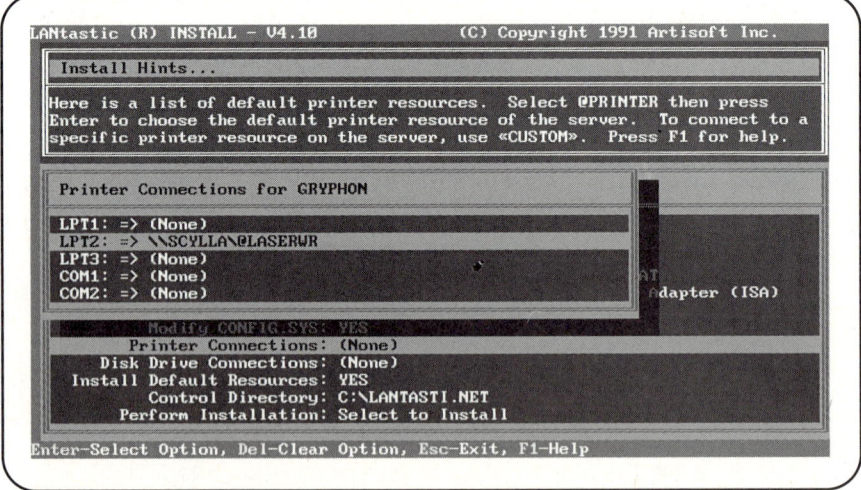

Figure 6.12 *The modified local devices screen.*

Installing LANtastic

Note: Whatever local port (LPT1, LPT2, and so on) that the remote printer is assigned doesn't have to be the same as the actual remote port that the printer is on. Thus, if you have an Apple LaserWriter II NT attached to COM1 on server GRYPHON, you could make that a network resource on LPT2 at a workstation.

5. You can continue to make any other connections required and then press Esc to return to the main screen. Once one or more printer connections have been made, the specification on the `Printer Connections:` line will be `Select to View or Modify`.

Note: This is where your detailed planning, which I covered in Chapter 4, "Planning Your Network," will pay off. You should have a list of all planned network resources, and it'll be easy to enter them. If you make any mistakes — for example, misspelling a printer name — you'll get an error message when you start the network.

Disk Drive Connections: (new installations only)

This option allows you to specify which disk drives should be connected to remote disk resources. Select the line and press Enter to bring up the window shown in Figure 6.13.

Note: The list of drives on this screen goes from A: to Z: no matter what specification for `LASTDRIVE` is given in CONFIG.SYS.

133

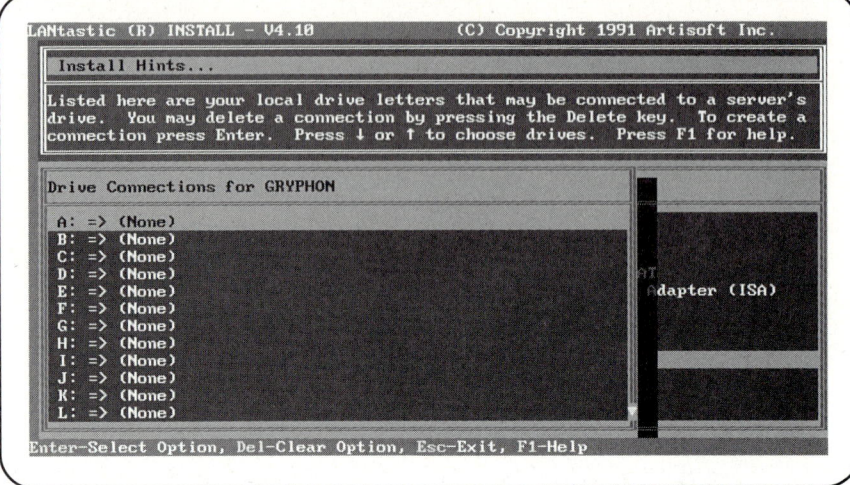

Figure 6.13 *The local drive connections.*

1. Select a drive that is to be connected to a remote disk drive and press Enter. The screen in Figure 6.14 will then appear. Type the name of the server whose disk resources you want this PC to use, and press Enter.

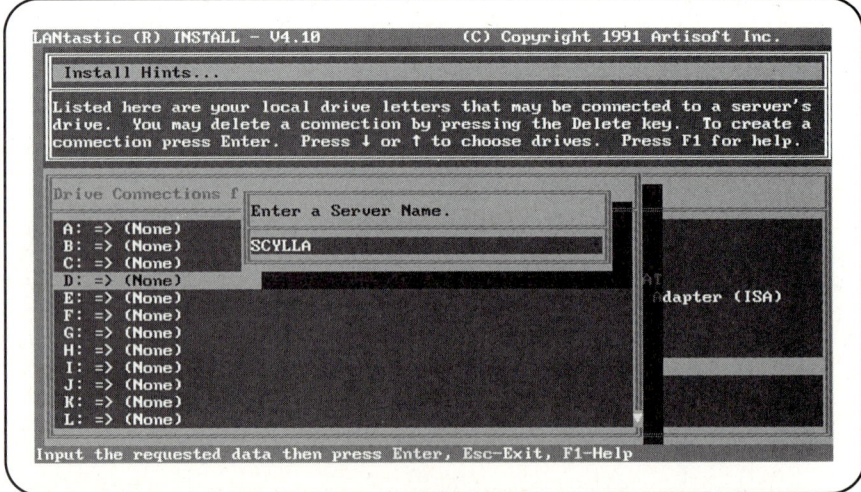

Figure 6.14 *Specifying the server whose disk resources are to be used.*

Installing LANtastic

2. The screen shown in Figure 6.15 will appear, listing the default disk drives. If the drive resource that you want to use on the specified server is either of the names listed, select it and press Enter. This will return you to the drive connections list (see Figure 6.13).

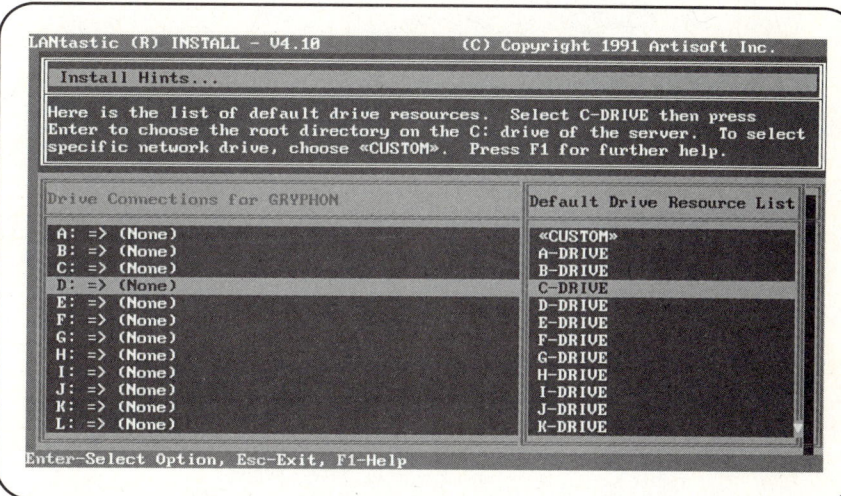

Figure 6.15 *The default drive resource list.*

3. Like the printer resources, if a drive on a server in your network has a customized name, you should select the <<CUSTOM>> device, and press Enter. A screen will be displayed, and you can enter the correct drive name and press Enter. You will be back at the drive connections list (see Figure 6.16).

Note: This is another step where your detailed planning will pay off. You will have already decided which disk resources will be made available to clients. If you make any mistakes, such as misspelling a disk resource name, you'll get an error message when you start the network.

135

Networking with LANtastic

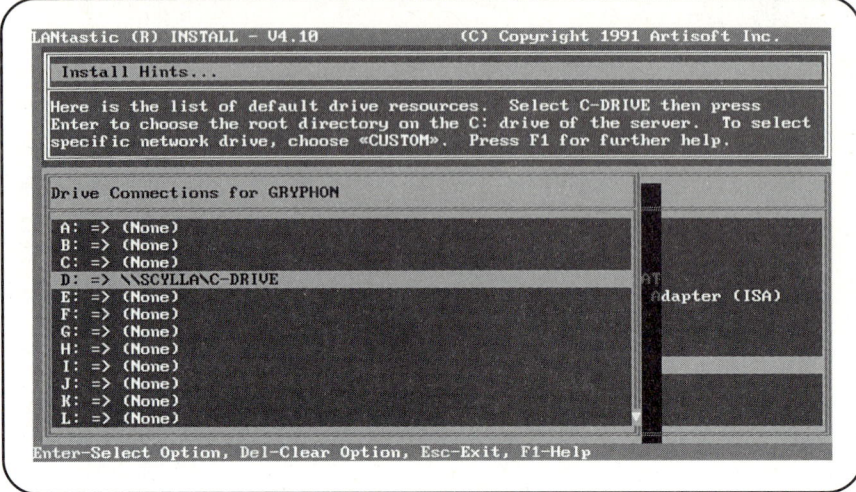

Figure 6.16 *The modified default drive resources list.*

4. Press Esc to return to the main screen.

Install Default Resources: (new server installations only)

This option can be toggled between Yes and No by pressing the Enter key repeatedly. If Yes is specified, the server will be installed with the default disk resources:

- A-DRIVE.
- B-DRIVE.
- C-DRIVE.
- A default printer, @PRINTER.
- The mail system (@MAIL).
- A group called *.

If you specify NO, no shared resources will be created and you can set them up later with the NET_MGR.EXE utility (see Appendix C, "Utilities Reference").

Installing LANtastic

Note: You'll have to finish the setup of the custom resource by using NET_MGR (see Appendix C, "Utilities Reference"). Although you've defined the custom resource, the rest of the setup is not automatic.

Control Directory: (server installations only)

This option defaults to `C:\LANTASTI.NET`. This directory holds various subdirectories and files that control the operation of the server system. Select this line and press Enter to bring up an editing window if you want to change the name of the control directory.

Note: As with the LANtastic utilities directory, using another directory rather than the default can lead to all sorts of problems and complexities. If you must change it, ensure that *every* server on the network uses the same named directory so that there's no possibility for confusion.

Perform Installation: Select to Install

Select this option and Enter when you're ready to go ahead with the installation. A window will appear (see Figure 6.17) asking if you want to continue or cancel.

- Press Enter to instruct the installation program to proceed.
- Press Esc to return to the main screen. All of the selections that you have made will still be set.

137

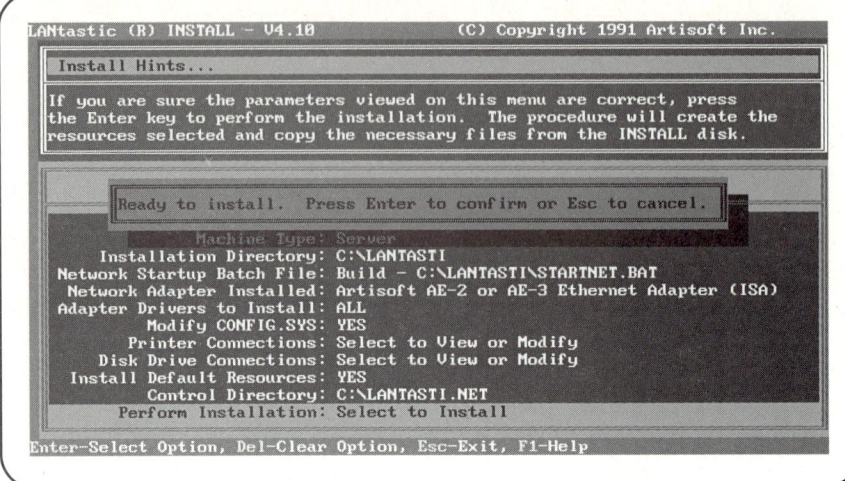

Figure 6.17 Installation confirmation window.

> **Note:** If you didn't give an installation directory ((NONE) was specified), a window will be displayed to tell you about the error and you'll be asked to enter one. Either enter a specification or press Esc to return to the main installation screen.

A window listing the files copied to the installation directory will appear, followed by a window showing the creation of shared resources (usually this happens so fast you can hardly read the details). And, if all is successful, Figure 6.18 will be displayed. When you press Esc, you will be returned to the DOS command line.

Installing LANtastic

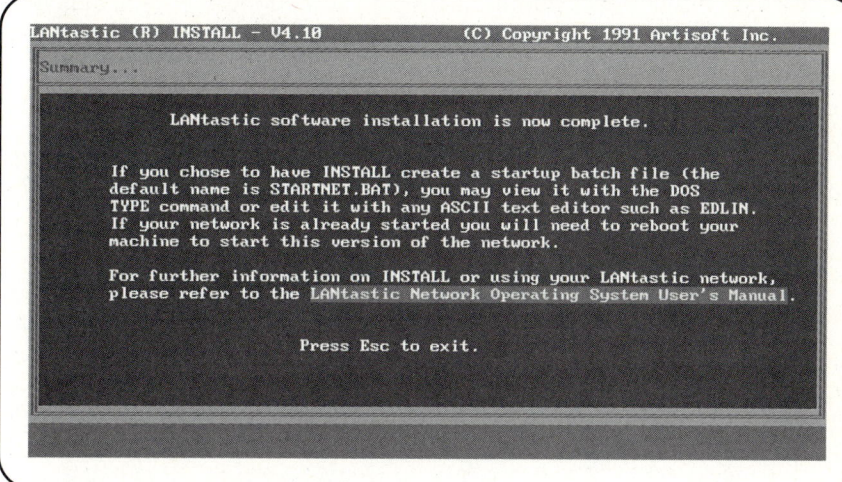

Figure 6.18 *Successful installation screen.*

Now it's time to check the network connections.

> **Note:** Congratulations! You have completed a LANtastic installation. For the more enthusiastic, it is acceptable to perform a short victory dance.

Testing the PC's Network Hardware

Now that you have installed the network software, you can run a basic check of the networking hardware. To do this, you need to:

- Load the network driver.
- Load the NETBIOS.
- Run the LANCHECK.EXE utility.

The following steps detail how to do these procedures.

139

1. From the DOS prompt, change to the installation directory (C:\LANTASTI by default).

Note: If you have already run the adapter driver and the NETBIOS for your adapter, or if the network is already running, you can skip ahead to step 4.

Note: If you are using Artisoft's 2Mbps adapters you can simply run the LANBIOS2 or LANBIOS3 program, and then skip ahead to step 4.

2. Run the driver program. The driver will be named according to the network adapter type: AEX.EXE or NE3.EXE for Artisoft EtherNet adapters, or, in the case of another vendor, whatever the correct filename is for their adapter driver.

Note: If your network adapter is configured in any way other than the standard settings (such as a different I/O address), you must tell the driver what configuration is being used on the command line.

3. Run the NETBIOS program for your particular adapter. The NETBIOS program for Artisoft products is named AILANBIOS (Adapter Independent Local Area Network Basic Input/Output System — what a mouthful!). AILANBIOS is used with Artisoft's EtherNet adapter, and with their serial port, parallel port, and modem drivers. For other vendors' products, the NETBIOS will have whatever name they give to it.

4. Now run the LANCHECK.EXE program. LANCHECK.EXE needs to be started with a command line that includes the name of the PC. For testing purposes, you can use any name you like. For the example PC (GRYPHON), the command would be entered like this:

LANCHECK GRYPHON

Installing LANtastic

 Tip: When you are running LANCHECK, it will be easier to follow what's happening if each PC uses the network name that you've planned that it will have in the final configuration.

5. If there is a problem with the system at the adapter level (for example, the board isn't properly configured and the driver can't see it) or at the software level (such that the NETBIOS can't work with the driver), either the driver or the NETBIOS will generate a warning message.

6. Once you press Enter and LANCHECK is running, the screen should look like Figure 6.19.

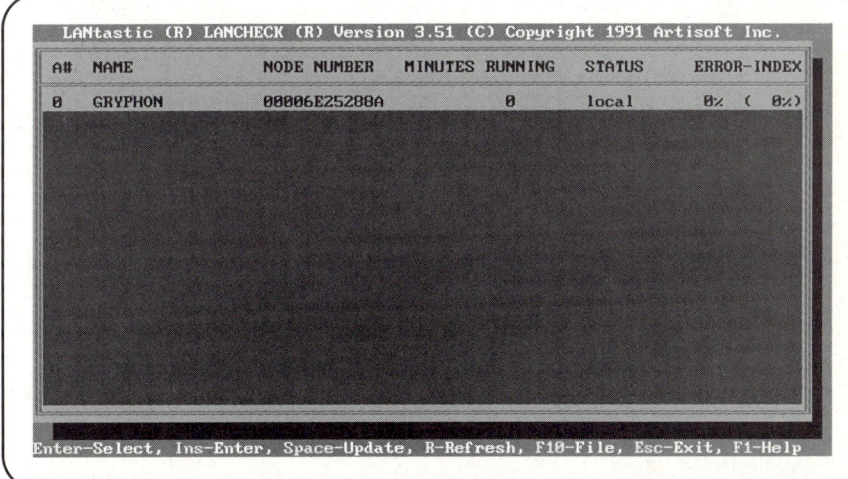

Figure 6.19 *LANCHECK.EXE running.*

7. Once LANCHECK is running, a hardware or software problem will be reported by LANCHECK.EXE either when it first tries to work with the network subsystem or when it shows the performance statistics for the network adapter.

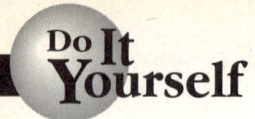

Networking with LANtastic

Note: If you have a problem on start-up or exit, check for the network adapter card conflicting with other hardware. You'll also want to check for missing or damaged cables, T-connectors, or cable terminators.

By pressing Insert and entering the workstation or server's name, you can check if other PCs running LANtastic are visible on the network.

Note: For a detailed description of LANCHECK.EXE's operation, see Appendix C, "Utilities Reference."

These tests, while not exhaustive, give you the assurance that the network hardware and low-level systems are working correctly. If the PC is to be a server, the next step is to configure its resources and operation.

Note: If the PC you are installing on is going to be a workstation only, skip ahead to the section, "The STARTNET.BAT File."

Server Configuration

Now that you have installed the network software, you need to configure the server's shared resources. You do this with the NET_MGR.EXE, which covers many functions other than server configuration. In this section, I'll discuss only those functions that are related to configuration. See Appendix C, "Utilities Reference," for a full discussion of NET_MGR.EXE.

NET_MGR.EXE allows you to modify the server start-up parameters and define users, groups, and shared resources as well as maintain various server facilities.

Installing LANtastic

Note: If you have included the LANtastic installation directory in your PATH specification or are running the network using STARTNET.BAT in the form created by the installation program, you only have to enter NET_MGR to access its facilities. If this is not the case, change to the installation subdirectory (C:\LANTASTI) and then enter NET_MGR.

Once you have defined the user's groups and resources, you need to plan the start-up of the PC. It is always better not to distract a PC user from doing his or her job. The best strategy requires that the user should be as unaware of the technology as possible. With LANtastic, the user should ideally be completely uninvolved with running network software — it should be "transparent" to his or her work.

You have two options as to how the PC can run the network software:

- Through the execution of the "AUTOEXEC.BAT" file.
- From the command line.

If you're going to use the first option, you can have the AUTOEXEC.BAT file "call" the LANtastic STARTNET.BAT file, or you can merge the contents of STARTNET.BAT into the AUTOEXEC.BAT file.

Caution: Until you're satisfied that the system is operating correctly, *don't* invoke or merge the STARTNET.BAT file with the AUTOEXEC.BAT file. The reason is that if anything goes wrong, the PC might "hang" and you'll have to boot off a floppy disk to recover. If you really want to be clever about it, you can invoke or include the STARTNET.BAT file and put a PAUSE statement immediately before the LANtastic commands. This will give you the chance to abort the AUTOEXEC.BAT process using Ctrl+Break or Ctrl+C when you reboot after a problem.

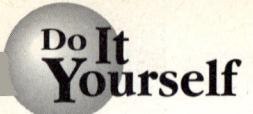

Networking with LANtastic

The STARTNET.BAT File

When a STARTNET.BAT file for a server or a workstation is created, it contains default commands that you might wish to change. For each command in this file, see Appendix C, "Utilities Reference," for full discussions of their use and what options are available.

> **Note:** A default in the installation is to configure the STARTNET.BAT file for servers to log into the server under the network name of the PC. Thus, if the assigned name is GRYPHON, this will be the attempted login name. Login will only be successful if either that name is actually defined, or if the group * or any other matching group exists.

The standard contents generated for the server LUCY (discussed in Chapter 4, "Planning Your Network") are:

```
@ECHO OFF
PATH C:\LANTASTI;%PATH%
AEX IRQ=15 IOBASE=300 VERBOSE
AILANBIO
REDIR LUCY LOGINS=4
SERVER C:\LANTASTI.NET
NET LOGIN/WAIT \\LUCY LUCY
NET LOGIN/WAIT \\GRYPHON LUCY
NET USE D: \\GRYPHON\C-DRIVE
NET USE E: \\GRYPHON\BACKUP
NET USE F: \\GRYPHON\DATABASE
NET USE LPT1: \\GRYPHON\@LASERWR
NET USE LPT2: \\GRYPHON\@DMATRIX
NET USE LPT3: \\GRYPHON\@HPLJII
NET LPT TIMEOUT 10
```

I'll discuss each grouping of lines separately. As the workstation STARTNET.BAT commands are a subset of the server STARTNET.BAT commands, I'll note those commands that apply to servers only.

1. `@ECHO OFF`
   `PATH C:\LANTASTI;%PATH%`

Installing LANtastic

The first two lines suppress screen output of the batch commands and add the installation directory (which holds the network utilities) to the "PATH" specification:

> **Note:** The command %PATH% references the existing path, so the existing path specification replaces this command in the batch file. See your DOS manual for more details.

You might want to remove the PATH command and include it in the AUTOEXEC.BAT file with any other PATH specifications.

2. `AEX IRQ=15 IOBASE=300 VERBOSE`
   `AILANBIO`

   These two lines start the network adapter driver and NETBIOS, for an Artisoft AE-2 EtherNet adapter. If a 2Mbps adapter is being used, this part will read (by default):

   `LANBIOS2 IRQ=3 IOBASE=280 RAMBASE=D800 VERBOSE`

   Obviously, if your configuration is different, you'll need to edit these lines accordingly.

3. `REDIR LUCY LOGINS=4`

   The next step is to start the redirector, REDIR.EXE, and specify the PC's name (in this case, LUCY). The number of servers this workstation can log into concurrently is also specified here and, by default, is set to 4. If your workstation is to connect to more or less than four servers, you may want to change this value.

4. `SERVER C:\LANTASTI.NET`

   This line is for servers only. Now the server software needs to be loaded. The default for this line is to specify the LANtastic control directory. If you specified a different control directory during installation, this line will reflect that specification.

5. `NET LOGIN/WAIT \\LUCY LUCY`
   `NET LOGIN/WAIT \\GRYPHON LUCY`

This section logs this PC into the local server (only if it exists) and the servers that were specified as having shared resources. The default is to log into each server using the machine name as given during installation (the first step of the section "General Options"). This is also the same name given to the redirector).

The instruction to /WAIT means that a client login should be repeatedly attempted until successful or the user aborts the attempt. The purpose of /WAIT is so that the network servers have enough time to start up before making client connections when networked PCs are started (for example, first thing in the morning).

If you want to add logins or change the name under which logins are attempted you should alter these lines accordingly. You might take all of these lines out and have logins performed by a separate batch file.

6. NET USE D: \\GRYPHON\C-DRIVE
   NET USE E: \\GRYPHON\BACKUP
   NET USE F: \\GRYPHON\DATABASE

Now that the servers have been logged into, each remote shared resource specified (the first step of the "Special Options" section) has a drive connected to it, starting with the first drive that isn't directed to a local resource.

These commands can be added or changed as you see fit. As with the server logins in step 5, you might leave these out and have them performed by a batch file. If you have deleted any server logins, you should check that the commands in this section can still be performed.

7. NET USE LPT1: \\GRYPHON\@LASERWR
   NET USE LPT2: \\GRYPHON\@DMATRIX
   NET USE LPT3: \\GRYPHON\@HPLJII
   NET LPT TIMEOUT 10

The printer resources defined during installation are now connected to, and the amount of time after which a print job is assumed to be finished is set to the default value of 10 seconds.

As with the server logins and resource connections in steps 5 and 6, any changes to the default printer assignments should be made here. If a server hasn't been logged into, the NET USE command will try to log you into the specified server with the machine name (see the first step of the section "General Options"). If your PC can't log in using that name, the redirection will fail.

Starting the Network

Now that the installation, testing, and configuration is complete, the node can be started. Simply reboot the PC and, if you've added the start-up batch file to the AUTOEXEC.BAT file, the process should begin.

If the AUTOEXEC.BAT file doesn't begin the start-up process, change to the directory containing the LANtastic utilities (\LANTASTI by default), type STARTNET, and press Enter (at the DOS prompt).

Solutions to Common Problems

Whether you start the network through the AUTOEXEC.BAT file, the STARTNET.BAT file, or by entering the command for each program by hand, there's a variety of problems that may come up.

- Command or filename not recognized. This is DOS's way of saying that either your command (or a command in a batch file) was misspelled or not where you said it was. Check the spelling and the location of the command and try again.

- Out of environment space. This is another DOS error message that indicates you need to alter your system. See your DOS manual for details on how to allocate more environmental space.

- One or more of the LANtastic components produces an error message that indicates it can't load. Check the LANtastic manuals for an explanation of the message. This kind of problem is very rare unless you've got a custom configuration of network hardware and software.

- If the NET LOGIN commands fail, the NET USE commands will also fail. Either ensure that the required server is on-line or remove the lines from the STARTNET.BAT file.

Networking with LANtastic

> **Note:** You can put these lines in a separate batch file and run it when the server is available.

Reconfiguring Applications and Utilities

Once the network servers and workstations have been set up, the applications and utilities that you'll be using need to be configured for the new environment.

In general, there are two ways of setting up the network environment for applications. The first is to make a fixed, or *static,* environment. In this situation, the workstation connects drives to the various resources needed, when it initializes. This setup then stays constant until the PC is restarted. The disadvantage of this plan is that for a complex system with many resources and many applications you may run out of drives to allocate (remember, there are 26 in total running from A to Z).

The alternative to a static setup is to make connections *dynamically* to network resources as required for each application. As yet, very few applications can directly set up network connections, so you'll probably have to use batch files to reconfigure the environment each time an application starts. The major disadvantage of this approach is that it may introduce a delay before the application is available.

For example, a static setup might have the following:

- Drive D: redirected to \\LUCY\WP for the word processing files.
- Drive E: redirected to \\BIGBOY\SS for the spreadsheet files.
- Drive F: redirected to \\GRYPHON\DB for the accounts data.

A dynamic setup would just redirect one drive, say, drive D: and switch the redirection as required for each program. This could be done using a batch file such as the one below (for full details on the NET commands used in this batch file, see Appendix C, "Utilities Reference"):

```
@ECHO OFF
CLS
rem DSETUP.BAT to manage a dynamic LANtastic setup
```

```
rem
rem We need to switch to drive C: as you can't "UNUSE"
rem a drive if it is your default drive.
rem
C:
NET UNUSE D:
rem
rem By putting the character tested for in both upper and
rem lower case, you don't have to worry about how the batch
rem file is run. This means that "DSETUP s", "DSETUP S",
rem "dsetup s", and "dsetup S" are all equivalent.
rem
IF %1 == W GOTO WP
IF %1 == w GOTO WP
IF %1 == S GOTO SS
IF %1 == s GOTO SS
IF %1 == D GOTO DB
IF %1 == d GOTO DB
NET ECHO
NET ECHO Ooops!
NET ECHO
NET ECHO You must enter one of the following:
NET ECHO
NET ECHO W for word processing
NET ECHO S for spreadsheet
NET ECHO D for database
NET ECHO
GOTO XIT
rem
rem The second parameter is the optional name of
rem the file for the application to use.
rem
rem Because the LOGIN is done without a user name,
rem the default user name and password is used.
:WP
rem
rem Login to server
rem
NET LOGIN \\LUCY
rem
rem Redirect the drive
rem
```

```
NET USE D: \\LUCY\WP
rem
rem Move to the drive and run the application
rem
D:
WORD %2
GOTO XIT
:SS
rem
rem Same principle as the last section
rem
NET LOGIN \\BIGBOY
NET USE D: \\BIGBOY\SS
D:
LOTUS %2
GOTO  XIT
NET LOGIN \\GRYPHON
NET USE D: \\GRYPHON\DB
PARADOX %2
rem
rem Tidy up and exit with the satisfaction of a job well done.
rem
:XIT
C:
NET UNUSE D:
```

Another application network configuration tactic that some sites use is to keep a single copy of each of the files that make up an application on one server to simplify management and reduce the amount of disk space used up on each PC.

For example, you might have all of the executable files for a word processing program on a single server. Any user who wants to use the word processor must be logged into that server and must load all of the components of the application across the network to their workstation. This organization works well for some applications, but it can put a huge load on the network and considerably reduce response at the workstation.

Installing LANtastic

Note: Check the license terms of each software package that you plan to organize in this way on your network. You may find that doing this will be, under the terms of the license, illegal. If in doubt, contact the manufacturer (I would recommend by letter) and try to get clearance for your site. You may find that they are unwilling to let you do so, and you'll then have to decide whether you still want to use the package and not centralize, or send back the software and give your business to one of their competitors.

Note: With Windows, holding a single, shared copy on a central server is not such a good idea. Although complex to set up correctly, it can be done, but the size of the files that must be sent across the network and the frequency with which Windows accesses its other system files can make the performance of even a fast network seem sluggish.

Some software may not work on a network at all. Although this is uncommon, some applications perform operations that are not compatible with the network environment and may disable network connections. Operations that are not network-compatible include direct input and output to serial ports, attempts at low-level disk access, and monopolizing processor time.

Some applications used to be very particular about where the files they used were kept. This was usually because they were designed for floppy-only systems. This is now uncommon, but if you do have programs that are unchangeable in their drive configuration, LANtastic allows you to connect any drive (including A and B) to shared resources.

Tip: You can even redirect your local A drive to be your B drive and vice versa. This can be very useful, for example, when you are installing software that must run from the A drive but comes on 3.5" floppy disks when your A drive is a 5.25" drive. You can also use a server PC's floppy drives as if they were your own. So, if you have no floppy drives or drives of the wrong size, you can now access any floppy drives you need to.

151

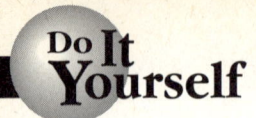

Networking with LANtastic

LANtastic's ability to redirect printer devices (COM1, COM2, LPT1, and so on) can also allow you to deal with software that won't recognize that printers can be on ports other than LPT1. And where software is incapable of driving the printer that you have, the spooler's job start-up and clean-up settings can often be used to configure the device as required.

Software that uses copy-protection mechanisms can often cause problems that cannot be avoided. For example, the application can't be loaded onto a network drive (in which case you may still be able to run it from a local drive and use it with files on the network), or the application won't allow access to any files on network resources.

> **Note:** Copy-protected software can create all sorts of difficulties even on stand-alone (non-networked) PCs, so consider using it with care on networks where the environment is much more complex.

Copy-protected software that uses a *dongle* (a hardware device that is either an add-in board or is attached to a serial or parallel port) may be less problematic, but test it out first or ask the software vendor if it is compatible with LANtastic. There are very few copy-protected applications that don't have non-copy-protected competitors, so don't feel that you are trapped into using a copy-protected package.

To find out whether a particular software package is LANtastic-compatible you have several sources you can turn to:

- *The manufacturer's sales department.* Frequently reliable but you'll usually find that they can't really help when specific network questions are raised unless it is a real network product.

- *The manufacturer's technical support group.* Usually reliable, but it depends very much on what kind of product they're handling and what kind of company it is.

- *The product manuals.* Unless the product has some relationship to networking, it probably won't help much.

- *Artisoft technical bulletins.* Always check Artisoft's ArtiFax service for information on applications and compatibility (see Appendix A, "Resources," for details). This system allows you to select technical bulletins and have them faxed to you.

- *Artisoft Technical Support.* While Artisoft Technical Support may not be able to give you a definite yes or no, they often will be able to point you in the right direction of someone who will.

- *Other users.* Usually among the best sources of intelligence on compatibility issues. Join a PC user group or get on CompuServe (see Appendix A, "Resources," for details).

- *A computer products dealer.* Unless they're really network specialists (rather than just saying so), they usually won't know. Many of the big dealers now let you try software on a 30-day evaluation. This is more than enough time to figure out for yourself if it works. Don't take the disks and manuals back and carry on using the copy you've got. The practice is illegal.

The last two options are often the best. Other users are the best sources but with a dealer, at the least, you can usually read the manual and, at best, you can actually try the product on your own system.

Reconfiguration of most software to make it compatible with the network environment is usually straightforward, as LANtastic creates a broadly DOS-compatible environment. If you have any questions about a particular application's network compatibility, ask whoever you're buying LANtastic from to research the issue for you.

Summary

Installing LANtastic can be broken down into five sections:

Preparation   Both well in advance, and immediately before, installation.

Installing Hardware   Laying the cable, configuring and installing the network interface cards in the PCs.

Installing Network Software   Running the installation program and testing the network hardware.

Configuring the System   Running the NET_MGR.EXE utility and setting up users, groups, resources, etc.

Reconfiguring Applications   Changing the disk directories and printers that applications use.

7

Shared Resources

You've read about shared resources in earlier chapters, but you haven't learned much about their details. Shared network resources are any devices (printer, plotter, disk storage, etc.) that are available remotely across the network. The LANtastic networking system supports three types of shared resources:

- Disk drives (hard disks, floppy disks, and CD-ROM drives).
- Printers on any of the serial or parallel ports.
- The mail system.

LANtastic also allows you to define these resources so as to hide the actual details (location, device) of a resource from the network user.

Shared resources are set up through the NET_MGR.EXE utility (see Appendix C, "Utilities Reference," for complete details). A shared resource has three components:

- The server it is on (for example, GRYPHON).
- The network name for the resource (such as C-DRIVE).
- The local specification of the resource (like C:\).

155

Networking with LANtastic

> **Note:** Network servers are always denoted by a double backslash before their name, thus: \\GRYPHON, \\ADGIBBS, \\LUCYSMITH.

Disk Resources

When you set up a network resource, you must give it a name by which users can refer to it in order to make a connection. In the case of disk resources, these names are totally independent of the true, local name of the resource.

For example, the local hard disk on the server \\GRYPHON might be drive C. The default name that LANtastic gives to this resource on installation will be C-DRIVE. You can change this name to anything you like as long as it follows these rules:

- It may be a maximum of eight characters long.
- It may include an optional three-character extension with a period (.) as a separator.
- It must not include any DOS delimiter characters other than the period (.) separator.

> **Tip:** It is always better to choose a readily identifiable name for resources if users are allowed to make their own connections. This also makes it easier from an administrative point of view.

Other LANtastic defaults at installation are:

- Each hard disk drive is made entirely available as a network resource.
- Each floppy disk is made available as a network resource.

Having an entire hard disk as a network resource means that the *root directory* of each drive (that is, the highest directory under which all other directories exist) and everything below it are, by default, accessible if you can log into that server.

Alternative Disk Resource Definitions

You can define a shared disk resource or change the definition of an existing one so that a subdirectory under the root directory is the highest directory network users can access. This directory will become, in effect, the root directory for that resource.

In Figure 7.1, after changing the definition of C-DRIVE, the root of the drive now appears to network users to be C:\DOCS rather than the actual root C:\.

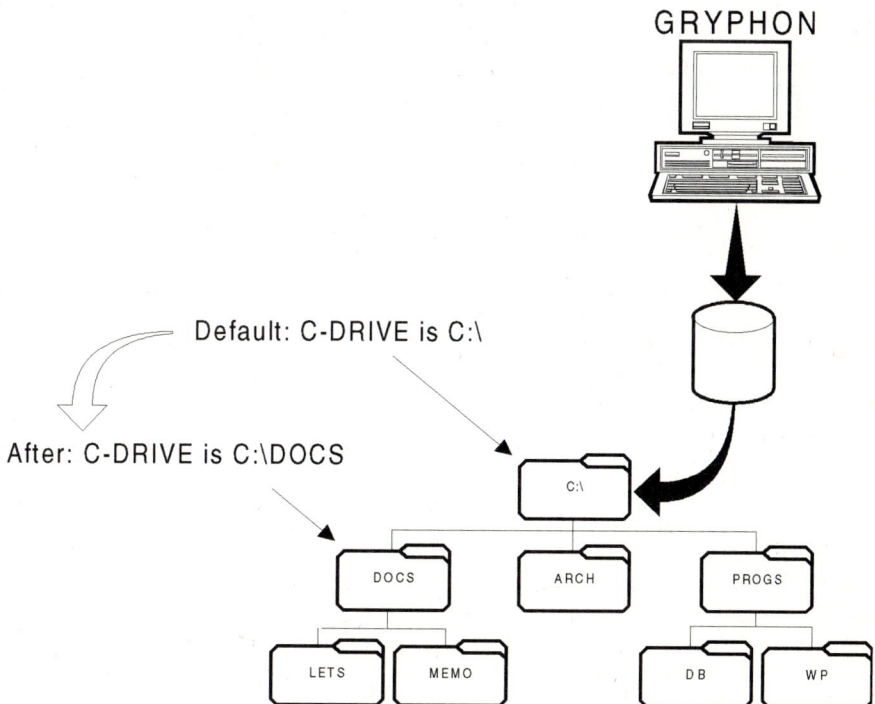

Figure 7.1   *Changing the specification of C-DRIVE on server GRYPHON.*

Making the effective root a subdirectory below the real root directory is an excellent mechanism for imposing control on users. Once a resource has been defined in this way, the user's freedom is strictly limited.

Networking with LANtastic

You can also define several disk resources that are on the same disk drive. For example, using the disk system in Figure 7.1, you could leave C-DRIVE as C:\ and define

- DOCUMENT as C:\DOCS
- WPPROG as C:\PROGS\WP
- DBPROG as C:\PROGS\DB

and so on.

Rights

As covered in Chapter 8, "Protecting Your Network," the default rights that users have will be:

RWCMLDKNEAI -

That is, the default rights include all rights except physical access. These access rights should be modified for each defined resource.

> **Caution:** A user's rights to access a shared disk resource applies to all directories under the directory that the resource is defined as.
>
> This means that you need to be careful in giving rights and in ordering access control lists. If you just accept the defaults that LANtastic uses for installation, users will have complete freedom in shared disk resources from whatever subdirectory is the starting point of a definition.
>
> The ultra-cautious approach is to set all access rights for the group * in the access control list for a shared disk resource to ------------, and then give specific rights to individual users.

Once a disk resource has been set up and is in use, you should avoid altering its definition. If you do, you'll probably have to change the configurations of all the users of that resource.

Shared Printers

LANtastic allows a user on one PC to use printers on other PCs that are set up as servers. By sharing printers across the network, you can use expensive devices such as plotters and laser printers much more efficiently and economically.

The output of data to shared devices is managed by a spooler system. A *spooler* is a mechanism that manages access to an output device, such as a printer or plotter. The purpose of the spooler is to make it appear as if the device were available to all programs that want to use it at the same time.

The spooler takes the stream of data produced by each remote user and stores it in a file. The files are stored ("queued") for output either on a first-in/first-out basis or according to some priority scheme. When the output device is available, the spooler starts to output the next file in the queue.

Note: LANtastic allows you to feed a single output device from more than one queue. This allows you to separate print jobs that require different paper or are different priorities.

Figure 7.2 shows the conceptual organization of a spooler system.

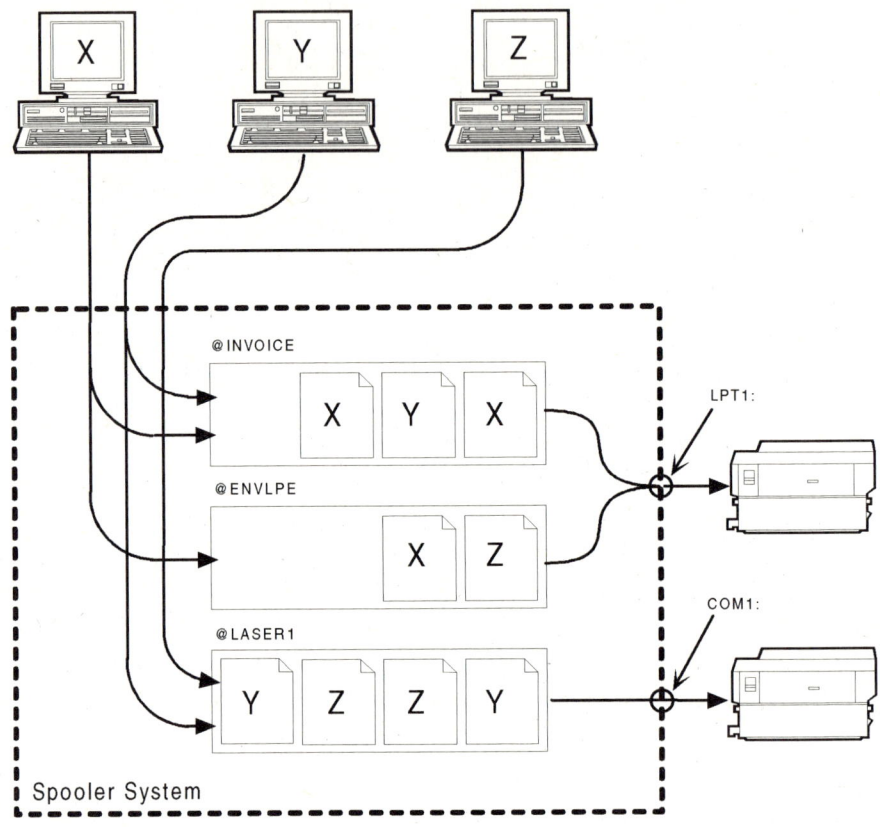

Figure 7.2 *The organization of a spooler system.*

Printer Resources

LANtastic's shared printer resources are similar to the shared disk resources. Each printer resource has a unique name that must be formed as follows:

- It must start with an at sign (@).
- It can include up to a maximum of seven characters (excluding the @).
- It may include an optional three-character extension with a period (.) as a separator.
- It must not include any DOS delimiter characters other than the peiod (.) separator.

Thus, @LASER, @MATRIX.DOT, and @LASER.001 are all valid names for printer resources.

The basic rights required as a user to access a printer resource are:

RWC - L - - - - - - -

- *Read:* You can look at the data in jobs waiting to be printed. Exactly which ones (either just your own or everyone's) will depend on what privileges you have (see Chapter 8, "Protecting Your Network").
- *Write:* You can add jobs.
- *Create:* You can start jobs.
- *List:* You can list the entries in the printer queue.

These rights are set up when the resource is created. Any other greater degree of access to allow the printer queues to be manipulated can be given by setting the Super Queue privilege for the user. A user with Super Queue privilege can delete print jobs, halt a printer, and so on. See Chapters 8, "Protecting Your Network."

> **Note:** Because Super Queue is a user privilege rather than a resource access right, a user who has that privilege on a server will be able to control *all* of the print resources on that server.

General Printer Configuration

When you create a printer resource, apart from giving it a name, you can specify its general configuration:

- Provide a description for the printer. This is just text that provides the opportunity to give the printer a more lengthy description.
- Designate which port the printer is on (LPT1, LPT2, LPT3, COM1, or COM2).
- Define the character sequence or the name of a file containing characters to set up the printer.
- Define the name of a file containing characters to "clean up" after printing.
- Set the amount of time (delay) required for the printer setup to complete and for the clean-up between print jobs.
- Set the rate at which characters are sent to the printer.
- Enable banner pages.
- Enable form feeds.
- Set the tab width.
- Set the paper width.

Note: "Clean up" is Artisoft's term for the process of resetting the state of a printer or plotter at the end of a job. Most devices don't need a clean-up, but the facility can be useful if the device is non-standard in any way.

A server could be configured to have printers on all ports that LANtastic supports. You could also specify that several printer resources use the same port. This would allow you, in conjunction with the setup and clean-up character sequences, to use different printer resources that use the same printer in different ways.

For example, a printer resource called @LASER.LND could be created to output to a laser printer on LPT1 in landscape mode. The characters specified as the setup would put the laser printer into landscape mode and do any other initialization required. Once the print job was finished, the clean-up data would reset the printer to portrait mode. A second printer resource could also be defined as @LASER.POR, to print on the same printer on LPT1. Again, using the setup and clean-up data would ensure that the printer was left in a known state.

The idea of setup and clean-up is to give you the greatest flexibility in controlling a printer in the network environment. Setup is used to configure before a print job is started. This could be to ensure that the correct paper bin and font are selected. After all the data has been saved to the printer, the clean-up sequence can be used to ensure that the job is completed.

For example, some applications might not ensure that the final page of output is ended with a form-feed character that tells the printer that the page is complete. Some laser printers won't actually print the data they've been sent without a form-feed, so the clean-up sequence can be used to force the printer to properly end the job.

Setup and clean-up are very important where more complex printers are used. For example, a laser printer with two paper hoppers and an envelope feeder receiving output from three printer resources could be left in a wide variety of states. Unless the printer was reset after each job, the chances of printing in the wrong format on the wrong paper would be very high.

You use delay settings for setup and clean-up to allow the output device adequate time to perform the operation. If the device is a plotter or a printer with multiple paper trays, this delay may be needed for pens to be changed or the paper tray to be switched. Any device that cannot cope with data when it is not in a ready state will need these delays set.

> **Note:** If you set the rate at which characters are sent to the device as 0, data will be sent to the printers as fast as possible without slowing down any other tasks that the server is doing. This value is set in the "Shared Resources Management" section of the NET_MGR utility (see Appendix C, "Utilities Reference").

The rate at which characters are sent to the device can be important in two situations. In the first, the device can only accept data at a rate lower than the server can supply it, and the device is unable to signal that the server should wait. The second situation is when you can improve server performance by slowing down the rate at which data is sent to the output device. For a server with five printers attached, this could make an important performance difference to users.

A banner page is a page of information output at the start of a print job. In a busy office environment, banner pages will make it much easier to identify who a print job belongs to. With LANtastic, a banner page looks like Figure 7.3.

```
************************************************************************

MM    MM  GGGGG    IIII   BBBBBB   BBBBBB    SSSSS
MMM  MMM  GG  GG    II    BB   BB  BB   BB  SS   SS
MMMMMMM  GG         II    BB   BB  BB   BB  SS
MM M MM  GG         II    BBBBB    BBBBB     SSSSS
MM   MM  GG GGGG    II    BB   BB  BB   BB       SS
MM   MM  GG   GG    II    BB   BB  BB   BB  SS   SS
MM   MM   GGGGG    IIII   BBBBBB   BBBBBB    SSSSS


 GGGGG   RRRRRR   YY   YY  PPPPPP   HH   HH   OOOOO   NN      NN
GG   GG  RR   RR  YY   YY  PP   PP  HH   HH  OO   OO  NNN     NN
GG       RR   RR   YY YY   PP   PP  HH   HH  OO   OO  NNNN    NN
GG       RRRRR      YYYY   PPPPP    HHHHHHH  OO   OO  NN NNNN
GG  GGG  RR   RR     YY    PP       HH   HH  OO   OO  NN   NNN
GG   GG  RR   RR     YY    PP       HH   HH  OO   OO  NN    NN
 GGGGG   RRR   RR    YY    PP       HH   HH   OOOOO   NN     NN










************************************************************************

                        Username  MGIBBS
                         Machine  GRYPHON
                         Comment
                            Date  92.03.12
                            Time  17:23:44
                         Printer  @PRINTER
                          Device  LPT1
                           Width  80
                            Tabs  0
                          Copies  1
                            File  \spool.net\1._SP
```

Figure 7.3 *A LANtastic print job banner page.*

Many applications and most printers don't automatically issue a form feed at the end of each print output. The problem with this is that the next print job could start printing on the last page of the previous job. As the new job would most likely expect that the printer is at the top of a new page to start with, the resulting output would be a mess. By enabling form feeds, the print spooler will send the printer a form feed after all other data has been sent.

> **Caution:** If you are using the setup and clean-up facilities, make sure that they don't send a form feed as well. In the worst case, you could get an end-of-job form feed, a clean-up form feed, and a setup form feed!

Finally, setting tabs, lines per page, and paper width is supported by LANtastic. If you enable tabs, whenever the spooler sees a tab character, it will replace that character with the number of spaces you specify. In general, this is only of use with very unsophisticated applications or for dumping pure text files into the printer. The tabbing facility is not a "smart" tabbing service that expands tabs to fixed positions on the page, and you may find that setting tabs will interfere with output from word processors.

> **Note:** For many devices, such as PostScript printers, enabling tabs and banner pages will confuse the device, and it will not print correctly. Use facilities such as tab expansion and page-width setting for truly simple printers.

If you set the lines per page value, after that many lines, the spooler will insert a form-feed character. This can be used when you want to ensure that the paper will be at the actual top-of-page for an application that expects a certain number of lines per page.

Setting the paper width allows the LANtastic spooler to print a banner of the appropriate width for the paper being used. In the case of 80-column printers, this setting will not need to be changed.

Serial Printer Configuration

For serial printers, additional information needs to be set:

- Baud rate.

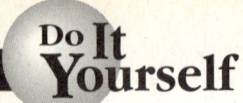

Networking with LANtastic

- Stop bits.
- Parity.
- Flow control.

The first three define the format and rate of data transfer and must be the same for the server and the output device.

Flow control needs to be set to ensure that the server doesn't send more data than the printer can handle. Flow control is the term used to describe the method by which the server and printer synchronize transferring data. With hardware flow control, signals on specific pins are used to indicate when a device is ready to receive data. Software flow control uses characters sent over the connection to indicate when a device is ready to receive. Some printers are fast enough to be always ready to accept data, so, in those cases, flow control is not required.

If flow control is needed, the server must know what kind is to be used. To determine the right type for your printer, check the printer's manual.

When a PC sends data to an output device, the device will often have an output rate that is less than the rate at which data can be supplied. For serial devices, there are three options for control of the data flow:

- *None*. The output device can keep up with the data rate.
- *XON/XOFF*. Otherwise known as *software control*.
- *Hardware control*. The output device indicates its ability to accept data through signals on the serial interface.

If the flow control type is not set correctly, you may find that your printer or plotter loses data or may not even begin taking it from the server.

Mail Resource

When a LANtastic server is set up, an electronic mail resource is configured by default. There is only one mail resource per server and it is always called @MAIL. This resource is a queue of files much like the printer-resource queues. When you send a message to someone using the NET.EXE utility (see Appendix C), a file containing the message is created and an entry is made in the queue. To read your message, you also use the NET.EXE program.

The LANtastic mail system is pretty simple and lacks many of the features that you might want if you have more than a few users. On the other hand, it is simple to learn, reasonably easy to use, and comes bundled with LANtastic.

To access your mail, you first need to select a server with a Mail resource. The NET.EXE utility is the application that is used to send and receive electronic mail messages (see Appendix C, "Utilities Reference"). If every server in your organization has a mail resource, it can be hard to find all of your mail, as you need to log in to each server to check for new messages.

Tip: Deleting the Mail resource on every server but one might be practical for your organization.

Once a Mail resource has been chosen, you can pick up your incoming mail and read it, delete it, forward it, or copy it to a file. You can also do the same with the mail you've sent to other people that they have not yet picked up.

Having only one mail system ensures that mail will only be routed through one server. This makes it easier to find your post and for the network supervisor to manage the system. It also makes the mail system more secure from unauthorized access.

LANtastic Mail provides an editor for creating messages and allows you to send files and (if you and the recipient have Artisoft Voice Adapter Boards) to send voice mail messages. The voice mail facility allows you to speak into a telephone-type handset and record a spoken message in a file on disk. You can then send the file as a mail message to another user. See Chapter 10, "Advanced Topics," for more details.

The basic rights required as a user to access a Mail system resource are:

RWC - - - - - - -

- *Read:* Allows you to read electronic mail messages.
- *Write:* Allows you to add data to a mail message.
- *Create:* Allows you to start a mail message.

Note: If the message recipient is on the network when you send an electronic mail message, he or she will get a pop-up message warning that mail is waiting.

These rights are set up when the resource is created. Any other greater degree of access to allow the mail queues to be manipulated can be given by setting the Super Mail privilege for the user. A user with Super Queue privilege can read, delete, copy, or forward anybody's messages. See NET.EXE in Appendix C, "Utilities Reference."

Note: The only management that the mail systems require is to remove old messages to conserve disk space.

Summary

LANtastic supports three types of shared resources:

- Shared disk drives defined as starting at either the root or any subdirectory.

- Shared printers attached to LPT1, LPT2, LPT3, COM1, or COM2 and fed by any number of printer resources each. Each resource is configurable to match the requirements of any particular printer. Printer queues may be fully managed by any user with Super Queue privilege.

- LANtastic Mail supports basic text message and file sending and receiving, and the rather more sophisticated voice messaging. The default setup for servers creates a single mail system (there is only one per server), and the entire Mail system may be fully managed by any user with the Super Mail privilege on that server.

Protecting Your Network

Any organization that invests in computer equipment does so expecting that they will be more productive and more organized through its use. But often the basic issues of maintaining the integrity of the systems are overlooked. The results? Loss of time, loss of data, theft, vandalism, and ultimately loss of money. In this chapter we'll look at protecting your network from the various threats that face it.

The Concept of Security

Security is the generic term used to refer to maintaining the integrity of computer systems. For networks, the security issues can be divided into two parts: physical and logical.

Physical security concerns the ability of someone or something to affect the material functioning or integrity of a network component (PCs, peripherals, cabling). The basis of physical security is accessibility. If, for

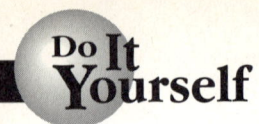

Networking with LANtastic

example, a PC is locked away and has controlled access, it can be considered physically secure. On the other hand, if the PC is in the middle of an office, anyone can read or copy the files on the hard disk, introduce a virus, or even walk off with the entire machine!

With a network, things get more complex. Because the network integrates so many resources, it becomes a more interesting system to thieves and vandals. It also becomes a greater potential liability to its owner. If the network is going to be used for anything confidential that others would be willing to try to discover or steal, then the issues of physical security are crucial.

Logical security concerns access that is restricted by a nonphysical control. For example, a combination lock is a physical security device, but the combination itself (three turns right to two, four turns left to three, and so on) is a logical feature. For a network, logical security covers the various privileges and rights associated with logging into a server, accessing directories, accessing files, accessing services, and monitoring activity.

Who and What Are You Protecting Your Network from?

There are a large number of potential threats to the security of a network. Many of them are uncommon and some are accidental, but few of them, if you are sufficiently prepared, will cause a lasting problem.

Physical Threats

The major physical threats are:

- Flood.
- Fire.
- Theft.

- General hardware failures.
- Cable failures.
- Hard disk failures.

Flood

A water source as innocuous as a leaking pipe can damage network cables. A full-scale flood, such as the triggering of a sprinkler system in the case of a fire, can damage PCs and peripherals. This threat is not common and is usually the result of other events like fire.

Fire

This fairly common threat may be started anywhere in the building housing the network and can, at the very least, damage or destroy cabling. PCs and peripherals such as printers, if left on, can be a fire risk. To counter this threat, use the correct cabling in walls (it's called *plenum type* and is designed not to produce toxic fumes when it burns), don't leave running equipment unattended unless there are fire controls, and maintain the normal kinds of fire precautions.

Theft

This is a very common threat. Unless you take specific action to prevent PCs and peripherals from being taken, there is always the possibility of theft. The larger the company, the greater the risk. You can prevent theft by locking PCs away, chaining them to desks (various companies offer anti-theft systems), and training staff to be vigilant.

General Hardware Failures

These are the most common source of physical problems with networks. There are various areas where hardware failure will affect a network. PCs can fail in many ways that range from the obvious (it simply won't work) to the subtle (a component may fail and prevent the network adapter from being accessed). Network cards can fail due to causes such as electrical

Networking with LANtastic

problems (static shocks transmitted through the PC case), component failure, and mechanical failure (connectors to the cabling can get damaged if treated roughly). The best strategy for dealing with these threats is to handle the equipment with respect and ensure that it is properly installed.

Cable Failures

By far the most common causes of network failures are cables and hard disk drives. Cable failures are easily caused by cables being bent or kinked, cut, or otherwise mangled, and finding a problem cable may be difficult without the right equipment and a methodical approach. Cable failures can be avoided by ensuring that cables are properly installed and protected from harm.

Hard Disk Failures

These are always major problems. It is often impossible, without considerable expense and time, to retrieve the data stored on a hard disk. The best defense against suffering down time (that is, loss of operational capability) is to take regular backups, have a good maintenance policy, and plan for what to do in the event of a failure.

> **Note:** If your server is going to handle very critical data, consider using software or hardware that supports *mirroring*. Mirroring keeps a copy of the data on two hard disks but is, of course, an extra expense in both additional software and hardware.

Nonphysical Threats

The nonphysical threats to networks are more subtle and require much more careful countermeasures. These threats fall into two categories: people and software. There are two major groups of people who can cause damage to a network: users and vandals.

Users

The most dangerous person to your network is the untrained or inadequately trained user. The command DEL *.* has caused much greater data losses than all of the hard disk failures, computer viruses, and program bugs combined.

In the hands of a novice user, even a word processing package can be lethal to files. Users can also wreak havoc simply by doing something that wasn't planned for, such as trying to send a 500-page report to a slow printer during the printer's busiest time of day.

There are two major strategies for preventing problems caused by users:

- Train your users — A trained user is much less likely to cause damage through ignorance.
- Control the network and the users — LANtastic offers a rich set of control services that allow you to restrict what is accessed and how.

Vandals

Vandals can include employees, hackers, and anyone with a grudge or mischievous intent. Vandals come in two types: technically ignorant and technically aware. Most of the time, the technically ignorant vandal is easily detected and his actions and effects are usually quite clear.

The technically aware vandal is just the opposite. This kind of vandal includes:

- Hackers (unwanted users whether local or remote, and whether or not they cause damage).
- Computer virus and Trojan software authors (who are almost always remote).

Both types of software are usually intended to affect your system in some way, either by playing a silly trick, such as displaying a message, or doing something more serious, such as reformatting your hard disk. The big difference between viruses and Trojans lies in the ability of viruses to reproduce themselves.

 *Networking with LANtastic*

A virus will find an uninfected file on whatever disk drives are accessible whether or not they are local or directed to another computer across the network. Again, using the LANtastic access controls will allow you to prevent unauthorized activities and control or even stop the spread of viruses.

Software-related Problems

These problems are the other type of nonphysical threat that can compromise a network. Despite extensive testing by the creator of an application or utility and even with a large number of users, it is still possible for a program to fail. In some cases, this failure may be catastrophic and might stop the PC from working. LANtastic is very robust under these circumstances and will usually continue to operate even if the application has "locked up."

The biggest software problem that PCs and networks face these days is from computer viruses. These programs are transmitted from one PC to another through executable files (that is, files that do things such as .EXE, .COM, .BAT, etc.). If you use the LANtastic network security controls and practice "safe computing," you are unlikely to experience any problems.

The LANtastic security controls can be used to prevent programs stored on a server from being infected by a client PC that has a virus.

Note: Once a program on a server is infected, any client that runs the program will infect its own local programs.

"Safe computing" means:

- Use one of the many available virus-checking programs at regular intervals to scan the PCs on your network (and those that aren't connected) for virus infections.

- Don't allow software supplied on either floppy disks or downloaded from bulletin boards to be put on any PC on the network unless it comes from a reputable source and has been scanned for viruses.

- Don't allow engineers who come to fix PCs to use their own diagnostic utilities (you should keep your own set for their use — the site they last visited may have been infected and it's unlikely that they check their disks).

These are some of the basic precautions you should take. They are particularly important if you are a business that provides services and takes in and/or supplies data on floppy disks. Passing a virus on to a client could, at the very least, lose you the client and might even result in a legal case! A selection of companies who provide anti-virus software can be found in the resources section.

Login Security

When you log into a server, you must give a name and a password. The purpose of a name is to identify you to the server and to other network users. This name can be:

- Your own name (for example, LUCYSMITH).
- Based on your name (LS).
- Any alias you like (THEBOSS).

The password is used to validate who you are. A correct combination of name and password is required to log in to a server although you can just omit the password if you feel it's not needed.

Note: It is always advisable to use passwords. Not using them is the equivalent of leaving the front door of your house unlocked. The first burglar who tries the door can get in. Once he's in, other controls may stop him (such as locking other internal doors), but he's in the position to steal or do some damage.

User Names

LANtastic allows users to have names of up to 16 characters and may not include commas, colons, semicolons, or spaces. Some examples of valid and invalid names are shown in Table 8.1.

Table 8.1   Valid and invalid user names.

Name	Status	Reason
ARIANNE GIBBS	Invalid	Contains a space.
SALES:ARIANNEDREWGIBBS	Invalid	More than 16 characters and contains a colon.
GIBBS,A.D.;SALES	Invalid	Contains a comma and a semicolon.
ARIANNE	Valid	
SALES_ADGIBBS	Valid	
!ADGIBBS	Valid	
AD$GIBBS	Valid	
@%$#$%^$#*&^&*!	Valid	

The length of 16 characters and the few disallowed characters allow for a tremendous flexibility in choosing names. In general, it is better to choose short, memorable names for users. In smaller organizations, using the person's first name is often adequate, although it is surprising how often a single company will have several Johns, Marks, and Janes.

Tip: A standard such as the *simple name format* is a good basis for defining network names. This standard uses the first initial, middle initial (optional), and as many characters of the last name to make the login name up to eight characters.

ADGIBBS fits the simple name format standard, whereas !ARIANNE-@SALES does not. Moreover, the latter will be hard to remember. Table 8.2 shows examples of the simple name format applied to various names.

Table 8.2   Examples of applying the simple name format to generate user login names.

Real Name	Login Name
Mark Gibbs	MGIBBS
Arianne Drew Gibbs	ADGIBBS
Quinn Kellog Redeker	QREDEKER (or QKREDEKE)
Edward Bradley Lay	EBLAY
Sally Bellovin	SBELLOVI

For Quinn Kellog Redeker, it would be better to use QREDEKER rather than QKREDEKE, because the first login name is more obvious, and easier for the user to remember.

Group Accounts

Group accounts allow anyone whose login name matches a *mask* (that is, a template specification of a name) and has the correct password to log into the server. A template name, as the term suggests, has characters that are tested for a match with the user's name. If there is a successful match, the user is given the rights and privileges assigned to that group on that server.

The purpose of groups is to simplify managing access to a server's resources. By defining a group of users, you can define their rights through the rights assigned to the group. If some of the users who are in that group require different rights, they can have specific accounts defined for them.

> **Note:** Groups can be useful in larger installations where you might have any number of users to define. LANtastic supports a maximum of 300 active, that is, logged-in users; however, you can define as many accounts as you like — at least until you run out of disk space. For most installations, it is easier to manage individuals rather than groups and much less error prone.

You create groups using the network management utility, NET_MGR.EXE (or WNET_MGR.EXE under Windows). Group names may be up to 15 characters long and must end with an asterisk (*). So, for example, the group SALES-* would allow a user called SALES-GLAEN to log in.

> **Note:** Groups are slightly different under LANtastic than under some other network systems. Rather than define a group and add existing accounts as group members, the group name is a prefix to a user name. This means that if you define a group account called ACCS_*, then PLSMITH is not a member but ACCS_PLSMITH is. The characters up to the asterisk (*) define the prefix that is common to all group members. If the user logs in as PLSMITH, he will only get the access rights and privileges associated with his account. Logging in as ACCS_PLSMITH gives him only the rights and privileges associated with the ACCS_* group. The weakness of this system of group accounts is that it excludes only those who don't have the password for the group account. This means that the same group account password must be given to several people. This is not desirable for the reasons covered in the section "Passwords" in this chapter.

Passwords

With LANtastic, you can build your access security from the most basic level by requiring that each user on a server actually has a password. To prevent others from guessing a user's password, the password should be reasonably complex and made up of at least six characters.

Furthermore, the password should not be predictable (like the name of the user's spouse or their telephone number), or used by more than one user. "One user, one password" should be the rule.

> **Note:** The issue of passwords not being predictable is important. A file of the most common passwords can be found on many bulletin boards. At the top of the list are words such as SECRET, PASSWORD, and FRED.

In most computer systems, it is easy to create a program that tests for these passwords, and tries to break into a particular user's account. LANtastic is no exception. Even if you use any sequence of letters or numbers, a program can just keep trying until it successfully logs in to the server.

> **Note:** Some systems managers don't set up passwords, or they give everyone the same password. For small networks this may be satisfactory, but in the long run, planning to control access to the network and developing a strategy for protecting the network resources will prevent loss of data and services.

Table 8.3 shows a selection of passwords for different users and how they rate for security. As you can see, the best passwords are phrases formed from two or three real words. There are so many combinations that random guessing will be virtually impossible, yet they are easily remembered. Being memorable is tremendously important, as complex passwords of random numbers or letters (such as FTHJIOUKL and 937854678) tend to get written down so that they're not forgotten.

Networking with LANtastic

Table 8.3 Login names and passwords and their security ratings.

Login Name	Password	Security Issues
EBLAY	(no password)	Could be easily guessed
LRSMITH	LUCY	Could be guessed and too short
QREDEKER	QR	Could be guessed and too short
PLAY	SECRET	Could be guessed
AJGIBBS	123456	Could be guessed
DANDARE	ROCKET	Could be guessed
PLSMITH	P9334SMITH	Guessable and hard to remember
GREDEKER	FTHJIOUKL	Good but hard to remember
TGIBBS	937854678	Good but very hard to remember
PJGIBBS	OIL-PRESSURE	Good and easily remembered
BREDEKER	SHALE-CIRCUS	Good and easily remembered

Protecting Passwords

The next issue in login security is making all users aware of the importance of protecting their passwords (not disclosing them to anyone) and the responsibility of the users to protect the network. In many companies, disclosing passwords or knowingly endangering or compromising the network can result in disciplinary action or grounds for dismissal!

Note: With LANtastic group accounts, the rule of "one user, one password" is broken. All users of a group account share a common group password. This increases the likelihood of someone passing on the password and makes it much more difficult to identify who divulged it. See the "Group Accounts" section in this chapter for more details.

To ensure that passwords don't become known, LANtastic can be set up by the network supervisor so that users have to change their passwords at regular intervals — for example, every 30 days. The system allows the user to log in once after the period passes, but requires that the password be changed before he or she can use the server.

Note: For group accounts, password changes could be difficult to handle, as one user would have to change the password and then tell everyone else. This problem is another reason to avoid using group accounts.

Controlling Access to the Server

Another valuable security feature is being able to control the times and days that a server can be accessed. This allows you to define when a server can be used by either all users or specific users. Any attempt to log in outside of the permitted times will fail. Also, if the user is logged in and the logout time is passed, messages will appear at intervals warning that the user will be logged out. After 15 minutes, if the user doesn't log out, the server does so automatically.

A related access feature is being able to set an account expiration date. This allows you to specify that a particular account will become unusable on a certain date.

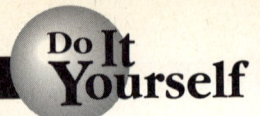

Networking with LANtastic

The final control is being able to set the number of concurrent logins for an account. This setting defines the maximum number of logins to that account that can occur at one time. This allows you to set up an account that can be used by more than one user, rather than having to specify the same access rights for several users.

> **Tip:** For most individual users, you'll want to set the number of concurrent logins to a value of 1. This means that the account can only be logged into once. Any further login attempts will fail. For group accounts, you should set this value to the number of users you want this account to support simultaneously.

> **Note:** The maximum total number of logins that the server can handle at one time is set by the Server Startup Parameters option in NET_MGR.EXE (see Appendix C, "Utilities Reference."

Guest Accounts

The GUEST account is often set up on network server systems. The purpose of this account is to allow minimal access to public resources such as printers and nonconfidential data and document files. This can be particularly useful in larger companies where each department takes responsibility for their own computer systems. Other departments can then access printers, mail queues, and disks that become corporate resources.

The only problem with guest accounts is ensuring that they are sufficiently limited so that they don't provide a "back door" for thieves, vandals, and computer viruses. The rights associated with guest accounts must be minimal, and changes in server systems need to be carefully considered if the guest accounts are not to prejudice security.

Access Rights

Access rights control what can be done with a shared resource once a user is logged into the system. This is done through *ACLs (Access Control Lists)*. ACLs define which access rights each user (or group of users) has when he or she uses a resource. LANtastic's ACLs apply to directories, printers, and the mail system. For each resource, though, each right has different meanings.

> **Note:** ACL rights are very important to the running of LANtastic and need to be understood if your network is to be well managed.

LANtastic's access rights are listed below (the letter in parentheses is the code used in all programs and documentation to denote that right):

- Directories can be searched to find files (L).
- Files can be read from (R).
- Files can be written to (W).
- Files can be created (C).
- Files can be deleted (D).
- Files can be renamed (N).
- File attributes can be changed (A).
- Files can be executed (if they are programs) (E).
- Indirect files (a special type of file — see NET INDIRECT in Appendix C, "Utilities Reference") can be created and used (I).
- Directories can be created (M).
- Directories can be deleted (K).
- *Physical access* (direct and unchecked) to devices is possible (P).

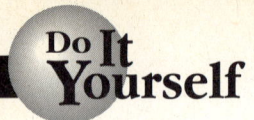

Caution: There are few reasons, if any, why anyone would want to use the physical access right. If you do use it, you may experience all sorts of complex and fatal problems. For these reasons, unless you're very brave and confident that you know what you're doing, don't mess with the physical access right — leave it turned *off*.

To understand the implications of each of these rights, we need to look at them as they apply to directories, printer queues, and mail queues. See Table 8.4 for a summary of the meanings of rights.

Note: For printer and mail queues, some access rights have no meaning. This means that whatever the setting of the right, the resource will not be affected.

Table 8.4 Access rights as applied to different resources.

Access Right	Effect on Files	Effect on Printer Queues	Effect on Mail Queues
Access Rights for File Operations			
Read	Files can be read from	Files sent for printing can be read by the person who enqueued the file	Mail messages can be read from the mail queue
Write	Files can be written to	The user can send data to a print job that they have started	Users can send messages to the mail queue
Create	Files can be created (without this you can only work with existing files).	The user can start a print job	Users can send files to the mail queue

Access Right	Effect on Files	Effect on Printer Queues	Effect on Mail Queues

Access Rights for File Operations

File Lookup	Directory searches can be made (without this, you need to know the name of the file to access it)	The user can list the jobs (files) in the printer queue	No meaning
Delete files	Files can be deleted	The user can delete their own files (jobs) from the printer queue	No meaning
ReName files	Files can be renamed	No meaning	No meaning
Change file Attributes	File attributes (hidden, system, read-only, archive) can be changed	No meaning	No meaning

Access Rights for Directory Operations

Make directory	Subdirectories in the resource directory can be created	No meaning	No meaning
K Delete directory	Subdirectories in the resource directory can be deleted	No meaning	
Execute programs	Program and batch files can be executed	Allows the print job to be output.	

continues

Table 8.4 Continued.

Access right	Effect on files	Effect on printer queues	Effect on mail queues
Access Rights for Special Operations			
Indirect file	Indirect files are supported in this directory	No meaning	No meaning
Physical access	Allows direct access to disk drives.	No meaning	No meaning

Tip: Table 8.5 shows which access rights for directories should be given to each type of user under different circumstances. The settings shown are for general cases. You may want to give the rights marked *Optional* in other situations where those types of access are required.

Table 8.5 LANtastic access rights and their applicability to different user types.

Right	Minimal Access	General Access	Network Supervisor	Network Manager
Read access	Yes	Yes	Yes	Yes
File Lookups	Yes	Yes	Yes	Yes
Create files	No	Yes	Yes	Yes
Write access	No	Yes	Yes	Yes
Delete files	No	Yes	Yes	Yes
ReName files	No	Yes	Yes	Yes
Execute programs	Optional	Optional	Yes	Yes
Indirect file	Optional	Optional	Optional	Yes
Change file Attribute	No	No	Optional	Yes

Protecting Your Network

Right	Minimal Access	General Access	Network Supervisor	Network Manager
Make directories	No	No	Optional	Yes
K Delete directories	No	No	Optional	Yes
Physical access	No	No	No	No

Some access rights fall into logical groupings because without other rights, the intended operations won't be allowed. These groups are:

- *Read with List files.* Without being able to list files, you must know the exact name of the file you need. For general purposes, the combination of these rights is the minimum needed.

> **Tip:** Giving users **R**ead access to a particular resource could be very useful in special situations, for example, if you are building a system with tight control of data or document files. By using program defaults, setting up macros, or simply giving the users a list of only the files they need, the contents of the directory would be difficult to determine.

- *Write, Read, and Create files.* All of these rights are needed if you want to be able to create a new file and put something in it.

For printer queues and the mail system, the default access rights of **R**ead, **W**rite, **C**reate, and **L**ist (RWCL) are the best choice for all normal configurations. If you need control for management purposes, setting the Super Queue or Super Mail Privileges will give you the required control capability.

As you can see, selecting the correct combination of access rights can be a complex task if you are trying to establish a specific set of constraints on how a resource can be accessed. The guidelines in table 8.5 give you the easiest set of selections for general purposes.

 *Networking with LANtastic*

How Access Control Lists Work

LANtastic's access control lists are a sort of filter. Each resource has its own list, which consists of one or more entries. Each entry contains a user name and the rights associated with that name.

> **Note:** You can skip this section if it seems complex and review it when you've had a chance to come to grips with the rest of LANtastic's features. To understand ACLs, it is helpful to be in front of a server and running NET_MGR (see Appendix C, "Utilities Reference" for information on running NET_MGR).

> **Note:** If you have no security concerns and want to keep your system simple and as open as possible, no further changes to ACLs are needed. If you are going to use LANtastic's access control lists to control shared resources, you'll find the changes to be pretty straightforward.

When a user's system requests access to a resource (a shared printer or disk), LANtastic reads the names defined in the access control list from top to bottom (the direction is very important), trying to match the requesting user's name with each name in turn. When a match is found with either a specific user name or a group name, the rights associated with that entry define what the user can do.

> **Note:** A default entry is created when a new resource is defined. This entry shows the group name * (for all users), and the assigned rights RWCMLDKNEAI-.

The default entry in the note above shows the group name * (for all users), and the assigned rights RWCMLDKNEAI-. If a right is not set, a – replaces it. So, in the default entry, all rights are given to the * group, except physical access.

Although it may seem strange to default to giving users all rights rather than giving them none at all (definitely the safest choice), Artisoft targeted LANtastic to users who want the simplest possible configuration.

This also means that the ordering of the access control list is vitally important. If you wanted to give PLSMITH the rights of RWC-LD-NEA--, the access control list in Table 8.6 would not work.

Table 8.6 An access control list that gives incorrect rights to ACCS_PLSMITH.

Entry #	User Name	Rights
1	GUEST	R---L-------
2	ACCS_*	RWC-LD-N----
3	ACCS_PLSMITH	RWC-LD-NEA--
4	*	------------

When a request from PLSMITH for use of that resource is to be handled, LANtastic will search the table starting with entry 1. There is no match, so entry 2 is tried. Because entry 2 has an asterisk (*) in it, there is a successful match and PLSMITH gets that set of access rights which exclude the execute (E) and change file attributes (A) that you wanted him to have. The correct access control list for this example is shown in Table 8.7 with the group for anyone, *, set to the safest set of rights.

Table 8.7 An access control list that gives the correct rights to "ACCS_PLSMITH."

Entry #	User Name	Rights
1	GUEST	R---L-------
2	ACCS_PLSMITH	RWC-LD-NEA--
3	ACCS_*	RWC-LD-N----
4	*	------------

Networking with LANtastic

ACLs are where you can use group names to set rights for several users. Any login name with an asterisk (*) at the end of it specifies that any name that starts with the same sequence of characters and ends with any other characters is a member of that group. For example, ACCS_* will include any user whose login name starts with ACCS_. Thus, ACCS_AJGIBBS, ACCS_PLSMITH, and ACCS_EDLAY all match with ACCS_*, so the rights associated with that entry would apply to all of them.

In general, access control lists should always be ordered beginning with specific names (PJGIBBS, ACCS_QKREDEKER, and so on) and ending with group names (ACCS_P*, ENG-*, and so on). The group names should be carefully ordered; the specific (ACCS_P*, ENG-RS*, and so on) coming before the general (ACCS_*, ENG-*, , and so on). And the asterisk (*) should always come last, as it matches to any name.

Note: There are several ways to avoid problems with ACLs giving the wrong rights to users. Set them to the default (* RWCMLDKNEAI-) so that all rights are available. Or set the default rights to none (* ----------) and then set the rights specifically for each user.

Caution: If you try to restrict a user's rights, for example, to prevent that user from writing to a particular file on a resource, his or her application software might not deal with the restrictions and might fail in an inelegant or even catastrophic manner.

Account Privileges

Account privileges control special types of access to shared resources, printer queues, mail, and audit services. These access types allow for the manipulation of the resources in potentially dangerous ways. For example, the ability to delete printer jobs is not something that you would want to make generally available. Only network managers and supervisors should be given account privileges on servers.

There are five privileges that can be given:

Super ACL allows a user to request and service without the server checking what ACL rights exist for that resource. This allows complete, uncontrolled access to a server's resources and is only suitable for people who will manage the server.

Note: Giving someone Super ACL privilege increases server performance slightly, as their requests don't have to be checked against the access control lists. However, the gain may not be significant.

Super Queue allows a user to manipulate the printer queues and spool system. This allows the user to start, stop, and pause the printer, as well as delete print jobs and so on.

Super Mail allows users to manipulate a server's mail queues similar to the way a Super Queue privileged user can work with a printer queue. A Super Mail user can read, delete, copy, and forward anybody's mail. This privilege should be assigned with care, as it removes any confidentiality that the mail system can have.

User Audit allows a user to add entries to the server's audit log. The audit log is a service that can be used to track various operations that occur, such as opening files or trying to open a file and failing (see the next section, "Audit Trails," for all of the events that can be tracked). This is a useful facility if you want to look for attempted security violations or misuse of facilities. The User Audit privilege can be used for many purposes to record the occurrence and/or status of an operation. For example, if an entry is made in the audit log at the start and end of an automatic backup, and the success (or otherwise) is noted, you could track how long the process was taking and whether it had succeeded.

System Manager allows a user to run a command on a remote server from their PC (see the section "NET RUN" in Appendix C, "Utilities Reference") or shut down a server from their PC (see the section "NET SHUTDOWN" in Appendix C, "Utilities Reference").

Table 8.8 summarizes who, as a general rule, should be given which privileges.

Networking with LANtastic

Table 8.8 Types of users and the suitability of assigning privileges to them.

Privilege	General User	Network Supervisor	Network Manager
Super ACL	Never	Possibly	Yes
Super Queue	Never	Yes	Yes
Super Mail	Never	Avoid	Possibly
User Audit	If required	If required	If required
System Manager	Never	Possibly	Yes

Audit Trails

The final component of LANtastic security is the audit trail system. *Audit trails* are records of access and use of resources. This allows you to monitor how often a facility is used and by whom. It also allows you to look for attempted break-ins and abuse of resources.

LANtastic servers support nine types of audit trail entries:

- Server started
- Server shut down
- User logged into server
- User logged off (or server connection broken)
- Access allowed to a server resource
- Access denied to a server resource
- Entry placed in server's printer queue
- Queue entry despooled to a printer
- User audit trail entry

> **Tip:** The audit trails can also reveal important network management data such as when servers fail or connections are lost. For example, when the audit trail is examined, what appears to be random losses of connection might show that groups of users whose PCs share a common power supply are being affected simultaneously. This, in turn, suggests that the power supply should be checked to see if it is subject to spikes or brownouts that could disrupt the PCs.

The audit trail can also show when repeated attempts to log in have failed. This would quickly reveal the automatic login program discussed above as well as a user who is just trying to "data surf" the network (the term "data surfing" is used to describe a user who is reading data files looking for useful information). In some cases, it may be idle curiosity, but in many cases the user is trying to find confidential information. Figure 8.1 shows an example of an audit trail viewed using the NET_MGR.EXE utility.

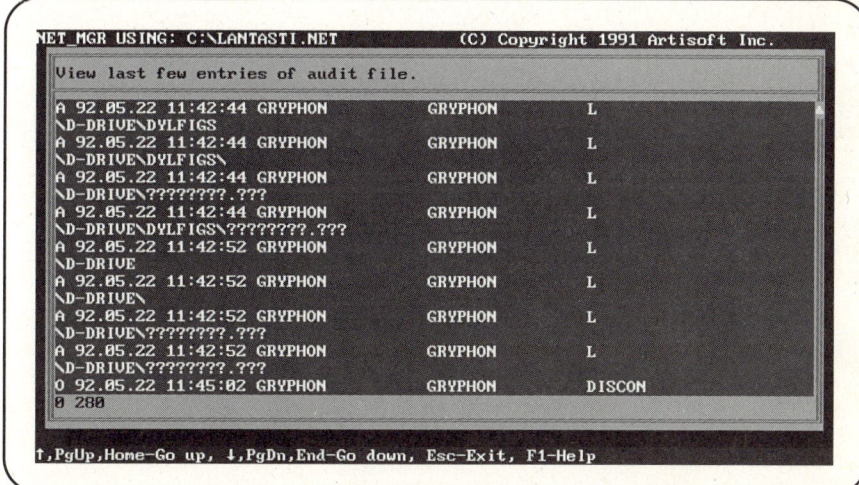

Figure 8.1 *An example of the contents of an audit trail.*

Another valuable use of the audit trail is to help assess the load that a server is handling. If a server is intended to support a large number of users and the audit trail shows that their use is much lighter than expected, the server's use might be expanded to meet other needs.

Note: If you do use the audit trail facility, ensure that you purge it regularly or else the server's performance will suffer.

Summary

There are two approaches to security on a network. The first is the easiest — just ignore it. For small networks, this will work fine as long as you will suffer only a minimal loss if the system is "trashed" by a virus or a vandal. For any network where money or time (which as we know, equals money) could be lost, the second approach is the best — address the problem.

Building a secure and robust network environment isn't hard or time-consuming — it just requires planning and maintaining to make it simple and cost-effective.

In this chapter, I discussed the threats to system integrity and security. I also covered the constraints and use of the security features of the LANtastic network system. The important issues of control with LANtastic are:

- **User Names:**

    16 characters maximum

    No DOS delimiters

    Preferably memorable

    The simple name format (first initial, optional middle initial, and last name joined, truncated to eight characters) is the easiest to use.

- **Group Names:**

    15 characters maximum

    Ending with a an asterisk (*)

    Not containing DOS delimiters

    Group names are useful, but they have administrative and implementation complexities that you might prefer to avoid.

- **Passwords:**

    16 characters maximum

    No DOS delimiters

    Preferably memorable

    Using pairs of common words separated by an allowed punctuation mark is the easiest and most memorable scheme to use.

- **Resource Access Rights:**

    RWCMLDKNEAIP — the basis of security of shared network resources.

    These access rights can be ignored for simple networks by using the default rights — all access rights given for directories, and those rights needed for printer queues and mail system. For networks of any real size (more than, say, six PCs), access rights are vital to protecting the network and its resources.

- **User Privileges:**

    AQMUS — These are very powerful permissions that need to be given sparingly.

- **Audit Trail:**

    Allows system events ranging from user logins to user-defined entries to be recorded. Very useful for monitoring system activity and determining system loading.

Protecting computer systems is an issue that many users ignore, preferring to deal with each crisis when it happens. But with a LAN, your liability is much greater. Loss of data on a single PC may be inconvenient, but on a network server it can bring the organization to a halt. All it takes to protect your investment is a little planning.

In the area of logical security, LANtastic is designed so that you can ignore its features and put it to work easily and quickly. But a little time spent learning how to make LANtastic a secure environment and implementing even the most basic features will pay off in the long run.

9

Avoiding and Solving Problems

This chapter is about avoiding and resolving problems in the LANtastic environment and dealing with problems when they arise. First, I'll discuss some of the best ways to avoid problems and then I'll outline techniques that are aimed at tracking down problems in a methodical way.

With any computer system, whether it's a stand-alone PC or a network of PCs, somewhere in the process of putting it together or using it you'll have problems of some kind. The problems fall into two main categories:

- Installation problems.
- Operational problems.

When you put your system together (installing hardware and software, configuration, and testing), you may have to deal with cabling faults, broken or damaged PCs, faulty floppy disks, and other hardware problems. You might find that you run out of disk space during critical parts of the installation process, or you might discover that some of the software components are incompatible.

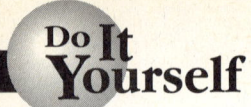
Networking with LANtastic

This is the phase where those people who have a short temper will discover how short it really is. Most of the problems in this phase are easily resolved and are due to easily diagnosed hardware faults, incorrect configurations, or not following installation instructions.

After you've gotten over the installation problems, you may find that hardware breaks or becomes unreliable, people may change settings and configurations without telling you, and users may press keys, delete files, or ignore what they've learned.

The number of things that can cause problems in live computer systems is remarkable. Once you've asked the right questions and started looking for the cause rather than the symptoms, these problems are often as simple as installation problems.

If you're dealing with stand-alone (that is, non-networked) PCs, you'll have a different set of problems than if you network them together. The stand-alone PC's environment is rich, but once it's on a network, it becomes part of a much bigger system.

The key to managing and troubleshooting networked PCs is organization. You need to know exactly what your network is made up of and how it is configured. You need to know when things should happen and whether they actually occur when they're supposed to. And when you have a problem that requires the help of a third party, you need to have the right information available and to present it coherently as it's asked for.

The Site Log

I've discussed the need for a site log in Chapter 6, "Installing LANtastic." The site log is one of your most important management tools. It should contain all of your plans, design notes, implementation notes, product purchasing information, and so on. In the following sections, I'll cover its contents. A good basis for your site log's structure follows:

1. The Site
2. Equipment
3. Configuration
4. Procedures and Standards
5. Documentation

The Site

The site section of the site log covers where the network components and the services that support them are.

Physical Site

This section includes maps of the site showing all of the relevant physical details: furniture, PCs, electrical outlets, and any other obstacles.

Power and Services

This is an inventory of electrical outlets and their loading, where fire extinguishers are, and anything else that is relevant to the health of your network.

Network Layout

This is a plan showing where the cables will go, with key problem areas or issues noted (such as the need for cable covers, routing around doors, and so on). This plan should show every server, workstation, printer, modem, and any other device connected to the network (including any Artisoft Central Station units, cabling concentrators and so on).

Equipment

This section is an inventory of all of the equipment on the network. The degree of detail depends on what you see as necessary, but in general, it is advisable to be as thorough and up-to-date as possible.

Personal Computers

This is a list of the hardware that makes up each PC (both servers and workstations) on the network and includes all adapter boards.

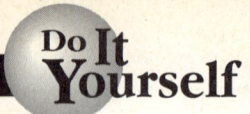

Networking with LANtastic

Printers

List each printer and its hardware configuration in this section. If you're going to use LANtastic's setup and clean-up facilities, list the details in the configuration section.

Other

This section is for miscellaneous network hardware such as modems and plotters.

Configuration

The configuration section should contain information on how each unit that can be configured is set up. This can be a vital resource if you have problems.

Server Configurations

You should maintain this section carefully. It should cover all of the utilities and their parameters so that you know exactly what you planned to do, and it should contain notes on all changes so that you know how you got where you are.

Workstation Configurations

The various parameters that define the configuration of each workstation should be recorded in this section.

Printer Configurations

Because printers can have quite complex setups, you should maintain a detailed log of how each printer has been configured. This should include the setup and clean-up instruction sequences, as well as the details of the wiring of printer cables.

Miscellaneous Configurations

This section is to record all of the relevant details for devices like plotters and modems. Again, comprehensive and up-to-date information will be very useful in problem solving.

Procedures and Standards

This section records how you plan to manage your network and what constitutes the basic levels of service or configuration that you expect to be maintained.

Password Management

You should record your plan for password management in this section. Include the details of how passwords are generated, given to users, stored (or not) in case users forget them, changed, and so on.

Backup and Restore Plan

To ensure that you don't lose data from workstations or servers, you should have a backup plan. See the section "Backup and Restore," and the sections which follow for a complete discussion. This section in the site log should include a detailed description of what will be backed up when, and where the backup media will be stored.

Rules and Policies

Every company has rules and regulations for conduct that they expect employees to obey. A network is like any other part of the company; it should have appropriate rules and policies for using the system. These rules should cover issues including the use of new software on the network, use of electronic mail services, disclosure of passwords, training plans, and staff instructions. All material used in connection with the network that is given to staff should be logged here.

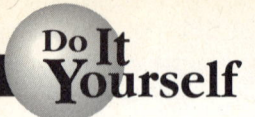 *Networking with LANtastic*

Documentation

Because a network has so many components, you'll wind up with lots of paperwork, including purchasing documents and manuals. This section shows you how to keep track of them and helps you identify what documentation exists and at what version or release level.

Receipts and Invoices

All documents regarding the purchase of network equipment should be filed here.

Warranties

Warranties vary according to manufacturer and type of equipment. Also, you may take up extended warranties on some items. This section is where this information should be recorded. An index should be created showing warranty expiration dates so you can determine the status of a piece of equipment with ease.

Hardware and Software Manuals

You're going to wind up with quite a few of these; use this section as an index to help you identify which manuals you've received and what their version numbers are. You will probably need to keep the manuals themselves elsewhere, so allocate an identification number for each one to tie them to the entries in this index.

History

All documents relating to planning, cost justification, and so on should be filed here for reference.

Problems

At any phase of your network you may encounter problems. This section is where you should keep a detailed record of what went wrong and why.

Backup and Recovery

Most PC owners are pretty casual about the integrity of their data. They assume that because their PC has started every weekday morning for the last year that it will operate perfectly today. Unfortunately, statistics are against them.

Hard disks fail, on average, after 24 months of service. As this is "on average," the life of the disk could be much greater . . . or much less. This is why backups are vital components of maintaining a computer system.

For stand-alone (non-networked) PCs, losing a disk drive can be catastrophic. If the drive contained a financial model or a document you had been working on for days and the disk it is on fails, you might consider that time spent wasted.

In a network environment, where many people may depend on the data on a single disk drive, losing it could affect the ability of those people to do their jobs. Worse still, the wasted time for any lost work is now multiplied by the number of people involved.

Backup is simply the process of copying data from one drive to another storage medium such as disk, tape, WORM drive, and so on. *Recovery* consists of restoring files from the backup data.

Network Backups

In the network environment, you can simplify the backup of user data by using shared network disk resources. To develop a backup system, the first thing you should do is establish the basic configuration of each PC. This basic configuration is the way each PC is set up before it is used. Because the PC will have no user data on it, the configuration can be reconstructed

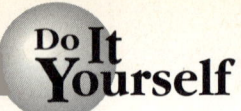

Networking with LANtastic

using the original installation disks for each application and utility. At this point, you have two choices:

- Make a backup of the entire basic configuration using whatever method you prefer. This allows for a fast reinstallation of the basic system to any machine. If there are two or three applications used by several people on the network, you only need to keep a single copy of the basic configuration.

- Do not bother making a backup of the basic configuration. This will use less backup storage but will be slower when you have to re-create a system, as you'll have to reinstall each program from scratch.

When the basic configurations are used, you can then restrict the backup of each PC to handle only the files that have changed. For a simple way to do backups, copy files to a server.

To organize the backed-up data in a workable scheme, create a directory on the server (for example, \NETBACK). Under this directory, create a subdirectory for each PC (such as \NETBACK\LUCY, \NETBACK\AJGIBBS, and so on). You can then either put all backup data in the PC's subdirectory, or you can create further subdirectories below that subdirectory for each application or type of data (for example, \NETBACK\LUCY\WP, \NETBACK\LUCY\ACCOUNTS, and so on).

When you want to back up the entire network system, all you need to do is back up the server that stores the user backups.

When to Back Up

With an active system, I recommend daily backups for user's data. Ideally, you should back up as part of the shutdown procedure of the PC. If you make backup part of the start-up procedure, the user will have to wait while it completes (this may not actually be very long), and you run the risk of losing data due to a hard disk failure on start-up (the most common time for disk failure).

> **Note:** A hard disk drive that has cooled to below normal operating temperature (that is, room temperature) is subject to strong mechanical forces when it is started. Powering up a PC system at room temperature puts tremendous stress on all mechanical and electronic components.

If you take backups of user data from their PC's hard disk and store them on other media or another PC, you greatly reduce the chances of totally losing a file. As I discussed in the last section, when you're using a LANtastic network, you can simplify daily backups by using one or more network servers as archival storage.

Beyond daily user backups, you should also establish a system of weekly or, at most, monthly server backups of all important data (including the user files) and control files. Keep these backups off-site so that you'll be able to recover critical data if a major disaster (such as a fire) occurs.

Backing Up the Minimum

The amount of storage a backup takes and how long the backup process lasts are important considerations when planning a backup system. If you have to back up all files, even those that haven't changed, you'll use more disk space and take more time than if you back up just those that have been modified.

So you can see that it is important both for performance and storage to back up only the data that has been newly created or changed.

Backup Systems

You have a wide range of choices for the program that you use to do backups. These choices include:

- *The DOS COPY command.* This is fairly fast but doesn't allow you to skip files that haven't changed. Also, COPY won't automatically access subdirectories under the current directory. This means that

you have to specify each directory explicitly and back up all files in that directory regardless of whether they have already been backed up. You will also need to have the same directory structure on the server to prevent overwriting files of the same name that are in separate directories on the PC being backed up. To restore files, you need to find them in the backup directories and copy them back. Also, there is no compression, no ability to back up hidden or system files, and too broad a specification of files and directories to back up will eat a lot of disk space. In short, don't try to use the COPY command. It will be totally impractical.

- *The DOS XCOPY (extended copy) command.* XCOPY is just a smarter version of COPY that will check and reset the archive attribute flag of specified files and search subdirectories. If the search finds files in a subdirectory that doesn't exist on the server, XCOPY will create that subdirectory on the server. These facilities make XCOPY a better choice than COPY, but you'll still wind up with a duplicate directory structure (although as it's automatically generated by XCOPY, it's less painful to use). Again, as there is no compression, too broad a specification of files and directories to back up will eat a lot of disk space. Restoring a file simply involves copying it from the backup files. Like COPY, XCOPY is hardly state of the art, although it may be of limited use.

- *The DOS BACKUP and RESTORE commands.* A little more sophisticated than COPY or XCOPY, the DOS BACKUP utility creates (if it doesn't already exist) a subdirectory under the root (for local drives) or the directory that is the definition of a shared disk resource, called BACKUP. This means that if you use the directory scheme recommended above, there will be another directory below the user's private directory also called BACKUP (that is, C:\BACKUP\username\BACKUP). When you specify the files to be backed up, an archive is created in this final directory called BACKUP.001. There is also an index of backed-up files called CONTROL.001. The .001 extensions are for floppy disk backups; the next floppy that is a continuation of the backup will contain the files BACKUP.002 and CONTROL.002. BACKUP supports subdirectory searching and checking file archive attribute flags, and will back up hidden and system files. Although BACKUP doesn't use compression, it does conserve some space by combining files together in the archive file.

Avoiding and Solving Problems

To restore a file, you can list the backup archive and select single or multiple files to restore. BACKUP is designed to create backups that span several disks so, unlike COPY or XCOPY, you won't have problems about which files have been copied and which haven't. BACKUP is better in some aspects than COPY or XCOPY, but it's a clumsy and antiquated system.

- *File compression utilities such as PKZIP and PKUNZIP.* The PKZIP utility from PKWARE, Inc., is a sophisticated archive system that allows you to store files in a format that, in some cases, can compress files by better than 80%. Files can be selected by many criteria including age, archive attribute flag status, path specification, and so on. Comments can be added to archive files, and files can be selectively handled on the basis of their hidden, system, and archive attribute flags. The tradeoff in using PKZIP is the extra time it takes to perform the compression. However, if the time penalty is too great and/or space isn't a problem, compression can be turned off. File restoring is done with the PKUNZIP utility, which allows you to specify files individually or as a range.

    This program is extremely cost-effective and is marketed under the shareware scheme. It offers great flexibility and can save significant space.

    For server backups, particularly onto floppies, the PKZIP utility probably won't be a good choice as its archives aren't designed to span multiple floppy disks.

- *Other commercial backup and restore utilities.* There are a large number of products in this category that you can select from. Their prices range from $10 to $100 and their capabilities are dependent on price. Some of them only support sophisticated media such as Digital Audio Tape (DAT), which makes them suitable only for server backups. Some of these systems are also incredibly powerful and designed to back up disk resources in the gigabyte (that's 1,000 megabytes) range.

You'll need to assess your needs relative to the depth of your pocket if these systems seem to be a solution to your particular problems.

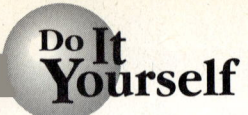 *Networking with LANtastic*

Server Backup Devices

As your system grows, backing up the server's data to a slow medium, such as floppy disks, may soon become very time-consuming. At that point, investing in a storage system such as a tape drive or a disk drive with exchangeable media may be necessary.

Your choice will be between those devices that can be made to look like DOS disk drives to a PC system and those devices that can only be used with special software. A device that looks like a DOS disk drive can usually be made available as a network resource. This means that user backups can be made directly to the device attached to the server and effectively eliminate the need for keeping the user backups on the server.

The Bernoulli drive from IOMega Corporation is a product that uses what looks like large, rigid floppy disks as storage media. These are called cartridges, and come in 20, 44, and 90 megabyte capacities. A major advantage of these drives is that, because they appear to the network to be a DOS drive, they can be both data resources (for example, to hold shared documents) as well as backup media. They are also fast, giving performance comparable to hard disks. These drives are more expensive than tape drives. They are priced in the $1000–$1600 range, and the cartridges cost between $90 (for 20MB) and $229 (for 90MB), but they offer unparalleled flexibility.

Tape drives are not usually available to the network as DOS devices. They can, however, hold large amounts of data, ranging from around 100 megabytes to over a gigabyte per tape. The Jumbo tape drives from Colorado Memory Systems, for example, offer 120- or 250-megabyte storage capacities for about $400 and $500 respectively, and tapes cost around $20 to $40. The tradeoffs are shown in Table 9.1.

Table 9.1 Comparison of Bernoulli drive and tape technologies.

Attribute	Bernoulli Drive	Tape Drive
Drive cost	$1000 to $1600	$400 to $500
Drive cost per MB	$12 to $82 per MB*	$3 to $2 per MB
Performance	1.5 to 2.5 MB/s	0.25 to 1.0 MB/s
Capacity	20 to 90 MB	120 to 250 MB
Media cost	$90 to $229	$20 to $40
Media cost per MB	$3 to $4 per MB	$.16 per MB
Flexibility	High	Low
Reliability	High	Low to high†

* *Higher capacity drives are less expensive per MB.*

† *Tape quality, handling, and storage conditions can reduce tape reliability considerably.*

The choice of which technology to use is a matter of determining your storage needs, your performance criteria, and what you can afford.

Creating a Backup Schedule

Whatever backup system you use, you'll need to plan how you'll actually handle backing up data. The schedule might be nightly user backups to a server (done as part of each user's shutdown procedure), with weekly backups from that server to floppy disks, tape or other media.

A commonly used routine is a rotating backup. This uses several sets of backup media (disks, tapes, etc.) that are used one after the other, in sequence. So if there are five sets of media, you use the first on Monday, the second on Tuesday, and the third on Wednesday, and so on. On the next Monday, you reuse the set used on the previous Monday; on Tuesday, you reuse the previous Tuesday's, and so on.

There are two ways that you can do backups:

- Back up the entire system each time.

- Back up the entire system the first time that the set is used. Then back up just those files with respect to what is on the backup (rather than which files have the archive attribute flag set). This approach will save time.

The result of this system is that it ensures that you have copies of the state of a file over the last five days. You can also extend this strategy to what is called a *grandfather, father, son* (GFS) backup. This means that you take backup copies of the entire system once a week and once a month, in addition to the daily backups.

So, rather than have a Friday backup using the daily backup sets, you have three additional sets of media to be used on the first, second, and third Fridays. This means that you can not only recover the file as it was on each of the last five days, but also as it was at the end of each of the last four weeks.

If you expand that scheme further still by storing away every fourth week's backup, you can now also recover files as they were for as many months ago as you choose.

Table 9.2 shows this five-day, weekly, and monthly scheme that needs a total of 10 sets of backup media. A complete cycle takes 12 weeks and the various versions available at the end of the 16th week are shown in bold. As you can see, this strategy gives you the best chance possible to recover from a major system corruption or the failure of a hard disk.

Table 9.2 A "grandfather, father, son" backup system.

Week	Monday	Backup Number Tuesday	Wednesday	Thursday	Friday
1	Day 1	Day 2	Day 3	Day 4	Week 1
2	Day 1	Day 2	Day 3	Day 4	Week 2
3	Day 1	Day 2	Day 3	Day 4	Week 3
4	Day 1	Day 2	Day 3	Day 4	**Month 1**
5	Day 1	Day 2	Day 3	Day 4	Week 1
6	Day 1	Day 2	Day 3	Day 4	Week 2
7	Day 1	Day 2	Day 3	Day 4	Week 3
8	Day 1	Day 2	Day 3	Day 4	**Month 2**
9	Day 1	Day 2	Day 3	Day 4	Week 1
10	Day 1	Day 2	Day 3	Day 4	Week 2
11	Day 1	Day 2	Day 3	Day 4	Week 3
12	Day 1	Day 2	Day 3	Day 4	**Month 3**
13	Day 1	Day 2	Day 3	Day 4	Week 1
14	Day 1	Day 2	Day 3	Day 4	Week 2
15	Day 1	Day 2	Day 3	Day 4	Week 3
16	**Day 1**	**Day 2**	**Day 3**	**Day 4**	**Month 1**

Archiving Files

You must consider which files are to be backed up. If you keep adding changed files to a backup, eventually you'll have many files that are no longer in use but are taking up space on the backup media. These files should either be archived in long-term storage or, if they are not impor-tant, deleted. This is where a "weeding" plan is needed.

Networking with LANtastic

For example, you might decide that any file that hasn't been modified for more than ninety days shouldn't be included in backups. This kind of plan allows you to exclude unused files from the backup storage even though they may still exist on the PCs or on server storage. A problem that may face you is how to deal with read-only or very infrequently changed documents. Some of the more sophisticated backup systems have complex strategies for managing these issues. You need to evaluate carefully the level of management that is required for the way your organization uses its data, and ensure that your backup system operates appropriately.

> **Note:** To back up the LANtastic control directory, you'll have to use the backup facility in NET_MGR because the various files are controlled by LANtastic. This also means that any other backup software you use should be configured to specifically ignore the LANtastic control directory. See Appendix C, "Utilities Reference," for details on using the NET_MGR utility to backup the control directory.

System Managers, Supervisors, and Network Management

As your network gets larger (more than about six PCs), you'll find that the need to manage the system increases. The more planned and documented the network is, the less time this will actually take.

System Managers

Every network needs a system manager to whom users can refer their problems, complaints, and queries. Even for a small network, a system manager should be assigned. Networks that are run by users (as opposed to controlled by a manager) are usually less cost-effective, and the problems

Avoiding and Solving Problems

with them can take much longer to resolve. The system manager's job is to control resources, resolve problems, and maintain the integrity of the network.

Without a central point of responsibility, authority, and control, a network (like any complex system) will tend to become disorganized, inefficient, and ultimately chaotic.

So what are a system manager's duties and responsibilities? The following list describes the job of a system manager for a large network. Which responsibilities and functions you select should be appropriate for your network's size and complexity.

- *User and group account maintenance.* Adding, deleting, and modifying user and group accounts.

- *Resource management.* Defining, controlling, and monitoring shared server disk and printer resources. Ensuring that ACLs give appropriate rights to individuals.

- *Security management.* Generating, assigning, and managing passwords. Allocating privileges. Monitoring and maintaining audit trails. Handling and reporting security violations.

- *Problem resolution.* Fielding, recording, and finding solutions to operational problems.

- *Performance monitoring.* Checking network performance and optimizing it where and when necessary.

- *Software management.* Installing, configuring, upgrading, and enhancing applications software. Ensuring that new and existing software is virus free. Ensuring that software is used within the terms of each package's license.

- *Hardware management.* Maintaining all PCs, printers, plotters, modems, and so on that are part of the network.

- *Reporting.* Generating status and performance reports for management and tracking purposes.

- *Training.* Educating end users in how to use and manage their network environments.

- *Housekeeping.* User and server backup and restore operations, file pruning, and availability of supplies (printer paper, floppy disks, backup tapes or cartridges, and so on).

This is a pretty broad range of responsibilities which, as your network grows, may well become a full-time job. If the network users can be trained to manage the network facilities that are close to them as well as their own PC environment, the system manager's work load can be vastly reduced.

The danger is that a single poorly trained or malicious user can wreak havoc, so it's vital to always keep a shield of responsible management and adequate security around critical server machines.

System Supervisors

There may come a time (when you have more than about 50 PCs on your network) when the system manager will get swamped by the sheer number of things that need to be managed, maintained, and controlled. At this point you should appoint system supervisors.

System supervisors should be put in day-to-day control of a group of PCs. The larger the number of PCs in the group, the more time-consuming their task will be. If you plan to use already busy people, either make their groups small or arrange for some of their job functions to be handled by others. Their role is to act as a filter for the system manager. This means that they should be able to handle most routine administrative tasks for the group of PCs they manage.

Diagnostic Disks

Computer systems (PCs and networks) go wrong. When they do, you want to spend as little time as possible finding and fixing problems. By creating a set of diagnostic disks, you'll have a toolkit prepared for such occasions.

Diagnostic disks allow you to:

- Boot DOS on any PC with floppy disks.
- Run PC system diagnostics.
- Run network diagnostics, such as LANCHECK.

- Load a server or workstation system.
- Support remote booting (if your network uses it).

You should always have at least two sets of these diagnostic disks, and keep one set in a secure place. Keeping two sets will allow you to recover from a lost or corrupt floppy disk.

These diagnostic disks have a very important role — they allow you to quickly determine the integrity of any network PC (other than diskless ones). And they ensure that, in emergencies or for maintenance purposes, you don't have to use disks with an unknown history.

For example, if an engineer comes to replace a failed hard disk, he or she will usually use his or her own utility disks. Unless this company is unusually advanced, these will probably be the same set of disks that have been used at another company. If that company's equipment was infected by a computer virus, using the disks on your network could infect the PCs he or she works on. Worse still, you've got a network! It's possible that all of your machines could wind up with an infection.

PC Diagnostics

There are many products to choose from to test, diagnose, and fix PC system problems. The main categories of products to include in your diagnostic disk set are:

- *DOS system.* These should be working copies (not originals) of the DOS disks ready for use. Ideally, you should have two sets, both write-protected. This ensures that the disks can't be infected by computer viruses or accidently changed.

- *Hard disk maintenance utilities.* Utilities (such as Spinrite) allow you to test, analyze, and correct hard disk problems. They are invaluable for both preventative and corrective maintenance.

- *LANtastic disk.* You should build a complete LANtastic system on a bootable floppy disk with a capacity of at least 720K bytes. You should have at least one version of this disk which loads only DOS and LANtastic — no other drivers or utilities should be run. This will allow you to boot the PC and start the network without interference from any other software — a very important step in tracking down problems.

- *Network utilities.* There are many utilities available that can make LANtastic problem solving much easier. Utilities to monitor NETBIOS activity, run performance tests, and check network status are available from commercial, shareware, and freeware sources. Artisoft's own bulletin board, ArtiFacts, and CompuServe are two excellent sources of shareware and freeware.

Training

One of the greatest tools in avoiding problems is to ensure that your network's users are trained. It's important to insulate users from the underlying network, but they also need to know enough to use the network properly at whatever levels are to be made available to them.

The idea of insulating users is to limit the amount they need to know about the network. The more they need to know, the more training will be required and the more opportunity there will be for them to make mistakes. You need to balance what users are allowed to do against their abilities and the amount of education you can afford to give them. In general though, there are some basic issues that network users need to be trained in.

To plan your training program, you must first decide what needs to be communicated. With a network, there are four basic areas in which network users should be instructed:

- *Background.* Why you have a network.
- *Services.* What the network does.
- *Use.* What you need to know to use the network.
- *Rules.* What you must, and must not, do.

Background—Why You Have a Network

It is important to explain to users why a network has been introduced and why it's important. Ideally, you should include the relevance of the network to the areas of operation and the impact that it will have on jobs and the future of the company.

The objective is to get the users involved. Most people, when they have a new tool forced upon them, will resist change. It's important to give the users a sense of responsibility and, if possible, enthusiasm.

Services—What the Network Does

Now you've got a hard task — you have to explain what a network is. Keep the explanation simple. Concentrate on the service and the concept of sharing resources.

Avoid speaking about technology. Unless your users are technically oriented, explaining access control lists, redirecting communications ports, and the function of the NETBIOS will probably send them into a deep sleep. Explain what they will have to deal with in terms of results rather than how the network achieves those results.

Use—What You Need to Know to Use the Network

The important thing for users to know is what they will have to do in the new environment. If they are going to have access to NET and LANPUP, you'll need to explain a lot of terminology and give them hands-on, supervised experience with the utilities before you turn them loose on the live system.

Rules—What You Must, and Must Not, Do

Finally, it is vital to establish the company's policies for the network. You should have policies for:

- *Security*. How seriously do you regard password use and disclosure?

 *Networking with LANtastic*

- *Electronic mail.* Are users allowed to use the E-mail services for private messages? Does the company reserve the right to read any messages on the system?

- *Reporting problems.* You should, on principle, have a policy for reporting problems with the network system. This should include who problems should be reported to, how to get help in emergencies, who is responsible for what services, and what actions the user is authorized to take.

- *Use of software.* Due to the increasing number of computer viruses, it is very important to have a policy limiting the use of personal software on the network. For example, a user may unknowingly have an infected program that he or she got from a friend or a bulletin board system. If that program is run on the network, it could cause a major disaster. Your network users should be encouraged to develop a sense of responsibility about the system.

The B.E.A.R. Approach to Solving Problems

To help you handle problems in a methodical way, I offer the B.E.A.R. approach. This is a simple and thorough way to deal with any PC problems. As I have said in other sections of this book, what appears to be a long procedure is, in fact, only an organized way to deal with a task.

You are free to use whatever method you choose, but it is normal that unless you're very lucky, an unstructured approach will take longer and may never actually get to the root of the problem.

The B.E.A.R. approach has four steps:

1. **Basics**
2. **Extend and test**
3. **Analyze**
4. **Repair**

 **Note:** Always ensure that you have a backup before doing any reconfiguration or repair work. Operations such as running the DOS utility CHKDSK or reformatting can delete some or all of your data. Even reinstalling files can result in the loss of complex configuration files.

Basics

Establish the basics — what components and subsystems are involved both overall and when the problem occurs. If a user has reported the problem, ensure that it can be duplicated by the user and then by you.

Make sure that any error messages and status data are recorded accurately. If you have to refer the problem to a vendor, these will be the first things they ask for. You should also document the environment thoroughly, although this information should already be at hand if you planned the system to begin with.

Extend and Test

Remove components until you have a "bare-bones" system which you are confident works properly. Add components and test after each addition until the combination that causes the problem is found. Once you've found the problem configuration, try all of the options.

This is also where using your diagnostic disks will simplify matters. You can use them to test the basic functionality of the PC, the integrity of its hard disk and other components, and the PC's connection to the network before getting involved with the complexities of the "live" network system.

Networking with LANtastic

Analyze

Determine as closely as possible what is happening (the sequence of events) when the problem occurs and what components are involved. Refer to the product manuals for the meaning and implication of error messages. If they don't help, you may need to refer to your vendor's technical support services.

> **Note:** Be aware that technical support groups can range from the good to the bad and the downright ugly. Some will be very helpful and go out of their way to chase down your problem; others will be next to useless. To get the best service, be aware of the pressure that most of these groups work under and have detailed information at hand. A problem that often comes up when you have to use a vendor's technical support service is that they disown the problem as it involves another vendor's product. Don't despair! (Refer to each vendor in turn, eliminating each area of interference between the products until the problem clearly relates to a specific product.

Repair

Fix the problem using whatever resources you have. These range from simply reconfiguring to upgrading or enhancing as needed. And be sure to document what has changed in the site log.

If your repairs have resulted in any operational differences (different use of redirections, reconfigured applications and utilities, or anything else that affects the way the system is used), make sure that the user is told and trained.

Although this a simple plan, approaching problem solving in a methodical way like this ensures that you'll lose nothing and be able to examine the problem thoroughly. It also helps you to be well-prepared if you need to refer your problem to a vendor's technical support group.

The Problem Log

In the section "The Site Log," I mentioned the need to log problems. It is amazing how many organizations solve the same computer problems over and over again. By not keeping records, they lose what knowledge they gain.

Obviously, there are problems that are so trivial that they aren't worth documenting. But by recording those that take a significant amount of time (say, more than ten minutes) to resolve, you'll not only develop a base of data for future problem solving, but you'll also be able to account for an element in the cost of running the network.

Figure 9.1 shows a form that can be used to log problem events.

Basic System Diagnostic Procedure

If you need to establish whether the basic system is operating correctly, the following guide will help you establish what is wrong. The objectives are to test:

- *The hardware.* You need to establish whether the components are operating correctly by themselves and together. This includes all of the PC components and the network adapter card.

- *The software.* Once you know the hardware is working correctly, you need to check that the operating system (DOS) and the network software are behaving as they should.

> **Caution:** With LANtastic, it is vitally important to ensure that all machines on the network are running the same version of software. If they aren't, it's likely that you'll see the servers and workstations behaving in strange and erratic ways.

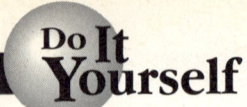 **Networking with LANtastic**

```
© Mark Gibbs, 1992                                    Form: DIY-015
                          Problem Report

Problem id:                        Date raised:
Raised by:                         Handled by:
Dept./location                     Extension:
Problem status:    Urgent / Rush / Configuration / Installation / Upgrade
PC      Manufacturer:
        Model:
        RAM:
        DOS type and version:
Adapter cards -
1                                  7
2                                  8
3                                  9
4                                  10
5                                  11
6                                  12
LANtastic version:
Node type:       Server & client  /  Workstation  /  Server only
Problem description:




















Prepared by:           Date:                      Page:

         This form is taken from "Do-It-Yourself Networking With LANtastic"
                          Published by SAMS (1992)
```

Figure 9.1 Form DIY-015: "Problem Report."

Avoiding and Solving Problems

If any of the following steps fail, you need to correctly identify the problem and start from step 1 again. Remember that a methodical and exhaustive approach will almost always work. Any other approach will almost always fail.

1. *Boot from a DOS diagnostic disk*. (See the section "Diagnostic Disks".) If it won't boot from this disk, either your machine is very sick, or something really silly is going on. You may have a major motherboard fault or other low-level fault (very sick). You may simply have loose cable connectors or adapter cards (silly). If you can't simply reconnect the loose cables or reseat the cards, and then reboot successfully, you'll need to refer to a PC repair company.

2. *Run PC diagnostics*. Various setup and test utilities come with PCs — you should use them as directed in the manuals. You can also buy various diagnostic tools, but many of these are more in-depth than you may want to deal with. The utilities supplied by most PC vendors should do the job. If these fail, either you will be able to immediately identify the exact cause of the fault or you'll have a generic error condition that won't point to a specific problem. In the latter case, you should follow the general B.E.A.R. strategy and simplify the system until the problem is found. If you're not comfortable with fault finding at this level, take the machine to a PC repair company.

3. *Run network hardware diagnostics*. Not all network adapters come with diagnostic software, so you may have to skip this step. This should result in one of three conditions: no response, a problem report, or an all clear. If the result isn't an all clear, check that the board is seated in the bus slot properly, that its jumpers and switches are correctly set, and that the board isn't damaged in any way. You should inspect the board for cracks and damaged components.

Caution: If your site is subject to power surges from lightning or someone manages to short the power supply to the network cabling (it really does happen), adapter card components can be fatally damaged.

4. *Load the correct low-level driver from the LANtastic diagnostic disk (see "PC Diagnostics" above)*. If the driver doesn't load

223

correctly, check that the driver's configuration is compatible with the network adapter card. (See the adapter card manual for detailed information on how to use the driver software.)

5. *Load the NETBIOS (either AILANBIO or manufacturer's version) from the diagnostic disk.* If the NETBIOS doesn't load correctly, ensure that it is configured to be compatible with the low-level driver. (See Appendix C, "Utilities Reference," for a detailed description of AILANBIO.)

6. *Run LANCHECK (from the LANtastic diagnostic disk) on the PC and on another network PC.* This will establish whether the PCs can communicate across the network and ensure that errors aren't being generated. (See Appendix C, "Utilities Reference," for a detailed discussion of LANCHECK.)

For the following steps, use the *default* configuration for each utility except where you know that a switch *must* be specified (for example, to avoid a interrupt conflict).

7. *Load REDIR from the diagnostic disk.* Again, if it doesn't load correctly, check that the various REDIR options are compatible with the NETBIOS. (See Appendix C, "Utilities Reference," for a detailed description of REDIR.)

Caution: If you're using LANCACHE or any other disk caching or memory resident utilities, *don't* use them while you're assessing the integrity of the basic configuration.

8. Load SERVER from the diagnostic disk, if this is a server. If it doesn't load correctly, check that the command line options for SERVER are compatible with the configuration of REDIR.

Note: Don't use software that is not from a diagnostic disk. The utilities on the PC may have been corrupted, which could be the cause of your problem. It is surprisingly often the case that corrupted software *seems* to work.

9. *Log in to a remote server and connect to a disk resource.* If you cannot log in and you can confirm that you have a valid, active account, try a different server.

> **Note:** If you hear audio warnings (beeps from the PC), investigate whether they are due to time-outs. (See Appendix C, "Utilities Reference," for a detailed description of audio warnings.) If they are, you have some kind of low-level problem that affects network communications. Ensure that all low-level drivers, NETBIOS programs, REDIR, and SERVER are up-to-date and configured correctly. If everything else has been tested, try using a different network cable and, where possible, connect the PCs directly to one another. This will eliminate any interference from other nodes.

In the following steps, any problems you experience will probably be due to add-on PC hardware, network hardware or cabling problems. Review these items and their configurations for damage, mismatched settings, memory conflicts, interrupt requests conflicts, and any other option settings.

If these checks are satisfactory, remove any coprocessor, communication, RAM expansion, and system enhancement cards (sound boards, and so on) and retry the tests.

10. *Using DOS COPY, copy a large file (at least 250 kilobytes) both to and from the remote server to a local disk drive.*

11. *If your PC is a server, connect to resources on this server from two or more remote workstations.* Then, using DOS COPY, copy large files (at least 250 kilobytes) both to and from the network resources. Use NET COPY from the remote workstations to copy the test files to other file specifications.

If you've got this far without problems, the basic configuration of your PC can be assumed to be functional. I say "assumed" because it may be that the basic configuration is incompatible with applications software that you're running.

Note: It is important to realize that some applications are simply not network-compatible. For these programs, the fact that LANtastic can be unloaded makes it possible to remove all of the network software, run the application, and then reload the network.

Another problem area is when you use applications that need to perform within certain constraints, such as handling serial port data or communicating with an adapter board at a certain rate. In these cases, the operation or configuration of the network may interfere or disable the application.

Tip: You'll often find that changing parameters such as the AILANBIO RUN_BURST value will cure the problem.

On the whole, you'll find that using an organized approach to investigating the problem will either solve it or at least simplify talking to your technical support resources.

Using Vendor Technical Support

Every one of your vendors will offer some kind of technical support. The more service-conscious will have free technical support, and some even offer a toll-free number.

Unless you have a very pressing need, it is best to avoid products whose vendors offer support on contract or per call. It is particularly worth avoiding pay-per-call schemes as any serious problems could make this kind of service very expensive.

If you are going to use a vendor's technical support group, you need to use it in such a way as to get the best possible service. If your problem isn't urgent or impeding work in a major way, then a written inquiry (via post, fax, or electronic mail) is the best choice.

Avoiding and Solving Problems

Not only can you communicate your problem more clearly, but you can also supply more detailed information that will help the technician understand the environment of the problem. Another option that is very cost-effective and usually has a quick turnaround is CompuServe. Many PC product vendors, including Artisoft, have product support "forums" where you can leave private or public messages requesting support. You'll usually get a response within 24 to 48 hours, although another user may know the answer and reply in a matter of minutes!

For urgent problems, telephone and fax are your best strategies. Telephoning can be used to establish a contact and ensure that your written query is being watched for.

Keep in mind that technical support groups aren't miracle workers. They can only work with what information you give them. They also can't know all possible configurations and equipment on the market, so the set-up of your system may or may not be familiar.

> **Note:** The issue of what can be supported raises an important point about planning your system. If you buy equipment that is obscure, "leading edge," or otherwise novel, you may benefit from the functionality but be left "high and dry" when you have a problem to resolve. If you want to play it safe, go for known brands and stable technologies.

Form *DIY-016* (see Figure 9.2) is a prototype that you might use to communicate with a vendor's technical support department. Fill out the relevant details as comprehensively as you can. Include any documentation from your site log that might be of use to them.

Form *DIY-017* (see Figure 9.3) can be used to track the problem's progress. The purpose of this form is to track what happens and when. This can be particularly useful if you have a complaint about a vendor's response time or a problem tracking the status of problems.

Do It Yourself — *Networking with LANtastic*

```
© Mark Gibbs, 1992                              Form: DIY-016
              Technical Support Report

Problem id:                      Date:
Name:                            Address:
Company:
Phone:
Fax:
Attached information:            Problem type:
    [ ] AUTOEXEC.BAT printout        [ ] Non-operation
    [ ] CONFIG.SYS printout          [ ] Intermittent operation
    [ ] STARTNET.BAT printout        [ ] Hanging
    [ ] Diskette                     [ ] Compatibility
    [ ] Network diagram              [ ] Performance
    [ ] Configuration data           [ ] Install/configuration
    [ ] Audit trail data             [ ] Documentation
    [ ] Screen print                 [ ] Suggested enhancement

Problem description:             Status:
                                     [ ] Urgent
                                     [ ] Rush
                                     [ ] Query




Prepared by:     Date:           Page:

     This form is taken from "Do-It-Yourself Networking With LANtastic"
                    Published by SAMS (1992)
```

Figure 9.2 Form DIY-016: "Technical Support Report."

Avoiding and Solving Problems

Problem ID	Event date	Event time	Details

© Mark Gibbs, 1992
Form: DIY-017
Problem Log

Prepared by: Date: Page:

This form is taken from "Do-It-Yourself Networking With LANtastic" Published by SAMS (1992)

Figure 9.3   *Form DIY-017: "Problem Log."*

 *Networking with LANtastic*

Summary

Problem solving is not difficult in the LANtastic environment. The error messages and warnings are complete and clear enough to guide you to a solution for most situations.

For the rare problem that requires research and external resources, an organized and methodical approach will lead you to a solution. At the very least, such an approach will ensure that when you have to communicate with a vendor for technical support, the data that you'll have on hand will make it easier for that vendor to help you.

Advanced Topics

LANtastic gives the do-it-yourself networker more than enough tools and facilities to build a basic network, configure it, and get it running. But if you want more facilities, enhanced manageability, or improved organization on your network, you have a wide range of services, products, and techniques at your disposal.

Many of these topics may seem to be esoteric, but as you get more comfortable with your network, you'll want to make it more manageable and cost-effective. These discussions are overviews of services and products rather than detailed how-to descriptions.

Some of the topics are "state-of-the-art" products such as Windows 3.1 (and LANtastic support for it) and DR DOS 6.0 (the MS-DOS alternative). Other topics are DOS and LANtastic enhancements that make networks easier to use, more organized, or more flexible.

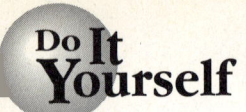 *Networking with LANtastic*

Working with Windows

The Microsoft Windows 3.x system has been one of the great successes in the PC world in the last couple of years. Artisoft has wisely ensured that they are not only compatible with Windows but have also rewritten the NET.EXE and NET_MGR.EXE programs as Windows utilities. Both LANtastic servers and workstations can run Windows.

The basic LANtastic version 4.1 release comes with windows drivers. To use LANtastic under Windows:

1. Follow the setup instructions in the LANtastic manual.

2. Start the network as usual (that is, use STARTNET.BAT or whatever your system is set up to use).

3. Start Windows.

> **Note:** Although you can run NET and NET_MGR as DOS applications under Windows, you'll find that you can run into all sorts of problems, as the changes that you make will apply only in that DOS session. Either don't use these utilities after you've started Windows, or use the Windows-specific LANtastic utilities discussed later in this section.

The LANtastic 4.1 upgrade manual has a chapter devoted to using LANtastic with Windows, and all of the basics of building a working system and troubleshooting are discussed.

For a greater degree of integration between Windows and LANtastic, you should consider purchasing the LANtastic for Windows package from Artisoft. The latest release of this software, version 4.10, is completely compatible with Windows 3.1. Installation is easy — you can even select the LANtastic "Tiny Ram" illustration as your Windows desktop.

The Windows versions of NET.EXE and NET_MGR.EXE (not surprisingly called WNET.EXE and WNET_MGR.EXE) differ from the DOS versions only in the use of the graphical interface.

WNET.EXE is the general user utility that allows you to log in and out of servers, redirect drives and printers, and so on. WNET_MGR.EXE, like its

Advanced Topics

DOS counterpart, is the server management tool. It allows you to create, modify, and delete users and resources, change server startup parameters, and so on. It is also an improvement over the DOS version, as it has enhanced mail features, an optional automatic login to servers, and automatic drive redirection facilities.

All of the DOS functions are there, but, because of the Windows interface, they are easier to use. To give you a feel for how the Windows programs look, I'll briefly run through some of the common operations.

WNET.EXE

Figure 10.1 shows the main window of WNET. Clicking the mouse on any of the panels will access the named set of services.

Figure 10.1 *The main window of WNET.*

If you access the Drives services, the window in Figure 10.2 will be displayed.

Tip: When you are in the Drive Connections window, you create a disk drive redirection by clicking and holding the mouse on a drive resource icon in the left-hand panel and dragging the icon to a local drive in the right-hand panel that you want to redirect.

233

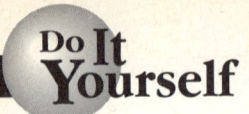

Networking with LANtastic

If the server you want to use isn't already listed along with its resource in the left-hand panel, you can use the Servers button to access the Server Connections window shown in Figure 10.3.

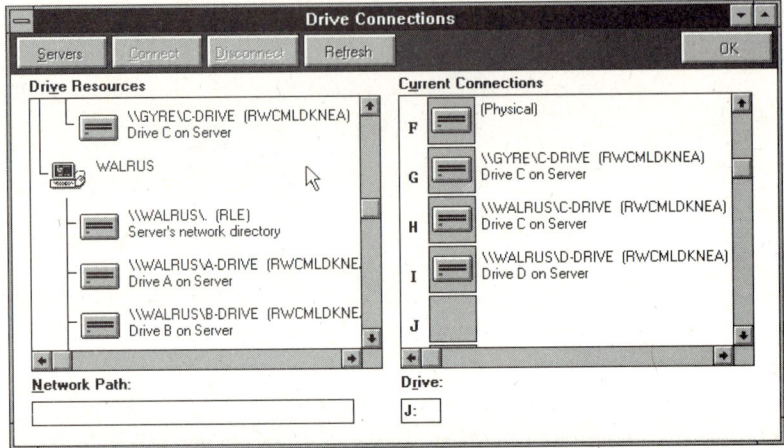

Figure 10.2 *The Drive Connections window of WNET.*

Figure 10.3 *The Server Connections window of WNET.*

When you select a server to log into or log out of, your default login will be used if the Use Default Name and Password box is checked. To set the login defaults, clicking on the Set Login Defaults button will produce the Login Defaults window shown in Figure 10.4.

Advanced Topics

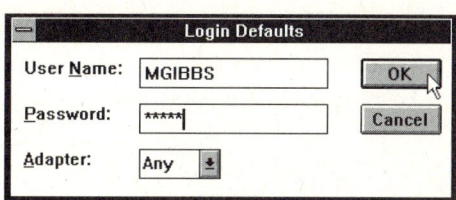

Figure 10.4   *The Login Defaults window of WNET.*

The printer redirection procedure is much the same as the procedure given for the Drive Connections window. The Printer Connections window is shown in Figure 10.5.

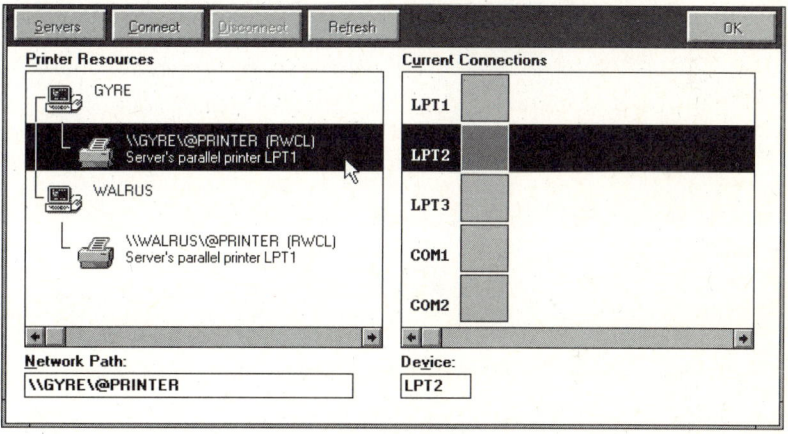

Figure 10.5   *The Printer Connections window of WNET.*

The other options — Mail, Chat, Queues, Login/Logout, and Account — are also functionally equivalent to their NET.EXE counterparts. The basic functions of Server Management are enhanced with a graphical display option for showing server activity (see Figure 10.6).

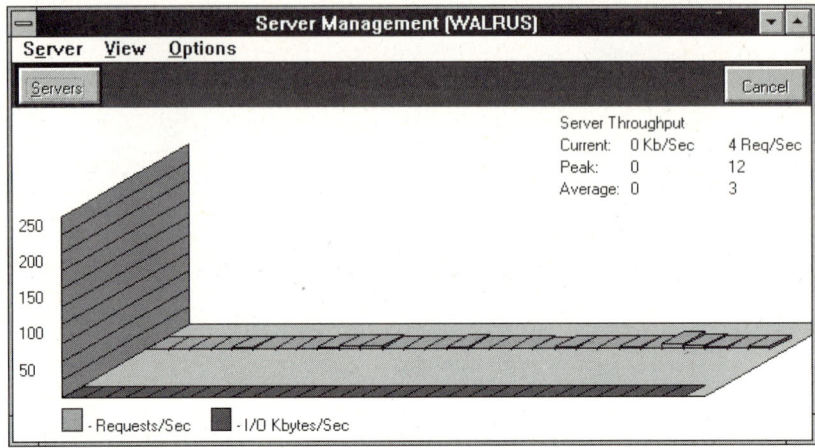

Figure 10.6   The WNET Server Throughput window.

WNET_MGR.EXE

WNET_MGR.EXE is basically the same as its DOS counterpart. Figure 10.7 shows WNET_MGR.EXE's main window.

WNET_MGR.EXE includes many nice enhancements; for example, you can select the icons for shared resources and use the mouse to define allowed login times for user accounts.

Figure 10.7   The WNET_MGR.EXE main window.

Dynamic Data Exchange (DDE)

The LANtastic for Windows utilities support various *Dynamic Data Exchange* (DDE) links to allow windows applications to directly access WNET.EXE and WNET_MGR.EXE functions. For example, you can add a button to the Word for Windows 2.0 Toolbar that will directly call up the WNET.EXE Drive Connections window. Then, if you need to access data on a remote server, you simply click on the button to go straight to the required service in WNET.

When you run the following Word for Windows macro, the Drive Connections window will appear:

```
Sub MAIN
'
'==============================================================
' NetDrives - A Word for Windows macro to call up a WNET "Drive
Connections" window
'
'==============================================================
'
' Just to play it safe, let's just save what we're working on
'
FileSave
'
' Now we'll build the DDE command string for WNET ...
'
X$ = "[CreateWindow(" + Chr$(34) + "Drives" + Chr$(34) + ")]"
'
' ... and then we'll open the channel and send WNET the command
'
ChanNum = DDEInitiate("WNET", "WNET")
DDEExecute ChanNum, X$
'
' Now we'll terminate the channel.
'
DDETerminate ChanNum
'
End Sub
```

By using the Word for Windows **T**ools **M**acros option, you can enter this text as a macro called, for example, NetDrives. Close the macro, and

then use **Tools Options** and select the Toolbar. Then set a Toolbar entry to whatever icon you like and associate it with the macro NetDrives. When you return to the main screen, the new tool will be on the Toolbar. Clicking on it will call up the Drive Connections window.

You can call nine other windows besides Drives using the CreateWindow command:

- *Account* calls up the user account functions.
- *Chat* accesses the chat facility.
- *Login* allows you to log into and log out of servers.
- *Mail* allows you to use the mail service window.
- *Popup* allows you to use the pop-up message window.
- *Printers* allows you to redirect printers.
- *Queues* accesses the print queue control services.
- *ServerMgt* accesses the server control options.
- *Timeout* sets the printer timeout.

There are four other WNET.EXE facilities that can be used by DDE-enabled applications:

- *MailFile*. This DDE command allows you to send files to other network users through the mail system. You can specify the file to be sent, the server that the mail system is on, the users the file is to be sent to, and a comment for the message.
- *PrintFile*. This command allows you to specify a file to print, the server the required printer is on, the name of the required shared printer resource, the number of copies, and a comment.
- *SelectServer*. This DDE command allows you to specify the name of the server that will be the WNET.EXE default server. This means that any WNET.EXE command that you execute that doesn't have a specified server will default to the server specified through SelectServer.
- *ExitNet*. To terminate the WNET.EXE program, issue a DDE ExitNet command. For example, after using any of the other commands (such as sending a file using the MailFile command), it would be an elegant touch to issue ExitNet to return to Word for Windows without any user intervention and would also free up memory.

Advanced Topics

 **Note:** The LANtastic for Windows package includes macros to add Save and Send menu options to the File menus of Microsoft Word for Windows and the Microsoft Excel spreadsheet program.

LANtastic for Windows is a great enhancement if you are a serious Windows user. It allows you to perform all of the functions required to control and manage the network from within the Windows environment through Windows utilities that are functionally equivalent to their DOS counterparts.

For organizations looking for greater integration of their applications with the LANtastic environment, the package offers some very exciting opportunities through Windows DDE services.

DR DOS

DR DOS 6.0 is an operating system from Digital Research that is designed to compete directly with Microsoft's MS-DOS. DR DOS offers several benefits, including memory-management tools and a set of performance- and facilities-enhancement utilities. If you are installing new PCs on a network, you can use either DR DOS or MS-DOS on either workstations or servers. You can also mix computers running either of the two operating systems on the same network.

Beyond its compatibility with Microsoft's MS-DOS 5.0, DR DOS 6.0 provides extended features that include:

- Simple installation through a menu-driven interface.
- Support for optimized memory use.
- Better memory-management features including the ability to load DOS into the High Memory Area so that more conventional memory space is left for applications.
- On-line command help.
- Disk caching and on-the-fly data compression utilities.
- A task switcher.

239

Networking with LANtastic

- Disk and file recovery utilities.
- Support for hard disk partitions up to 512MB.
- Free and unlimited lifetime (the lifetime of DR DOS, defined as expiring one year after the release of the next version) technical support.

The memory-management system is very sophisticated and consists of a collection of utilities that are collectively called MemoryMAX. All MemoryMAX services may be used in conjunction with LANtastic.

Although DR DOS doesn't allow real multitasking (that is, running several programs at the same time), it features a task switcher system called TaskMAX. This allows you to load several tasks and switch between them. When you switch tasks, the new task gets the full attention of the system, and the task that is switched out becomes inactive. The switcher can be used on either a LANtastic server or a workstation.

Connections to shared disk resources made before starting TaskMAX will be available to all tasks, while those made within a particular task will be accessible only within that task. However, printer redirections made within any task are available to all tasks.

To help the user deal with the system and avoid the command-line interface, DR DOS offers ViewMAX. This utility provides a graphical interface for DR DOS.

A very useful feature, particularly in the network environment, is DR DOS's security service. When enabled, this facility requires a user to enter a password each time the computer is booted before any access to files or programs is allowed. It is fully compatible with LANtastic.

DR DOS also offers support for virtual disks, disk caching, deletion tracking, and on-the-fly disk data compression. All of these features, bundled under the name of DiskMAX, may be used with LANtastic 4.0 with the following exceptions:

- The DiskMAX Super PC Kwik disk-caching utility must be configured with delayed write caching disabled if it is going to be used on a server (see the entry for the LANCACHE utility in the appendix "LANtastic Utilities Reference" for an explanation of delayed write caching).
- The DELWATCH utility that monitors file deletions and allows deleted file recovery cannot be used on network drives or on a machine running SERVER. However, it should work correctly on the local disk drive of a workstation.

Advanced Topics

- Before enabling data compression via the DiskMAX SuperStor device driver in conjunction with LANtastic, Artisoft and Digital Research recommend that users obtain Technical Tip #1200 from Digital Research.

DR DOS is an extremely well-designed replacement for MS-DOS and introduces a range of features and facilities that make the system an outstandingly good buy. These features, DR DOS's total compatibility with MS-DOS, and high quality documentation make it well worth considering as a PC platform whether you're networking or not.

Batch Files for Networking

One of the quickest ways to improve the manageability of your network is to automate frequently used processes. And the simplest way to do this is to use batch files.

Batch files have some major drawbacks however. There are a limited range of batch commands that DOS supports, and batch files run relatively slowly. They can also be easily modified or accidentally corrupted by any over-enthusiastic user with a word processor. To get around this problem, you might consider using a batch file compiler such as Builder 2.0 from Hyperkinetics, Inc. This system may be a little more than you'd expect; it is a complete programming system in its own right. Builder scores in taking existing batch files and turning them into programs (a process called *compiling*).

By learning the additional commands that Builder supports (a good tutorial is included), you can create very slick menu systems to protect your users from the DOS environment. Perhaps more importantly, you can use these menu systems to protect the DOS environment from the users! Builder contains a simple menu builder that allows you to specify the titles of menu items and then builds an outline Builder program so that you can fill in the actions.

In the network environment, being able to build custom menu systems, handle errors, and control batch procedures in a sophisticated way makes control and administration much simpler. For example, you can use batch files to create users to standard profiles. These batch files would run the NET_MGR.EXE commands CREATE USER *uname* and SET USER *uname*

Networking with LANtastic

`pw logins privs accexp pwexp` (see Appendix C, "Utilities Reference," for a full explanation of these commands). This is considerably simpler than entering the commands by hand. Using Builder, you can make this process a full-screen menu interface system tailored to your organization's specific needs.

Central Station

The Central Station product from Artisoft is intended to be a low-cost way to solve various problems, such as providing network access for laptops and creating printer servers. There are many functions, such as servicing a group of printers, that you may not want to dedicate a PC for. This is the reason that Artisoft created their Central Station product.

Central Station is a microprocessor-based device designed to support the low-cost connection of printers, laptops, and other devices to the network (see Figure 10.8). It has a variety of input/output ports that include:

- A thin coaxial port to allow connection to any EtherNet network.
- A port for connection to any unshielded twisted pair (UTP) EtherNet network.
- A parallel port for high speed connection to a PC (labelled *PC*).
- Two bidirectional serial ports with DB9 connectors (labeled *COM1* and *COM2*).
- One additional serial port with a DB9 connector that supports only software (XON/XOFF) flow control (labeled *AUX*).
- One IBM PC-type parallel port with a DB25 connector (labeled *LPT1*).
- One internal SCSI port for connecting to disk drives, etc.

The PC port connection can be used in two ways. First, it can be used to connect laptops and other PCs that can't use or don't support network adapter cards to a LANtastic network (this is referred to as a "slotless" LAN connection).

The second use is for downloading what Artisoft calls *Stationware* through a connected PC into the memory of the Central Station. Stationware is utility software that allows the Central Station unit to perform a service function.

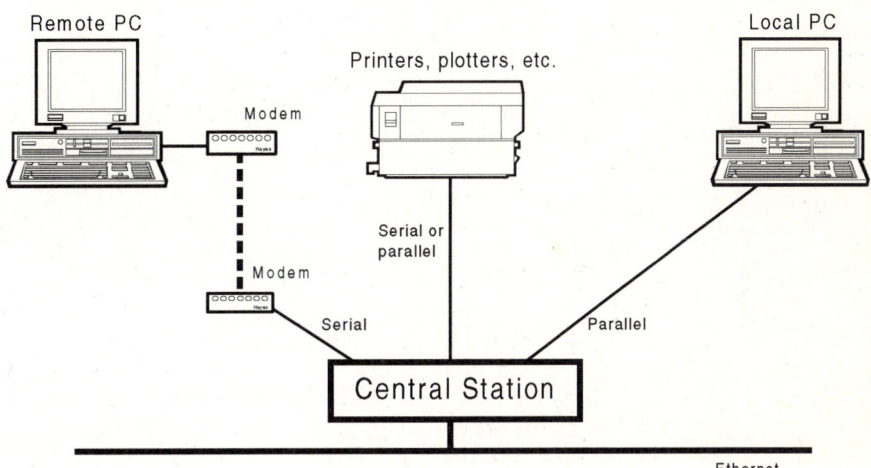

Figure 10.8 *The role of Artisoft's Central Station in a network environment.*

> **Note:** The only service built into the Central Station units is network support for allowing PCs to access the network through parallel port connections.

Currently, Artisoft offers Stationware that allows a Central Station to be a print server for either a LANtastic or a NetWare network. These packages support any mixture of the Central Station ports COM1, COM2, and LPT1 as printer ports. The installation of Stationware is fairly simple and integrating the printer services with the existing network should be straightforward.

Future Stationware services will include the ability to connect to the network through a modem (Dial-Up connections). This will come in varieties to support remote connections from either LANtastic or NetWare workstations. Another future product is a developer's kit, so that third parties can develop Stationware applications.

Depending on your needs and budget, Central Station could be a powerful solution for supporting casual connections for laptops and acting as a printer server. The remote modem connection support will be a useful service but will be limited by the performance of the modem connection (see the comments under "LANtastic Z").

Mixing LANtastic and NetWare

The lion's share of the networking market is held by Novell's NetWare operating system. This networking solution is a server-based system that doesn't use DOS on the server. The NetWare system is used on large networks and supports very high performance, advanced security and management, and sophisticated communications services.

The trade-off for this power is complexity (NetWare requires a lot of network experience to install and configure), cost (significant compared to LANtastic), and a continuing network management overhead (again, significant compared to LANtastic).

Many organizations that use NetWare may find that internal groups (such as branch offices, departments, and corporate project teams) will want to use LANtastic. This may be in place of, or in addition to, NetWare.

The flexibility and relative simplicity of LANtastic offers a style of working that may be more in line with group needs. But if the organization has already invested in NetWare, there will probably be a need to get the best of both worlds, allowing LANtastic users to use the shared resources of both systems simultaneously.

This combination of the services of LANtastic and NetWare is what is offered by Artisoft's LANtastic for NetWare software. The package includes the normal LANtastic networking software with specific support for Novell's implementation of NETBIOS.

The integration is not complete, and in reality the two systems simply coexist. There are several areas where conflicts can arise, such as trying to use the same printer for despooling from both LANtastic and NetWare. Recommendations and techniques for avoiding these problems are discussed in the LANtastic for NetWare manual.

A basic problem is that the commands to use NetWare are totally different from those for LANtastic. You might look at using batch files to control a mixed LANtastic and NetWare environment so that the difference between the two command sets are completely hidden from the user. Using a batch file compiler, such as Builder, could result in a very elegant and efficient solution.

LANtastic for NetWare is a good way to combine the benefits of peer-to-peer networking with the key server-based network product.

Multiple Network Adapters

It is possible to use more than one network adapter in a LANtastic server or workstation. The limitation on this is that the networks each adapter is connected to are logically separate. This means that in Figure 10.9, the user on the server GYRE can use the server GRYPHON but won't know the whereabouts of either of the servers JHOFFA or ELVIS. The user on GRYPHON, however, will be able to see both of them and the server GYRE.

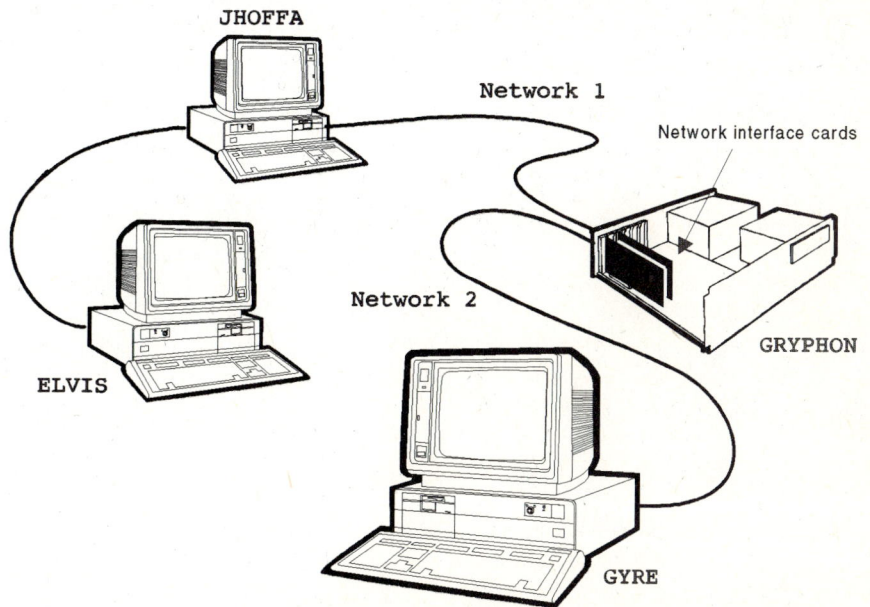

Figure 10.9 *Two networks with a common server.*

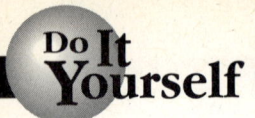

Networking with LANtastic

This means that a server on a network other than the one your PC is on is effectively invisible, even though the networks meet at a common server or workstation. It doesn't stop users from accessing the same data files, sharing printers, and exchanging electronic mail on their common servers.

A possible advantage of this limitation is that it allows you to separate networks by department or functional group but still leave them with common facilities.

> **Note:** For lower-performance technologies like ARCNET, having separate networks reduces the traffic on each network (as compared to having a single network) and therefore improves performance.

There are some configurations for which having multiple network adapters may be required or at least of great benefit. While not entirely easy to implement (getting the right combination of interrupt and memory address settings can take time, patience, and experimentation), careful planning and testing can give you a sound and effective system.

Remote Control and Monitoring

Two important services for physically large networks, training, and control of PCs are remote control and monitoring. There are many reasons why you might want to avoid having to physically go to a network PC. Some of them are:

- If your network is spread out over a large area, going to it to check the work of the operator or start a program running could take considerable time.

- If you want to run a program or check the status of a running program that is any distance from you.

- If you're training users and want to monitor progress or show your screen to several users at once.

Advanced Topics

There are several products that allow you to monitor and/or control a remote PC across the network. Artisoft's offering is called The Network Eye.

The Network Eye is easy to install on any NETBIOS network. It can be run as either a memory-resident service monitoring up to thirty-two remote PCs or as a stand-alone monitor to communicate with a single remote computer.

Note: You should check with Artisoft first to see if a particular NETBIOS implementation other than Artisoft's is supported.

Each PC (whether a server or a workstation) running The Network Eye can be set up as a Master, a Workstation, or both at the same time. Masters monitor Workstations, and you can set up your network to have as many of each as you need.

A Master can be configured just to monitor the remote workstation or to monitor and control it (the Master's keyboard can act as the remote Workstation's keyboard). Additionally, the Workstation can be password-protected and configured to display a warning when being remotely monitored.

Note: A limitation of The Network Eye is that it only works with character-based screen data. If you are a Master and the workstation switches to a graphical application, the screen will blank, but (if enabled) you can still enter keyboard commands.

The memory-resident mode of the Master program is very powerful. You can monitor up to 32 screens at once and move between them at will. Each screen is initially shown in a small window that can be repositioned on the screen and shrunk or enlarged as required. Each window can be set to display a particular region of the remote PC screen or automatically follow the cursor's position. You can also set The Network Eye Master to display each screen, one after another automatically.

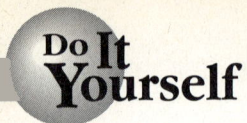 *Networking with LANtastic*

If there's some data that you want to save from a remote screen, you can copy it to a special screen called the clipboard. The contents of the clipboard can then be pasted into a text-based application on any of the remote computers you are monitoring and have keyboard control of. Because The Network Eye isn't multitasking, it can't paste the saved data into a local application.

The Network Eye is a great tool for monitoring the network and controlling remote PCs, and its performance is good. Its price makes The Network Eye attractive, and its only real drawback is that it is limited to text-only displays.

Sharing Modems

There are several reasons why you might want to share modems on the network rather than give one to each user:

- *Cost.* A modem for each user gets expensive, particularly if all the users want high-performance models. Worse still, they won't be making continuous use of the device. Being able to share a number of modems among a group of users will decrease the cost per user, but at the risk that a modem will not always be available.

- *Control.* If modems are freely available, you may have a problem with people using them at times and to destinations that are not authorized.

Artisoft's network product to meet these needs is called ArtiCom. This program allows you to pool up to two modems (using COM1 and COM2), or if you use a multiport serial communications board, up to eight modems. A multiport serial communications board is a card that allows you to have more than the basic two serial ports, and ArtiCom supports multiport boards from ARCnet, DigiBoard, Star Gate, and Quatech.

> **Note:** Although the ArtiCom product is discussed here, and in its documentation, as supporting remote access to modems, the serial connections could be to any serial device. This would allow you to support access across the network to any system that supports serial terminals or is intended for direct connection to a PC.

Each PC that is going to share one or more modems runs a utility called A-SERVER.EXE. This is a small (6 kilobytes), memory-resident utility that could be thought of as performing a similar function to the LANtastic SERVER.EXE software, except that it allows you to share serial connections rather than disks and printers.

On another PC, you run the A-REDIR.EXE software which, as you might expect, is a redirector for serial communications. To use a modem, you can use the ACOM.EXE communications package that comes bundled with the ArtiCom system. This utility allows you to select a modem server and serial port and then enters a full-featured terminal emulator.

The emulations available include ANSI BBS, several DEC terminal types, and up to four external terminal emulator packages supplied by third parties. You can use almost any communications package that supports Int 14 connections (refer to any terminal emulator vendor on this question to establish if they do, in fact, support it). The terminal emulators that Artisoft lists as compatible include Crosstalk, DynaComm, Mirror, Procomm Plus, and WinComm.

ArtiCom also offers a number of features that add to network management. For individual port definitions, you can:

- Disable the ability for remote users to change the port parameters.
- Set limits to the duration of sessions.
- Restrict access by time-of-day.
- Require a password for access.

Being able to use third-party communications packages makes up for ACOM's biggest deficiency — the lack of a script language. Scripting allows the package to interact with the incoming data and take appropriate action. Thus, you could have a script to log onto CompuServe, pick up any mail messages, and then log off.

Voice Mail

Although LANtastic's electronic mail is relatively simple, it boasts one very sophisticated feature — voice mail.

Networking with LANtastic

If you install voice mail on your network, you can use it for sending memos or creating a virtual telephone system that can be used anywhere the network reaches.

Voice mail is supported by creating a sound file using a low-level driver called LANVOICE.EXE with Artisoft's Voice Adapter card and attaching the file to an electronic mail message. This card is a half-length board that comes with a handset. You can also connect microphones, CD players, cassette recorders, and amplifiers to the Voice Adapter.

This configuration allows you to use the voice version of the NET CHAT service with other network users who have the same setup. This allows you to have a spoken conversation using the Voice adapters and the supplied handsets rather than typing messages. There are probably many odd situations where this could be of great use. For example, you might want to communicate with a user in a remote corner of a warehouse where there is no telephone, but you have a PC connected to the network.

The cost of the Artisoft Voice Adapter is very low, and the sound quality is good. The NET CHAT feature is interesting, but the real use is to enhance electronic mail. As the Voice Adapter system records to and replays from files, you can use the software with most electronic mail systems.

LANtastic Z

If you want to create a cheap networking connection between any pair of PCs without using any network hardware, LANtastic Z is a good solution. This system is sold as a separate package and is, in fact, a complete LANtastic system with special low-level drivers. LANtastic Z software is designed to support three types of connections between two PCs. These connections are:

- Serial ports COM1 and COM2.
- Parallel ports LPT1, LPT2, or LPT3.
- A modem on either of the serial ports.

These connections can support communications between the two PCs on a serial connection at rates up to 56000 baud or the maximum available from your parallel port configuration (usually about 150 kilobytes per second).

The LANtastic Z software consists of three low-level drivers, related utility software, and the rest of the regular LANtastic utilities. If the connection is through modems, a utility is used to define the telephone dialing list, establish and break connections, and monitor the connection status. The modem connection can be defined as a call-in connection (a remote computer will call this computer) or a dial-up connection (this computer will dial the remote computer). A wide range of modems can be accommodated by editing the various modem command strings.

The LANtastic Z system is very useful for supporting connections between two PCs or between a laptop and a server on a network. The drawback with the system is that the connection is, in fact, a separate network, so the limitations that were discussed in the section "Using Multiple Adapters" apply also to LANtastic Z connections.

Another limitation is performance. Compared to EtherNet, LANtastic Z through a direct parallel connection is about a tenth of the speed and through 2400 baud modems is more than 4000 times slower! This means that the connections should be limited to very restricted uses such as picking up electronic mail and transferring small files (on modem links, *very* small files). Figure 10.10 summarizes the LANtastic Z environment.

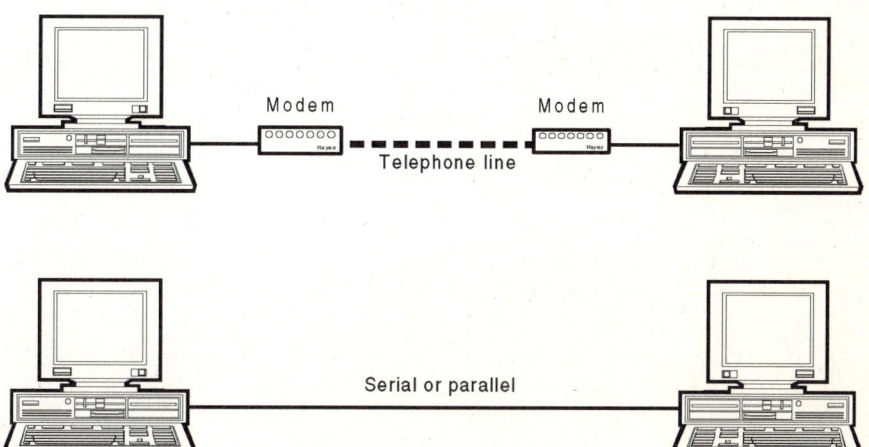

Figure 10.10 *The LANtastic Z environment.*

To support a LANtastic Z setup as well as another network on a single PC, you need to install the appropriate LANtastic Z driver, a copy of AILANBIO.EXE for it, the drivers for the other network adapters, and a copy of NETBIOS for each adapter. If the PC is to be a server, you must then run

 **Networking with LANtastic**

NET_MGR.EXE and specify the number of adapters that are being supported in the section "Server Start-up Parameters." When the network is reloaded, the server will accept requests from all adapters including the LANtastic Z connections.

LANtastic Z is a good solution for supporting laptops and casual, low-volume access via modems. It is not a workable solution if you want to transfer large files or perform a lot of network transactions.

Expanding Your Disk Space

For many small networks, the problem of running out of disk space is a regular occurrence. The more useful a computer system is, the more it is asked to do. As a result, you must deal with increasingly large volumes of data and keep that data available.

An excellent solution to increasing your disk capacity is to use an "on-the-fly" data compression system such as Stacker from Stac Electronics. This is a software system that can achieve a compression ratio of up to 2 to 1; that is, it effectively doubles your disk capacity! To improve performance, there is also a coprocessor board, which takes the processing load for compression and decompression off the PC.

The basis of this software is some very slick and sophisticated programming that takes each data block being written to disk and encodes the data in such a way as to decrease its size. When you read data blocks from the disk, the Stacker software decompresses the data and hands you back the original.

Stacker is completely compatible with LANtastic, and, because it caches data, you'll notice a small performance improvement just using the software version. If you use the coprocessor (on either a workstation or a server), you'll see a slight performance improvement that reportedly increases as the load increases.

Installation is fairly simple, and the product has received many rave reviews. As an alternative to buying larger hard disk drives (say, upgrading a 40-megabyte drive), the cost of Stacker is roughly 80 percent of the cost of an 80-megabyte drive. Stacker is definitely a product well worth considering as a simple and effective upgrade to your network storage.

Advanced Topics

Summary

This has been a brief survey of some of the areas in which you can enhance or augment the power and facilities of a LANtastic network. The most important aspect of the products discussed is that, at worst, some could be tricky to implement correctly. Most of them are actually pretty easy and straightforward to both implement and use.

There are hundreds of other products you might also consider using. The best sources for opinion on what is good and what isn't are other users. If you haven't joined a local user group, do so. Whether it's a PC-oriented one or you're lucky enough to find a LANtastic users group, you'll almost always be able to find someone who knows the ins and outs of a product. Artisoft now runs a LANtastic forum on CompuServe that will give you excellent intelligence on LANtastic and compatible products.

 Resources

Artisoft

Artisoft offers free, unlimited technical support for their products. The wait can be fairly long, so it's often worth trying their bulletin board (ArtiFacts) or the fax support service (FaxFacts) first. For basic product information, call their sales number.

>Artisoft, Inc.
>691 East River Road
>Tucson, AZ 85704
>
>Main switchboard: (602) 293-4000
>Customer service/sales: (800) 846-9726
>Technical support: (602) 293-6363
>ArtiFacts BBS: (602) 293-0065
>General fax: (602) 293-8065
>FaxFacts: (602) 293-1397

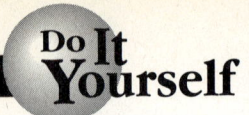
Networking with LANtastic

CompuServe

CompuServe is a global bulletin board system with about one million users. It has sections (called *forums*) covering a huge range of topics and boasts over 1,700 databases. For the do-it-yourself networker, CompuServe is an invaluable service, hosting a support forum for Artisoft (GO ARTISOFT) as well as many other network product vendors.

One of the great benefits to this service is that technical questions are usually answered in less than 24 hours. And if you want to know about software compatibility or the best way to do something, other users will always give their opinions and share their knowledge.

Customer support: (800) 848-8199 or (614) 457-8650

Microsoft Corporation

Microsoft offers a large range of products, many of which have specific support for networking.

Microsoft Corporation
One Microsoft Way
Redmond, WA 98052-6399

Main switchboard: (206) 882-8080
Sales and service: (800) 541-1261 or (206) 936-8661

Uninterruptable Power Supplies

If you are going to build a network that is at all critical to your business, providing uninterruptable power supply protection to at least the servers is crucial. The following are some of the UPS vendors whose products are cited by Artisoft as being compatible with LANtastic.

American Power Conversion: (800) 800-4272 or (401) 789-5735

PARA Systems: (800) 238-7272 or (214) 446-7363

SOLA: (708) 439-2800

Tripp Lite: (312) 329-1777

Magazines

There are now a huge number of PC-related magazines to choose from. The following are a selection of those that regularly cover networking at a do-it-yourself level:

- *Byte*
- *PC Magazine*
- *PC Computing*

For more in-depth information on networking, try:

- *LAN Magazine*
- *LAN Technology*
- *Network Computing*

Forms

These "Do It Yourself" forms will help you plan and manage your LANtastic network. You'll also find them helpful when trouble arises on your network. They will form the backbone of your site log, if you choose to assemble one.

Of course, these forms will be useful only if you use them. You can enlarge them to full size, using a photocopier with an enlargement feature (the optimum enlargement would be around 140%). Then, you can make additional copies of the enlarged forms.

Figure B.1 *DIY-001, Needs Analysis: Problems.*

Forms

© Mark Gibbs, 1992   **Needs Analysis: Goals**   Form: DIY-002

#	Description

Prepared by: Date: Page:

This form is taken from "Do-It-Yourself Networking With LANtastic"
Published by SAMS (1992)

Figure B.2   *DIY-002, Needs Analysis: Goals.*

Figure B.3 *DIY-003, Site Analysis: Layout.*

Figure B.4 DIY-004, Site Analysis: Power.

Title & name	PC configuration	Printer & port	Notes

Site Analysis: Equipment (Form: DIY-005, © Mark Gibbs, 1992)

Prepared by: / Date: / Page:

This form is taken from "Do-It-Yourself Networking With LANtastic" Published by SAMS (1992)

Figure B.5 DIY-005, Site Analysis: Equipment.

Figure B.6 *DIY-006, Solutions.*

Figure B.7 *DIY-007, Purchase List.*

Location	Type	Function	Machine name

© Mark Gibbs, 1992
Form: DIY-008
Network Configuration

Prepared by: Date: Page:

This form is taken from "Do-It-Yourself Networking With LANtastic"
Published by SAMS (1992)

Figure B.8 *DIY-008, Network Configuration.*

Server name		Location	
Control dir.		Install dir.	
Mail system	Enabled	Server user	
Startup file			

Directory structure:

Prepared by: Date: Page:

© Mark Gibbs, 1992   Form: DIY-009

Network Server Configuration #1

This form is taken from "Do-It-Yourself Networking With LANtastic" Published by SAMS (1992)

Figure B.9   DIY-009, Network Server Configuration #1.

Forms

© Mark Gibbs, 1992   Form: DIY-010

Network Server Configuration #2: Users

Server name			
Real name		User name	
Status		Privileges	
Acc. expiration		Login days	M T W T F
Renew password	days	Login times	: to :
Real name		User name	
Status		Privileges	
Acc. expiration		Login days	M T W T F
Renew password	days	Login times	: to :
Real name		User name	
Status		Privileges	
Acc. expiration		Login days	M T W T F
Renew password	days	Login times	: to :
Real name		User name	
Status		Privileges	
Acc. expiration		Login days	M T W T F
Renew password	days	Login times	: to :
Real name		User name	
Status		Privileges	
Acc. expiration		Login days	M T W T F
Renew password	days	Login times	: to :
Real name		User name	
Status		Privileges	
Acc. expiration		Login days	M T W T F
Renew password	days	Login times	: to :
Real name		User name	
Status		Privileges	
Acc. expiration		Login days	M T W T F
Renew password	days	Login times	: to :
Prepared by:	Date:	Page:	

This form is taken from "Do-It-Yourself Networking With LANtastic"
Published by SAMS (1992)

Figure B.10 DIY-010, Network Server Configuration #2: Users.

Networking with LANtastic

Server name					Res. name						
Local definition											
Order	User				Access rights						
	*	R	W	C	M	L	D	K	N	E	A	I	P
	GUEST	R	W	C	M	L	D	K	N	E	A	I	P
		R	W	C	M	L	D	K	N	E	A	I	P
		R	W	C	M	L	D	K	N	E	A	I	P
		R	W	C	M	L	D	K	N	E	A	I	P
		R	W	C	M	L	D	K	N	E	A	I	P
		R	W	C	M	L	D	K	N	E	A	I	P
		R	W	C	M	L	D	K	N	E	A	I	P
		R	W	C	M	L	D	K	N	E	A	I	P
		R	W	C	M	L	D	K	N	E	A	I	P
		R	W	C	M	L	D	K	N	E	A	I	P
		R	W	C	M	L	D	K	N	E	A	I	P
		R	W	C	M	L	D	K	N	E	A	I	P
		R	W	C	M	L	D	K	N	E	A	I	P
		R	W	C	M	L	D	K	N	E	A	I	P
		R	W	C	M	L	D	K	N	E	A	I	P
		R	W	C	M	L	D	K	N	E	A	I	P
		R	W	C	M	L	D	K	N	E	A	I	P
		R	W	C	M	L	D	K	N	E	A	I	P
		R	W	C	M	L	D	K	N	E	A	I	P
		R	W	C	M	L	D	K	N	E	A	I	P
		R	W	C	M	L	D	K	N	E	A	I	P
		R	W	C	M	L	D	K	N	E	A	I	P
		R	W	C	M	L	D	K	N	E	A	I	P
		R	W	C	M	L	D	K	N	E	A	I	P
Prepared by:		Date:						Page:				

This form is taken from "Do-It-Yourself Networking With LANtastic"
Published by SAMS (1992)

© Mark Gibbs, 1992   Form: DIY-011
Network Server Shared Disk Resources

Figure B.11 *DIY-011, Network Server Shared Disk Resources.*

© Mark Gibbs, 1992   Form: DIY-012

Network Server Shared Printer Resources

Server name					Resource name			@			
Printer											
Port		COM1:		COM2:	LPT1:		LPT2:		LPT3:		
Baud rate					Banner						
Form feeds					Lines/page						
Immed. despool					Despool timeout					seconds	
Tab width					Paper width						
Chars/second					Handshake			H/W	S/W	None	
Setup delay					Cleanup delay						
Order	User	Access rights (R WCL are standard)
8	*	R	W	C	M	L	D	K	N	E	A	I	P
1	GUEST	R	W	C	M	L	D	K	N	E	A	I	P
2	LRSMITH	R	W	C	M	L	D	K	N	E	A	I	P
3	AJGIBBS	R	W	C	M	L	D	K	N	E	A	I	P
4	PLAY	R	W	C	M	L	D	K	N	E	A	I	P
5	GREDEKER	R	W	C	M	L	D	K	N	E	A	I	P
6	ELAY	R	W	C	M	L	D	K	N	E	A	I	P
7	BREDEKER	R	W	C	M	L	D	K	N	E	A	I	P
		R	W	C	M	L	D	K	N	E	A	I	P
		R	W	C	M	L	D	K	N	E	A	I	P
		R	W	C	M	L	D	K	N	E	A	I	P
		R	W	C	M	L	D	K	N	E	A	I	P
		R	W	C	M	L	D	K	N	E	A	I	P
		R	W	C	M	L	D	K	N	E	A	I	P
		R	W	C	M	L	D	K	N	E	A	I	P
		R	W	C	M	L	D	K	N	E	A	I	P
		R	W	C	M	L	D	K	N	E	A	I	P
		R	W	C	M	L	D	K	N	E	A	I	P
		R	W	C	M	L	D	K	N	E	A	I	P
		R	W	C	M	L	D	K	N	E	A	I	P
Prepared by:		Date:					Page:				

This form is taken from "Do-It-Yourself Networking With LANtastic"
Published by SAMS (1992)

Figure B.12 *DIY-012, Network Server Shared Printer Resources.*

Figure B.13 *DIY-013, Equipment Received Log.*

Forms

```
© Mark Gibbs, 1992                                      Form: DIY-014
                      PC Hardware Configuration
```

PC Location*:				User*:		
Network name*:				Type*: Server-only / Server & WS / WS*		
Manufacturer:				Model:		
Display:	Herc. / CGA / EGA / VGA / _____				Mono / Color	

	Port	Exist?	Attached device
Input / Output*	COM1:		
	COM2:		
	COM3:		
	COM4:		
	LPT1:		
	LPT2:		
	LPT3:		

	Type:	Serial number:
Network adapter*	Manufacturer	I/O address:
	Remote boot ROM Installed / Not installed	IRQ

Notes:

Prepared by:	Date:	Page:

This form is taken from "Do-It-Yourself Networking With LANtastic"
Published by SAMS (1992)

Figure B.14 *DIY-014, PC Hardware Configuration.*

```
© Mark Gibbs, 1992                                      Form: DIY-015
                          Problem Report

Problem id:                        Date raised:
Raised by:                         Handled by:
Dept./location                     Extension:
Problem status:      Urgent / Rush / Configuration / Installation / Upgrade
PC      Manufacturer:
        Model:
        RAM:
        DOS type and version:
Adapter cards -
1                                  7
2                                  8
3                                  9
4                                  10
5                                  11
6                                  12
LANtastic version:
Node type:         Server & client  /  Workstation  /  Server only
Problem description:





















Prepared by:            Date:                    Page:
         This form is taken from "Do-It-Yourself Networking With LANtastic"
                          Published by SAMS (1992)
```

Figure B.15 *DIY-015, Problem Report.*

Figure B.16 *DIY-016, Technical Support Report.*

Networking with LANtastic

© Mark Gibbs, 1992　　　　　　　　　　　　　　　　　　　　Form: DIY-017

Problem Log

Problem ID	Event date	Event time	Details

Prepared by:	Date:	Page:

This form is taken from "Do-It-Yourself Networking With LANtastic" Published by SAMS (1992)

Figure B.17   DIY-017, Problem Log.

C

Utilities Reference

Parameters	285
Switch Files	286
The REMOVE Switch	287
AILANBIO.EXE	289
Description	289
General Form	289
@	290
ACK_TIMEOUT	290
ADAPTER	291
BUFFERS	292
FORCE_ACK_MODE	293
HELP or ?	293
INITIAL_SEND_SIZE	294
MAX_NAMES	295
MAX_NCBS	296
MAX_SESSIONS	297
MPX	299

NCBS	299
REMOVE	300
RETRY_PERIOD	300
ROM_PATCH	301
RUN_BURST	302
SESSIONS	303
SIZE	303
TIMEOUT	304
VERBOSE	305
AIMOVE.EXE	**307**
Description	307
General Form	307
ALONE.EXE	**309**
Description	309
General Form	310
LANCACHE.EXE	**311**
Description	311
General Form	313
@	313
AFTER_IO_DELAY	314
CACHE_SIZE	314
DISABLE	315
DISK	315
ENABLE	316
FAST_IRQ	316
FLUSH	317
HELP or ?	317
LONG_WRITE_DELAY	318
RELEASE	319
REMOVE	319
RESET	320
SHUTDOWN_KEY	320
STAT	321
TYPE	322
VERBOSE	322
WITH_WINDOWS	323
LANCHECK.EXE	**325**
Description	325
General Form	325
nname	325
/MONO	326

Utilities Reference

LANPUP.EXE	**327**
Description	327
General Form	327
LINE	327
REMOVE	328
STAND_ALONE	328
STACK	328
Usage Notes	329
NBSETUP.EXE	**339**
Description	339
General Form	339
CHECK	340
HELP or ?	340
MAX	341
NCBS	341
SESSIONS	342
VERBOSE	342
NET.EXE	**345**
Description	345
General Form	345
ATTACH	346
AUDIT	347
CHANGEPW	347
CHAT	348
CLOCK	348
COPY	349
DETACH	350
DIR	350
DISABLEA	352
ECHO	353
EXPAND	353
FLUSH	355
HELP	356
INDIRECT	357
LOGIN	358
LOGOUT	359
LPT	359
MAIL	362
MESSAGE	362
/MONO or no switches	363
NOERROR	363

PAUSE	364
POSTBOX	364
PRINT	365
QUEUE	366
RECEIVE	368
RUN	368
SEND	369
SHOW	370
SHUTDOWN	371
SLOGINS	373
STREAM	373
STRING	376
TERMINATE	379
UNLINK	380
UNUSE	380
USE	381
USER	382
NET_MGR.EXE	**383**
Description	383
General Form	383
BACKUP	383
COPY USER	384
CREATE USER	386
DELETE	387
HELP or ?	388
RESTORE	389
SET	389
SHOW	391
REDIR.EXE	**393**
Description	393
General Form	393
@	393
BEEP_CYCLE	394
BEEP_DELAY=n	394
BUFFERS=n	395
HELP or ?	396
LOGINS	397
MONO	397
NOCHAIN	398
POPUP_DURATION	399
POPUP_LINE	399

Utilities Referemce

REMOVE	400
SIZE	400
VERBOSE	401
SERVER.EXE	**403**
Description	403
General Form	403
ADAPTERS	404
DESPOOLER_STOPPED	405
FILES	405
FLOPPY_DIRECT	406
HELP or ?	407
LOCK_HOLD_TIME	407
LOGINS	409
NETWORK_BUFFER_SIZE	410
NETWORK_TASKS	411
PRINTER_BUFFER_SIZE	411
PRINTER_TASKS	412
REMOVE	413
REQUEST_SIZE	413
RESOURCE_CACHE	414
RPL	415
RUN_BUFFER_SIZE	417
RUN_BURST	417
SEEK_CACHE	418
SEND_SERVER_ID	419
SHUTDOWN_KEY	420
VERBOSE	421
UPS.EXE	**423**
Description	423
General Form	425
@	425
BROWNOUT_SECONDS	426
CANCEL_SECONDS	427
DEVICE	427
HELP or ?	428
IOBASE	429
LOW_BATTERY	430
NO_CANCEL	431
NO_POWER_DOWN	431
POWER_DOWN_CYCLE	431
REMOVE	432

SHUTDOWN_MINUTES	432
WARNING	433
LANtastic Special Strings	**435**
!"DATE"	436
!"DAY"	437
!"DIRECTORY"	437
!"ETEXT=n"	437
!"FILE=file"	437
!"INSTALLED"	438
!"LOGIN=sname"	438
!"NODEID"	438
!"MACHINEID"	438
!"PROGRAM"	439
!"TIME"	439
!"USER"	439
Prompts	439
Audio Warnings	**440**
The Menu Interfaces	**441**
LANCHECK	**443**
Starting LANCHECK	443
The LANCHECK Main Screen	445
NET.EXE	**451**
Network Disk Drives and Printers	452
Printer Queue Management	453
Mail Services	456
Chat With Another User	458
Login or Logout	459
User Account Management	460
Monitor & Manage Server Activity	462
NET_MGR.EXE	**469**
Individual Account Management	470
Group Account Management	474
Shared Resources Management	477
Server Start-up Parameters	484
Maximum Users	485
Printer Buffer	488
Audit Trail Maintenance	494

Utilities Reference

Queue Maintenance	496
Password Maintenance	496
Boot Image Maintenance	497
Control Directory Maintenance	498

 *Networking with LANtastic*

LANtastic comes with all of the basic utilities that you need to configure, use, and manage your network. They fall into two categories:

- System utilities that are used to enable, enhance, or modify the characteristics of a networked PC.
- User utilities that allow you to control and manage LANtastic.

The user utilities can be run in either of two modes:

- *Command line mode.* The utility's function is specified as part of the command line. This is used for batch file operations or where you know exactly what service you want.
- *Menu-driven mode.* You can select functions through a full-screen menu system. This is useful if you don't remember all of the options and format conventions of the command line mode.

The LANtastic utilities are summarized in Table C.1.

Table C.1 Summary of LANtastic utilities.

File name	Type	Modes*	Functions
AILANBIO.EXE	System	CL	Part of network operating system.
AIMOVE.EXE	System	CL	Configuration utility for diskless workstations.
ALONE.EXE	System	CL	Puts server into dedicated server mode.
LANCACHE.EXE	System	CL	Adds a cache to improve performance.
LANCHECK.EXE	User	M	Checks and monitors network communications and status.
LANPUP.EXE	User	M	Pop-up version of NET.EXE
NBSETUP.EXE	System	CL	Used to configure a third party NETBIOS.
NET.EXE	User	CL/M	Controls session and user settings.
NET_MGR.EXE	User	CL/M	Used to configure server system.
REDIR.EXE	System	CL	Part of network operating system.
SERVER.EXE	System	CL	Part of network operating system.

Utilities Referemce

File name	Type	Modes*	Functions
UPS.EXE	System	CL	Supports UPS to sense power supply condition.

* CL = command line interface, M = menu interface.

Parameters

When the utilities are run in command line mode, they may have various *parameters* following the name of the command. Parameters specify the modes and operations that the command is to use or perform. There are two types of parameters — *variables* and *switches*.

Variables are parameters that occur in a fixed order on the command line. For example, if the command is LANCHECK, the next item (a variable) on the command line must be the name of the node. If the name you want to use is FRED (the variable), the command line would be LANCHECK FRED.

Switches specify different options and their settings. A switch is either a word or character that identifies the option to the command. Some switches don't have values; their presence alone indicates that something is to be done (or not done). Alternatively, the switch may be followed by text or a value that is the required setting.

For example, for AILANBIO /MAX_NAMES=25, AILANBIO is the command and /MAX_NAMES is the switch. The value specified by the switch is 25.

Switches can be specified as follows:

- Although Artisoft says that either a space or a slash (/) can be used to separate a command from its switches or one switch from the next, in most cases you'll find that for a switch (not a variable) which immediately follows a command, the only separator that will be accepted is slash (/). This means that NET MONO will be considered an error, but NET/MONO will be accepted. In general, use the formats shown in the command explanations below.

- Switch values may be separated from the switch itself by either a colon (:) or an equal sign (=). In general, either SWITCH:VALUE or SWITCH=VALUE will work.

285

- For any command, you can abbreviate the switch characters to as few as you like so long as the switch remains uniquely identifiable. Thus, for the command AILANBIO.EXE, you could abbreviate /MAX_SESSIONS to /MAX_S. You couldn't, however, use MAX, as that could be /MAX_BUFFERS.

In the descriptions of the utilities, I'll use the following conventions to explain how the command line for a utility should be composed:

- Items between braces ({}) are optional.
- Items separated by vertical bars are choices, and only one can be made. Thus, for {A}, you can choose to use option A or not. For {A¦B¦C}, you can choose only one of A or B or C.
- A text item in lowercase italic letters is a variable.

For example:

NET {USE *drive sname*¦UNUSE *drive*}

- The command is NET.
- USE and UNUSE are switches. You can use either but not both.
- *drive* and *sname* are variables.
- If you use USE you must specify *drive* and *sname*, if you use UNUSE you need only to specify *drive*.

Switch Files

Some of the LANtastic utilities allow you to put the specification of switches in a text file called a *switch file*. This means you can avoid entering complex command line specifications. The name of the switch file is preceded by an at sign (@). The general form of this switch is @*file*.

The name of the switch file, *file*, can be any legal DOS filename optionally preceded by the file's path. Thus, you could have @SRVRLUCY.SWI, if the file is going to be in the current directory, or @C:\LANTASTI\SRVRLUCY.SWI, if you want to be certain of finding the file. These files don't have to have an .SWI extension, but it does make it easier to find them.

The switch files can reference other switch files to any depth you like. However, you should avoid this, as you can get confused about which switches will actually be used.

The contents of the switch files are one line per switch, and blank lines are allowed. Comments can be put into the switch file on any line by using a semicolon (;) followed by the comment text. A line can be a comment, a switch, or a switch followed by a comment. For example:

```
;
; This is just a comment line.
;
; The next line is just a switch ...
4SWITCH1 = 1
;
; The next line is a switch that is followed by a comment.
SWITCH2 = 64 ; A comment.
;
```

A real example might be:

```
;
; AILANBIOS switch file, LUCYAILB.SWI
;
MAX_NCBS = 64          ; Set max. # of NETBIOS Control Blocks
MAX_SESSIONS = 64      ; Set to max. # of NETBIOS sessions
NCBS = 64              ; Must match MAX_NCBS
SESSIONS = 64          ; Must match MAX_SESSIONS
VERBOSE                ; Display the configuration
```

The REMOVE Switch

Many terminate-and-stay-resident utilities offer a REMOVE switch. You cannot remove a program if any other memory-resident programs have been loaded. This applies to utilities (things like command line editors and key faking programs), drivers (for mice, scanners, and so on), and applications (such as SideKick). You'll first need to remove all programs that were loaded after the program you want to remove. If you're in doubt whether a LANtastic program can be taken out with its REMOVE switch, try it. You'll get an error message if it can't be removed.

AILANBIO.EXE

(System) Low-level network OS component.

Description

AILANBIO.EXE is Artisoft's Adapter Independent NETBIOS. This program is a system utility that, along with the low-level network driver, forms the basic communications components for the network. In general, most of the default settings for AILANBIO are fine for normal network configurations.

If you plan to change any settings, try it in a safe environment first. A safe time is when the network isn't being used and when there's adequate time to "soak test" the changed system. This involves running software that will exercise the network in much the same way as users would. Weekends, after work, and the wee hours of the night are best.

General Form

```
AILANBIO {HELP¦?}¦{REMOVE}¦{switches}
```

Where {switches} are any combination of:

@file	ACK_TIMEOUT=n
ADAPTER=n	BUFFERS=n
FORCE_ACK_MODE	INITIAL_SEND_SIZE=n
MAX_NAMES=n	MAX_NCBS=n
MPX=n	NCBS=n
RETRY_PERIOD=n	ROM_PATCH
RUN_BURST=n	SESSIONS=n
SIZE=n	TIMEOUT=n
VERBOSE	

@

AILANBIO @*file*

Variables

file is a DOS file name and optional path, maximum size 4096 bytes.

Example

AILANBIO @C:\LANTASTI\AILANBIO.SWI

Description

See the section "Switch Files" in this appendix.

ACK_TIMEOUT

AILANBIO /ACK_TIMEOUT=*n*

Variables

$n = \{0 \ldots 254\}$ ticks. One tick is 0.055 seconds (55 milliseconds). Default: 2 ticks.

Example

AILANBIO /ACK_TIMEOUT=8

Description

For many transactions between network nodes (reading data, writing data, and so on), LANtastic sends and receives acknowledgments that the transaction has succeeded. ACK_TIMEOUT is the amount of time in ticks that this copy of the NETBIOS will wait for an acknowledgment from another node.

If an acknowledgment isn't received in the timeout period, the transaction data will be sent again. The value for ACK_TIMEOUT might need to be increased if the node starts to make one or more single beeps during network accesses. This signals that there have been timeouts that may be due to:

- A heavily loaded network making the node wait too long for a response.
- A cabling problem causing retries.

If you know that network activity is high at the time of the indication and it happens frequently, you may want to increase the value just to stop the irritating noise. In general, don't. The beep isn't really that bad, and increasing the value may cause you to miss a more serious network problem.

If the low-level driver sets this value, the ACK_TIMEOUT value is ignored anyway.

> **Caution:** *Don't* set this to a value of 0, or timeouts will occur immediately. Not only will the beeping drive you to distraction, but the node won't operate correctly.

ADAPTER

```
AILANBIO ADAPTER=n
```

 *Networking with LANtastic*

Variables

n = {0 . . . 255}; default = 0

Example

```
AILANBIO ADAPTER=2
```

Description

This switch tells the copy of NETBIOS which network adapter it is working with. See Chapter 10, "Advanced Topics," for more details on how to use multiple adapters.

BUFFERS

```
AILANBIO BUFFERS=n
```

Variables

n = {0 . . . 254} buffers; default = 1 buffer

Example

```
AILANBIO BUFFERS=4
```

Description

If you increase the value set by this switch, performance may improve. It isn't possible to say precisely how much performance will improve, as it will vary with each situation (what application, how it works, and so on). The trade-off is that each buffer takes the number of bytes of memory set by the SIZE switch.

Utilities Referemce

Note: If LANCACHE.EXE is in use, the BUFFERS switch value must be set to zero.

Note: In general, don't mess with this switch unless you're willing to run benchmarks to establish whether performance for a particular environment improves as you increase the value.

FORCE_ACK_MODE

    AILANBIO FORCE_ACK_MODE

Description

This switch controls whether acknowledgments will be required before a remote mode can proceed with whatever transaction it is conducting with this node. If you're using Artisoft's Central Station (see Chapter 10, "Advanced Topics") or a regular PC as a dial-in modem-connection service to a remote PC, you may want to set this switch to prevent problems. If you're getting problems, they'll be indicated by beeps (see "Audio Warnings," later in this appendix) and by very poor performance.

HELP or ?

    AILANBIO HELP

Description

If you use this switch, AILANBIO.EXE will display a list of all of the switches available (see Figure C.1).

```
C:\> AILANBIO /HELP
Adapter Independent AI-LANBIOS(R) V3.01 - (C) Copyright 1992 ARTISOFT Inc.


Valid command line switches:
    ACK_TIMEOUT= Range 0 to 254 decimal
    ADAPTER= Range 0 to 255 decimal
    BUFFERS= Range 0 to 254 decimal
    FORCE_ACK_MODE
    HELP
    INITIAL_SEND_SIZE= Range 1 to 65535 decimal
    MAX_NAMES= Range 1 to 253 decimal
    MAX_NCBS= Range 1 to 255 decimal
    MAX_SESSIONS= Range 1 to 254 decimal
    MPX= Range C0 to FF hex
    NCBS= Range 1 to 255 decimal
    REMOVE
    RETRY_PERIOD= Range 0 to 254 decimal
    ROM_PATCH
    RUN_BURST= Range 0 to 254 decimal
    SESSIONS= Range 1 to 254 decimal
    SIZE= Range 1 to 4300 decimal
    VERBOSE
    ?
    @ Range 0 to 4096 byte switch file
             ---- AI-LANBIOS(R) NOT installed ----
```

Figure C.1 *The output from the help switch of AILANBIO.EXE.*

INITIAL_SEND_SIZE

```
AILANBIO INITIAL_SEND_SIZE=n
```

Variables

$n = \{1 \ldots 65535\}$ bytes; default = 570 bytes.

Example

    AILANBIO INITIAL_SEND_SIZE=640

Description

When a LANtastic node sends the first message of a sequence across the network to another node, the size of that first packet of data is determined by this setting. This allows a transaction (the complete sequence) to complete faster, but each packet will use the network longer. In a lightly loaded environment, increasing this may give you better performance if you are moving large amounts of data between nodes. If you change this setting from the default value, you must change it for every node on the network.

> **Note:** From the point of view of managing your network, it is much easier not to change this setting, as you must make sure all nodes use the same value.

MAX_NAMES

    AILANBIO MAX_NAMES=n

Variables

$n = \{1 \ldots 253\}$ names; default = 32 names

Example

    AILANBIO MAX_NAMES=16

Description

In a NETBIOS network, each node has at least one name, and sometimes several. The local copy of NETBIOS registers the names for the machine it's on. If you run out of names, you'll get a message `Name Table Full`. Each additional name requires 16 bytes of memory.

> **Note:** REDIR.EXE requires five names to operate. If remote booting is enabled, a sixth name is needed for SERVER.EXE. For the single-node version of LANtastic that uses Artisoft's adapter-independent NETBIOS, one more name is needed.

MAX_NCBS

```
AILANBIO MAX_NCBS=n
```

Variables

$n = \{1 \ldots 255\}$ NCBs; default = 32 NCBs

Example

```
AILANBIO MAX_NCBS=16
```

Description

Network Control Blocks, or NCBs, are data blocks that are used by programs to communicate with the NETBIOS. Each NCB requires 48 bytes of memory. If the switch NCBS specifies a value greater than MAX_NCBS, the NCBS switch determines the number allocated. As the default for NCBS is 32, the default for MAX_NCBS, 8, is ignored.

 **Note:** You need to set MAX_NCBS equal to the number required at maximum by applications that use the NETBIOS. To calculate the required number, see Table C.2.

Table C.2 Calculating the value of the MAX_NCBS switch for AILANBIO.

Program	NCB requirements	Value
REDIR	Total requirement	4
SERVER	Basic requirement	3
	Number of logins	___
	Number of server tasks	___
	Number of adapters	___
NET CHAT	Total requirement (optional)	(8)
Other	(for other NETBIOS programs)	___
	MAX_NCBS value	___

MAX_SESSIONS

```
AILANBIO MAX_SESSIONS=n
```

Variables

$n = \{1 \ldots 254\}$ sessions; default = 32 sessions

Networking with LANtastic

Example

```
AILANBIO MAX_SESSIONS=64
```

Description

A connection between two computers is called a *session*. Each node on a LANtastic network that is involved in a session must have resources allocated to support it. This switch controls the number of simultaneous sessions that a node can support. If you are only a client or a dedicated server, each login to a server or from a client counts as one session. If you are a combined client and server, you must be able to support enough sessions for each server login you make and for each login that is made to your local server (including any you make to that local server). Each session requires 80 bytes of memory.

> **Note:** The value of MAX_SESSIONS must be high enough to allow one session for each login you make to other servers, one for each login to the local server (if loaded), and two if you will be logging into your local server. You can use Table C.3 to calculate the value required for MAX_SESSIONS.

Table C.3 Calculating the value of the MAX_SESSIONS switch for AILANBIO.

Logins to other servers	___
Remote logins to local server	___
Local login to local server (optional)	(2)
MAX_SESSIONS value	___

MPX

    AILANBIO MPX=n

Variables

$n = \{C0 \ldots FF\}$; default = C7

Example

    AILANBIO MPX=C8

Description

The MPX, or MultiPleX number, is a setting that identifies the "channel" used to communicate with the low-level driver. Each driver is started with a unique MPX number, and a separate NETBIOS is required for each driver. You need to change this only if you're using multiple network adapters (see Chapter 10, "Advanced Topics," for more details about using multiple adapters) or if some other component of your PC has already used the default MPX.

NCBS

    AILANBIO NCBS=n

Variables

$n = \{1 \ldots 255\}$ NCBs; default = 32 NCBs

Example

    AILANBIO NCBS=64

Description

The NCBS switch specifies the number of Network Control Blocks that the NETBIOS should use. A value higher than that set for MAX_NCBS causes the NCBS value to be used.

REMOVE

    AILANBIO REMOVE

Description

The REMOVE switch removes the NETBIOS from memory if there is nothing else (for example, REDIR or SERVER) loaded on top of it. This is useful if you want to reclaim memory in order to use a very large application.

RETRY_PERIOD

    AILANBIO RETRY_PERIOD=n

Variables

$n = \{0 \ldots 254\}$ ticks (0.055 seconds, 55 ms each); default = 2 ticks (0.11 seconds)

Example

```
AILANBIO RETRY_PERIOD=8
```

Description

The RETRY_PERIOD switch controls the amount of time that a node should wait before retrying an operation (after you hear the beep). For very slow nodes or in the case of heavily loaded networks, increasing this value will cure the problem. Don't increase it too high, or serious network problems may be hard to recognize as they'll be masked. Like ACK_TIMEOUT, if the low-level driver sets this, the RETRY_PERIOD switch will be ignored.

> **Note:** You may find that decreasing the value of this switch improves performance for high-performance network adapters, such as EtherNet, where the network isn't heavily loaded. Where the network is heavily loaded or slow (such as with LANtastic Z or Central Station, see Chapter 10, "Advanced Topics"), decreasing the value of this switch may make performance worse.

ROM_PATCH

```
AILANBIO ROM_PATCH
```

Description

This switch is only used for network adapters that have the AILANBIOS in an on-board remote boot ROM chip (Read-Only Memory). For these adapters, the ROM_PATCH switch enhances the performance of the NETBIOS.

RUN_BURST

    AILANBIO RUN_BURST=n

Variables

$n = \{0 \ldots 254\}$ ticks (0.06 seconds or 60 ms each); default: 10 ticks (0.6 seconds)

Example

    AILANBIO RUN_BURST=20

Description

To control how much processing time an application receives, the RUN_BURST switch specifies the maximum number of ticks that the NETBIOS can run before returning control to the application or DOS. The larger this value, the lower the performance of applications that are run on that node. If you find that the network performance of the node is slow, this value may be increased to compensate. This switch is ignored if the low-level driver sets the value.

> **Note:** For people trying to optimize performance with applications running on a server, the following may help you understand the interaction of AILANBIO with the rest of the system. AILANBIO receives control on three different events: when the network adapter causes an interrupt, when there is a timer interrupt, and when there is a call to the NETBIOS by an application. If your application does anything out of the ordinary, such as disabling or trapping interrupts, you'll find that you can lose connections or, at the very least, have poor server performance. Increasing RUN_BURST may, in some instances, improve this situation.

SESSIONS

AILANBIO SESSIONS=n

Variables

n = {1 . . . 254} sessions; default = 32 sessions

Example

AILANBIOS SESSIONS=64

Description

This switch allows you to determine how many sessions out of those specified by MAX_SESSIONS should be used. If this value is higher than MAX_SESSIONS, the MAX_SESSIONS value will be used. This switch doesn't affect the amount of memory used.

SIZE

AILANBIO SIZE=n

Variables

n = {1 . . . 4300} bytes; default = 570 bytes

Example

AILANBIO SIZE=640

Description

The SIZE switch controls the number of bytes of RAM that each buffer allocated by the BUFFERS switch will use. The larger the buffer size, the better the performance. The trade-off is obviously RAM use — each buffer takes up memory. All computers on the network must use the same SIZE value.

> **Note:** In general, *don't* change this value. You'll wind up having to change for all nodes, and this could prove to be a major pain if you have to upgrade, reconfigure, or install a new node.

TIMEOUT

```
AILANBIO TIMEOUT=n
```

Variables

n = {1 . . . 254} ticks (0.5 seconds or 500 ms each); default = 8 ticks (4 seconds)

Example

```
AILANBIO TIMEOUT=16
```

Description

For certain network transactions, the TIMEOUT switch value specifies how long to wait before signaling (with a beep) that there's a problem and retrying the operation. The value defines how many ticks the timeout will be. This switch is ignored if the low-level driver sets the value.

Utilities Referemce

Note: If many users are each logging into a server at the same time and this value is too low, some users may experience timeout beeps. If you're getting a lot of beeps on a work station, set this to a higher value (say,16), and it should stop.

VERBOSE

```
AILANBIO VERBOSE
```

Description

The VERBOSE switch causes the AILANBIOS to display configuration data when it finishes loading and initializing. Figure C.2 shows a sample output from using this switch.

```
C:\>AILANBIO /VERBOSE
Adapter Independent AI-LANBIOS(R) V3.01 - (C) Copyright 1992
ARTISOFT Inc.
AEX AI-LANBIOS(R) driver V3.01 - (C) Copyright 1992 ARTISOFT Inc.

Command line                   verbose
Adapter number                 0         Low level MPX number         C7
Maximum number of NCBs         32        Run burst time in ticks      10
Maximum number of sessions     32        System timeout in 1/2 seconds 8
Maximum number of names        16        Retry period in ticks        2

Variables:
Default number of NCBs         32        ACK timeout in ticks         2

Variables:
Default number of sessions     32        Number of buffers            1
Buffer size                    570       Initial send size            570
Bytes of memory used           15168
```

Figure C.2 *Output from using the VERBOSE switch with AILANBIOS.*

305

AIMOVE.EXE

(System) Performance enhancement (remote boot nodes only)

Description

AIMOVE.EXE is a system utility program that moves the AILANBIOS code out of a network adapter's remote boot ROM and into regular memory. This allows the AILANBIOS code to execute faster. It reportedly improves performance by more than 50% and uses only 7 KB of RAM.

General Form

AIMOVE

ALONE.EXE

(System) Performance enhancement

Description

If you have a *dedicated* server (that is, a server that does nothing else and does not run any local applications), you can run ALONE.EXE to increase its performance. When ALONE is running, it displays status information (see Figure C.3) on what logged-in users are doing.

When ALONE is running, the screen display shows two lines per user. The top line gives:

- The user's unique identification number.
- Name.
- The name of the machine they're using.
- The last command they executed.
- The number of bytes that they've read and written from the server.
- The number of requests that user has made.
- The user's privileges.

The second line gives:

- The number of minutes until that user will be logged out automatically.
- The complete specification of the last file that the user accessed.

There are four actions that can be taken when ALONE is running:

- Press F1 to show help information. Pressing Z will switch between a large and a small help window. The help window contains a complete description of all of the data displayed.
- Press F2 to enable or disable the display of the names of files accessed. Selecting display off gives a slight performance improvement.

Networking with LANtastic

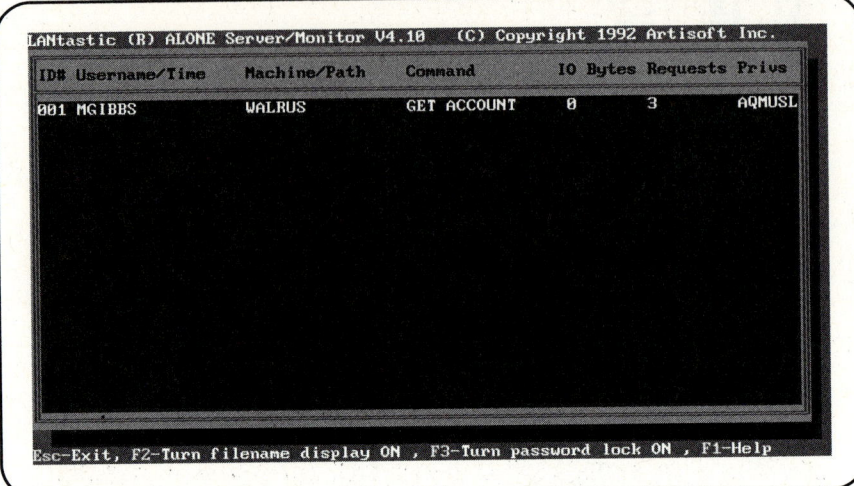

Figure C.3 The monitor screen of the ALONE utility.

- Press F3 to enable or disable password access to exit from ALONE. The first time you press F3, you'll be asked to enter a password twice with no echo (the second time for verification). By pressing F3 again or Esc, you'll be asked for the password.

- Press Esc to exit the ALONE utility.

General Form

ALONE

LANCACHE.EXE

(System) Performance enhancement.

Description

LANCACHE is a disk-caching utility that boosts the network performance of a node. The theory behind LANCACHE.EXE's operation is that because hard disks are mechanical devices, there are several factors that slow down the speed at which you can store and retrieve data (see Figure C.4). The first factor is moving the read/write heads to the correct track. This could be as small a movement as from one track to the next or as large as from the outermost to the innermost track. The average time for this operation is called the *seek time*. The next factor is that when the heads get to the correct track, the data block you want may not be ready to read. In that case, you have to wait for the disk to rotate so that the block is readable. This is called the *latency* of the disk.

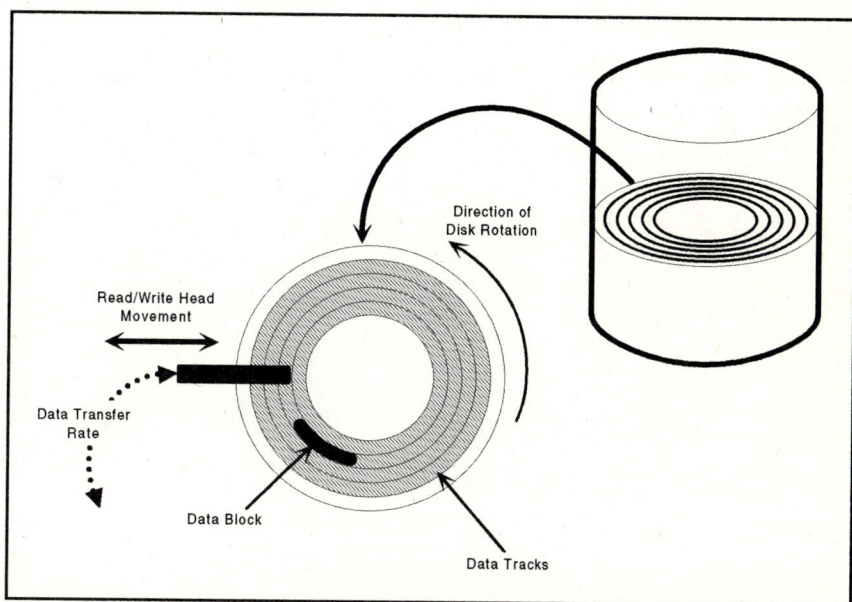

Figure C.4 *The issues of disk performance.*

Finally, the rate at which data can be read and transferred to the PC's memory affects performance. Some hard disks are interfaced to the PC through very high speed controllers, but, as always, the performance of the controller and hard disk is a trade-off against cost.

LANCACHE.EXE sits between the hard disk and the rest of the system and, by intelligently handling disk reads and writes, can significantly boost the overall system response. LANCACHE.EXE relies on two main techniques to improve performance:

- *Read-ahead buffering* reads not only the data blocks your program asks for, but also as many more blocks as will fit into the cache size you specify. This means that if the next data blocks you want have already been read into the buffer, there won't be any delay due to waiting for the hard disk. This obviously will improve the performance of programs that read a file *sequentially*, that is, from beginning to end. For *random access files* (files structured into records of a set size that can be read from, and written to, at any position within the file), LANCACHE.EXE will improve performance for large records that require multiple transfers across the network.

- *Write-behind* (also called *delayed write*) is a technique that queues disk writes in the cache so that they can be written in sequence. When several users are reading and writing to different files in different locations on the disk, the disk heads (the components that read and write data) have to move from location to location, pretty much at random. LANCACHE.EXE accumulates write data in the cache until the cache is full, the system is not busy (a user-definable period and called *variable delayed writes* by Artisoft), or a preset time limit is reached. At this point, LANCACHE.EXE writes the data to disk and, because the writes are done in track order (called *elevator seeking*), the process is as efficient as possible.

Because LANCACHE.EXE is tightly integrated with the rest of the system, input and output to the system can occur even while disk reads and writes are being done in the background. Artisoft refers to this as *overlapped CPU and I/O functions*.

General Form

LANCACHE {/HELP|/?}|{/REMOVE}|{*switches*}

Where {*switches*} are any combination of:

{@*file*}	{AFTER_IO_DELAY=*n*}
{CACHE_SIZE=*n*}	{DISABLE}
{DISK=*n*}	{ENABLE}
{FAST_IRQ=*n*}	{FLUSH}
{HELP}	{LONG_WRITE_DELAY=*n*}
{RELEASE}	{REMOVE}
{RESET}	{SHUTDOWN_KEY=*key*}
{STAT=*op*}	{TYPE=*type*}
{VERBOSE}	{WITH_WINDOWS}

LANCACHE @*file*

Variables

file is a DOS file name and optional path; maximum size 1000 bytes.

Example

LANCACHE C:\LANTASTI\LANCACHE.SWI

Description

See the section "Switch Files" earlier in this appendix.

AFTER_IO_DELAY

LANCACHE AFTER_IO_DELAY=n

Variables

n = {0 . . . 3600} seconds; default = 3 seconds

Example

LANCACHE AFTER_IO_DELAY=6

Description

When data is written to the cache, a timer is set to the value of AFTER_IO_DELAY. If there has been no read or write request and the amount of time (in seconds) specified by this switch passes, any data in the cache waiting to be written will be "flushed" to disk (the data will be written). If a read or write occurs before AFTER_IO_DELAY passes, the timer is reset and the countdown starts again. This value must be less than LONG_WRITE_DELAY or the LONG_WRITE_DELAY value will be used.

CACHE_SIZE

LANCACHE CACHE_SIZE=n

Variables

$n = \{16 \ldots 16000\}$ kilobytes; default = (see below).

Example

`LANCACHE CACHE_SIZE=640`

The CACHE_SIZE switch sets the amount of memory that LANCACHE will use. The exact amount used may be less than you specify as LANCACHE will round down to the exact amount that it can use. The default if the CACHE_SIZE switch isn't set will depend on the setting of the TYPE switch. If the TYPE is not set, LANCACHE will use either 384 KB of normal memory or all of extended memory if it is available. If the type is set, LANCACHE will use all of the available memory of that type.

DISABLE

`LANCACHE DISABLE`

Description

The cache is flushed (that is, all outstanding disk writes are done) and the cache is no longer used.

DISK

`LANCACHE DISK=n`

Variables

$n = \{0 \ldots 3\}$; default = 0

Example

```
LANCACHE DISK=1
```

Description

Specifies which physical disk drive will be cached. Only one drive at a time may be cached, but if you cache a physical drive that is partitioned into logical drives (for example, physical drive 0 might be partitioned into logical drives C and D), all logical drives will be cached.

> **Note:** If you aren't using the first hard disk (drive 0), you *must* specify the DRIVE switch on the command line.

ENABLE

```
LANCACHE ENABLE
```

Description

If you issued a LANCACHE command with the DISABLE switch, you can restart the caching system using the command again with the ENABLE switch specified.

FAST_IRQ

```
LANCACHE FAST_IRQ=n
```

Variables

$n = \{0 \ldots 15\}$; default = (none)

Description

This is a very technical facility that allows you to specify that a particular interrupt routine triggered by the specified IRQ number is not to be intercepted by LANCACHE. This allows routines that provide timing-sensitive services to execute without delays. This might be of use if you have a slow PC that is running LANtastic with LANCACHE and is losing characters that are being received on a serial port. Setting FAST_IRQ to a value of 4 if COM1 is being used or 3 for COM2 may cure the problem.

FLUSH

LANCACHE FLUSH

Description

This switch simply forces a flush of the cache to write all unwritten data to disk. This does not stop caching (use DISABLE to both flush and disable).

HELP or ?

LANCACHE HELP

Description

If you use this switch, LANCACHE.EXE will display a list of all of the switches available (see Figure C.5).

```
C:\> LANCACHE /HELP
LANtastic (R) Cache (LANCACHE) V2.17 - (C) Copyright 1992 ARTISOFT Inc.

Valid command line switches:
    AFTER_IO_DELAY= Range 0 to 3600 decimal
    CACHE_SIZE= Range 16 to 16000 decimal
    DISABLE
    DISK= One of the following choices:
        0 1 2 3
    ENABLE
    FAST_IRQ= Performs special action
    FLUSH
    HELP
    LONG_WRITE_DELAY= Range 0 to 3600 decimal
    RELEASE
    REMOVE
    RESET
    SHUTDOWN_KEY= One of the following choices:
        A B C D E F G H I J K L M N O P Q R S T U V W X Y Z DEL
    STAT= One of the following choices:
        INFO RESET
    TYPE= One of the following choices:
        CONVENTIONAL EMS EXTENDED XMS
    VERBOSE
    WITH_WINDOWS
    ?
    @ Range 0 to 1000 byte switch file
            ---- LANtastic Cache NOT Installed ----
```

Figure C.5 The output from the help switch of LANCACHE.EXE.

LONG_WRITE_DELAY

LANCACHE LONG_WRITE_DELAY=n

Variables

$n = \{0 \ldots 36000\}$ seconds; default = 12 seconds

Example

```
LANCACHE LONG_WRITE_DELAY=20
```

Description

The LONG_WRITE_DELAY value is the maximum amount of time that LANCACHE will allow to pass before it writes any cached data to disk. If you set this to 0, LANCACHE will immediately write data to disk as soon as it is intercepted (effectively making LANCACHE of no use). This value should be greater than AFTER_IO_DELAY.

RELEASE

```
LANCACHE RELEASE
```

Description

The RELEASE switch flushes the cache, disables caching, and returns all memory that it was using for caching back to the system without removing the LANCACHE program itself. The cache can be restarted using the command LANCACHE ENABLE.

REMOVE

```
LANCACHE REMOVE
```

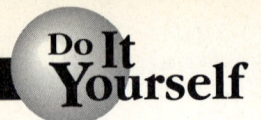

Description

REMOVE does everything that RELEASE does and removes the LANCACHE program from memory as well. See "General Notes" earlier in this appendix for more details.

RESET

LANCACHE RESET

Description

RESET is the same as FLUSH but also sets to zero all of the counters that provide statistical and performance data. This is useful if you are running benchmarks to establish the best configuration.

SHUTDOWN_KEY

LANCACHE SHUTDOWN_KEY=key

Variables

key = {A . . . Z|DEL}; default = DEL

Example

LANCACHE SHUTDOWN_KEY=Z

Description

When the specified character combined with Ctrl-Alt is typed, the cache is flushed. This is useful if there is a program that intercepts the default (Ctrl-Alt-Del).

STAT

    LANCACHE STAT {INFO¦RESET}

Examples

LANCACHE STAT INFO

LANCACHE STAT RESET

Description

The STAT switch either gives information about the performance (INFO) of LANCACHE or resets (RESET) the various statistics counters. Figure C.6 shows the output for the value INFO.

```
C:\> LANCACHE /STAT=INFO
LANtastic (R) Cache (LANCACHE) V2.17 - (C) Copyright 1992 ARTISOFT Inc.

              LANtastic (R) LANcache statistics
              ---------------------------------

        Minutes cache active 0        Cache size in K bytes 2227
           After-I/O delay 3             Long-write delay 12

         Total read requests 8         Total write requests 1
          Actual disk reads 12          Actual disk writes 0
     Actual disk sectors read 187  Actual disk sectors written 0
       Number of track flushes 0     Number of cache flushes 0
            Read cache hits 3             Write cache hits 1
          Read cache misses 12          Write cache misses 0

        Read cache hit rate 20%       Write cache hit rate 100%
C:\>
```

Figure C.6 *Sample output from the command LANCACHE /STAT=INFO.*

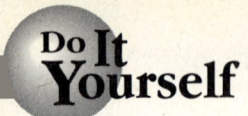

TYPE

LANCACHE TYPE=type

Variables

type = {CONVENTIONAL|EMS|EXTENDED|XMS}; default = EXTENDED

Example

LANCACHE TYPE=XMS

Description

The TYPE switch specifies what type of memory LANCACHE should use. For EMS, extended, and XMS memory, you must have an appropriate driver installed. Conventional memory is usually not much use, as there's not enough of it to make a decent-sized cache.

> **Note:** If you're using extended memory, you can omit this switch.

VERBOSE

LANCACHE VERBOSE

Description

The VERBOSE switch causes the LANCACHE to display configuration data when it finishes loading and initializing. Figure C.7 shows a sample output from using this switch.

```
C:\>LANCACHE    /TYPE=XMS/VERBOSE
LANtastic (R) Cache (LANCACHE) V2.17 - (C) Copyright 1992 ARTISOFT Inc.

Command line              /TYPE=XMS/VERBOSE

Cache memory type         XMS        Cached disk drive number 0
After-I/O delay           3          Long-write delay         12
K byte cache memory size  2227       Conventional memory used 29456
              ---- LANtastic Cache Installed ----

C:\>
```

Figure C.7   *Sample output from using the VERBOSE switch with LANCACHE.*

WITH_WINDOWS

```
LANCACHE WITH_WINDOWS
```

Description

Use this switch to let LANCACHE know Windows will be used (see Chapter 10, "Advanced Topics"). If this switch is given, AFTER_IO_DELAY and LONG_WRITE_DELAY must both be set to 0.

LANCHECK.EXE

(System) Connection testing and performance evaluation.

Description

See the section "The Menu Interfaces" later in this appendix.

General Form

LANCHECK {name}{/MONO}

nname

LANCHECK name

Variables

name is any name for this copy of LANCHECK to identify itself with.

Example

LANCHECK LUCY

Description

Assigns a name to the node. If the PC already has a machine name specified from running REDIR, then *nname* can be omitted.

 *Networking with LANtastic*

/MONO

LANCHECK {*nname*} /MONO

Example

LANCHECK LUCY /MONO

Description

If the MONO switch is specified, the display will be in monochrome. This makes it easier to read on laptop PCs and monochrome monitors.

LANPUP.EXE

(User) Network environment control.

Description

LANPUP is a pop-up (terminate-and-stay-resident) utility that is almost a memory-resident equivalent of the NET utility. I say *almost* because the functions available are organized a little differently from NET's layout. LANPUP covers four main functional areas:

- *Session control.* Logging into and out of servers.
- *Resource connections.* Managing connections to shared resources.
- *Printer queue management.* Managing printer queue jobs.
- *Electronic messaging.* Sending and receiving electronic mail.

General Form

    LANPUP {switches}

LINE

    LANPUP LINE=n

Variables

$n = \{0 \ldots 20\}$; default = 4

Description

The LINE switch specifies on what line of the screen the pop-up should appear. Zero is the top line of the screen.

REMOVE

LANPUP / REMOVE

Description

Removes the LANPUP utility from memory. See "General Notes" earlier in this appendix for more details.

STAND_ALONE

LANPUP STAND_ALONE

Description

The STAND_ALONE switch tells LANPUP to operate as a non-memory-resident program. This is a rather odd use of the term stand-alone which is usually used to describe non-networked PCs or programs. When you finish with LANPUP, having been started in this mode, the program exits leaving nothing in memory.

STACK

LANPUP STACK

Description

When LANPUP pops up, it needs to use a facility call a *stack*. To conserve memory, it will use the stack of whatever program it pops up over. In the case of programs that have small stacks, such as Microsoft Works, this will cause problems such as stack overflow messages or even mysterious software crashes. If you pop up LANPUP and everything falls apart (the system crashes on pop-up, the application that you popped up over crashes when you return to it, and so on), try using this switch.

Usage Notes

If LANPUP was not started with the STAND_ALONE switch, it is activated by pressing the key combination Ctrl-Alt-L. The first display, either when LANPUP is popped up or run "stand-alone," is the window shown in Figure C.8.

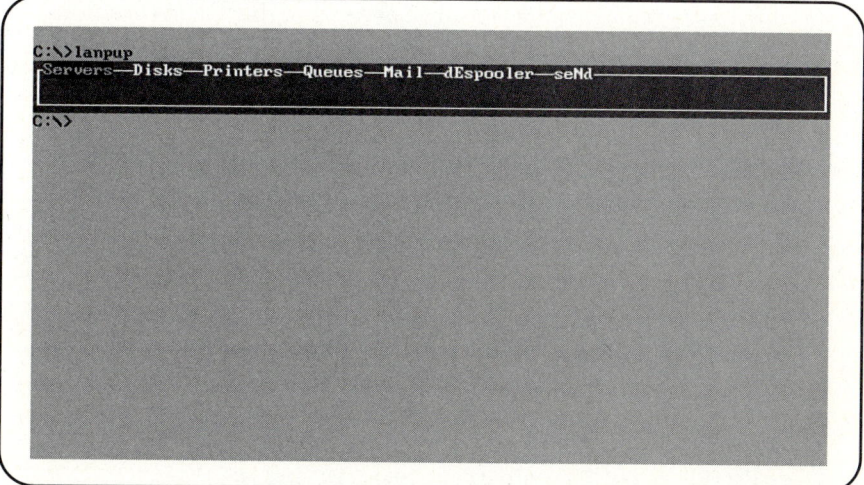

Figure C.8 *The first screen of the LANPUP utility showing the main options.*

Select the function you want from those listed at the top of the box using the space bar to move to the next option on the right, the right arrow and the left arrow, or the capitalized letter of an option. When the highlight is on the option you want, press Enter to start the option. The LANPUP program has option lists under some of the main options. To return to a previous option list or cancel an operation, press Esc. To quit LANPUP, press Esc when you're at the main options.

Servers

Allows you to log into or out of servers.

To log into a server, either:

- Use the up arrow and the down arrow to select the correct server from the list of servers you are currently logged into. This allows you to log in again under another user name.

Or

- Press Ins and enter the server's name, or use the up arrow and the down arrow to scroll through the list of servers you are currently connected to. Once the target server's name is correct, press Enter and then enter your name and password.

To log out of a server, use the up arrow and the down arrow to find the correct server and press Del. You'll be asked to confirm or cancel.

Disks

To connect to, or disconnect from, a shared disk resource, select Drives.

Note: If you want to redirect a drive that is currently redirected, you don't need to disconnect the drive first; just use the following procedure to redefine the connection.

To connect to a server's disk resource, select the local drive to redirect by using the up arrow and the down arrow or enter the drive's letter (the drive's current assignments are shown). Press Enter and the name of a server that you are logged into (whichever is alphabetically the first) will be displayed in flashing characters. If this is not the server you want, either:

- Use the up arrow and the down arrow to select the correct server from the list of servers you are currently logged into.

- Press Ins and enter the target server's name. Once the target server's name is correct, press Enter and then type your name and password.

The first shared disk resource for that server is then displayed. Use the up arrow and the down arrow to scroll through the resources until you find the one you want and press Enter.

To disconnect a local drive from a shared disk resource, select the drive by using the up arrow and the down arrow or enter the drive's letter. When the correct drive is displayed, press Del. You'll be asked to confirm or cancel the operation.

Printers

To redirect, or cancel the redirection of, printer output to shared printer resources, select Printers from the main options.

> **Note:** If you want to redefine a port that is currently redirected, select the port and press Delete to disconnect the port from the printer resource first; then use the following procedure to make a new connection.

To redirect a port, use the up arrow and the down arrow to scroll through the ports (their current assignments are shown). When the correct port shows, press Enter. The name of a server that you are logged into (whichever is alphabetically the first) will be displayed in flashing characters. If this is not the server you want, either:

- Use the up arrow and the down arrow to select the correct server from the list of servers you are currently logged into.

  Or

- Press Ins and enter the target server's name. Once the target server's name is correct, press Enter and then type your name and password.

The first shared printer resource for that server is then displayed. Use the up arrow and the down arrow to scroll through the printer resources until you find the one you want and press Enter.

To disconnect a port from a shared printer, select the port by using the up arrow and the down arrow or enter the drive's letter. When the correct drive is displayed, press Del. You'll be asked to confirm or cancel the operation.

Queues

The Queues option allows you to manipulate the printer queues of a server.

> **Note:** Although Artisoft's Technical Manual version 2.01 says that "LANPUP allows you to look through the printer and mail queues and control the entries listed there," the Queues: option allows you to do this only with printer queues. Use the Mail option to manage Mail queues.

You need to have the Super Queue (Q) privilege to do anything to the queues. When you select the option, a list of suboptions appears (see Figure C.9).

```
C:\>lanpup
Servers  Disks  Printers  Queues  Mail  dEspooler  seNd
         Hold  reLease  Delete  Read  rUsh
C:\>
```

Figure C.9 *The suboptions under Queues.*

The display will show (alphabetically) the first server you're logged into. If this is not the server you want, either:

- Use the up arrow and the down arrow to select the correct server from the list of servers you are currently logged into.

  Or

- Press Ins and enter the target server's name. Once the target server's name is correct, press Enter and then type your name and password.

Use the up arrow and the down arrow to select the required printer queue and press Enter. You can then use the up arrow and the down arrow to scroll through the entries in the selected queue. Pressing the key for the capitalized letter of one of the suboptions will invoke that function. The functions are:

Hold   Prevents a print job from being serviced until you select the reLease option for that job.

reLease   Allows a print job that was on Hold to be serviced.

Delete   Removes a print job.

Read   Allows you to read the data in a print job.

rUsh   The rUsh option makes a print job move to the head of the queue. It will be serviced as soon as the job being currently serviced (if there is one) finishes.

Mail

When you select the Mail option, the display will show the (alphabetically) first server you're logged into. If this is not the server whose mail queue you want to look at, either:

- Use the up arrow and the down arrow to select the correct server from the list of servers you are currently logged into.

  Or

- Press Ins and enter the target server's name. Once the target server's name is correct, press Enter and then type your name and password.

You can now Read, Delete, or Send mail (see Figure C.10).

Networking with LANtastic

```
C:\>lanpup
 Servers─Disks─Printers─Queues─Mail─dEspooler─seNd
         Read─Delete─Send
C:\>
```

Figure C.10 The suboptions under Mail.

The first item in your list of mail is displayed. You can use the up arrow and down arrow to scroll through the message headings, and whatever suboption you select will be performed on the currently displayed item.

Read

If you select Read, you are asked for a file name. You can now do three things with the mail item:

- Entering a name will store the current message in a file.
- Entering CON (for console) or pressing Enter will display the message on the screen.
- Entering a printer port (COM1, COM2, LPT1, LPT2, LPT3) will send the message contents to whatever printer (local or network) is connected to it.

Delete

This suboption (unsurprisingly) deletes the message.

Send

When you select Send:

1. You'll be asked for a user name. Type the user's login name and press Enter.

2. You will be asked to enter a comment (you can leave the line blank). Press Enter.

3. You'll be asked if you're attaching a voice file (see Chapter 10, "Advanced Topics"), if so, type Y and press Enter. You'll be asked for the name of the file containing the voice mail message. Type in the name and press Enter. You'll be returned to the suboptions list.

4. If you answer N to the voice file question, you'll be prompted for a filename. Enter either the path and name of an existing file, CON, or press Enter. Entering CON or pressing Enter allows you to enter text from the console. Finish the text entry by pressing Esc. The editor is very simple and allows you only to move the cursor right and left and change from Insert mode to Overtype mode. You'll now return to the suboptions list.

dEspooler

To use this option, you need to have the Super Queue (Q) privilege. The output to a shared printer is controlled by a piece of software called a *spooler*. The process of queuing data for a printer is called *spooling*, and outputting to a printer is called *despooling*. When you select the dEspooler option from the main options, the display will show the (alphabetically) first server you're logged into. If this is not the server whose mail queue you want to look at, either:

- Use the up arrow and the down arrow to select the correct server from the list of servers you are currently logged into.

    Or

- Press Ins and enter the target server's name. Once the target server's name is correct, press Enter and then type your name and password.

Once you've selected a server, a set of suboptions are displayed (see Figure C.11).

```
C:\>lanpup
 Servers—Disks—Printers—Queues—Mail—dEspooler—seNd
LPT1 ENABLED
 Halt—Stop—Pause—sIngle—sTart—Restart
C:\>
```

Figure C.11   *The suboptions under dEspooler.*

This facility allows you to control the despooling operations in several ways:

Halt   Stops despooling immediately and abandons the current job.

Stop   Stops despooling at the end of the current job.

Pause   Stops despooling temporarily (doesn't abandon the current job).

sIngle   Allows the next ready job in the printer queue to print then stops the despooler.

sTart   Starts the spooler if it has been halted, stopped, or paused.

Restart   A job that is currently printing, has been halted, or has been paused can be restarted from the beginning.

seNd

This option allows you to send a message of up to 64 characters to a user or group of users. Selecting this option will give you a prompt `To machine:`.

Type the user or group name and press Enter. Then type the message and press Enter again.

Table C.4 summarizes the functions supported by LANPUP.

Table C.4   Summary of LANPUP's functions.

Service	Operation	Main option
Drives	Connect to a network drive	Disks
	Disconnect from a network drive	Disks
	List drive connections	Disks
Login	Log into a server	Servers
	List servers logged into	Servers
Logout	Logout from a server	Servers
Mail	Send electronic mail	Mail
	Read electronic mail	Mail
	List electronic mail messages to screen	Mail
	Print electronic mail message	Mail
	Save electronic mail to file	Mail
	Delete electronic mail	Mail
	Delete any mail item	Mail
	Read any mail item	Mail
Message	Send a message to another user	seNd
Printing	Halt all printing (Q)	dEspooler
	Pause printing (Q)	dEspooler
	Stop printing after current job (Q)	dEspooler
	Print a job then stop (Q)	dEspooler
	Restart a job (Q)	dEspooler
	Start printing all ready jobs (Q)	dEspooler
	Select a network printer	Printer
	Hold a print job (Q)	Queues
	Move a print job to head of queue (Q)	Queues
	Delete a print job	Queues

Note: Operations marked (Q) require Super Queue privilege to use.

NBSETUP.EXE

(System) Performance enhancement.

Description

NBSETUP allows you to modify the setup of a non-Artisoft NETBIOS so that is can be used with a LANtastic system. This utility needs to be used only with NETBIOS programs that don't have their own configuration utility. A NETBIOS may need to be configured because one written to conform to the IBM PC Network Adapter NETBIOS or the IBM Token Ring NETBIOS is usually set to support a maximum of 6 sessions and 12 NCBs. The default settings for AILANBIO are 32 sessions and 32 NCBs. If you use lower values, the number of logins to a server or server connections from a workstation is lower. Note that this will only work with NETBIOSes on adapter 0. NBSETUP can only be run *after* the NETBIOS is loaded and *before* any other network software (REDIR, for example) is run.

To use this utility, you need first to determine whether the NETBIOS you plan to use can support the configuration you need. If the documentation doesn't make it clear what it does and does not support, just execute the NETBIOS and then run NBSETUP CHECK. If this shows that there aren't enough NCBs or sessions, run NBSETUP with switches set as required. Then run NBSETUP again to check that the NETBIOS has reconfigured as required. If you find that it hasn't, you will either have to get an update from the manufacturer of the NETBIOS or live with whatever capabilities it has.

General Form

NBSETUP{/HELP¦/?}¦{/REMOVE}¦{switches}

Where {switches} are any combination of:

{CHECK}   {MAX}

{NCBS=n}   {SESSIONS=n}

CHECK

        NBSETUP CHECK

Description

This switch causes NBSETUP to report on the number of sessions and NCBs supported by the NETBIOS. No matter what other switches are specified with CHECK, they will be ignored.

HELP or ?

        NBSETUP{ /HELP ¦ ?}

Description

If you use this switch, NBSETUP.EXE will display a list of all of the switches available (see Figure C.12).

```
C:\> NBSETUP /HELP
LANtastic (tm) NBsetup V1.0 - (C) Copyright 1988 ARTISOFT Inc.

Valid parameters are
  VERBOSE     Displays NETBIOS information after setting it
  MAX         Sets maximum NCBs and sessions that NETBIOS supports
  NCBS=n      Sets maximum NCBs to n
  SESSIONS=n  Sets maximum sessions to n
  CHECK       Displays current NETBIOS information but does not set it
  ? or HELP   Displays this help text
        ---- NETBIOS parameters have NOT been altered ----

C:\>
```

Figure C.12 The output from the help switch of NBSETUP.EXE.

MAX

NBSETUP MAX

Description

The MAX switch sets the NETBIOS to the greatest number of sessions and NCBs that it can support. The maximum for many NETBIOS programs is often 32 sessions and 32 NCBs but some support 128 of each. Use this switch with caution as you may wind up allocating more resources than you'll need at the expense of memory. Also note that if either the NCBS or SESSIONS switches are set, they will override the MAX switch. Thus,

NBSETUP /NCBS=16/MAX

will set NCBS to 16 and SESSIONS to the maximum value. The defaults for the MAX switch will be as set by other switches or NETBIOS defaults.

NCBS

NBSETUP NCBS=n

Variables

n = {1, 2, 3 . . .} NCBs; default depends on the NETBIOS defaults

Example

NBSETUP NCBS=32

Description

Sets the number of NCBs available. If this value is either zero or more than the NETBIOS can support, the NETBIOS will probably reset itself to its defaults (depending on the implementation).

SESSIONS

    NBSETUP SESSIONS=n

Variables

n = {1, 2, 3 . . .} sessions; default depends on the NETBIOS defaults

Example

    NBSETUP=32

Description

Sets the number of sessions available. If this value is either zero or more than the NETBIOS can support, the NETBIOS will probably reset itself to its defaults (depending on the implementation).

VERBOSE

    NBSETUP VERBOSE

Description

The VERBOSE switch causes the NBSETUP to display configuration data when it finishes loading and initializing. Figure C.13 shows a sample output from using this switch.

Utilities Referemce

```
C:\>NBSETUP /VERBOSE
LANtastic (tm) NBsetup V1.0 - (C) Copyright 1988 ARTISOFT Inc.

Command line:
 verbose
            Configured maximum NCBs 32
         Configured maximum sessions 32
         ---- NETBIOS parameters have been altered ----


C:\>
```

Figure C.13 *Sample output from using the VERBOSE switch with LANCACHE.*

343

NET.EXE

(User) Session control.

Description

The NET utility allows users to:

- Connect drives and printers to shared network resources.
- Manage printer queues (if they have Super Queue [Q] privilege).
- Create, receive, and handle electronic mail (if they have Super Mail [M] privilege).
- "Chat" with another user.
- Log into, and log out from, servers.
- Manage their accounts.
- Show the activity of a server.

NET has two modes of operation: *command line* and *windowed*. The command line options are covered in the following listing of parameters and the windowed mode in the section "The Menu Interfaces" at the end of this appendix.

General Form

NET {HELP¦?}¦{REMOVE}¦{switches}

Where, {switches} are any combination of:

{ATTACH...}	{AUDIT...}	{CHAT...}
{CHANGEPW...}	{CLOCK...}	{COPY...}
{DETACH...}	{DIR...}	{DISABLEA...}
{ECHO...}	{EXPAND...}	{FLUSH...}

Networking with LANtastic

{INDIRECT...}   {LOGIN...}   {LOGOUT...}
{LPT...}   {MAIL...}   {MESSAGE...}
{/MONO}   {/NOERROR}   {PAUSE...}
{POSTBOX...}   {PRINT...}   {QUEUE...}
{RECEIVE...}   {RUN...}   {SHOW...}
{SEND...}   {SHUTDOWN...} {SLOGINS...}
{STREAM...}   {STRING...}   {TERMINATE...}
{UNLINK...}   {UNUSE...}   {USE...}
{USER...}

ATTACH

NET ATTACH{/VERBOSE} sname

Variables

sname = server name

Example

NET ATTACH/VERBOSE \\GRYPHON

Description

Attach all of the resources of sname to whatever drives are available. If you include the VERBOSE switch, detailed information on the connections established will be produced.

Note: Be careful with this command, as the order in which new drives are attached will vary according to which drives have already been redirected.

AUDIT

NET AUDIT sname reason message

Variables

sname = server name

reason = maximum eight characters

message = maximum 64 characters

Example

NET AUDIT \\GRYPHON BACKUP "Lucy's WP files"

Description

Add an entry to the audit trail on sname. The text of the entry will be reason followed by message.

> **Note:** You must have the User Auditing (U) privilege to use this switch.

CHANGEPW

NET CHANGEPW sname old_pw new_pw

Networking with LANtastic

Variables

sname = server name
old_pw = old password
new_pw = new password

Example

NET CHANGEPW LRSMITH MANAGER DERVISH-WHIRL

Description

Change your current password (*old_pw*) to a new password (*new_pw*).

CHAT

NET CHAT

Description

Allows you to establish a connection to another computer and exchange text messages with that computer's current user (see the description "Chat With Another User" in the section "The Menu Interfaces" later in this appendix).

CLOCK

NET CLOCK *sname*

Variables

sname = server name

Example

```
NET CLOCK \\GRYPHON
```

Description

Reset the local date and time to that of the server *sname*.

COPY

```
NET COPY from_file to_file
```

Variables

from_file = file specification

to_file = file specification

Example

```
NET COPY \\GRYPHON\C-DRIVE\DATA.TXT \\GRYPHON\C-DRIVE\DOCS\DATA.NEW
```

Description

The copy switch copies a file, *from_file*, from one location on a server to another file, *to_file*, on the same server. The actual copy operation is done on the server, by the server, and therefore reduces network traffic. Normal copy operations would read the file data across the network to the client who would then write it back across the network to the destination file. The NET COPY does not only reduce network traffic; it is also faster. The trade-off is that it takes server resources, so if you use this service on a very heavily loaded server, you may reduce the server's throughput.

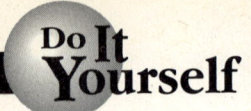

DETACH

NET DETACH sname

Variables

sname = server name

Example

NET DETACH \\GRYPHON

Description

The DETACH switch is the opposite of the ATTACH switch. It removes all of the connections the node you are on has to the server sname.

DIR

NET DIR{/ALL} path{file}

Variables

path = directory path specification

file = file name

Example

NET DIR/ALL \\GRYPHON\C-DRIVE\DOCUMENT\

Description

Displays file and directory information for the specified *path* and optionally the *file*. This differs from the regular DOS DIR command in that it shows extra network information including indirect files. Figure C.14 shows the output from a NET DIR command. The output shows the file name, the attributes, file size (in bytes), creation date, and creation time. Without the /ALL switch, system and hidden files are not displayed.

```
C:>NET DIR/ALL \\GRYPHON\C-DRIVE\DOCUMENT\
        Directory of \\GRYPHON\C-DRIVE\DOCUMENT\

    .              --D----              9-Mar-1992  16:22:12
    ..             --D----              9-Mar-1992  16:22:12
    DYL            --D----              9-Mar-1992  16:22:26
    FLDR-TOC.DOC   -------     5077    13-Mar-1992  12:39:46
    FILEWARE.DOC   -A-----    20131    28-Sep-1991  20:33:30
    FORMS.DOC      -A-----     6378    12-Dec-1991  09:27:06
    AVRY5262.DOC   -------    14491    29-Mar-1992  22:40:46
    IDEAS.DOC      -A-----     2019    29-Aug-1991  01:01:38
    INFOPARA.IND   IA-----    \C-DRIVE\CONTRACT\PARA301.DOC
    KEYCAPS.DOC    -A-----    10921     7-Feb-1991  12:00:06
    MLA-LET.DOC    -------     2871    12-Feb-1992  20:18:26
    MLA-LET2.DOC   -------     3072    12-Feb-1992  20:04:52
    MLA-RES.SYS    -A--SH-     5297     5-Feb-1992  20:07:56
    TEMP.DOC       -A-----    12804     5-Feb-1992  08:46:24
    TEMP2.DOC      -A----R     2272     5-Feb-1992  20:41:12
```

Figure C.14 The output from a NET DIR command.

Note: Although Artisoft documentation refers to DIR showing "attributes," some of these, such as the Directory and Volume label attributes, aren't. These attributes can't be changed without deleting the file, so they are really indicators of the item's type.

The attributes and indicators are:

- **I**   Indirect (LANtastic specific)
- **A**   Archive (DOS attribute)
- **D**   Directory (indicator)
- **V**   Volume label (indicator)
- **S**   System file (DOS attribute)
- **H**   Hidden file (DOS attribute)
- **R**   Read-only file (DOS attribute)

DISABLEA

```
NET DISABLEA sname pw
```

Variables

sname = server name

pw = password

Example

```
NET DISABLEA \\GRYPHON DERVISH-WHIRL
```

Description

This switch is used to disable your account (the name that you logged in with) from further use. The effect of this switch is to set the concurrent logins for your account to zero. To reenable the account use NET_MGR and set concurrent logins to greater than zero.

Utilities Referemce

> **Note:** You can't use DISABLEA to disable your account on the node you're actually on. For example, the user LRSMITH who uses the server named \\LUCY and is logged in on that machine will be denied access if he or she issues a DISABLEA request from that machine for his or her own account on that machine. You can have only one concurrent login to the server when you issue the DISABLEA command.

ECHO

```
NET ECHO message
```

Variables

message = text to remaining length of buffer

Example

```
NET ECHO "The backup process was successful!."
```

Description

The ECHO switch is a more versatile version of the DOS ECHO command. This switch can also be used with LANtastic Special Strings (see "LANtastic Special Strings," later in this appendix).

EXPAND

```
NET EXPAND{/PHYSICAL¦/RECURSE} file
```

Variables

`file` = file name

Example

`NET EXPAND/RECURSE INFOPARA.IND`

Description

The EXPAND switch is used to find the physical, network, or redirected path of a file. Without /PHYSICAL or /RECURSE, the output will show the network path to the file. With /PHYSICAL, the actual path on the server is displayed. /RECURSE is only used for indirect files. It tracks each redirection to reveal the file that an indirect file refers to, no matter how many redirections are involved.

For example, LRSMITH is the user on the server \\LUCY who is logged into the server \\GRYPHON. \\GRYPHON is set up with the following disk resources:

- C-DRIVE refers to C:\.
- STDDOCS refers to C:\DOCUMENT.

\\GRYPHON's indirect files are set up as follows:

- C:\NET.IND refers to C:\ARCHIVE\PARA301.DOC.
- C:\DOCUMENT\PARA.DOC refers to C:\NET.IND.

Table C.5 shows different commands and their results for LRSMITH, who has connected a drive to \\GRYPHON\STDDOCS and is using that drive as the default drive.

Table C.5   Examples of using the NET EXPAND command.

Command	Result
NET EXPAND PARA.DOC	\\GRYPHON\STDDOCS\PARA.DOC
NET EXPAND/P PARA.DOC	C:\DOCUMENT\PARA.DOC
NET EXPAND/R PARA.DOC	\\GRYPHON\C-DRIVE\DOCUMENT\PARA301.DOC
NET EXPAND/P/R PARA.DOC	C:\DOCUMENT\PARA301.DOC

Note: The /PHYSICAL and /RECURSE switches can be abbreviated to /P and /R.

FLUSH

    NET FLUSH sname

Variables

   sname = server name

Example

    NET FLUSH \\GRYPHON

Description

The FLUSH switch is used to force the writing of data in the random-access cache and LANcache (if it's running) to disk on the specified server *sname*. The contents of the resource cache will also be updated from the server's hard disk. This ensures that changes that have been made to accounts or files are made. This is particularly useful if you've modified a user's account and want the change to be immediately effective. You must have System Manager (S) privilege to use this switch.

HELP

NET HELP command_name

? command_name

Variables

command_name = name of a NET command

Example

NET HELP EXPAND

Description

Provides help on the use of each switch (see Figure C.15).

```
C:\>NET HELP
Help is available for the following global switches:

        /HELP      /?         /MONO      /NOERROR

Help is available for the following commands:

        ATTACH     AUDIT      CHAT       CHANGEPW   CLOCK      COPY
        DETACH     DIR        DISABLEA   ECHO       EXPAND     FLUSH
        HELP       INDIRECT   LOGIN      LOGOUT     LPT        MAIL
        MESSAGE    PAUSE      POSTBOX    PRINT      QUEUE      RECEIVE
        RUN        SHOW       SEND       SHUTDOWN   SLOGINS    STREAM
        STRING     TERMINATE  UNLINK     UNUSE      USE        USER
        ?

Help is available for the following topics:

        MACROS     ERRORS     SYNTAX

Type "NET HELP item-name" to see help on an individual item.
C:\>
```

Figure C.15 *NET.EXE: output from the HELP switch.*

INDIRECT

NET INDIRECT *ind_file file*

Variables

ind_file = network path to indirect file name

file = file name

Example

```
NET INDIRECT NET.IND \C-DRIVE\DOCUMENT\PARA.DOC
```

Description

The INDIRECT switch creates an indirect file that refers to another file. Any operations on the indirect file are actually performed on the referenced file. Both the indirect file and the actual file must be on the same server.

LOGIN

```
NET LOGIN{/WAIT} sname {uname pw}
```

Variables

sname = server name

uname = user name

pw = password

Example

```
NET LOGIN/WAIT \\GRYPHON LRSMITH DERVISH-WHIRL
```

Description

LOGIN establishes your connection to a server. The *uname* is an account on that server. Any operations that you perform on, or connections you establish with, the server are limited by the rights assigned to the account.

LOGOUT

```
NET LOGOUT sname
```

Variables

sname = server name

Example

```
NET LOGOUT \\GRYPHON
```

Description

LOGOUT cancels your connection to the server *sname* and removes any drive or printer connections that you established with that server.

LPT

```
NET LPT{ COMBINE¦{/ENABLE¦/DISABLE} NOTIFY¦ FLUSH¦ SEPARATE¦ TIMEOUT seconds}
```

Variables

seconds = {0 . . . 3600} seconds; default = 0 seconds

Networking with LANtastic

Examples

```
NET LPT COMBINE

NET LPT/ENABLE NOTIFY

NET LPT FLUSH

NET LPT SEPARATE

NET LPT TIMEOUT 10
```

Description

The LPT switch and its subswitches control the behavior of the print spooling system. The subswitches COMBINE, FLUSH, and SEPARATE are used in batch files. The termination of the batch file cancels the effect that the subswitch has.

- COMBINE is an LPT subswitch used in batch files. It allows you to join printer output that would normally be treated as separate jobs. For example, the following batch file would create a single job although there are actually four separate printer outputs.

```
NET COMBINE
ECHO "Test for NET LPT subswitches.">LPT1:
COPY TEST1.TXT LPT1:
COPY TEST2.TXT LPT1:
COPY TEST3.TXT LPT1:
```

- NOTIFY instructs the spooler to send you a message when your print job finishes printing. This is useful if the printer is in another room.

- FLUSH is an LPT subswitch for use in batch files. When a COMBINE has been issued, FLUSH is used to start a new job. The COMBINE feature is still in operation after the FLUSH. The following batch file creates two printer jobs, although there are actually four printer outputs:

Utilities Referemce

```
NET COMBINE
ECHO "Test for NET LPT subswitches.">LPT1:
COPY TEST1.TXT LPT1:
rem
rem Start next job using FLUSH
rem the COMBINE is still in effect
rem
NET FLUSH
COPY TEST2.TXT LPT1:
COPY TEST3.TXT LPT1:
```

- SEPARATE is another LPT subswitch for use with batch files. After a COMBINE has been used, SEPARATE cancels its effects. The following batch file creates three printer jobs although there are actually four printer outputs:

```
NET COMBINE
ECHO "Test for NET LPT subswitches.">LPT1:
COPY TEST1.TXT LPT1:
rem
rem Start job #2 by canceling COMBINE
rem
NET SEPARATE
COPY TEST2.TXT LPT1:
rem
rem Start job #3
rem
COPY TEST3.TXT LPT1:
```

- TIMEOUT is used to specify how long the spooler should wait after receiving a character before assuming that the print job has ended. If this value is too low, what should be a single print job will be split. This problem can be caused by software that pauses when producing printer output. If the value is too high, printer output that should be two or more jobs will be treated as if it were a single job. The default value is 0 seconds.

Note: The minimum recommended value is 10 seconds. If you're going to print graphics, a value of 40 or 50 may be needed.

361

MAIL

```
NET MAIL{/VOICE} file sname uname{message}
```

Variables

file = file name

sname = server name

uname = user name

message = text to buffer length

Example

```
NET MAIL/VOICE C:\VCE.MEM \\GRYPHON ELAY Hi!
NET MAIL C:\PARA301.DOC \\GRYPHON LUCY "Legal para you asked for."
```

The MAIL switch allows you to send either voice mail (see Chapter 10, "Advanced Topics") or any kind of file to user *uname* on server *sname*.

MESSAGE

```
NET MESSAGE{/ENABLE¦/DISABLE}{ /BEEP¦ /POP}
```

Example

```
NET MESSAGE/ENABLE /BEEP
NET MESSAGE/DISABLE /POP
```

The MESSAGE switch allows you to control whether messages cause a beep, pop up, both, or neither when they arrive.

/MONO or no switches

    NET {/MONO¦no switches}

Examples

    NET

    NET /MONO

Description

The NET utility executed with either no switches or just the MONO switch will run in the menu interface mode (see "The Menu Interfaces" later in this appendix). The MONO switch specifies that only black and white are to be used. This makes using the program with a monochrome display easier.

NOERROR

    NET/NOERROR {any switches}

Example

    NET/NOERROR AUDIT \\GRYPHON TEST "Test entry."

Description

The NOERROR switch tells the NET utility to suppress any error messages that may be generated. The NOERROR switch must be the first switch on the command line after the command itself. This is useful if you don't care about the result of a network operation and don't want unnecessary messages generated. The actual status of the command is stored in a special environment variable if it exists. See the section "LANtastic Special Strings" for a complete description.

PAUSE

NET PAUSE{/NEWLINE} message{ seconds}

Variables

message = text to buffer limit

seconds = {0 . . . 999} seconds; default = 0 seconds (wait for key press)

Example

NET PAUSE "Waiting 10 seconds" 10

NET PAUSE/NEWLINE "Press any key to continue."

Description

The PAUSE switch is like the DOS PAUSE command except that you can specify whether a new line should be generated after the message (NEWLINE) and how long the pause should last (seconds_999). If no time value is given, the pause will last until a key is pressed. If a time value is given, pressing a key ends the pause before the time expires.

POSTBOX

NET POSTBOX

Example

NET POSTBOX

Description

To check for electronic mail on all of the servers you're currently logged into, use the POSTBOX switch. The result will be a list of which servers have post waiting for you and how many items there are.

PRINT

```
NET PRINT{/BINARY}{/DELETE}{/DIRECT}{/NOTIFY} {/NONOTIFY}{/VER-
BOSE} file (nprinter¦LPTn¦COMn) { message} {copies}
```

Variables

file = file name

nprinter = network printer specification

LPTn = LPT1, LPT2, LPT3

COMn = COM1, COM2

message = text to buffer limit

copies = {1 . . .} copies; default = 1 copy

Example

```
NET PRINT/BINARY TEST1.TXT \\GRYPHON\@LASER
NET PRINT/DELETE/DIRECT *.PRN \\GRYPHON\@MATRIX "Dumping old files."
NET PRINT/VERBOSE/NOTIFY RE??.* LPT2 "LUCY" 10
```

Description

The PRINT switch sends the contents of *file* to a network printer or redirected local device (*LPTn* or *COMn*). Any combination of the following switches can be specified:

/BINARY   Prevents any tab replacement or suppression of control characters.

/DELETE   Deletes the specified file(s) after they have been queued for printing. This works only in conjunction with the /DIRECT switch.

/DIRECT   For files that are on the given server, the DIRECT switch specifies that they should not be copied to the spool area but should be read directly from the original file.

> **Note:** If you use the /DIRECT switch, be sure not to move or delete the specified files before they are printed.

NOTIFY   Generates a notification message when the print job is finished. This will override the NET LPT/DISABLE NOTIFY command.

NONOTIFY   Suppresses notification of print jobs finishing if NET LPT/ENABLE NOTIFY has been issued.

VERBOSE   Displays the name of each file as it is queued.

QUEUE

NET QUEUE (HALT¦PAUSE¦RESTART¦SINGLE¦START¦STATUS¦STOP) *sname*{*LPTn*¦*COMn*¦"ALL"}

Variables

sname = server name

LPTn = LPT1, LPT2, LPT3

COMn = COM1, COM2

Example

```
NET QUEUE HALT \\GRYPHON COM1
NET QUEUE SINGLE \\GRYPHON LPT1
NET QUEUE STATUS \\GRYPHON ALL
```

Description

The QUEUE switch gives you control over the despooler system on the server *sname*. The output port can be specified and the ALL switch will generate a report for all enabled ports. With the exception of STATUS, these are the same functions supported by LANPUP (see "LANPUP" earlier in this appendix). These functions are:

HALT   Stops despooling immediately and abandons the current job.

PAUSE   Stops despooling temporarily (doesn't abandon the current job).

RESTART   A job that is currently printing, has been halted, or has been paused can be restarted from the beginning.

SINGLE   Allows the next ready job in the printer queue to print and then stops the despooler.

START   Starts the spooler if it has been halted, stopped, or paused.

STATUS   Displays the status of all printer ports specified.

STOP   Stops despooling at the end of the current job.

RECEIVE

NET RECEIVE {*position seconds*}

Variables

position = {0 . . . 23} line number; default = no pop-up and text display

seconds = {0 . . . 65539} seconds; default = none

Example

NET RECEIVE 23 30

Description

The RECEIVE switch causes the last message sent to you to be displayed. If *position* and *seconds* aren't given, the message is just echoed to the screen. If *position* and *seconds* are given (if one is specified, the other must also be entered), the message is displayed in a pop-up box as specified. If you have disabled pop-up messages, this will allow you to retrieve them.

RUN

NET RUN{/NOCR} *sname message*

Variables

sname = server name

message = text to buffer limit

Example

```
NET RUN \\GRYPHON "DEL \DOCUMENT\*.BAK"
NET RUN/NOCR \\GRYPHON "1D3"
```

Description

The RUN switch is a powerful tool. With it, you can, if you have the System Manager (S) privilege, send command lines to a server and have them executed. The length of the command line is limited by both the local machine and the server's keyboard buffers (normally 128 characters), and Enter is automatically added to the end of the string. If a program is running on that server, the command (*message*) can be used to drive the program. If you're sending keystrokes to an application, use the NOCR switch to suppress the Enter at the end of the command, which would otherwise be interpreted as an additional keystroke by the application.

SEND

```
NET SEND mname {sname message}
```

Variables

mname = name of user *uname*'s machine

uname = user name

sname = name of server *uname* must be logged into to receive the message; default is all server.

message = text to buffer limit

Example

```
NET SEND PC3 TGIBBS LUCY "Hey! Time for Uncle Voddie."
```

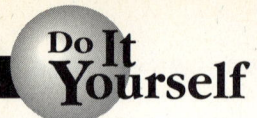

Description

Allows you to send a one-line message, *message*, to user *uname* on the PD that has the name *mname*. If you specify *sname*, the target user must be logged into that server to receive the message. To send a message to a user when you don't know which machine name or server name is correct, use the following command:

```
NET SENT * TGIBBS * "'Twas brillig and..."
```

Messages will not be seen or even known about if the target node has suppressed messages using MESSAGE/DISABLE POP BEEP.

SHOW

```
NET SHOW{/BATCH}
```

Example

NET SHOW

NET SHOW/BATCH

Description

The SHOW switch displays information on the connections and setup of the node it's run on. The BATCH switch displays it in a form that is suitable for redirecting to a batch file. This allows the current environment to be saved and recreated when needed by running the batch file. For example, **NET SHOW/BATCH>ENV01.BAT** would store the commands to setup the current environment in the file ENV01.BAT. Examples of the output of the SHOW switch are shown in Figure C.16.

```
C:>NET SHOW
LANtastic (R) Connection Manager V4.10 - (C) Copyright 1991 ARTISOFT Inc.
Machine LUCY is being used as a Redirector and a Server
File and record locking is currently ENABLED
Unsolicited messages will BEEP and NOT POP-UP
LPT notification is DISABLED
LPT timeout in seconds: 10
Autologin is ENABLED with username LUCY
Logged into \\LUCY as LRSMITH on adapter 0
Logged into \\GRYPHON as LRSMITH on adapter 0
Disk F: is redirected to \\GRYPHON\C-DRIVE
Printer LPT2 is redirected to \\GRYPHON\@LASER

C:>NET SHOW/BATCH
NET MESSAGE/ENABLE BEEP
NET MESSAGE/DISABLE POP
NET LPT/DISABLE NOTIFY
NET LPT TIMEOUT 10
NET USER LUCY ^"Enter password: "
NET LOGIN \\LUCY LRSMITH ^"Enter password: " 0
NET LOGIN \\GRYPHON LRSMITH ^"Enter password: " 0
NET USE F: \\GRYPHON\C-DRIVE
NET USE LPT2 \\GRYPHON\@LASER
```

Figure C.16 *The output from the NET SHOW and NET SHOW/BATCH commands.*

SHUTDOWN

NET SHUTDOWN{/CANCEL¦/HALT¦/REBOOT¦/SILENT} *sname* {*minutes*} {*message*}

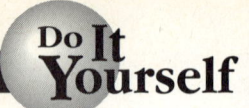

Variables

sname = server name

minutes = {0 . . . 9999}; default = 0

message = text to 79 characters

Examples

```
NET SHUTDOWN/REBOOT \\GRYPHON 15 "Closing down in # minute$."
NET SHUTDOWN/CANCEL
```

Description

The SHUTDOWN switch allows you to shut down, or cancel the shutdown of a server, *sname*, remotely. You can set the time before shutdown, the message to be sent out, and the manner of shutdown:

CANCEL   Cancels a shutdown that is in progress.

HALT   When shutdown occurs, the PC will stop processing and "freeze." You'll have to reboot the machine to do anything on it.

REBOOT   When shutdown occurs, the PC will reboot. This is useful if you want to change something in the server's environment that requires restarting to take effect and the node is remote from you. For example, this could be changing the release of a NETBIOS on the server GRYPHON. You would replace the old NETBIOS and then issue the command:

```
NET SHUTDOWN/REBOOT \\GRYPHON 15 "Rebooting in # minute$. Will restart immediately."
```

SILENT   This shuts the server down without sending a message to logged-in users. Not recommended on a live production system as users might lose data if they have no warning.

If included in the message, the # is replaced by the minutes remaining and the $ by an s if that time is greater than one minute.

Note: You must have System Manager (S) privilege for a NET SHUT-DOWN command to succeed.

SLOGINS

    NET SLOGIN{/ENABLE¦/DISABLE} sname

Variables

sname = server name

Description

The SLOGIN switch is used to enable or disable users from logging into *sname*. You must have System Manager (S) privilege to complete this operation. Any users who are logged in when this command is successfully issued are not affected; however, if they log out, they won't be allowed to log in again until logins are enabled.

STREAM

    NET STREAM{/ENABLE¦/DISABLE} sname stream_index stream_spec

Variables

sname = server name

stream_index = {0 ... 20}; default = none

stream_spec = file name format

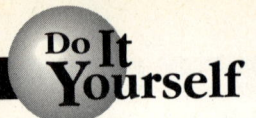

Networking with LANtastic

Examples

`NET STREAM \\GRYPHON`

Shows all stream control table entries on server \\GRYPHON.

`NET STREAM \\GRYPHON 4`

Shows only stream control table entry 4 on server \\GRYPHON.

`NET STREAM/ENABLE \\GRYPHON 4`

Enables the stream defined by stream control table entry 4 on server \\GRYPHON.

`NET STREAM/ENABLE \\GRYPHON 6 @EPSONFX`

Defines a stream called @EPSONFX in the stream control table entry 6 on server \\GRYPHON and enables it.

`NET STREAM/DISABLE \\GRYPHON 6`

Disables the streams specified by stream control table entry 6 on server \\GRYPHON.

Description

When you send data to a networked printer, it is sent to a *logical stream*. A *stream* is a queue of print jobs that are to be sent to a serial or parallel port. As more than one stream may be associated with a single port and streams can be configured to set up a printer and control the format of the output, there is a wide scope for managing the use of printers. The control of whether a stream is active is supplied by a stream control table that allows you to define up to 20 stream specifications and their associated status (either enabled or disabled). The position of an entry in the table is *stream_index*. If a *stream_spec* is given, it is used as the specification of a stream and assigned to the table entry defined by the *stream_index*. Its status is set according to whether ENABLE or DISABLE is given. When the STREAM switch is used with just an *sname* and no other switches, the entire stream control table of *sname* is shown (see Figure C.17). If a *stream_index* is given, the status of only that entry is displayed.

`C:>\NET STREAM \\GRYPHON`

```
0:    LSRWRTR.     ENABLED
1:    HPLJ2.       ENABLED
2:    EPSONFX.     ENABLED
3:                 DISABLED
4:                 DISABLED
5:                 DISABLED
6:                 DISABLED
7:                 DISABLED
8:                 DISABLED
9:                 DISABLED
10:                DISABLED
11:                DISABLED
12:                DISABLED
13:                DISABLED
14:                DISABLED
15:                DISABLED
16:                DISABLED
17:                DISABLED
18:                DISABLED
19: ????????.???  ENABLED
C:\>
```

Figure C.17 *The output from the NET STREAM command for a server that has had stream specifications defined.*

The stream control table is always empty when the server first starts, so any changes that you make are lost when the server is shutdown. If you want to set up stream specifications, you need to modify the STARTNET batch file to:

- Disable despooling for the server at start-up (see the DESPOOLING switch for the SERVER utility later in this appendix).

- Issue NET STREAM commands to build the table entries.

- Issue a NET QUEUE START ALL command (see the QUEUE switch description previously in this appendix).

The ENABLE and DISABLE switches (not surprisingly) enable and disable the stream specified by $stream\_index$, which will have a value between 0 and 19. The purpose of the $stream\_spec$ is to allow you to create

"generic" specifications that allow you to enable a single stream or a group of streams. For example, if the specification @LASER??.??? is enabled and comes before @LASER01 and @LASER02, a job from either stream will be available for printing regardless of whether the @LASER01 and @LASER02 entries are enabled or disabled. The @LASER01 and @LASER02 entries would be redundant, as the @LASER??.??? specification status will always determine their status.

The reason that print jobs are described as "available" is that they will only be printed if the port hasn't been paused or stopped.

Note: It's very important to remember that the stream control table is scanned from entry zero upwards, so the ordering of entries is important.

The default entry, ????????.???, will match all streams, so if it's the first entry in the table, all other entries will have no effect.

Tip: Unless you have some very special needs, it is a lot easier to avoid the generic specifications and use exact matches. It's very easy to make a mistake and find that a generic specification is matching the wrong stream.

STRING

        NET STRING{/LEFT=n}{/RIGHT=n} env_var message1 {message2}

Variables

env_var = existing environment variable

message1,*message2* = text total length to buffer limit and edited length to length of *env_var*

Examples

```
NET STRING/LEFT=1/RIGHT=-12 COMPATH %COMSPEC%
```

Extracts the path from the COMSPEC environment variable and puts it in the environment variable COMPATH.

```
NET STRING DTG !"DATE"
```

Puts the date into the environment variable DTG.

```
NET STRING DTG "The time is " !"TIME"
```

Combines the text "The time is " with the actual time and stores it in the environment variable DTG.

Description

The STRING switch is a powerful tool for building smart batch files in the network environment. The result of the operation is put into the environment variable specified by *env_var*. *env_var* must exist before you try to use it. You can create environment variables using the DOS command SET. See your DOS manual for details.

> **Note:** The number of characters that is allocated to the specified environment variable limits how much data can be stored in it. If the result of a STRING operation is greater than the variable can hold, the excess characters will be lost. Thus, if the result is ABCDEFG, and it's to be put into a four character environment variable, only ABCD will be stored.

The last two variables, both *message* types, define the *result*, that is, what is to become the contents of *env_var*. If only the first variable is defined, its value is used. If both are defined, their values are joined together. This allows you to produce more complex environment variable values. The first switches, LEFT and RIGHT, specify what portion of the result is to be stored in the environment variable. LEFT is the position of the first character to include and RIGHT is the last character to include, both counted from the left-hand end of the text. If either value is negative, the position is counted from the right. For example, using the text ABCDEFGH:

/LEFT=2/RIGHT=5 results in BCDE.

/LEFT=-2/RIGHT=-5 results in GH (RIGHT is ignored because it's on the left of LEFT).

/LEFT=-5/RIGHT=-2 results in DEFG.

/LEFT=-2/RIGHT=5 results in GH (again, RIGHT is ignored because it's on the left of LEFT).

/LEFT=-5/RIGHT=2 results in DEFGH (yet again, RIGHT is ignored because it's on the left of LEFT).

/LEFT=2/RIGHT=-5 results in BCD.

Note: The important thing to remember when using LEFT and RIGHT to edit text in a NET STRING command is that LEFT must be left of RIGHT. If it is not, all characters from LEFT to the end of the text will be kept.

For the two *message* variables, you have three choices:

- Plain text such as "The time is ".
- A DOS environment variable.
- A LANtastic *special string*.

To use a DOS environment variable, it must be enclosed in percent signs (%), for example, %COMSPEC%.

Note: Referring to DOS environment variables by placing them between a pair of percent signs will not work on the command line. It will only work in batch files.

LANtastic special strings are described later in this appendix.

TERMINATE

```
NET TERMINATE sname uname {mname} {mins}
```

Variables

sname = server name

uname = user name

mname = machine name

mins = 0 . . . 999; default = 0 (immediate)

Examples

```
NET TERMINATE \\GRYPHON BREDEKER * 10
```

Terminates BREDEKER's connection on server GRYPHON in 10 minutes.

```
NET TERMINATE \\GRYPHON
```

Immediately terminates all users logged in on server GRYPHON.

```
NET TERMINATE \\GRYPHON ACCS-* * 5
```

Terminates all logged-in users of server GRYPHON whose login name starts with ACCS- in five minutes.

```
NET TERMINATE \\GRYPHON * ALICE
```

Immediately terminates the connection to the server GRYPHON of the user who is on the node that has a machine name of ALICE.

Description

The TERMINATE switch allows you to terminate the connection to *sname* of either the user named *uname* or the user who is on the machine *mname*. The number of minutes before the user's connection is terminated can be specified and if left out, defaults to zero (immediate logout).

UNLINK

NET UNLINK sname

Variables

sname = server name

Example

NET UNLINK \\GRYPHON

Description

The UNLINK switch is used with remote-booted PCs to enable them to use their local drives A and B. This is because the remote boot system redirects these drives to the boot image (see Chapter 10, "Advanced Topics").

UNUSE

NET UNUSE {drive¦LPTn¦COMn}

Variables

drive = {A: ... Z:}

LPTn = {LPT1|LPT2|LPT3}

COMn = {COM1|COM2}

Examples

NET UNUSE F:

    Disconnects disk drive F from the network-shared disk resource it is redirected to.

NET UNUSE COM1

    Cancels the printer redirection for COM1.

Description

The UNUSE switch cancels the redirection of the specified disk drive or printer port.

USE

NET USE {(drive shared_disk)¦ {(LPTn¦COMn) shared_printer}

Variables

drive = {A: . . . Z:}

shared_disk = server disk resource specification

LPTn = {LPT1|LPT2|LPT3}

COMn = {COM1|COM2}

shared_printer = server printer resource specification

Examples

NET USE F: \\GRYPHON\DOCUMENTS

    Connects drive F to the shared disk resource DOCUMENTS on the server \\GRYPHON.

Networking with LANtastic

```
NET USE LPT1: \\GRYPHON\@LSRWRTR
```

Connects the port LPT1 to the shared printer resource @LSRWRTR on the server \\GRYPHON.

Description

The USE switch connects a local disk drive (A through Z) or a local port (LPT1, LPT2, LPT3, COM1, or COM2) to a shared disk or printer resources respectively. The shared resource specification must include the name of the server and the resource.

USER

```
NET USER{/DISABLE} uname {pw} {adapter}
```

Variables

uname = default username for autologins

pw = password to use for autologins

adapter = Optional adapter number to log in through

Example

```
NET USER LRSMITH COAL-PONG
```

Description

Sets the default username, *uname*, password, *pw*, and adapter number, *adapter*, to be used for automatic login to servers. If the adapter number, *adapter*, is not specified, login will be tried on all adapters. The /DISABLE switch disables automatic logins.

NET_MGR.EXE

(User) System management.

Description

The NET_MGR utility allows network managers to:
- Back up and restore a server's control directory.
- Manage user and group accounts.
- Change the server's start-up configuration (menu interface only).
- Manage the server's shared resources (menu interface only).
- Maintain the server's audit file (menu interface only).
- Maintain the server's boot image for remote-booting PCs (menu interface only).
- Maintain the printer queues on a server (menu interface only).

General Form

```
NET_MGR {HELP|?}|{switches}
```

Where, {*switches*} are any combination of:

{/CONTROL}	{/MONO}	{COPY}
{SHOW}	{DELETE}	{CREATE}
{SET}	{BACKUP}	{RESTORE}

BACKUP

```
NET_MGR BACKUP control_dir file
```

Variables

`control_dir` = network control directory specification

`file` = file name

Example

NET_MGR BACKUP C:\LANTASTI.NET A:\LUCY.NBU

Description

If you have specified any reasonably large number of users and shared resources, re-creating them could be a tedious process (especially if you don't plan your network and document it as you build it). To ease this chore, you can back up the LANtastic control directory (by default called LANTASTI.NET). The BACKUP switch copies all of the files and subdirectories under the specified control directory, `control_dir`, to the file `file`.

> **Note:** You must have System Manager (S) privilege to use the BACKUP switch. Also, the server that uses the control directory must not be running. If you do try to perform a backup, you'll get a sharing violation, and the backup will fail.

The control directory contains hidden files that may defeat normal backup programs. Even more importantly, the entire control directory can be reconstructed using the RESTORE switch described below.

COPY USER

NET_MGR{/C=control_dir}{/P=pw} {/DC=control_dir}{/DP=pw} COPY USER uname {uname}

Variables

control_dir = network control directory specification

pw = password

file = file name

uname = user name

Examples

NET_MGR/C=C:\LUCY.NET/P=POLO-GASKET /DC=F:\LANTASTI.NET/P=LEFT-SELTZER COPY USER MGIBBS

　　Copies the user account MGIBBS and its settings from the control directory C:\LUCY.NET to the same user in the control directory F:\LANTASTI.NET. The password for the source control directory data is POLO-GASKET, and for the destination directory, it is LEFT-SELTZER.

NET_MGR COPY USER MGIBBS TGIBBS

　　Copies the user MGIBBS and all that user's related settings to the user TGIBBS on the same server using the default control directory C:\LANTASTI.NET.

Description

The COPY USER switch is used to copy a user account to an account with a different name on the same server, the same name on a different server, or a different name on a different server. If either or both of the control directories are password protected, you must have the passwords to complete the operation.

Note: You must have System Manager (S) privilege for this operation.

CREATE USER

NET_MGR {/C=control_dir} {/P=pw} CREATE USER uname

Variables

control_dir = network control directory specification

pw = password

file = file name

uname = user name

Examples

NET_MGR/C=C:\LUCY.NET/P=POLO-GASKET CREATE USER PJGIBBS

Creates a user called PJGIBBS in the specified control directory. The control directory, LUCY.NET, is password protected (the password is POLO-GASKET).

NET_MGR CREATE USER PJGIBBS

Creates a user called PJGIBBS in the default control directory, C:\LANTSTI.NET.

Description

The CREATE USER switch allows you to create a user.

Note: You must have System Manager (S) privilege for this operation.

The account is set up with:

- No privileges.
- No password or account expiration.

- No login restrictions.
- No password renewal requirement.
- One concurrent login.

Note: For a system with a serious plan for security, it would be better to create one or more standard accounts (called something like USER1, USER2, and so on) and copy them to create new accounts rather than use the CREATE USER switch. That way, the privileges and access rights for a new user can be more easily and exactly controlled.

DELETE

NET_MGR{/C=control_dir}{/P=pw} DELETE (USER¦GROUP)uname

Variables

control_dir = network control directory specification

pw = password

uname = user name

Examples

NET_MGR/C=C:\LUCY.NET/P=POLO-GASKET DELETE USER PJGIBBS

Deletes a user called PJGIBBS in the specified control directory. The control directory, LUCY.NET, is password protected (the password is POLO-GASKET).

NET_MGR DELETE GROUP ACCTS-*

Deletes a group called ACCTS-* in the default control directory, C:\LANTSTI.NET.

Description

The DELETE switch allows you to remove a user's account.

 **Note:** You must have System Manager (S) privilege for this operation.

HELP or ?

```
NET_MGR HELP

NET_MGR ?
```

Description

If you use this switch, NET_MGR will display a list of all of the switches available (see Figure C.18).

```
C:\>NET_MGR HELP

These are the valid command line switches:

        /CONTROL   /MONO

Help is available for the following commands:

        COPY      SHOW      DELETE     CREATE     SET        BACKUP
              RESTORE    ?         HELP

Type "NET_MGR HELP command-name" to see help on an individual command.
C:\>
```

Figure C.18 *Display from NET_MGR SHOW command.*

RESTORE

    NET_MGR RESTORE file control_dir

Variables

file = file name

control_dir = network control directory specification

Example

NET_MGR RESTORE F:\LUCY.NBU C:\LUCY.NET

Restores the backup of a control directory in the file F:\LUCY.NBU to the control directory C:\LUCY.NET.

Description

The RESTORE switch restores the contents of a control directory from a backup file.

> **Note:** You must have System Manager (S) privilege to use the RESTORE switch. Also, the server that uses the control directory must not be running. If you do try to perform a backup, you'll get a sharing violation, and the backup will fail.

SET

    NET_MGR{/C=control_dir}{/P=pw} SET (USER uname¦GROUP gname)
    ({USERNAME=(uname¦gname)} {PASSWORD=pw} {PRIVILEGES=prvs}
    {ACTT_EXP=date} {PW_EXP=date}

Variables

control_dir = network control directory specification

pw = password

uname = user name

gname = group name

prvs = privileges {A}{Q}{M}{U}{S}

date = date {*dd-mmm-yyyy* | *mm/dd/yyyy*}

Examples

NET_MGR/C=C:\LUCY.NET/P=POLO-GASKET SET USER PJGIBBS PASSWORD=OIL-PRESSURE PRIVILEGES=S

Sets the password to OIL-PRESSURE and the privileges to system manager, M, for the user PJGIBBS in the control directory LUCY.NET that has a password of POLO-GASKET.

NET_MGR SET GROUP ACCS-* ACCT_EXP=21-JUN-1992

Sets the expiration date for the group account ACCS-* to June 21, 1992.

Description

The SET switch allows you to change one of six attributes of an account.

Note: You must have System Manager (S) privilege to complete this operation.

The attributes are:

USERNAME   The name that you want to change the user or group name to.

PASSWORD   The new password for the user or group.

PRIVILEGES   The privileges that are to be assigned to that account; any combinations of the privileges A, Q, M, U, and S (see the detailed discussion of privileges in Chapter 8, "Protecting Your Network").

ACTT_EXP   The date on which the account is to become unusable. This may be specified in two forms; either *dd-mmm-yyyy* (for example, 21-JUN-1992) or *mm/dd/yyyy* (as in 06/21/1992).

PW_EXP   The date on which the account password is to become unusable. This may be specified in two forms; either dd-mmm-yyyy (for example, 21-JUN-1992) or mm/dd/yyyy (as in, 06/21/1992).

SHOW

```
NET_MGR{/C=control_spec}{/P=pw} SHOW (USER uname¦GROUP gname)
```

Variables

control_dir = network control directory

pw = password

uname = user name

gname = group name

Examples

NET_MGR/C=C:\LUCY.NET/P=POLO-GASKET SHOW USER PJGIBBS

Shows the status of the user PJGIBBS using the control directory C:\LUCY.NET with the password POLO-GASKET.

NET_MGR SHOW GROUP *

Shows the status of all groups using the default control directory C:\LANTASTI.NET with the no password.

Description

The SHOW switch displays the account description, privileges, number of concurrent logins, account and password expiration dates, and last login date (see Figure C.19).

```
C:\>NET_MGR SHOW LRSMITH
               USER NAME:  LRSMITH
     ACCOUNT DESCRIPTION:  Office Manager
      ACCOUNT PRIVILEGES:  MUS
        CONCURRENT LOGINS: 8
 ACCOUNT EXPIRATION DATE:  NONE
PASSWORD EXPIRATION DATE:  NONE
         LAST LOGIN DATE:  1-Apr-1992
C:\>
```

Figure C.19 *Display from NET_MGR SHOW command.*

REDIR.EXE

(System) Basic network software.

Description

The redirector is the network software component that provides client access to servers and interfaces the server software to the network. See Chapter 3, "The LANtastic Networking System," for more information.

General Form

REDIR{/REMOVE¦/HELP¦/?}¦mname{switches}

Where, {switches} are any combination of:

{@file}	{BEEP_CYCLE=n}	{BEEP_DELAY=n}
{BUFFERS=n}	{HELP or ?}	{LOGINS=n}
{MONO}	{NOCHAIN}	{POPUP_DURATION=n}
{POPUP_LINE=n}	{REMOVE}	{SIZE=n} {VERBOSE}

@file

Variables

file is a DOS file name and optional path, maximum size 1000 bytes.

Example

```
REDIR GRYPHON @C:\LANTASTI\RCFG.SWI
```

Description

See the section "Switch Files" earlier in this appendix.

BEEP_CYCLE

```
REDIR mname BEEP_CYCLE=n
```

Variables

mname = machine name

$n = \{1 \ldots 3600\}$ seconds; default = 4 seconds

Example

```
REDIR GRYPHON BEEP_CYCLE=10
```

Description

Sets the interval between the warning beeps (see "Audio Warnings" later in this appendix).

BEEP_DELAY=n

```
REDIR mname BEEP_DELAY=n
```

Variables

mname = machine name

n = {1 ... 3600} seconds; default = 4 seconds

Example

REDIR GRYPHON BEEP_CYCLE=10

Description

Sets the delay before REDIR generates warning beeps (see "Audio Warnings" later in this appendix).

BUFFERS=n

REDIR *mname* BUFFERS=*n*

Variables

mname = machine name

n = {1 ... 64} buffers; default = 1 buffer

Example

REDIR GRYPHON BUFFERS=2

Description

Sets the number of buffers allocated for network traffic. If you allocate more buffers, you will get better performance when using NET CHAT and other NETBIOS applications such as the Network Eye (see Chapter 10, "Advanced Topics"), but it will use more memory. If you're using applications that do

Networking with LANtastic

mainly sequential rather than random file access, increasing the number of buffers will improve performance. This can make a great difference if you're using a word processor or graphics package.

HELP or ?

```
REDIR HELP
REDIR ?
```

Description

This switch will display a list of all of the REDIR switches available (see Figure C.20).

```
C:\>REDIR HELP
LANtastic (R) Redirector V4.10 - (C) Copyright 1992 ARTISOFT Inc.
U.S.A. version only - NOT FOR EXPORT.

USAGE: REDIR machine-name [switches...]

Valid command line switches:
    BEEP_CYCLE= Range 1 to 3600 decimal
    BEEP_DELAY= Range 0 to 3600 decimal
    BUFFERS= Range 1 to 64 decimal
    HELP
    LOGINS= Range 1 to 255 decimal
    NOCHAIN
    MONO
    POPUP_DURATION= Range 0 to 3600 decimal
    POPUP_LINE= Range 0 to 24 decimal
    REMOVE
    SIZE= Range 512 to 32768 decimal
    VERBOSE
    ?
    @ Range 0 to 1000 byte switch file
C:\>
```

Figure C.20 *Display from NET_MGR SHOW command.*

LOGINS

    REDIR mname LOGINS=n

Variables

mname = machine name

n = {1 ... 255} logins; default = 2 logins

Example

    REDIR GRYPHON LOGINS=8

Description

The LOGINS switch specifies how many sessions can be established between the client and servers (including those that are remote and local). If this switch value is less than the number of servers on your network, the NET menu will only display that many names. Each login requires extra memory, so if you want to run large programs, you'll want to keep the number of concurrent logins as low as possible.

> **Note:** If you know all of the servers that you want to connect to, and if you have planned how many you'll want to access simultaneously, you can reduce your logins (and therefore the memory required) to the minimum and make all of your server connections using batch files. To support 255 logins requires about 14,224 more bytes of memory than to support one login.

MONO

    REDIR mname MONO

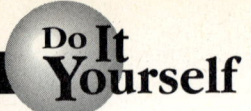

Variables

mname = machine name

Example

REDIR GRYPHON MONO

Description

The MONO switch tells REDIR to pop up messages using only black and white. This improves readability for monochrome or CGA displays.

NOCHAIN

REDIR *mname* NOCHAIN

Variables

mname = machine name

Example

REDIR GRYPHON NOCHAIN

Description

Used the NOCHAIN switch for NETBIOS implementations that don't support the CHAIN command correctly.

Note: There are very few NETBIOS implementations that don't support the CHAIN command. Reportedly, these include IBM's Token-Ring NETBIOS and the CBIS NETBIOS. If you are thinking of using a non-Artisoft NETBIOS, check with the vendor and, failing success there, Artisoft Technical Support.

POPUP_DURATION

```
REDIR mname POPUP_DURATION=n
```

Variables

mname = machine name

n = {0 . . . 3600} seconds; default = 10 seconds.

Example

```
REDIR GRYPHON POPUP_DURATION=20
```

Description

Defines the length of time a pop-up message will stay on the screen after being received.

POPUP_LINE

```
REDIR mname POPUP_LINE=n
```

Variables

mname = machine name

n = line {0 . . . 23} ; default = line 5

Example

```
REDIR GRYPHON POPUP_LINE=0
```

Description

Defines the line on the screen where pop-ups will appear.

REMOVE

```
REDIR REMOVE
```

Description

The REMOVE switch removes the redirector from memory if there is nothing else (SERVER, LANCACHE, and so on) loaded on top of it. This is useful if you need to reclaim memory so that you can run a very large application. See the discussion on using REMOVE earlier in this appendix.

SIZE

```
REDIR mname SIZE=n
```

Variables

mname = machine name

n = {512 . . . 1024} bytes; default = 1024 bytes

Example

```
REDIR GRYPHON SIZE=4
```

Description

The buffers allocated by the BUFFERS switch (above) will be of the size specified by the SIZE switch. Increasing the size of the buffers may improve performance but will use additional memory.

VERBOSE

```
REDIR VERBOSE
```

Description

The VERBOSE switch causes REDIR to display configuration data when it finishes loading and initializing. Figure C.21 shows a sample output from using this switch.

```
C:\>REDIR /VERBOSE
LANtastic (R) Redirector V4.10 - (C) Copyright 1992 ARTISOFT Inc.
U.S.A. version only - NOT FOR EXPORT.

Command line            GRYPHON LOGINS=8 VERBOSE
Machine name            GRYPHON         Maximum logins       8
Number of buffers       1               Buffer size          1024
Beep cycle              4               Beep delay           4
Pop-up duration         15              Pop-up line          5
Chain sends             ENABLED         Bytes of memory used 14208

          ---- LANtastic (R) Redirector Installed ----
C:\>
```

Figure C.21 *Output from using the VERBOSE switch with REDIR.*

SERVER.EXE

(Network)

Description

The server component of a LANtastic system is supplied by the SERVER utility.

General Form

SERVER{HELP¦?}¦{REMOVE}¦{cdir}{switches}

Where, {switches} are any combination of:

{@files}   {ADAPTERS=n}
{DESPOOLER_STOPPED=yn}   {FILES=n}
{FLOPPY_DIRECT=yn}   {HELP}
{LOCK_HOLD_TIME=n}   {LOGINS=n}
{NETWORK_BUFFER_SIZE=n}   {NETWORK_TASKS=n}
{PRINTER_BUFFER_SIZE=n}   {PRINTER_TASKS=n}
{RPL=op}   {RUN_BUFFER_SIZE=n}
{RUN_BURST=n}   {SEEK_CACHE=n}
{SEND_SERVER_ID=yn}   {SHUTDOWN_KEY=key}
{VERBOSE}

Note: If you have been adventurous and changed the control directory to something other than LANTASTI.NET, you'll need to specify the name of the control directory, *cdir*, whenever you use the SERVER command.

Variables

`file` is a DOS file name and optional path; maximum size 1000 bytes.

Example

`SERVER @C:\LANTASTI\SCFG.SWI`

Description

See the section "Switch Files" earlier in this appendix.

ADAPTERS

`SERVER ADAPTERS=n`

Variables

$n = \{1 \ldots 6\}$ adapters; default = 6 adapters

Example

`SERVER ADAPTERS=2`

Description

The ADAPTERS switch specifies the number of adapters that are installed in your computer. The maximum number of adapters that your computer can support depends on the type of network adapter. Some adapters use limited addressing or interrupts, so you must use less than the maximum that SERVER can support.

DESPOOLER_STOPPED

SERVER DESPOOLER_STOPPED=yn

Variables

yn = {YES|NO}; default = NO

Example

SERVER DESPOOLER_STOPPED=YES

Description

By setting DESPOOLER_STOPPED to YES, you can prevent print jobs from being despooled. This allows you to set up the stream control table (see *NET STREAM*) or use the attached printers as dedicated rather than shared devices. Spooling may be restarted with either NET QUEUE START or NET QUEUE SINGLE (see *NET QUEUE*).

FILES

SERVER FILES=n

Variables

n = {0|50 . . . 5100} files; default = 0 files

Example

SERVER FILES=60

Description

The maximum number of simultaneously open files that DOS can support is 255. For large server systems, this may not be enough. The default setting uses whatever FILES parameter has been set in the CONFIG.SYS file. If you set the SERVER FILES value between 50 and 5100, SERVER allocates its own files for network users.

FLOPPY_DIRECT

SERVER FLOPPY_DIRECT=yn

Variables

yn = {YES|NO}; default = YES

Example

SERVER FLOPPY_DIRECT=YES

Description

When remote users access a floppy disk drive, two operations require direct access: FORMAT and CHKDSK. Setting FLOPPY_DIRECT to NO prevents remote users from performing either function.

> **Note:** Using the **FLOPPY_DIRECT=NO** switch to prevent remote users from formatting a server's floppy disks is a very good idea if floppy disk drives are defined as shared network resources. You might consider making your server floppy disk drive inaccessible to remote users on principle.

HELP or ?

SERVER HELP or SERVER ?

Description

This switch will display a list of all of the SERVER switches available (see Figure C.22).

LOCK_HOLD_TIME

SERVER LOCK_HOLD_TIME=n

Variables

n = {DISABLED|2|3|4|5|9|13|18|27|36|45|54|63|72|81|90|108|126|144} ticks (1/18 seconds, 55.5 ms); default = 9

Example

SERVER LOCK_HOLD_TIME=18

```
C:\>SERVER HELP
LANtastic (R) Server V4.10 - (C) Copyright 1992 ARTISOFT Inc.
U.S.A. version only - NOT FOR EXPORT.

USAGE: SERVER [network-control-directory] [/switches...]

Valid command line switches:
    ADAPTERS= Range 1 to 6 decimal
    DESPOOLER_STOPPED= One of the following choices:
        YES NO
    FILES= Range 0 to 5100 decimal
    FLOPPY_DIRECT= One of the following choices:
        YES NO
    HELP
    LOCK_HOLD_TIME= One of the following choices:
        DISABLED 2 3 4 5 9 13 18 27 36 45 54 63 72 81 90 108 126 144
        162 180
    LOGINS= Range 1 to 300 decimal
    NETWORK_BUFFER_SIZE= One of the following choices:
        2K 4K 6K 8K 10K 12K 14K 16K 20K 24K 28K 32K 40K 48K 56K
    NETWORK_TASKS= Range 1 to 32 decimal
    PRINTER_BUFFER_SIZE= One of the following choices:
        512 1K 2K 3K 4K 5K 6K 8K 10K 12K 14K 16K 18K 20K 24K 28K 32K
    PRINTER_TASKS= Range 0 to 5 decimal
    REMOVE
    REQUEST_SIZE= Range 14 to 2048 decimal
    RESOURCE_CACHE= Range 1 to 50 decimal
    RPL= One of the following choices:
        DISABLED READ-ONLY READ-WRITE
    RUN_BUFFER_SIZE= Range 0 to 1024 decimal
    RUN_BURST= Range 1 to 255 decimal
    SEEK_CACHE= One of the following choices:
        NONE 1K 2K 4K 8K 12K 16K 20K 24K 28K 32K 40K 48K 56K 64K
    SEND_SERVER_ID= One of the following choices:
        YES NO
    SHUTDOWN_KEY= One of the following choices:
        A B C D E F G H I J K L M N O P Q R S T U V W X Y Z DEL
    VERBOSE
    ?
    @ Range 0 to 1000 byte switch file
```

Figure C.22 *Display from NET_MGR HELP command.*

Description

When a program locks a record, it will hold that lock for a period of time. For well-behaved applications, this time period is as short as possible. But even when the application is well behaved, it still takes time to perform a record update or complete some other file operation. Because of this, you may want to set the value of LOCK_HOLD_TIME so that other users won't automatically fail when one user locks record. This switch sets the time that the server will wait before failing the attempt to lock the record. If, for example, you know that the average record update time for your invoice system is 5 seconds, LOCK_HOLD_TIME might be set to a value of 108 ticks (or 6 seconds) to prevent a record lock attempt from failing. If used with the right applications, LOCK_HOLD_TIME can improve the response time of the system.

LOGINS

```
SERVER LOGINS=n
```

Variables

$n = \{1 \ldots 300\}$ logins; default = 5 logins

Example

```
SERVER LOGINS=24
```

Description

The LOGINS switch defines the number of simultaneous user connections the server will support. The more connections you support, the more memory is used.

> **Note:** Remember that the total number of sessions to be supported is the maximum defined for REDIR (the LOGINS switch) and for SERVER (also the LOGINS switch). This total value mustn't exceed that set by the NETBIOS SESSIONS and MAX_SESSIONS switches for AILANBIO or the setup done for other NETBIOS implementations. See the adapter vendor's documentation for the correct setting method.

NETWORK_BUFFER_SIZE

```
SERVER NETWORK_BUFFER_SIZE=n
```

Variables

n = {2K|3K|4K|5K|6K|8K|10K|12K|14K|16K|18K|20K|24K|28K|32K|40K|48K|56K} bytes; default = 4K bytes

Example

```
SERVER NETWORK_BUFFER_SIZE=8K
```

Description

Increasing the NETWORK_BUFFER_SIZE will increase performance but will use more memory. How much memory depends on the NETWORK_TASKS switch setting. Performance increases will be noticed only when programs that read and write large amounts of data are being used. For example, if you're copying files using COPY or XCOPY, performance will improve as NETWORK_BUFFER_SIZE increases. If the reads and writes on your network involve small amounts of data, such as database record access, little performance improvement will be noticed.

NETWORK_TASKS

SERVER NETWORK_TASKS=n

Variables

n = {1 . . . 32} tasks; default = 1 task

Example

SERVER NETWORK_TASKS=4

Description

To handle several user requests at the same time, SERVER needs multiple buffers. The more tasks, the better the performance, but the more memory is used.

PRINTER_BUFFER_SIZE

SERVER PRINTER_BUFFER_SIZE=n

Variables

n = {512|1K|2K|3K|4K|5K|6K|8K|10K|12K|14K|16K|18K|20K|24K|28K|32K} bytes; default = 512 bytes

Example

SERVER PRINTER_BUFFER_SIZE=8K

Description

To improve the performance of the spooler system, you can increase the value of PRINTER_BUFFER_SIZE. This, of course, will use more memory, the amount depending on the number of buffers set by PRINTER_TASKS discussed below.

PRINTER_TASKS

        SERVER PRINTER_TASKS=n

Variables

$n = \{0 \ldots 5\}$ tasks; default = 1 task

Example

        SERVER PRINTER_TASKS=4

Description

If you don't allocate as many server printer tasks as there are printers, the spooler has to do a lot of juggling to keep feeding data to the printers. If the value of PRINTER_TASKS is set to zero, despooling is disabled and cannot be started, as there are no resources for the spooler to use.

Note: You should never have more printer tasks than printers.

REMOVE

    SERVER REMOVE

Example

    SERVER REMOVE

Description

The SERVER switch removes the redirector from memory if there is nothing else loaded on top of it. This is useful if you need to reclaim memory so that you can run a very large application. See the discussion on using REMOVE earlier in this appendix.

REQUEST_SIZE

    SERVER REQUEST_SIZE=n

Variables

$n = \{14 \ldots 2048\}$ bytes; default = 14 bytes

Example

    SERVER REQUEST_SIZE=48

Description

To handle user requests, SERVER needs a place to store incoming messages. The *request buffers* are where the incoming messages are stored. If the buffer isn't big enough to hold the whole message, the client will have to send the rest of the message later. This increases the load on the network and the response of the server. Increasing SERVER REQUEST_SIZE will improve performance for some operations such as file lookups and random access file writing. The trade-off in improving the performance is using more memory. The amount of memory used depends on the value set for maximum users in the server start-up parameters and the value of REQUEST_SIZE.

> **Note:** Artisoft recommends setting the value of REQUEST_SIZE to the same value as INITIAL_SEND_SIZE (in AILANBIO.EXE) to get the best performance on EtherNet networks. If you're not using one of Artisoft's NETBIOS implementations, check the manual or ask the vendor for that product's equivalent switch to INITIAL_SEND_SIZE. The default size of 14 bytes is the smallest size available. This will only allow a few operations to be performed optimally (that is, in a single network data transfer). Setting REQUEST_SIZE to 570 bytes will optimize for all operations other than large writes. This parameter is worth experimenting with if you're looking to improve performance.

RESOURCE_CACHE

SERVER RESOURCE_CACHE=*n*

Variables

n = {1 . . . 50} resources; default = 1 resource

Example

```
SERVER RESOURCE_CACHE=4
```

Description

To handle the shared resources, LANtastic keeps a set of data either on disk or in memory. If the data is on disk, it must be read into memory to be used. The resource caches are where that data is held. If there are less caches than resources, and if a user accesses a different resource than the one currently in the cache, LANtastic must swap out the data for one of the cached resources to allow it to handle the required resource. This puts an overhead on the operation that, for a heavily used server, can degrade performance seriously. You can improve performance greatly by increasing the value of the RESOURCE_CACHE switch. Each cache requires 580 bytes of memory.

> **Note:** You can have only one boot server on a network. If you have more than one, the first to boot up will become the boot server, and all others will be automatically discarded.

> **Note:** There is no advantage to having a higher value for RESOURCE_CACHE than the total number of shared resources. For optimization purposes, RESOURCE_CACHE should be equal to the maximum number of resources that will be simultaneously used.

RPL

```
SERVER RPL rplmode
```

Variables

rplmode = {DISABLED|READ-ONLY|READ-WRITE}; default = DISABLED

Example

SERVER RPL=READ-ONLY

Description

When a server downloads a boot image to a remote booting client, the client has access to that boot image. The boot image is a file on the server that contains a one-for-one copy of a floppy disk. This image includes the installed DOS operating system, the NETBIOS, and so on. The data from the boot image is requested from the server by the Boot ROM (installed on the adapter card), and the data is sent across the network into the requesting PC's memory. Once received, the boot image data is used as if it were data direct from a floppy disk and the PC boots up. As it has access to all of the required files to join the network, connections can be made to whatever servers are needed. When the remote booting PC first connects to the network, the boot image is all that it can "see" as drives A and B are both redirected to the image. The RPL switch defines whether the PC can read data from the image but not write (READ-ONLY), or both read from and write to the image (READ-WRITE). Setting the RPL switch to DISABLE prevents any PC from remote-booting from that server.

> **Note:** If you allow remote-booting PCs to write to the boot image, it is possible to delete the NETBIOS, REDIR, and so on. If this boot image is shared by all remote booting clients, you stand the risk of disabling remote booting for the whole network. It is generally better to set the RPL switch to READ-ONLY.

RUN_BUFFER_SIZE

SERVER RUN_BUFFER_SIZE=n

Variables

n = {0 . . . 1024} bytes; default = 127 bytes

Example

SERVER RUN_BUFFER_SIZE=256

Description

The RUN_BUFFER_SIZE switch specifies how much buffer space (memory) to allocate for commands issued by using the NET RUN command. If you set the value to zero, you disable the feature. Setting RUN_BUFFER_SIZE to a high value allows you to queue up several commands. Increasing the buffer size increases the server's memory use by the amount specified.

RUN_BURST

SERVER RUN_BURST=n

Variables

n = {1 . . . 255} ticks ($1/_{18}$ seconds, 0.056 ms); default = 14 ticks (0.78 seconds, 0.778 ms)

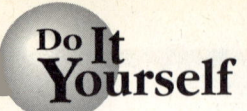

Example

```
SERVER RUN_BURST=36
```

Description

This switch has the same function as the AILANBIOS switch of the same name. To control how much processing time an application receives, the RUN_BURST switch specifies the maximum number of ticks that SERVER can run before returning control to the application or DOS. The larger this value, the lower the performance of applications that are run on that node. If you find that the network performance of the node is slow, this value may be increased to compensate.

SEEK_CACHE

```
SERVER SEEK_CACHE=n
```

Variables

n = {NONE|1K|2K|4K|8K|12K|16K|20K|24K|28K|32K|40K|48K|56K|64K}; default = NONE

Example

```
SERVER SEEK_CACHE=4K
```

Description

The seek cache is used (if enabled) to store information about random access operations. By doing so, you can increase the performance of the system for database-type applications (ones that use random-access) that keep files greater than 100 KB open for long periods of time and perform frequent access to data records. The larger the seek cache, the better the performance and the more memory that it will use.

Note: This is definitely worth testing to improve the performance of database applications. Unoffical benchmarks show throughput improvements of up to 25%.

Note: For the technically and mathematically inclined, you can find the option SEEK_CACHE size by taking the size of the most frequently used large database file and dividing its size by the drive's cluster size (usually 4096 bytes). This gives you the number of clusters used (NumClusters), each of which needs 32 bytes of cache. Each open file (totaling NumFiles) will also need 32 bytes. So, to calculate the optimum cache size, use the following formula:

CACHE_SIZE >= 32(NumClusters + NumFiles)

SEND_SERVER_ID

    SERVER SEND_SERVER_ID=yn

Variables

yn = {YES|NO}; default = YES

Example

    SERVER SEND_SERVER_ID=NO

Description

This switch instructs the server to broadcast its name when requested. When you use a program that displays a list of available servers, any server that has had SEND_SERVER_ID set to NO will not appear. To access the server that has SEND_SERVER_ID set to NO, the user needs to know its name.

Note: If you are building a very tightly controlled network, setting all server's SEND_SERVER_ID switches to NO is another tactic to make the network less vulnerable to unauthorized access.

SHUTDOWN_KEY

SERVER SHUTDOWN_KEY=key

Variables

key = {A . . . Z|DEL}; default = DEL

Description

When the specified character is pressed with Ctrl and Alt, the server pops up a shutdown menu. Where the PC is also running a program that intercepts the default (Ctrl-Alt-Del) and prevents the server from seeing the sequence, the SHUTDOWN_KEY switch allows you to change key to be recognized.

VERBOSE

SERVER VERBOSE

Description

The VERBOSE switch causes SERVER to display configuration data when it finishes loading and initializing. Figure C.23 shows a sample output from using this switch.

```
C:\>SERVER /VERBOSE
LANtastic (R) Server V4.10 - (C) Copyright 1992 ARTISOFT Inc.
U.S.A. version only - NOT FOR EXPORT.

Command line              /VERBOSE

Machine name              GRYPHON         Adapters in use         1
Maximum open files        in CONFIG.SYS   Maximum logins          8
Initial despooling        ACTIVE          Remote program load     DISABLED
Floppy direct access      YES             Send server ID          YES
Network buffer size       4096            Network tasks           1
Printer buffer size       512             Printer tasks           1
Initial request size      14              Cached resources        1
Run buffer size           127             Run burst               2
Random access cache KB    0               Record lock hold time   9
Shutdown key              Ctrl-Alt-DEL    Bytes of memory used    30928

          ---- LANtastic (R) Server Installed ----
```

Figure C.23   *Output from using the VERBOSE switch with SERVER.*

UPS.EXE

(System) Availability and integrity support.

Description

The UPS utility allows LANtastic to sense and act on the status of the AC power supply as reported by an intelligent Uninterruptable Power Supply (UPS) system.

> **Note:** UPS.EXE can only be used if SERVER.EXE has been loaded.

The function of a UPS unit is to prevent:

- *Spikes*. Also called *line noise*, these are short duration (a few milliseconds or less) power increases that can cause hardware damage. The voltages range in the thousands of volts. Spikes are typically caused by noisy electrical motors and lighting.

- *Surges*. These events can also cause hardware damage. Surges are power increases that last for anything up to a couple of seconds and are usually about 30% over nominal voltage (around 140 or 285 volts). They may be caused when heavy electrical equipment is started.

- *Power supply failures*. The power supply can fail in two ways: the voltage can drop (a *sag* or *brownout*) or disappear (a *blackout*). These events can cause loss of data.

UPSs come in many specifications covering different capabilities such as the degree of spike and surge suppression and backup power supply duration. The types of UPS that the LANtastic UPS utility supports are the "intelligent" models that can send status information to a computer.

To understand the operation of an intelligent UPS you need to understand the power conditions that it senses:

- *Normal power*. The line voltage is within normal limits (generally plus or minus about 10% of the nominal voltage). The UPS just maintains the charge level of its batteries.

- *Surge or spike*. The line voltage exceeds 110% of nominal voltage. The UPS suppresses these events.

- *Brownout*. The line voltage has dropped below about 90% of the nominal voltage. The UPS takes over supplying power to the computer by either boosting the line voltage to a normal value (this may not be available on all UPS units) or switching to battery supply. At this point, an intelligent UPS unit will warn the PC. The PC will either begin shutdown immediately or wait until the *battery low* condition occurs.

- *"Deep" Brownout or Blackout*. The line voltage has dropped below a level where it can be boosted (around 80% of nominal voltage) or has disappeared altogether. An intelligent UPS will start or continue the same warning to the PC as generated by going to brownout supply. The PC will either begin shutdown immediately or wait until the battery low condition occurs.

- *Battery power low*. The UPS unit has taken over supplying power but its batteries are running low. An intelligent UPS unit will signal the PC to warn of this new condition. If the PC hasn't already shutdown, this will usually be considered the last opportunity to do so before power fails completely.

Note: If UPS protection is applied only to the server, you'll be able to prevent an unplanned server shutdown, but you may still lose data if the clients don't have UPS service. You should, at the very least, consider putting UPSs on the nodes that are critical to conducting your business.

An intelligent UPS can also switch off power on receipt of a signal from the PC. This allows you to avoid running until the UPS unit's power fails. The actual setup of the UPS utility depends on the capabilities of the UPS unit.

Utilities Referemce

Note: If you're going to use intelligent UPSs to support your LANtastic network servers — highly advised if you are even slightly serious about your network — check the vendor's specifications for LANtastic compatibility. If in doubt, check with LANtastic's technical support services (see Appendix A, "Resources").

General Form

UPS{/HELP¦ ?}¦{REMOVE}¦{switches}

Where, {switches} are any combination of:

{@file}	{BROWNOUT_SECONDS=n}
{CANCEL_SECONDS=n}	{DEVICE=COMn}
{IOBASE=n}	{LOW_BATTERY=n}
{NO_CANCEL}	{NO_POWER_DOWN}
{POWER_DOWN_CYCLE=n}	{SHUTDOWN_MINUTES=n}
{WARNING=msg}	

Note: A shutdown that has been scheduled by the UPS utility can be canceled by the command NET SHUTDOWN/CANCEL.

@file

Variables

file is a DOS file name and optional path, maximum size 3000 bytes.

Example

UPS @C:\LANTASTI\RCFG.SWI

Description

See the section "Switch Files" earlier in this appendix.

BROWNOUT_SECONDS

UPS BROWNOUT_SECONDS=*n*

Variables

$n = \{0 \ldots 1800\}$ seconds; default = 10 seconds

Example

UPS BROWNOUT_SECONDS=30

Description

The BROWNOUT_SECONDS value determines how long after a brownout starts before the UPS software begins shutting down the server. Setting BROWNOUT_SECONDS to zero causes an immediate shutdown as soon as a brownout occurs. As soon as the shutdown sequence starts, logged-in users will receive a message.

CANCEL_SECONDS

UPS CANCEL_SECONDS=n

Variables

n = {0 . . . 1800} seconds; default = 10 seconds

Example

UPS CANCEL_SECONDS=30

Description

If power is restored after a server shutdown is scheduled and before the UPS unit runs out of power, you may want to wait for a period of time before canceling the shutdown to ensure that the power supply is stabilized. The value of CANCEL_SECONDS defines how long to wait before the UPS utility cancels the shutdown. If the shutdown is canceled, logged-in users will be notified.

> **Note:** If the scheduled shutdown occurs before the expiration of CANCEL_SECONDS, the shutdown will still happen.

DEVICE

UPS DEVICE=COMn

Variables

COMn = {COM1|COM2|COM3|COM4}; default = COM1

Example

UPS DEVICE=COM2

Description

An intelligent UPS unit communicates with a LANtastic server running the UPS utility through a serial port. You have four choices available: COM1, COM2, COM3, or COM4.

> **Note:** If you are planning to have two serial printers on your PC, you'll need to install a serial adapter to add COM3 and/or COM4 to your system. Remember that LANtastic can't support COM3 or COM4 as a shared network printer.

HELP or ?

UPS HELP

UPS ?

Description

This switch will display a list of all of the UPS switches available (see Figure C.24).

Utilities Referemce

```
C:\>UPS HELP
LANtastic (R) UPS Monitor Utility V1.09 - (C) Copyright 1992
ARTISOFT Inc.

Valid command line switches:
    BROWNOUT_SECONDS= Range 0 to 1800 decimal
    CANCEL_SECONDS= Range 0 to 1800 decimal
    DEVICE= One of the following choices:
        COM1 COM2 COM3 COM4
    HELP
    IOBASE= Range 0000 to FFFF hex
    LOW_BATTERY= One of the following choices:
        IGNORE 0 1 2 3 4 5
    NO_CANCEL
    NO_POWER_DOWN
    POWER_DOWN_CYCLE= Range 0 to 60 decimal
    REMOVE
    SHUTDOWN_MINUTES= Range 0 to 300 decimal
    WARNING= character string
    ?
    @ Range 0 to 3000 byte switch file
                ---- UPS utility NOT installed ----
```

Figure C.24   Display from UPS HELP command.

IOBASE

UPS IOBASE=n

Variables

$n = \{0000h \ldots FFFFh\}$; default = none

Example

If you have a nonstandard COM port configuration, you can use the IOBASE switch to specify its port address. If you set this switch, its value will override that set by the DEVICE switch.

LOW_BATTERY

    UPS LOW_BATTERY=n

Variables

n = {IGNORE | 0 . . . 5} minutes; default 1 minute

Example

    UPS LOW_BATTERY=3

Description

When the UPS unit has been running for some time, its battery will get low. At a point that depends on the vendor's design and whether the UPS unit can be configured, it will generate a battery low warning. The LOW_BATTERY switch specifies the amount of time after the UPS unit signals that the battery is low that a server shutdown will be forced. Thus, if a shutdown is due in, say, 15 minutes, and the UPS unit signals that its battery is low, shutdown will be scheduled in however many minutes are specified by the BATTERY_LOW switch. If a shutdown is going to occur in less time than the BATTERY_LOW value, the existing shutdown schedule is maintained.

NO_CANCEL

UPS NO_CANCEL

Description

The NO_CANCEL switch specifies that once a UPS-originated shutdown is underway it won't be canceled even if the AC power is restored. If NO_CANCEL and CANCEL_SECONDS are both specified, NO_CANCEL overrides.

NO_POWER_DOWN

UPS NO_POWER_DOWN

Description

If the NO_POWER_DOWN switch is specified, the UPS will not be instructed to switch off after the server is shutdown.

POWER_DOWN_CYCLE

UPS POWER_DOWN_CYCLE=n

Variables

$n = \{0 \ldots 60\}$ seconds; default = 5 seconds

Example

UPS POWER_DOWN_CYCLE=30

Description

The POWER_DOWN_CYCLE switch sets the duration of signal that the UPS utility must send to the UPS unit to tell it to switch off the power. The value set causes the utility to send the signal for that amount of time, stop signaling for that amount of time, signal again, and so on. Check the documentation of the UPS to determine the correct setting.

REMOVE

```
UPS REMOVE
```

Description

The REMOVE switch removes the UPS utility from memory if there is nothing else (SERVER, LANCACHE, and so on) loaded on top of it. This is useful if you need to reclaim memory in order to run a very large application. See the discussion on using REMOVE earlier in this appendix. If a shutdown was scheduled by the UPS utility, it will still be in effect after it is removed. Shutdown can be canceled by command NET SHUTDOWN/CANCEL.

SHUTDOWN_MINUTES

```
UPS SHUTDOWN_MINUTES=n
```

Variables

$n = \{0 \ldots 300\}$ minutes; default = 15 minutes

Example

```
UPS SHUTDOWN_MINUTES=10
```

Description

The value of SHUTDOWN_MINUTES determines how long after an event which requires a shutdown occurs, that the actual shutdown will happen. A value of zero causes an immediate shutdown.

WARNING

```
UPS WARNING=message
```

Variables

message = up to 79 characters

Example

```
UPS WARNING="Sorry folks, we're having a power failure. Shutting down in # minute$."
```

Description

This switch allows you to specify the message that will be sent to users during the interval before shutdown. If included in the message, the # is replaced by the minutes remaining and the $ by an *s* if that time is greater than one minute.

LANtastic Special Strings

LANtastic special strings are available for use with any NET commands where variables are used. These special strings are indicated by a leading exclamation point and are enclosed in quotation marks, for example, !"DATE", !"TIME", and !"PROGRAM". Table C.6 summarizes all of the LANtastic special strings except the prompts and gives a sample of their outputs using the NET ECHO command.

Table C.6 Examples of the results of using LANtastic's special strings.

Command line	Result
NET ECHO !"DATE"	2-Apr-1992
NET ECHO !"DAY"	Thursday
NET ECHO !"DIRECTORY"	C:\
NET ECHO !"ETEXT=0"	No Error
NET ECHO !"FILE=TEST.TXT"	This the first line of TEST.TXT
NET ECHO !"INSTALLED"	NRS-
NET ECHO !"LOGIN=GRYPHON"	TRUE
NET ECHO !"LOGIN=GRYPPON"	FALSE
NET ECHO !"NODEID"	00006E25288A
NET ECHO !"MACHINEID"	LUCY
NET ECHO !"PROGRAM"	C:\LANTASTI\NET.EXE
NET ECHO !"TIME"	15:41:56
NET ECHO !"USER"	LRSMITH

In all LANtastic strings that have an equal sign (=) in them, you must ensure that there is no space between the equal sign (=) and the data that follows. Thus, if you are logged into a server called GRYPHON, the command:

NET ECHO !"LOGIN=GRYPHON"

will return TRUE but,

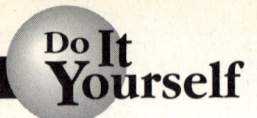

```
NET ECHO !"LOGIN= GRYPHON"
```

will return FALSE.

The LANtastic NET.EXE switch STRING operates on environment variables only. These are shown in the following examples as *evar*. See the section "STRING" under the section "NET.EXE" for more details. These environment variables must already exist before you try to use them.

Another important feature with environment variables is LANtastic's use of NET_ERROR. This is set as the result of any NET.EXE command that uses the /NOERROR switch. Also remember that the NET_ERROR environment variable must be predefined before a NET/ERROR command can use it. See the section "NET.EXE" for more details.

There are twelve LANtastic special strings, which will be discussed in the following sections.

> **Note:** *evar* is a DOS environment variable that must be set with the DOS SET EVAR= command. This must be done before you use it in a special string, and it must be at least as many characters as the special string will generate.

!"DATE"

Returns the current date in the form *dd-mmm-yyyy* (eleven characters). Examples are 1-Apr-1992 and 21-Jun-1992. Note that when the numbers for the day of the month are less than 10, a space is put in front of the digit to keep the text to 11 characters.

Useful substrings:

Day of the month:	NET STRING/R=2 *evar* !"DATE"
Short month ("Jun"):	NET STRING/L=4/R=6 *evar* !"DATE"
Full year (1992):	NET STRING/L=8 *evar* !"DATE"
Short year (92):	NET STRING/L=10 *evar* !"DATE"

Utilities Referemce

!"DAY"

Returns the name of the day of the week in full. Thus, the result will be: Monday, Tuesday, Wednesday, Thursday, Friday, Saturday, or Sunday. The maximum string length is nine characters, the minimum is six characters.

There are two ways to generate unique day identifiers of fixed length:

Three characters (Mon): `NET STRING/R3=` *evar* `!"DAY"`

Two characters (Mo): `NET STRING/R2=` *evar* `!"DAY"`

!"DIRECTORY"

Returns the disk and directory that is your default, or current, disk location. There may be any number of characters from three upwards (the drive letter followed by a colon and a backslash, for example, C:\, will be the shortest path specification), and the characters will always be in capital letters.

> **Note:** You can find your current drive with `NET STRING/R=2` *evar* `!"DIRECTORY"`

!"ETEXT=n"

Returns the text that describes the error number *n* returned by the NET utility. This is useful in batch files for determining the cause of failure of a NET command if the /NOERROR switch has been used.

!"FILE=file"

Will print the first line of the file specified by *file*. Only the first 128 characters of the first line will be displayed, and if the first line is over 772 characters, an error will be reported.

437

!"INSTALLED"

This is a very useful special string that causes NET to test for the various LANtastic network components and returns characters indicating their presence or absence. The components detected are indicated by: N for NETBIOS (any NETBIOS, not just Artisoft's), R for the redirector (REDIR.EXE), S for the server (SERVER.EXE), L for the LANPUP pop-up, and - (hyphen) for a missing component. Not all combinations are logical; N---, NR--, NRS-, NRSL, and NR-L are the only valid results.

Useful substrings:

NETBIOS status: `NET STRING/L=1/R=1` *evar* `!"INSTALLED"`

REDIR status: `NET STRING/L=2/R=2` *evar* `!"INSTALLED"`

SERVER status: `NET STRING/L=3/R=3` *evar* `!"INSTALLED"`

LANPUP status: `NET STRING/L=4/R=4` *evar* `!"INSTALLED"`

!"LOGIN=sname"

Returns TRUE if you are logged into the server *sname* and FALSE if you're not.

!"NODEID"

Will return a unique NETBIOS node number of 12 digits, for example, 00006E25288A. This is very useful for creating things like unique file names in shared directories.

!"MACHINEID"

Expands to the name of the machine (that is, the machine name specified when REDIR was executed).

!"PROGRAM"

Returns the full path and name of the NET.EXE program, for example, C:\LANTASTI\NET.EXE. This is useful if the installation directory isn't the default C:\LANTASTI and you need to identify where the LANtastic program files are.

To extract:

The drive:	NET STRING/R=2 *evar* !"PROGRAM"
Full path:	NET STRING/R=-8 *evar* !"PROGRAM"
Short path:	NET STRING/L=3/R=-8 *evar* !"PROGRAM"

!"TIME"

Expands to the current time in the 24-hour format including seconds. The result will be between 00:00:00 and 23:59:59.

Useful substrings:

Hours and minutes:	NET STRING/R=5 *evar* !"TIME"
Hours:	NET STRING/R=2 *evar* !"TIME"

!"USER"

Returns the name of the default login name, if one was set using the NET program (see the section "NET" under "Login or Logout" later in this appendix).

Prompts

Are used to interactively ask the user for a value to input as a switch value or variable. There are two types of prompts: echoing and nonechoing. An echoing prompt is specified by quoted text preceded by a ◆, and a

nonechoing prompt is quoted text preceded by a ^. For example, in Figure C.25, `Enter server:` and `User:` are both echoed prompts and `Password:` isn't. You'll notice that the nonechoing prompt prints a ◆ for every character entered. This supports the entry of passwords and anything else you want to keep private.

```
C:\>NET LOGIN ?"Enter server: " ?"User: " ^"Password: "
Enter server: \\GRYPHON
User: MGIBBS
Password: ◆◆◆◆◆◆◆◆
```

Figure C.25 *The use of prompts with the NET LOGIN command.*

Audio Warnings

Both AILANBIO and REDIR use beeps to indicate timeout conditions that you should be aware of. There are five different sequences used to indicate errors:

- *One beep:* Your print job has been sent to the print queue (this also occurs when you press Ctrl-Alt-PrintScreen to force an end of job).

- *Two beeps:* You pressed Ctrl-Alt-Del to reboot a PC that is a server. A pop-up window will appear to offer you the choice of pressing Ctrl-Alt-Del again to immediately reboot, S to shut down the server (and remove it if there's nothing loaded below it), or any other key to continue.

- *Three beeps:* Unless you disable beeping on receiving messages (by using NET MESSAGE/DISABLE BEEP), you'll hear three beeps for each message received.

- *Low-high beep:* Your PC, as a client, made a network request and the server failed to respond before the client software timed out. The beeps will continue until the server responds or is shut down.

- *High-low beep:* If a server shutdown is pending and you cancel it, the server will generate a high-low beep.

Utilities Referemce

The Menu Interfaces

The three utilities LANCHECK.EXE, NET.EXE, and NET_MGR.EXE can be run in a menu-interface mode.

All of the programs share similar features:

- Select menu items by using the up arrow and the down arrow to move the highlighted bar and pressing Enter to execute the item.

- Press Esc to return to the previous menu or to DOS if you're at the main menu.

- Any window that has a small triangle at the top and/or bottom of the right-hand side of the border (see Figure C.26) has information that is too long to display in the window. A top triangle indicates there is data above and a bottom triangle that there is data below. This convention applies to text screens and to lists of servers, users, and so on. Press Home, End, PgUp, PgDn, the up arrow and the down arrow to view all of the text.

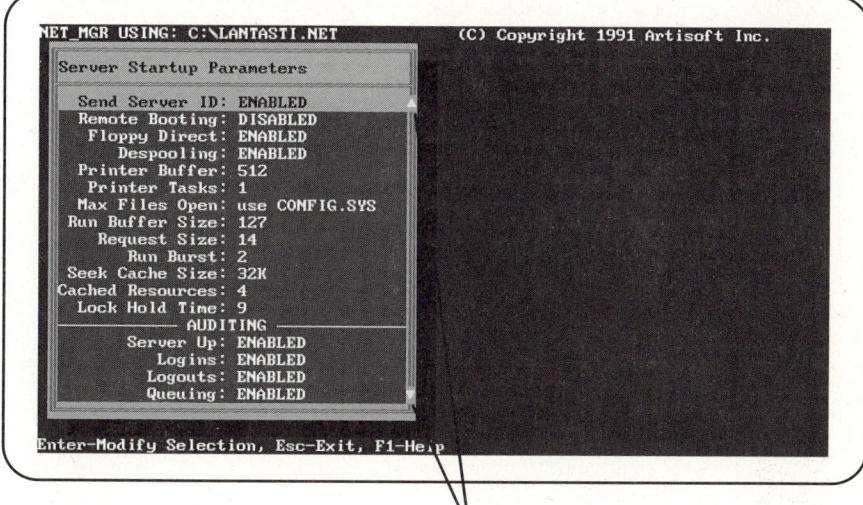

These triangles indicate that more detail is available for this screen

Figure C.26 *The "more data" triangles.*

441

Press F1 for help at any point in the program. When a help screen is displayed, you can press Z (for Zoom) to toggle the help window between being half and the whole of the window. Many of the help screens are longer than can be displayed, so press Home, End, PgUp, PgDn, the up arrow and the down arrow to view the rest of the text.

Utilities Referemce

LANCHECK

LANCHECK allows you to test and analyze the performance of network connections. LANCHECK reports on:

- Whether there is a connection to the network.
- Whether the local and remote network adapters are detecting error conditions.
- Error statistics.

LANCHECK can be run with none or all LANtastic network operating system components (REDIR, SERVER, and so on), but the low-level driver (if required) and the NETBIOS must be running. LANCHECK can show information on:

- The local node.
- Other nodes that are running LANCHECK.
- Other nodes that are not running LANCHECK.

Starting LANCHECK

There are four ways to start LANCHECK. If REDIR has been loaded:

LANCHECK

This starts LANCHECK with a color display, using the existing machine name.

LANCHECK /MONO

LANCHECK starts in monochrome mode using the existing machine name.

If REDIR hasn't been started or you want to give your PC a different name for testing purposes:

LANCHECK *mname*

443

This starts LANCHECK in color using the name you specify. For example, type **LANCHECK LUCY**.

LANCHECK *mname* **/MONO**

LANCHECK will run in monochrome using the given machine name. For example, type **LANCHECK LUCY /MONO**.

> **Note:** If you have already loaded the redirector and you don't give LANCHECK a name when it's started, LANCHECK will use the machine name that was specified for REDIR. If you do specify a name, LANCHECK will use that name and ignore the existing machine name. Note also that the name specification is case-sensitive, so LUCY and Lucy are different names. In general, use the name of the PC as you have planned it to be. This will make it easier to identify the PC if you run LANCHECK from another node.

Figure C.27 shows the display produced by running LANCHECK started with the name WALRUS.

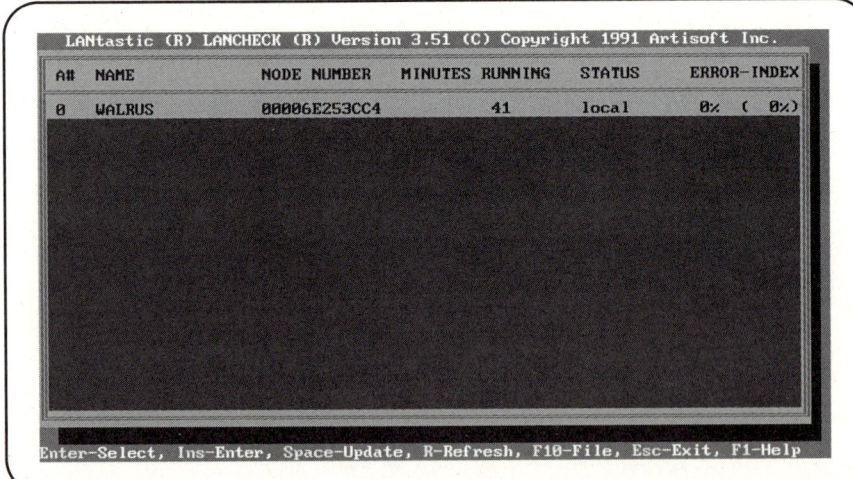

Figure C.27 *The LANCHECK main display.*

The display shows the following statistics for each node (PC) running LANCHECK:

A#   The network adapter to which the node is connected.

NAME   The name specified when LANCHECK was started.

NODE NUMBER   The node number assigned to an adapter. Every adapter must have a unique node number.

MINUTES RUNNING   The number of minutes the node has been active.

STATUS   An adapter can be active, inactive or local (installed in your computer — in which case it is active if LANCHECK is using it).

ERROR-INDEX   The occurrence of various error conditions are totaled (CRC errors, alignment errors, and bad transmissions) and divided by the number of successful transmit and receive operations, and multiplied by 100 to give a general indication of the PC's network health. The percentage figure in parentheses beside it is the highest percentage recorded during the current session.

The LANCHECK Main Screen

There are five functions available to you when you're at the main screen of LANCHECK:

- Press the space bar to update the display.

- Press R to specify how frequently the display should be automatically updated (between 0 and 3600 seconds).

- Press F10 to save information for all entries from the current display in a file.

- Select an entry from the list and press Enter (or press Ins and enter the target PC's machine name) to get detailed statistics about any PC's adapter.

- Press Esc to return to DOS.

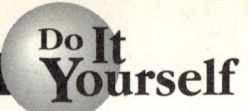

Saving the Report in a File

You can choose a short (summary) or long (detail) report. Figures C.28 and C.29 show each type of report.

```
            4-Apr-1992  10:08 AM
    A#   NAME       NODE NUMBER   MINUTES RUNNING   STATUS      ERROR-INDEX
    ===========================================================================
    0    LUCY       00006E25288A        114         local       0%  (  0%)
    0    GRYPHON    00006E251C45        114         active      0%  (  0%)
```

Figure C.28   *The LANCHECK summary adapter status report.*

Detailed Statistics about a Network Adapter

If the node is not shown in the LANCHECK display, you can press insert and then, at the prompt, enter the target machine's name. If the node is shown in the LANCHECK display (because it too is running LANCHECK), use the up arrow and the down arrow to move the highlight to the required name and press Enter. A screen similar to Figure C.30 will be displayed.

The following data is shown in the detailed adapter status display:

- *Adapter Number.* The number of the network adapter on the node which is connected to the network we're testing.

- *Node Number.* The unique node number assigned to the node.

- *Software Version.* The version number of the NETBIOS software the node is running.

- *Minutes Running.* The number of minutes the node has been active.

- *CRC Errors.* An error associated with corruption of data as it passes through the network.

Utilities Referemce

```
4-Apr-1992   10:12 AM
===============================================================
                 Adapter Status of: LUCY
                    Adapter Number: 0
                       Node Number: 00006E25288A
                  Software Version: 3.01
---------------------------------------------------------------
    TRAFFIC AND ERROR STATISTICS  ¦  ADAPTER RESOURCE STATISTICS
---------------------------------------------------------------
         Minutes Running: 117      ¦     NCBs Available: 26
             CRC Errors: 0         ¦     NCBs Allocated: 32
       Alignment Errors: 0         ¦   Max NCBs Possible: 32
             Collisions: 0         ¦     Active Sessions: 4
       Bad Transmissions: 0        ¦  Sessions Allocated: 32
      Good Transmissions: 3741     ¦   Sessions Possible: 32
           Good Receives: 8139     ¦     Max Packet Size: 1470
          Retransmissions: 0       ¦     Number of Names: 6
         Resource Exhaust: 0       ¦
===============================================================
===============================================================
                 Adapter Status of: GRYPHON
                    Adapter Number: 0
                       Node Number: 00006E251C45
                  Software Version: 3.01
---------------------------------------------------------------
    TRAFFIC AND ERROR STATISTICS  ¦  ADAPTER RESOURCE STATISTICS
---------------------------------------------------------------
         Minutes Running: 117      ¦     NCBs Available: 26
             CRC Errors: 0         ¦     NCBs Allocated: 32
       Alignment Errors: 0         ¦   Max NCBs Possible: 32
             Collisions: 0         ¦     Active Sessions: 4
       Bad Transmissions: 0        ¦  Sessions Allocated: 32
      Good Transmissions: 21854    ¦   Sessions Possible: 32
           Good Receives: 17372    ¦     Max Packet Size: 1470
          Retransmissions: 0       ¦     Number of Names: 7
         Resource Exhaust: 0       ¦
===============================================================
```

***Figure C.29**   The LANCHECK detail adapter status report.*

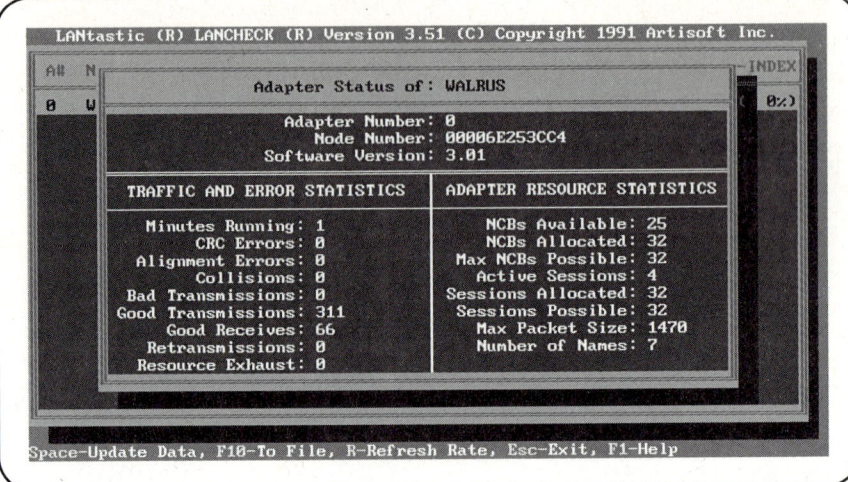

Figure C.30 *The LANCHECK detail adapter status display.*

- *Alignment Errors.* An error associated with receiving data.

- *Collisions.* A normal occurrence on networks such as EtherNet. Collisions become more frequent as the network traffic increases.

- *Bad Transmissions.* The number of unsuccessful transmissions (the receiving node didn't get an error-free transmission).

- *Good Transmissions.* The number of successful transmissions.

- *Good Receives.* The number of error-free receives this node has made.

- *Retransmissions.* Number of times a retransmission was necessary due to an error.

- *Resource Exhaust.* Number of times a receive could not be made because there were no buffers available to receive the data.

- *NCBs Available.* The number of available Network Control Blocks (NCBs).

Utilities Referemce

- *NCBs Allocated.* The number of NCBs allocated for the adapter by the Reset command.
- *Max NCBs Possible.* Maximum number of NCBs the adapter can support.
- *Active Sessions.* Number of active sessions.
- *Sessions Allocated.* Maximum number of sessions supported by the adapter as configured by the Reset command.
- *Sessions Possible.* Maximum number of sessions the adapter can support.
- *Max Packet Size.* Maximum size of a data packet.
- *Number of Names.* The number of names present on the local NETBIOS name table.

While you are examining the data from the status display, you can:

- Press R to change the refresh rate.
- Press F10 to send the display data to file (the detailed data for the displayed entry is saved).
- Press the space bar to update the display.
- Press Esc to return to the main display of LANCHECK.

449

Utilities Referemce

NET.EXE

The NET utility allows you to control your network environment. Its options include:

- Managing network disk drives and printers.
- Printer queue management.
- Accessing mail services.
- Chatting with another user.
- Server logins and logouts.
- Managing your user account.
- Monitoring and managing server activity.

There are two ways to start NET. **NET** starts with a color display. **NET /MONO** starts NET in monochrome mode.

When NET starts the main options menu is displayed (see Figure C.31).

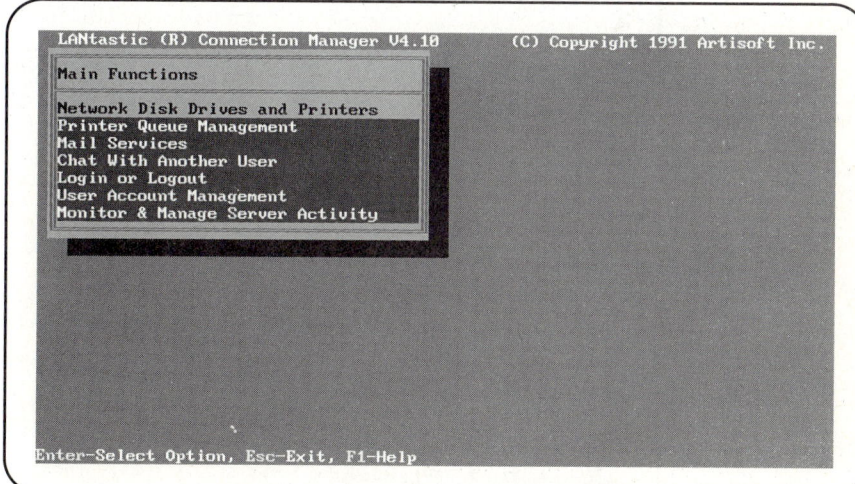

Figure C.31 *The main screen of NET.EXE.*

451

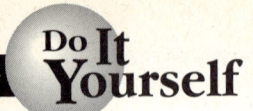

Networking with LANtastic

When you are at the main menu, you can press Esc to exit to DOS. If you need help anywhere in the program, press F1.

Network Disk Drives and Printers

This option offers equivalent functions to NET USE. When you select this option, a list of local devices (ports and drives) is shown with their current assignments (see Figure C.32).

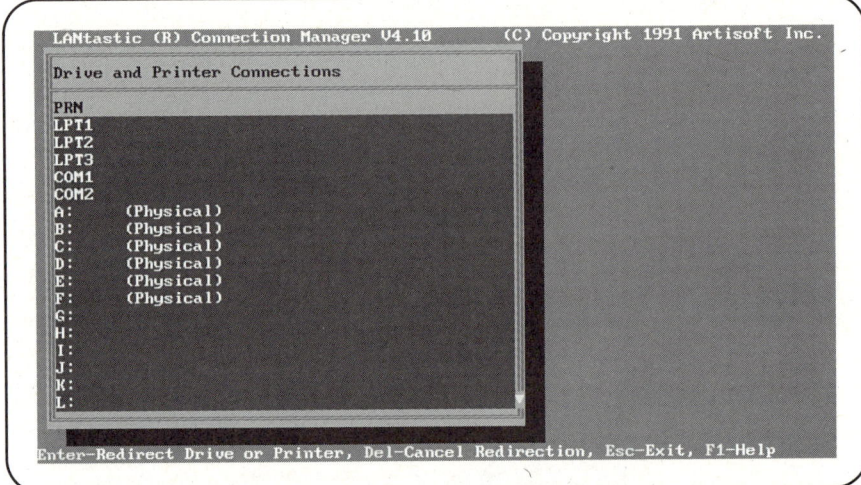

Figure C.32 NET.EXE: The Drive and Printer Connections screen.

There are two operations that can be performed:

- *Disconnect from a resource.* To disconnect from a resource, select it and press Del. Press Esc at the main screen for Network Disk Drives and Printers to return to the main options menu.

- *Connect to a resource.* To create a new connection, the device must not be already connected. Press Enter or Ins and select a server from the displayed list. If the server you want isn't listed, press Ins and enter the required server name. Select the required resource from the list. Press Esc at the main screen for Network Disk Drives and Printers to return to the main options menu.

452

Printer Queue Management

This option offers the same functions as the NET PRINT, NET QUEUE, and NET STREAM commands. When this option is selected, you'll first be asked to choose a server. The screen in Figure C.33 appears.

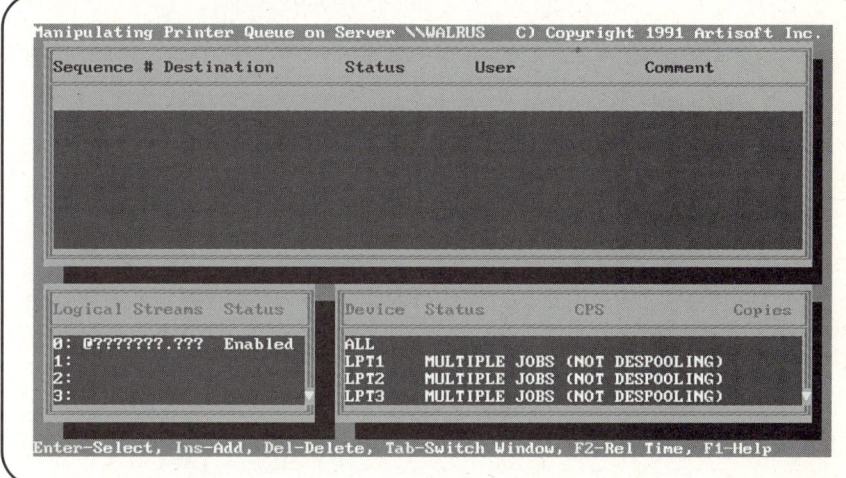

Figure C.33 *NET: The Manipulating Printer Queue on Server screen.*

There are three windows to choose from:

- The print job queue.
- The stream control table.
- The output devices.

Note: You can move to any window by pressing Tab or Shift-Tab.

Networking with LANtastic

Print Job Queue Window

The print job queue window shows the print jobs that are queued for output, their job numbers, which print stream they're destined for, the user who created the job, and the comment attached to the job. There are six status conditions:

DESPOOLING   Data from the job is currently being sent to the printer.

IMMEDIATE   The device has immediate despooling enabled and has begun to print even though all of the data for the job has not been queued.

WAITING   The job is waiting to be despooled. Jobs remain waiting until the printer is available.

HELD   The job has been held. A held job won't be despooled until it is released.

DELETED   The job is in the process of being deleted. A job is marked as deleted only if it was in the process of being printed, and it will remain in the deleted status until a (*CANCELED*) message is printed.

RUSH   The job has been "rushed" by a user with the Q privilege. Rushed jobs are printed before any other jobs.

There are two sets of operations that can be performed in the print job queue window:

- *Adding a job to the queue.* Press Ins and you'll be offered two ways to add a job: Use Screen Editor or Copy Text File to Queue. Whichever you choose, you'll first be asked to select a target output stream (one of the defined printer resources). When you've entered the data using the editor or specified the file, you'll be asked for an optional comment and the number of copies you want.

- *Controlling the status of queue entries.* Select the job that you want to change the status of and press Enter. You'll be offered a menu of status options:

Show Gives detailed information about the selected job.

Delete Removes the selected job from the queue.

Hold Suspends despooling of the selected job.

Release Allows the selected job to be despooled after it was put on hold.

View Views contents of the selected job.

Copy Copies the selected job to a file.

Rush Gives the selected job top priority.

The Streams Control Window

This window allows you to manage print streams individually or in groups using the print stream control table. Use the up arrow and the down arrow to move to an entry (there are 20 of them). Press Del to clear an entry, Enter to edit the entry's mask, and F5 to toggle the entry from Enabled to Disabled.

The Device Control Window

This window allows you to check and change the status of each output port (a change to ALL affects every port). The status conditions are:

DISABLED Despooling is disabled for the printer on that port.

MULTIPLE JOBS Output to the printer on that port has been enabled to despool more than one job.

HALT AT EOJ The printer on that port will print one job and then stop.

PAUSED The printer on that port has been paused.

NOT DESPOOLING The printer port is enabled, but there is nothing to print.

The CPS value is the rate at which the printer is currently accepting data. A value of zero means that either the printer is off-line or too busy to accept more data. Copies shows the number of copies of the job that have been printed.

Networking with LANtastic

Use the up arrow and the down arrow to select a device. Press Enter to select a new status for that port or ALL ports:

Halt Halts all despooling.

Stop Stops despooling at end of current job.

Pause Temporarily suspends despooling.

One-Job Despools one job, and then stops output to the port(s).

Start Begins despooling if paused or stopped.

Restart Restarts printing the current job from beginning.

Pressing Esc at the main screen for Manipulating Printer Queue on Server will take you back to the main options menu.

Mail Services

When you select this option, you will first be asked to choose a server. The screen in Figure C.34 will then appear.

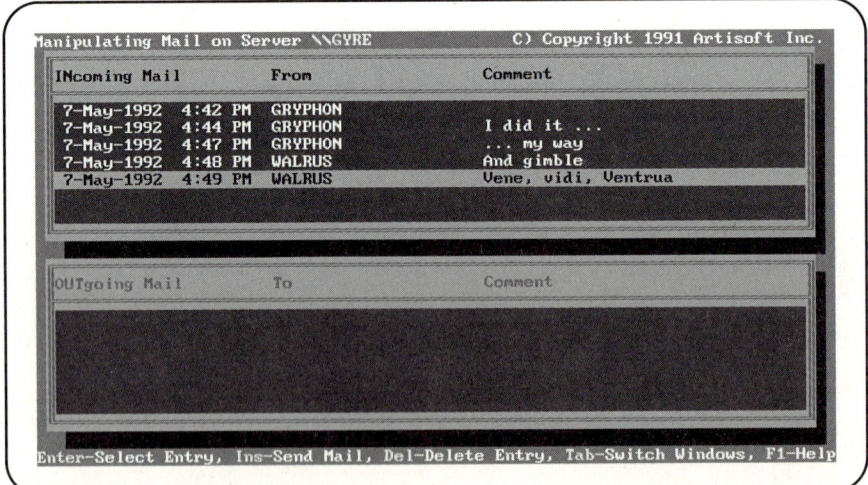

Figure C.34   NET: the Manipulating Mail on Server screen.

This screen offers two windows, INcoming Mail and OUTgoing Mail. Tab allows you to jump from one to the other. Each window shows the date and time the message was sent, the sender or receiver, and the comment line. Any mail item showing V before the comment is a voice mail item (see Chapter 10, "Advanced Topics," for information on voice mail). If you have Super Mail (M) privilege, you'll see all of the mail that is waiting on the server for all users, and you can perform any of the mail-handling options on that mail as well as on your own. Use the up arrow and the down arrow and press Enter to select a mail item. At this point, there are four mail handling options:

- *Read Mail or Listen to Mail.* Allows you to view or hear the contents of a text or voice mail message.

- *Forward Copy of Mail.* This option allows you to send a copy of the message to another user. You'll be asked to specify a user name or press F10 to choose a user from the server's user list. You'll also be allowed to enter an optional comment.

- *Copy Mail to File.* Allows you to copy the mail message to a file. You'll be asked to specify a file name.

- *Delete Mail.* Allows you to remove a mail item from the mail queue. You'll be asked to confirm deletion.

If you want to send a message (it doesn't matter which of the mail handling windows you're in), press Ins. You'll be offered the choice of using the built-in editor, sending an existing text file, or sending a voice mail message. Again, you'll be asked to specify a user name or press F10 to choose a user from the server's user list. You'll also be allowed to enter an optional comment.

Note: This option is the same as the NET MAIL command.

Pressing Esc at the main screen for mail will take you back to the main options menu.

Networking with LANtastic

Chat With Another User

This option allows you to establish a conversation over the network with another user. When you type a message, the other user will see it immediately and respond by typing back. When you select this option, you'll be presented with the screen in Figure C.35.

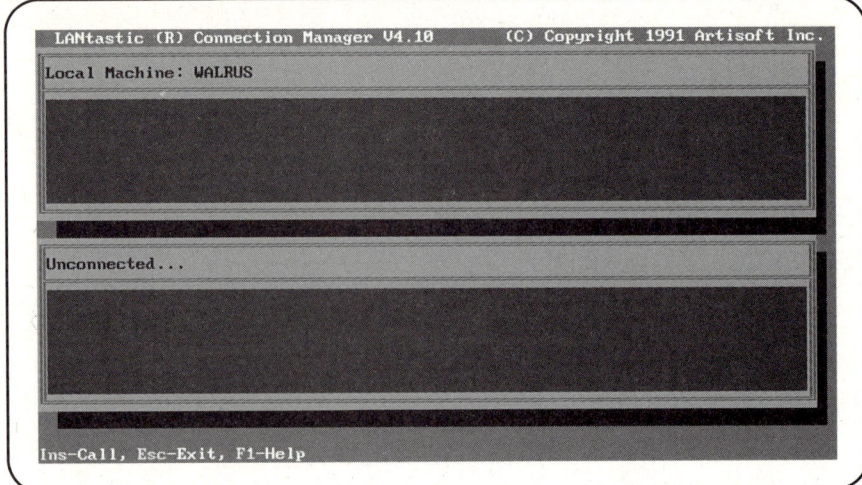

Figure C.35 *NET: The chat screen.*

The upper window displays what you type and the lower window shows what the remote user types. Initially, unless you're answering a call, you won't have anything in either window. To establish a connection to another user, press Ins and enter their machine name. If you don't know the user's correct name (the name specified with REDIR), there's no way to list the network nodes. If the user has messages enabled, he or she will hear a beep, the message will pop-up, or both. If the user doesn't respond within about 15 seconds, the message will pop up again and continue to do so until the user responds or the caller aborts the call. The remote user can respond by using either the NET command and selecting the Chat With Another User option, or by using the **NET CHAT** command. If both users have the Artisoft Voice Board installed, they can pick up their handsets and talk as if they were using a normal telephone (see Chapter 10, "Advanced Topics," for information on voice mail). If either user presses Del, the conversation will be terminated. They will still be in the "chat" option and can make another call. Press Esc to return to the main menu.

Login or Logout

To make or break a connection to a server, use the Login or Logout option. Select this option to display the screen shown in Figure C.36.

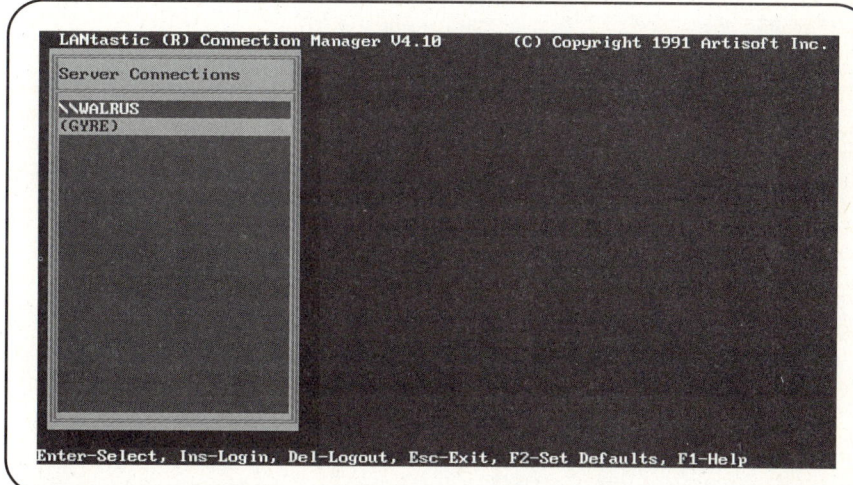

Figure C.36   *NET: The Login or Logout screen.*

The menu shows all the servers for which SERVER.EXE was started with the SEND_SERVER_ID switch set to YES (the default value). The servers that you are logged into appear as *sname*; those that you are not attached to are shown as (*sname*). There are three operations that can be performed from this window:

- *Set your default login parameters.* Press F2 and enter the account name and the password that you want to use as your default login details when you select a server. If no name is set, all logins will prompt for a user name and password. You'll be returned to the Server Connections window. You can press Esc at this point to return to the main menu.

- *Log out from a server.* Use the up arrow and the down arrow to move the highlight to the required server and press Del. You'll be asked to confirm the logout. You'll be returned to the Server Connections window. You can press Esc at this point to return to the main menu.

Note: This option is the same as the NET LOGOUT command.

- *Log into a server.* Use the up arrow and the down arrow to move the highlight to the required server and press Enter. You'll be logged in with your default name and password if they are set, or prompted for the details if not. If the server you want to log into isn't shown, press Ins and enter the server's name. If default login isn't set, enter your account name and your password. If your account name and password are correct, you'll be asked if you want to synchronize your PC's date and time with that of the server. You'll be returned to the Server Connections window. You can press Esc at this point to return to the main menu.

Note: This option is the same as the NET LOGIN command.

User Account Management

If you select this option, you will be asked to select a server. You will then see the display shown in Figure C.37.

The User Account Management option allows you to perform the following maintenance operations on your own account:

- *Switch to New Username.* This option lets you enter a new name and password so that you can change to a different account. If

Utilities Referemce

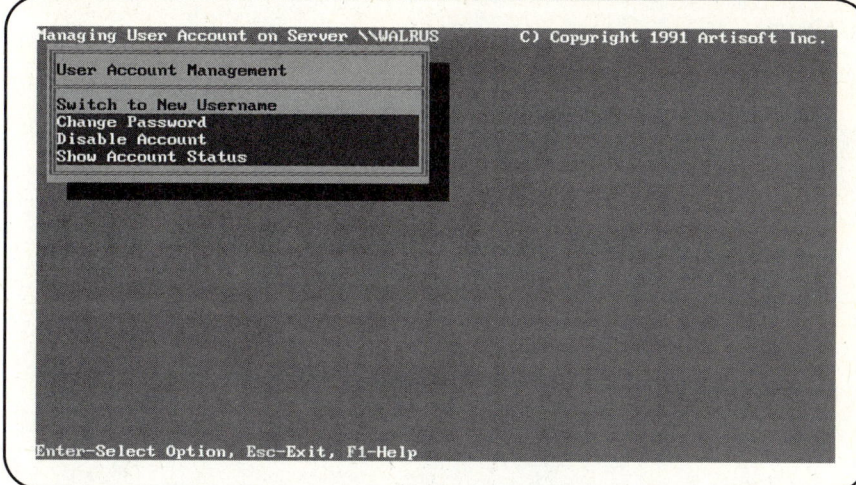

Figure C.37 *NET: The User Account Management screen.*

your account name and password are correct, you'll be asked if you want to synchronize your PC's date and time with that of the server. You'll be returned to the User Account Management window. You can press Esc at this point to return to the main menu.

- *Change Password.* This option allows you to set a new password. You must first enter your current password, and then the new password twice. The reason for entering it twice is that you could lock yourself out of your account if you got it wrong the first time (and as it doesn't echo the characters you type, you wouldn't know). You'll be returned to the User Account Management window. You can press Esc at this point to return to the main menu.

- *Disable Account.* If you are going on vacation or need to make your account inaccessible for some other reason, this option disables your account. Only someone with the System Manager (S) privilege can reinstate your account. You'll be returned to the User Account Management window. You can press Esc at this point to return to the main menu.

Networking with LANtastic

Note: This is the same as the NET DISABLEA command.

- *Show Account Status.* This displays the status of your account (see Figure C.38). You'll be returned to the User Account Management window. You can press Esc at this point to return to the main menu.

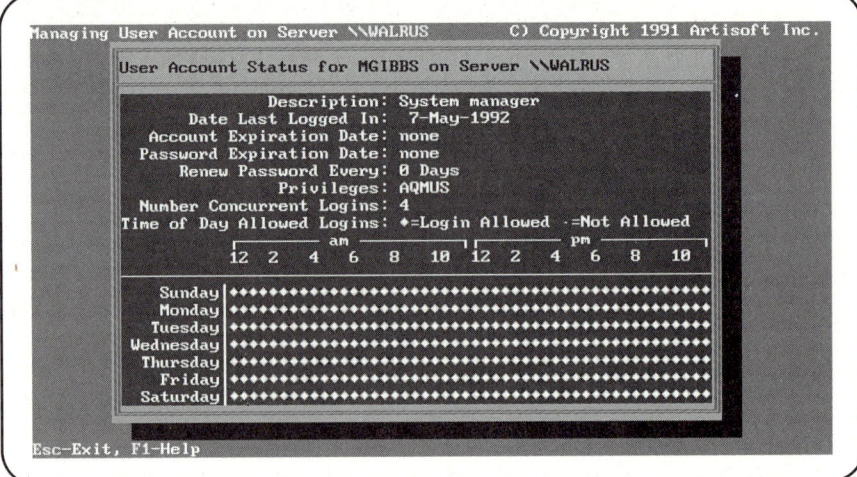

Figure C.38 *NET: The Show Account Status display under the User Account Management option.*

Monitor & Manage Server Activity

If you select this option, you will be asked to select a server. You will then see the display shown in Figure C.39.

Utilities Referemce

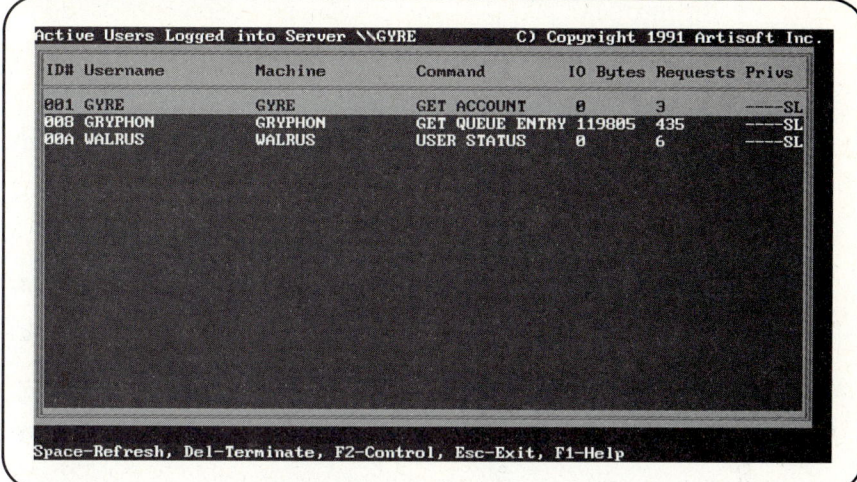

Figure C.39 *NET: The Monitor & Manage Server Activity screen.*

The display shows all of the logged-in users and their details, which are discussed in the following sections.

ID#

The user's identification on this server (the number of your account's entry in the account database).

Username

The user's login name.

Machine

The user's machine name (the REDIR name).

Command

The last command that the user issued to the server.

AUDIT ENTRY   The user created a user audit entry.

CANCEL SHUTDOWN   The user canceled a server shutdown.

CHANGE PASSWORD   The user changed a password.

CHANGE USERNAME   The user changed a username.

CLOSE FILE   The user closed a file.

COMMIT FILE   The user committed file data to disk.

CONTROL QUEUE   The user modified a queue entry or controlled the despooler.

COPY FILE   The user requested a server-based file copy.

CREATE DIR   The user created a directory.

CREATE FILE   The user created a file. An existing file with the same name may have been overwritten.

CREATE INDIRECT   The user created an indirect file.

CREATE NEW FILE   The user created a new file.

DELETE DIR   The user deleted a directory.

DELETE FILE   The user deleted a file.

DISABLE ACCOUNT   The user disabled an account.

FILE READ   The user read data from a file.

FILE WRITE   The user wrote data to a file.

FIND DISK SPACE   The user requested information about the amount of free disk space.

FIND FIRST FILE   The user performed a find first operation.

FIND NEXT FILE   The user performed a find next operation.

FLUSH CACHE   The user flushed the server's caches.

GET ACCOUNT   The user requested account information.

GET INDIRECT   The user accessed the contents of a file referenced through an indirect file.

GET LINK INFO   The user requested information about a directory/device Access Control List.

GET QUEUE ENTRY The user obtained queue entry information.

GET RESOURCE The user obtained detailed information on a resource.

GET SERVER TIME The user obtained the current server time.

GET STREAM The user requested information about a logical printer stream.

GET USERNAME The user retrieved a username from the account file.

LOCK RANGE The user locked a file region.

LOGIN The user is in the process of logging in.

MULTI-MODE OPEN The user performed a multi-mode file open.

OPEN FILE The user opened a file.

PRINTER STATUS The user requested current printer status.

RENAME FILE The user renamed a file.

RUN COMMAND The user submitted a command string.

SEEK POSITION The user performed a file seek.

SERVER CONTROL The user retrieved server control parameters.

SET ATTRIBUTE The user changed a file's attributes.

SET QUEUE ENTRY The user modified queue entry information.

SET STREAM The user modified stream information.

SHUTDOWN The user initiated a server shutdown.

TERMINATE USER A user was terminated by operator request.

TERMINATE The user exited a program.

TRANSLATE PATH The user requested a network pathname translation.

UNIQUE FILE The user created a new file with a unique name.

UNLOCK RANGE The user unlocked a file region.

USER STATUS The user requested user status information.

WRITE W/COMMIT The user wrote data and it was committed to disk.

10 bytes

The amount of data input and output that the server has performed for the user. The value may be followed by a K (for kilobytes), an M (for megabytes), or a G (for gigabytes). For example, 40M would mean that the user has read and written a total of 40 megabytes of data.

Requests

The number of server commands performed since the user logged in.

Privs

The privileges the user has been granted. Table C.7 shows what each code indicates.

Table C.7 Codes returned by the Privs command.

Code	Stands for	Meaning
A	Super ACL	The user's requests are not checked against resource ACLs.
Q	Super Queue	The user is allowed to manipulate the despooler and all printer queue entries.
M	Super Mail	The user can manipulate everyone's mail.
U	User Audit	The user may place an entry in the audit trail with NET AUDIT.
S	System Manager	The user has system manager privileges.

Utilities Referemce

Operations That Can Be Performed

There are two operations that can be performed, but you must have System Manager (S) privilege to complete them:

- To forcibly terminate a user, use the up arrow and the down arrow to highlight a user and press Del. You can enter the number of minutes until termination; zero forces immediate termination. If the value is greater than zero, the user will receive warning messages before being terminated.

> **Note:** This option is the same as the NET TERMINATE command.

- If you press F2, you can control the server. The options available allow you to:

    Schedule Server Shutdown. You can set the number of minutes before shutdown (zero equals immediate shutdown), specify whether the server is to halt, reboot, or continue after shutdown, whether user should be notified, and what the shutdown message sent to logged-in users should be.

> **Note:** These are options available with the NET SHUTDOWN command.

    Cancel Server Shutdown. If a server shutdown has been scheduled, this option allows you to cancel it.

> **Note:** This option is the same as the NET SHUTDOWN/CANCEL command.

    Disable Logins or Enable Logins. This option toggles whether the server will allow users to log in.

467

 **Networking with LANtastic**

 **Note:** This option is the same as the NET SLOGIN command.

- Press Esc to return to the main menu screen.

Utilities Reference

NET_MGR.EXE

The NET_MGR utility allows you to manage network servers, their resources, and environment. Its options include:

- Managing user and group accounts.
- Defining the servers shared printer and disk resources.
- Defining the server's start-up parameters.
- Managing the server's printer and mail queue system.
- Managing the audit trail system.
- Setting a server management password.
- Maintaining the remote boot image file.
- Maintaining the LANtastic control directory.

There are two ways to start NET_MGR. **NET_MGR** starts with a color display. **NET_MGR /MONO** starts NET_MGR in monochrome mode.

If you have set a password (see "Password Maintenance" later in this appendix), you'll be asked to enter it before NET_MGR will display its main menu. When NET_MGR starts, the main options menu is displayed (see Figure C.40).

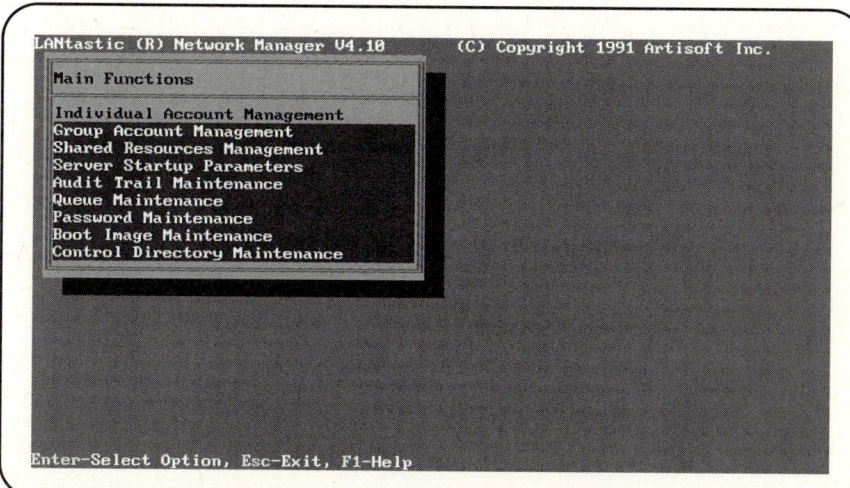

Figure C.40 *The main screen of NET_MGR.EXE.*

469

When you are at the main menu, you can exit back to DOS by pressing Esc. If you need help anywhere in the program, press F1.

Individual Account Management

Selecting this option allows you to perform various operations on user accounts. The screen shown in Figure C.41 will be displayed.

Five operations can be performed on the current users list; they are discussed in the following sections.

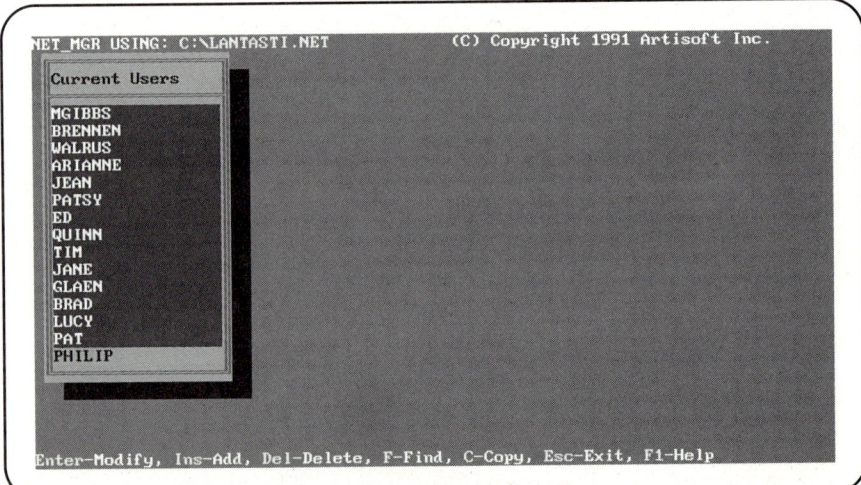

Figure C.41 NET_MGR.EXE: The current user accounts list.

Modify an Existing User Account's Details

Selecting this option will display the window shown in Figure C.42.

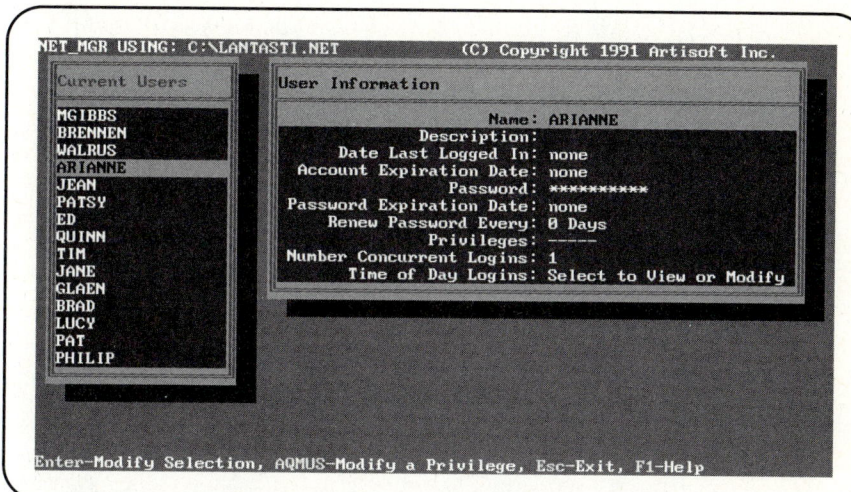

Figure C.42 *NET_MGR.EXE: The user account modification window.*

There are ten choices in the user account modification window:

Name If you change the user account name, be sure that any users of that account have their logins changed appropriately.

Description An optional description of the user account that you can change. Descriptions might be System Manager, Chief Financial Officer, Chief Tap Dancer, and so on.

Date Last Logged In This field is not editable.

Account Expiration Date Selecting this field will pop-up a window that allows you to set the user account expiration date.

Password Setting the user's password is handled a little differently here than setting your own password in NET. You aren't asked to reenter the password; since the characters aren't echoed, it's easy to make a mistake that can cause a user some problems. Always test a user's login if you change the password using this facility.

Password Expiration Date Selecting this attribute will pop up a date-setting window.

Renew Password Every If a value is set here, the user will be forced to change their password every time that many days elapse.

Privileges This option allows you to assign privileges to the user account (see Chapter 8, "Protecting Your Network").

Number Concurrent Logins This attribute defines the number of times this user account can be simultaneously logged into.

Time of Day Logins If you select this option, the window shown in Figure C.43 will be displayed.

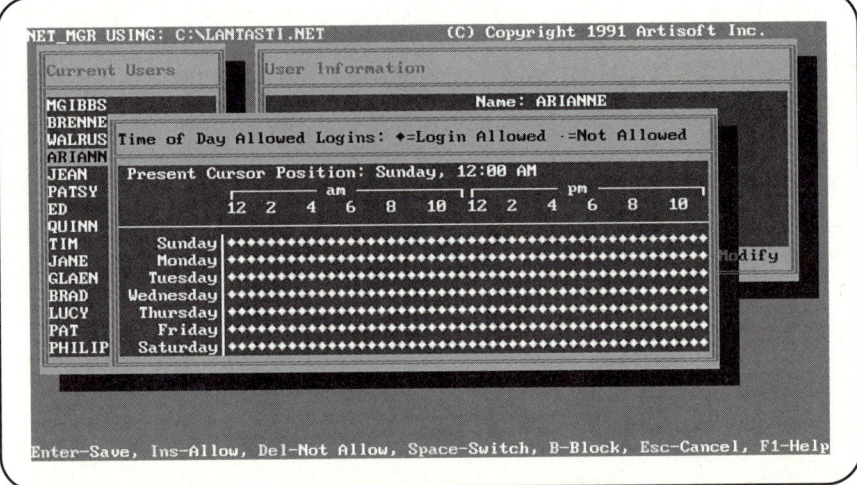

Figure C.43 *NET_MGR.EXE: The Time of Day Logins modification window.*

To enable or disable a block of time for user account logins, move the cursor to the starting day and time using the arrow keys. As you move the cursor, the day and time position are displayed. Press B and then move the cursor to the ending day and time. Press Ins to allow logins or press Del to disallow logins for that entire time block. When you press Enter, you save the settings and return to the modification options menu. If you press Esc, you'll abandon any changes you made and be returned to the modification options menu. You can set as many blocks as you like.

Utilities Referemce

Add a User Account

Press Ins and enter the user name, password, description (optional), and number of concurrent logins.

Delete a User Account

Press Del and confirm deletion.

Find a User Account

You can press F to enter a name of a user. Wildcard characters can be used so that you can, for example, specify TECH-* to find the first user whose name starts with TECH- (such as TECH-TIM or TECH-TGIBBS). The highlight bar will move to the first entry that matches the specification.

Copy a User Account to Another User Account

You can press C to copy the currently highlighted account to a differently named account on the same server, or you can copy the same or differently named account on a different server. (You can change the target server by editing the control directory specification.) You can also specify the password for the destination account and specify whether the account should be overwritten if an account of that name already exists. To change any of the parameters, select the Replace option. Repeatedly select the Replace option to toggle between Yes and No.

> **Note:** Be careful of overwriting an existing group account. If you have planned your groups' accounts carefully, you can make overwriting a safe process. If you haven't planned the accounts, be prepared for surprises and problems.

473

Group Account Management

Selecting this option allows you to perform the same operations on group accounts that you can perform on individual user accounts. The screen shown in Figure C.44 will be displayed.

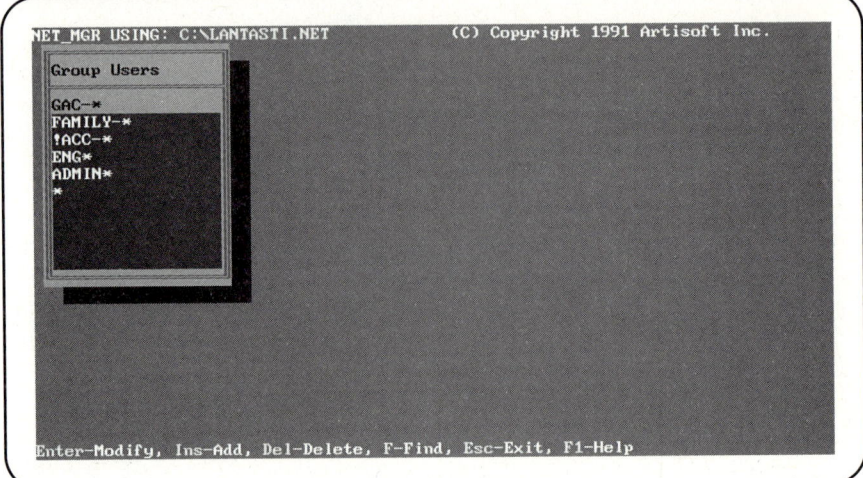

Figure C.44   *NET_MGR.EXE: The current group user accounts list.*

Five operations can be performed on the group users list; they are discussed in the following sections.

Modify an Existing Group Account's Details

Select this option to display the window shown in Figure C.45.

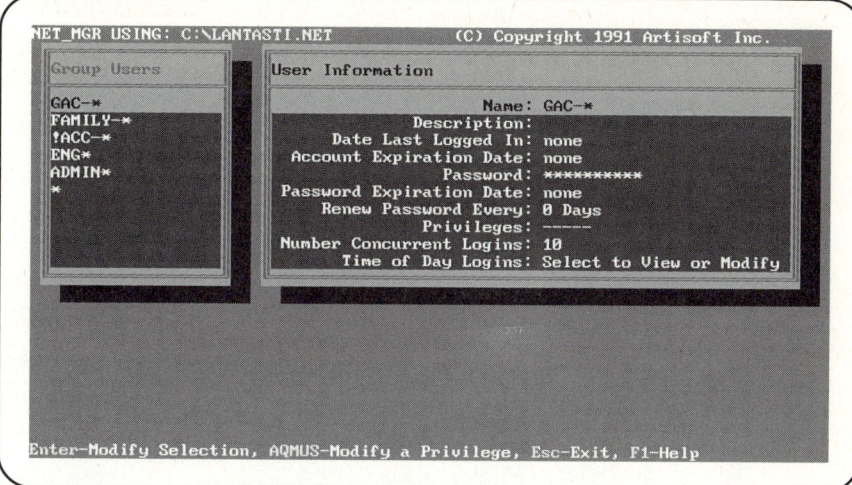

Figure C.45 *NET_MGR.EXE: The group account modification window.*

There are 10 items in the group account modification window:

Name   If you change the group account name, be sure that any users of that group account have their logins changed appropriately.

Description   An optional description of the group account that you can change. Descriptions might be `Accounts users`, `Engineering department`, `Tap-dancing squad`, and so on.

Date Last Logged In   This field is not editable.

Account Expiration Date   Selecting this field will pop up a window that allows you to set the group account expiration date.

Password   Setting the group's password is handled a little differently here than setting your own password in NET. You aren't asked to reenter the password; since the characters aren't echoed, it's easy to make a mistake that can cause a user some problems. Always test the group's login if you change the password using this facility.

Password Expiration Date   Selecting this attribute will pop up a date setting window.

Renew Password Every   If a value is set here, the group will be forced to change their password every time that many days elapse.

Networking with LANtastic

Privileges This option allows you to assign privileges to the group (see Chapter 8, "Protecting Your Network").

Number Concurrent Logins This attribute defines the number of times this group account can be simultaneously logged into.

Time of Day Logins If you select this option, the window shown in Figure C.46 will be displayed.

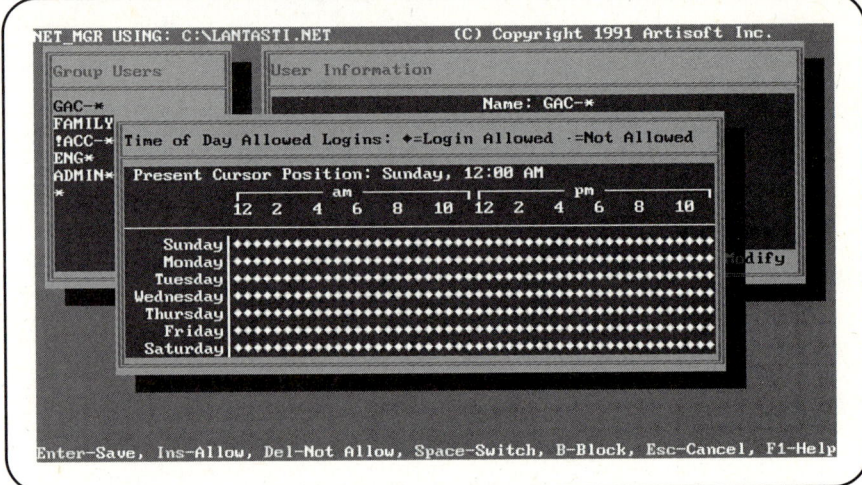

Figure C.46 NET_MGR.EXE: The Time of Day Logins modification window.

To enable or disable a block of time for user account logins, move the cursor to the starting day and time using the arrow keys. As you move the cursor, the day and time position are displayed. Press B and then move the cursor to the ending day and time. Press Ins to allow logins or press Del to disallow logins for that entire time block. When you press Enter, you save the settings and return to the modification options menu. If you press Esc, you'll abandon any changes you made and be returned to the modification options menu. You can set as many blocks as you like.

Add a Group Account

Press Ins and enter the group name, password, description (optional), and number of concurrent logins.

Utilities Referemce

Delete a Group Account

Press Del and confirm deletion.

Find a Group Account

You can press F to enter a name of a group account. Wildcard characters can be used, so you can, for example, specify T* to find the first group whose name starts with T (such as TECHSERV or TRAINING). The highlight bar will be moved to the first entry that matches the specification.

Copy a Group Account to Another Group Account

You can press C to copy the currently highlighted account to a differently named account on the same server, or you can copy the same or differently named account on a different server. (You can change the target server by editing the control directory specification.) You can also specify the password for the destination account and specify whether the account should be overwritten if an account of that name already exists. To change any of the parameters, select the Replace option. Repeatedly selecting the Replace option will toggle it between Yes and No.

> **Note:** Be careful of overwriting an existing group account. If you have planned your groups' accounts carefully, you can make overwriting a safe process. If you haven't planned the accounts, be prepared for surprises and problems.

Shared Resources Management

This option allows you to create, delete, and modify shared resources. When you select this item, the window shown in Figure C.47 will be displayed.

477

Do It Yourself *Networking with LANtastic*

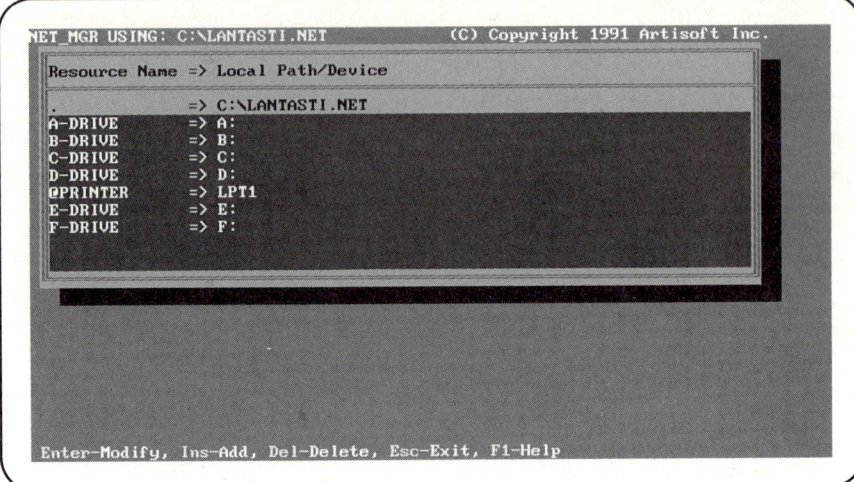

Figure C.47 NET_MGR.EXE: The Resource Name => Local Path/Device list.

The Resource Name => Local Path/Device list shows which resources have been created and what directory path (for disk resources) or port (for shared printers) they are defined as.

You have four options:

- Modify a resource.
- Add a resource.
- Delete a resource.
- Exit.

Modify a Resource

Use the up arrow and the down arrow to highlight a shared resource, and press Enter to display a window for editing the resource's attributes.

You can modify two types of resources:

- Shared disk resources.
- Shared mail resources.
- Shared printer resources.

The window for modifying shared disk resources is shown in Figure C.48.

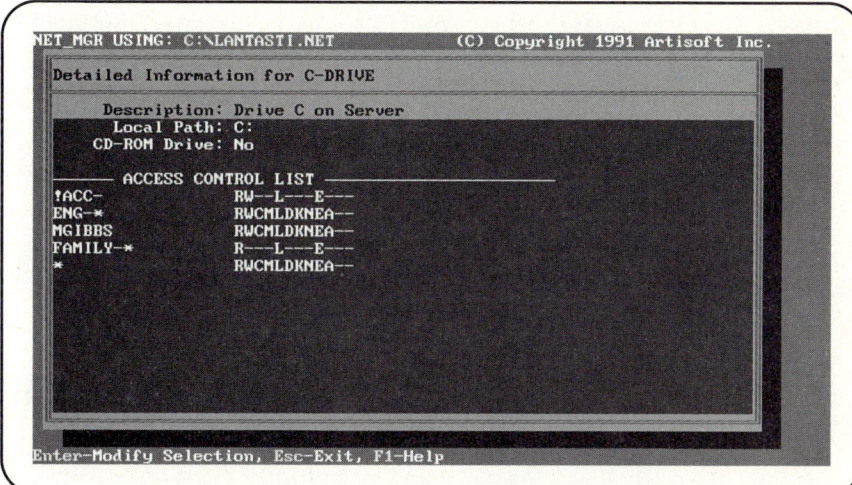

Figure C.48 *NET_MGR.EXE: The Detailed Information for* disk_resource *window.*

The attributes shown are:

- *Description.* Selecting this attribute will allow you to change the optional description of the resource.

- *Local Path.* This is the definition of the path that defines the resource. Selecting this option allows you to edit the specification.

- *CD-ROM.* If the resource is to be treated as a CD-ROM (slower access and, consequently, a low server-processing overhead and read-only), this should be set to Yes. Selecting this attribute toggles the field from Yes to No.

- *The Access Control List.* There are several operations that can be performed on the ACL for a disk resource:

    Modify the entry's name Select any entry other than * to modify the name associated with those rights.

    Change the entry's rights Highlight an entry and press any of the letters for rights (RWCMLDKNEAIP) to toggle the right between enabled and disabled (if the right's identifying letter isn't shown, that right is disabled).

Create an entry Pressing Ins allows you to make an entry. Once you have given the name, the entry is created with a set of rights that only lacks I and P.

Delete an entry To delete an entry, highlight it, press Delete, and confirm the operation.

Set all normal rights Press F3 to set the entry's rights to RWCMLDKNEA--.

Clear all rights Press F4 to clear all rights so that the line reads ------------.

Store current ACL Press F9 to store the current ACL settings.

Restore ACL Press F10 to restore the last version of the ACL that was stored.

Return to Resource Name => Local Path/Device list Press Esc to return to the previous window, and any ACL changes that weren't saved will be stored automatically.

The window for modifying shared printer resources is shown in Figure C.49.

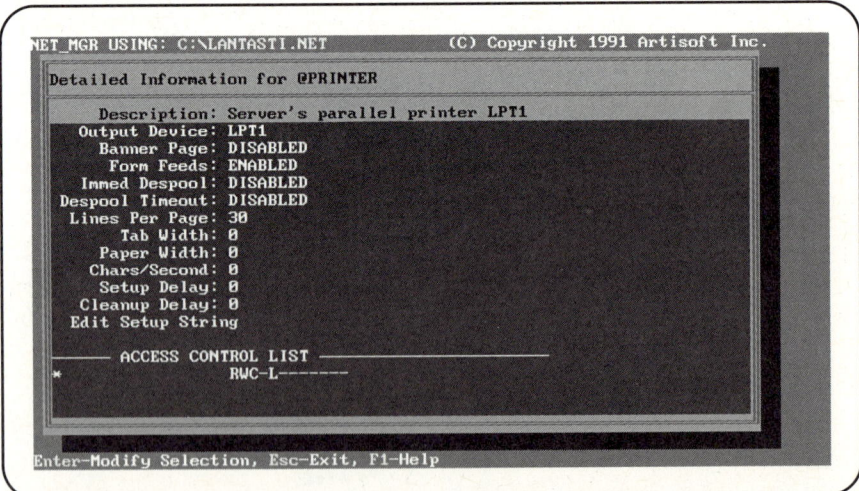

Figure C.49 *NET_MGR.EXE: The Detailed Information for @printer_resource window.*

The attributes that are shown are:

- *Description.* Optional text description. Select to change.

- *Output Device.* Selecting this field will bring up a list of ports to select from.

- *Banner Page.* Select to toggle between Enabled and Disabled. When enabled, the spooler prints a banner page before the job. See Chapter 7, "Shared Resources."

- *Form Feeds.* Select to toggle between Enabled and Disabled. When enabled, the spooler sends a form feed after the completion of a print job. See Chapter 7, "Shared Resources."

- *Immed Despool.* Select to toggle between Enabled and Disabled. When enabled, this allows the spooler to start printing the job even though the job hasn't been completed.

- *Despool Timeout.* Select to set a value. A value of zero is shown as Disabled and there will be no timeout. When set, this value specifies how long the spooler will wait when an immediate despool job has begun printing after characters have stopped being received. When this period expires, the job is automatically ended so that another job can print.

- *Lines Per Page.* Select to set the page length in lines.

- *Tab Width.* Select to set the number of spaces that tab characters should be expanded to.

- *Paper Width.* Select to set the width of the page in characters to allow the banner page to print correctly. The default for this field is 80 characters even though it displays as zero.

- *Chars/Second.* Select to set the rate at which the spooler will send characters to the port. If you need to increase the user-perceived performance of a server that is handling several printers, setting this parameter to a low value for the printers that the system would have to service frequently (the faster ones) will give more processing time for user data access requests.

- *Setup Delay.* Select to set the delay before the spooler sends output data to the printer to allow the printer to setup for the next print job.

- *Cleanup Delay.* Select to set the delay before the spooler sends output data to the printer to allow the printer to cleanup after finishing a print job.

- *Edit Setup String.* Selecting this option allows you to select which of the printer control sequences to edit:

  Setup String   When you select this option, enter the characters that will set up the printer. The Printer Setup String windows will appear (see Figure C.50). Pressing Ins pops up another edit window that lets you enter setup data one character at a time. If you enter two digits, it is taken as a character's value. A single character is taken literally as that character.

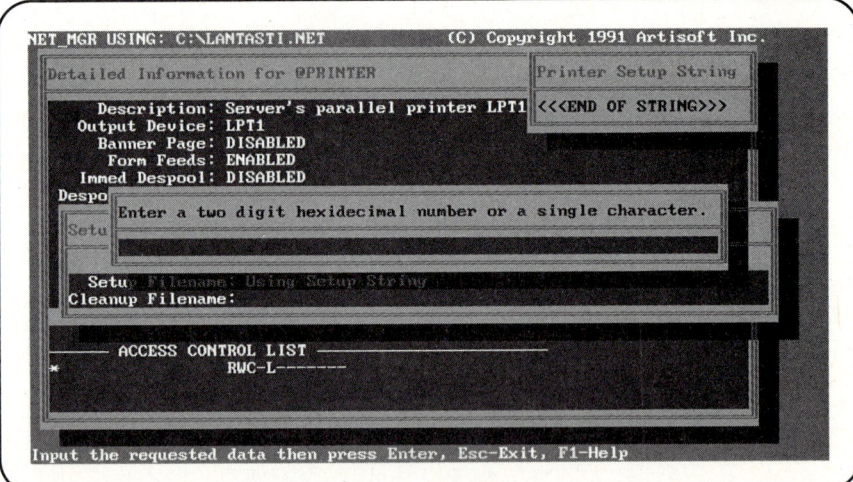

Figure C.50   *NET_MGR.EXE: The Printer Setup String and character entry windows.*

You can move the highlight up and down the list of entered characters in the Printer Setup String to select a character to delete or to insert a new character.

Setup Filename   Selecting this item allows you to specify a file and its path which contains the printer setup character sequence.

Cleanup Filename   Selecting this item allows you to specify a file and its path which contains the printer cleanup character sequence.

● *The Access Control List.* There are several operations that can be performed on the ACL for a disk resource:

Modify the entry's name   Select any entry other than * to modify the name associated with those rights.

Change the entry's rights   Highlight an entry and press any of the letters for rights (RWCMLDKNEAIP) to toggle the right between enabled and disabled (if the right's identifying letter isn't shown, that right is disabled).

Create an entry   Press Ins to make an entry. Once you have given the name, the entry is created with the rights RWC-L-------.

> **Note:** For most situations for shared printer resources, the rights RWC-L------- are the only practical combination to allow.

Delete an entry   To delete an entry, highlight it, press Del, and confirm the operation.

Set all normal rights   Press F3 to set the entry's rights to RWC-L-------.

Clear all rights   Press F4 to clear all rights so that the line reads ------------.

Store current ACL   Press F9 to store the current ACL settings.

Restore ACL   Press F10 to restore the last version of the ACL that was stored.

Return to Resource Name => Local Path/Device list   Press Esc to return to the previous window; any ACL changes that weren't saved will be stored automatically.

Add a Resource

Press Ins to pop up a window where you can enter the name of a new resource.

- To create a new disk resource, enter a name that doesn't start with an @. You'll be asked to specify a path to define the resource.

- To create a new printer resource, enter a name that starts with an @. You'll then be asked to select a port to associate with that resource.

Delete a Resource

Use the up arrow and the down arrow to highlight a resource and press Del. You'll be prompted to press Enter to actually perform the deletion or press Esc to cancel.

Exit

Press Esc to return to the main menu.

Server Start-up Parameters

Selecting this option will display the window in Figure C.51. This window allows you to modify the server's start-up configuration.

Utilities Reference

```
NET_MGR USING: C:\LANTASTI.NET          (C) Copyright 1991 Artisoft Inc.
┌─Server Startup Parameters──────┐
│     Maximum Users: 5           │
│    Network Buffer: 4096        │
│   Number Adapters: 6           │
│     Network Tasks: 1           │
│    Send Server ID: ENABLED     │
│    Remote Booting: DISABLED    │
│     Floppy Direct: ENABLED     │
│        Despooling: ENABLED     │
│    Printer Buffer: 512         │
│     Printer Tasks: 1           │
│    Max Files Open: use CONFIG.SYS │
│   Run Buffer Size: 127         │
│      Request Size: 14          │
│         Run Burst: 2           │
│   Seek Cache Size: 32K         │
│  Cached Resources: 4           │
│     Lock Hold Time: 9          │
│──────── AUDITING ──────────────│▼
Enter-Modify Selection, Esc-Exit, F1-Help
```

Figure C.51 *NET_MGR.EXE: The Server Start-up Parameters window.*

Maximum Users

Select to set the maximum number of users the server can support. This value is used by SERVER.EXE but cannot be set anywhere else other than here.

> **Note:** Make sure that you set this value to the required maximum number of users from the default of two before you start your system in "live" operation. This value can also be set by the LOGINS switch in SERVER.EXE.

Network Buffer

Select this option to specify the size of the buffers used for network communication. The default value is 4096 (4K) bytes. Increasing the network buffer value will increase performance but will use more memory. How much memory depends on the value of Network Tasks.

485

Note: This option is also controlled by the SERVER.EXE switch NETWORK_BUFFER_SIZE, and the value of the switch as specified on SERVER's command line will override the value set under the NET_MGR Server Start-up Parameters option's Network Buffer suboption.

Number of Adapters

Select this option to specify the number of adapters that are installed in your computer. The maximum number of adapters that your computer can support depends on the type of network adapter. Some adapters are limited in the addressing or interrupts they use, so you can only use less than the maximum that can be supported.

Note: This option is also controlled by the SERVER.EXE switch ADAPTERS, and the value of the switch as specified on SERVER's command line will override the value set under the NET_MGR Server Start-up Parameters option's Network Adapters suboption.

Network Tasks

Selecting this option allows you to specify the number of tasks that will be allocated to handle simultaneous user requests. The more tasks, the better the performance but at the cost of memory. The memory required will be the number of network tasks multiplied by the size set for Network Buffer.

Note: This option is also controlled by the SERVER.EXE switch NETWORK_TASKS, and the value of the switch as specified on SERVER's command line will override the value set under the NET_MGR Server Start-up Parameters option's Network Tasks suboption.

Send Server ID

Select this option to toggle between Enabled and Disabled. This determines whether the server will broadcast its name when requested. When you use a program that displays a list of available servers, any server that has SEND_SERVER_ID set to NO will not appear. To access the server that has SEND_SERVER_ID set to NO, the user needs to know its name.

> **Note:** If you are building a very tightly controlled network, setting all server's SEND_SERVER_ID switches to NO is another tactic to make the network less vulnerable to unauthorized access.

Remote Booting

Select this option to toggle between Enabled and Disabled. This determines whether a remote PC can read data from the boot image but not write (READ-ONLY) or both read from and write to the boot image (READ-WRITE). If this option is set to DISABLE, remote booting is not supported by this server. See the NET RPL command for more detail.

> **Note:** This option is equivalent to the SERVER RPL command. The setting of the SERVER RPL switch will override the value set under the NET_MGR Server Start-up Parameters option's Remote Booting suboption.

Floppy Direct

Select this option to toggle between Enabled and Disabled. When remote users access a floppy disk drive, there are two operations that require direct access: FORMAT and CHKDSK. Setting Floppy Direct to Disable prevents remote users from performing either function.

Note: Disabling the Floppy Direct option to keep remote users from formatting a server's floppy disks is a very good idea if floppy disk drives are defined as shared network resources. You might consider making your server floppy disk drive inaccessible to remote users on principle.

Note: This option is also controlled by the SERVER.EXE switch FLOPPY_DIRECT, and the value of the switch as specified on SERVER's command line will override the value set under the NET_MGR Server Start-up Parameters option's Floppy Direct suboption.

Despooling

Select this option to toggle between Enable or Disable to control the print despooling service when the server starts. If you want to create a print stream control table, you'll need to set this to Disable, build the table with NET STREAM commands, and then issue a NET QUEUE START command to enable despooling.

Note: This option is also controlled by the SERVER.EXE switch DESPOOLER_STOPPEC. The state of the switch as specified on SERVER's command line will override the state set under the NET_MGR Server Start-up Parameters option's Despooling suboption.

Printer Buffer

Select this option to specify the size of the print buffer used to transfer data from disk to the printer ports. To improve the performance of the spooler system, you can increase the value of Printer Buffer. This, of course, will use more memory, the amount depending on the number of buffers set by Printer Tasks.

Utilities Referemce

Note: This option is also controlled by the SERVER.EXE switch PRINTER_BUFFER_SIZE. The state of the switch as specified on SERVER's command line will override the state set under the NET_MGR Server Start-up Parameters option's Printer Buffer suboption.

Printer Tasks

Select this option to specify the number of printer tasks that can be allocated. If you don't allocate as many server printer tasks as there are printers, the spooler has to do a lot of juggling to keep feeding data to the printers. Allocating more buffers will improve the performance of the printers at the expense of memory. If the value is set to zero, despooling is disabled and cannot be started as there are no resources for the spooler to use.

Note: Do not set the number of printer tasks to be greater than the number of printers.

Note: This option is also controlled by the SERVER.EXE switch PRINTER_TASKS. The state of the switch as specified on SERVER's command line will override the state set under the NET_MGR Server Start-up Parameters option's Printer Tasks suboption.

Max Files Open

Selecting this option allows you to specify the maximum number of simultaneously open files that the server system can support. The DOS limit is 255, and this may not be enough for a large server system. The default setting (use CONFIG.SYS or zero) uses whatever FILES parameter has been set in the CONFIG.SYS file. If you set the value between 50 and 5100, SERVER allocates its own files for network users.

Note: This option is also controlled by the SERVER.EXE switch FILES. The value of the switch as specified on SERVER's command line will override the value set under the NET_MGR Server Start-up Parameters option's Max Files Open suboption.

Run Buffer Size

Select this option to specify how much buffer space (memory) to allocate for commands issued by using the NET RUN command. If you set the value to zero, you disable the feature. Setting buffer to a high value allows you to queue up several commands. The amount of memory used will be equal to the size of the buffer.

Note: This option is also controlled by the SERVER.EXE switch RUN_BUFFER_SIZE. The value of the switch as specified on SERVER's command line will override the value set under the NET_MGR Server Start-up Parameters option's Run Buffer Size suboption.

Request Size

Selecting this option allows you to specify the size of the request buffers where the incoming messages are stored. If the buffers aren't big enough to hold the whole message, the client will have to send the rest of the message later. This increases the load on the network and the response of the server. Increasing the value of Request Size will improve performance for some operations, such as file lookups and random access file writing. The trade-off in improving the performance is using more memory; the amount of memory used depends on the value set for maximum users in the server start-up parameters and the value of Request Size.

Note: This option is also controlled by the SERVER.EXE switch REQUEST_SIZE. The value of the switch as specified on SERVER's command line will override the value set under the NET_MGR Server Start-up Parameters option's Request Size suboption.

Run Burst

To control how much processing time an application receives, the Run Burst option allows you to specify the maximum number of ticks that the server can run before returning control to the application or DOS. The larger this value, the lower the performance of applications that are run on that node. If you find that the network performance of the node is slow, this value may be increased to compensate.

Note: This option is also controlled by the SERVER.EXE and AILANBIO.EXE switches called RUN_BURST. The value of the switch as specified on SERVER's command line will override the value set under both AILANBIO's switch and the NET_MGR Server Start-up Parameters option's Run Burst suboption.

Seek Cache Size

The seek cache is used (if enabled by setting a value greater than zero) to store information about random access operations. By doing so, you can increase the performance of the system for database-type applications. The larger the seek cache, the better the performance and the more memory that it will use.

Note: This option is also controlled by the SERVER.EXE switch SEEK_CACHE. The value of the switch as specified on SERVER's command line will override the value set under the NET_MGR Server Start-up Parameters option's Seek Cache Size suboption.

Networking with LANtastic

Cached Resources

To handle the shared resources, LANtastic keeps a set of data either on disk or in memory. If the data is on disk, it has to be read into memory to be used. The resource caches are where that data is held. If there are less caches than resources and if a user accesses a different resource than the one currently in the cache, LANtastic must swap out the data for one of the cached resources to allow it to handle the required resource. This puts an overhead on the operation that, for a heavily used server, can degrade performance seriously. By increasing the value of the Resource Cache option, you can gain some major performance improvements.

> **Note:** This option is also controlled by the SERVER.EXE switch RESOURCE_CACHE. The value of the switch as specified on SERVER's command line will override the value set under the NET_MGR Server Start-up Parameters option's Cached Resources suboption.

Lock Hold Time

When a program locks a record, it will hold that lock for a period of time. For well-behaved applications, this time period is as short as possible. But even when the application is well behaved, it still takes time to perform a record update or complete some other file operation. Selecting this option allows you to set the value of Lock Hold Time so that other users won't automatically fail when a record is locked by one user. This switch sets the time that the server will wait before failing the attempt to lock the record. If, for example, you knew that the average record update time for your invoice system was 5 seconds, you might set this parameter to a value of 108 ticks or 6 seconds to prevent a record lock attempt from failing. If used with the right applications, LOCK_HOLD_TIME can improve the response time of the system.

Utilities Referemce

Note: This option is also controlled by the SERVER.EXE switch LOCK_HOLD_TIME. The value of the switch as specified on SERVER's command line will override the value set under the NET_MGR Server Start-up Parameters option's Lock Hold Time suboption.

Auditing

For each server, you can specify what system operation you want the audit trail to include and exclude records of. Selecting one of the following operations will toggle its status between ENABLED and DISABLED:

- *Server Up.* An entry is made whenever the server is started.
- *Logins.* An entry is made whenever a user logs into the server.
- *Logouts.* An entry is made whenever a user logs out of the server.
- *Queuing.* An entry is made whenever a mail item or a print job is added to a queue.
- *Printing.* An entry is made whenever the server finishes printing a job.

Note: If you abandon a job (that is, stop or delete it) and the audit options for Queuing and Printing are enabled, you'll see that the audit trail has an entry when the job was created but no corresponding entry for being printed.

- *User Entry.* Disable this to prevent the creation of user audit entries with the NET AUDIT command.

Select the following entries to edit the rights that are to be audited for access allowed or denied:

- *Access Allowed.* When a user performs an operation that requires one of the rights specified and access is allowed, an audit entry will be made. If the rights that are specified are - - - - - - - - - - - -, no access allowed audit entries will be made.

Networking with LANtastic

- *Access Denied.* When a user performs an operation that requires one of the rights specified and access is denied, an audit entry will be made. If the rights that are specified are - - - - - - - - - - - -, no access denied audit entries will be made.

Note: You should be very selective as to which audit trail options you enable. Each entry takes an average of about 80 characters, so you can use up a lot of disk space fairly quickly if many options are enabled.

Audit Trail Maintenance

The audit trail is a list of all events that you have defined through the Server Start-up Parameters auditing section should be recorded. Selecting this option allows you to do three operations:

- *View Last Few Audit Entries.* Allows you to examine the last few entries. When you select the option, a window will open showing the data (see Figure C.52).

Figure C.52   *NET_MGR.EXE: The View Last Few Audit Entries display window.*

- *Copy Audit Trail File.* Allows you to copy the audit trail to a file. When you select this, you'll be asked to give an output path and file name.
- *Clear The Audit Trail File.* Clears out the audit trail entries.

The audit trail entries are in the form:

`Type Date Time Username Machine Reason Variable`

The individual entry components are:

- `Type`.

    - `*`   Server started.
    - `!`   Server shut down.
    - `I`   A user successfully logged into the server.
    - `O`   A user logged off server, or the server connection was broken.
    - `A`   Access was allowed to a shared resource.
    - `D`   Access was denied to a shared resource.
    - `Q`   An entry was placed in the queue.
    - `S`   A queue entry was despooled to a printer.
    - `U`   A user requested to write an audit entry.

- `Date`. A date entry is in the form *YY.MM.DD* where *YY* represents the year, *MM* is the month, and *DD* is the day.
- `Time`. Time entry is in the form *HH:MM:SS* where *HH* represents hours, *MM* is minutes, and *SS* is seconds.
- `Username`. The name of the user who created or caused the audit entry to be made.
- `Machine`. The machine name (REDIR name) of the PC the user was on when the entry was made.
- `Reason`. An eight-character text field (user specified with the NET AUDIT command).
- `Variable`. A 64-character text field (user specified with the NET AUDIT command).

Networking with LANtastic

Queue Maintenance

This option is not available if the server is running. The queue maintenance option allows you to do two operations; to change the spool area and to delete all entries in the current spool area.

Change Spool Location

The spool area is a directory, by default C:\LANTASTI.NET\SPOOL.NET. You can change the spool area to any directory you like as long as it is on a local disk drive. This means that you can't put the spool area on another server but you could put it on a floppy disk (a very bad idea), a hard disk drive, or a RAM disk drive. If you use the latter, you can get some improvement in printing performance, but you'll be limited in the size of the print queue.

Clear Spool Area

When you select this operation, you'll be asked for the spool area's path (the default path or, if you changed it, the current path will be shown). Press Enter to delete any jobs that haven't been despooled and reset the job numbering to one.

Password Maintenance

If you have not currently enabled a password, selecting this option will give you a single option, Enable Password Access for NET_MGR. If you select this, you'll be asked to enter a password twice, and you'll be returned to a menu now showing two options: Disable Password Access for NET_MGR and Change Password. Now you'll have to enter that password whenever you start NET_MGR. Also, if you want to access Password Maintenance, you'll be asked to enter the password again before you can continue (just in case you left a password-protected NET_MGR running on your PC, and somebody decides to try to disable password access).

Select Disable Password Access for NET_MGR to change the menu to the single item Enable Password Access for NET_MGR again. Select Change Password to change to a new password.

Press Esc to return to the main options menu.

> **Note:** By setting a password on NET_MGR, you effectively prevent unauthorized interference in any of the aspects of the server that are controlled by NET_MGR. This really provides protection only against unauthorized NET_MGR access across the network. If someone can get to your PC physically, your security can be easily breached.

Boot Image Maintenance

This option can't be used if the server is running. Select it to access an option list of two types:

- If a boot image doesn't exist, there will be only one option: Build Boot Image.
- If a boot image exists, there will be two options available: Build Boot Image and Delete Boot Image.

If you select Build Boot Image, you'll be asked to specify a source drive (A or B are the only options) which contains a disk prepared to be the contents of the image. A display of progress will be shown as the image file is built.

> **Note:** Once you have built a boot image, you must enable the Remote Booting option under Server Start-up Parameters for remote booting to work.

If you select Delete Boot Image, you'll be asked to confirm or cancel. If you do delete the boot image, the Remote Boot option in Server Start-up Parameters will automatically be disabled.

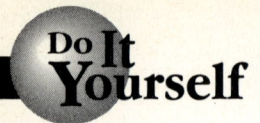

Control Directory Maintenance

Selecting this option offers you a menu of five options:

- *Change Control Directory.* Selecting this option allows you to specify a different control directory to be used.

> **Note:** If the actual network control directory isn't C:\LANTASTI.NET, you can use this option to tell NET_MGR.EXE which directory to use. Alternatively, you can start NET_MGR.EXE with the /CONTROL= switch.

- *Backup Control Directory.* Allows you to make a backup copy of the information in the control directory to file. This is vitally important if you have a complex list of users, groups, and shared resources.

- *Restore Control Directory.* Allows you to restore the network control directory from the data in a file that was created with the Backup Control Directory option.

- *Delete Control Directory.* Deletes the currently selected control directory.

- *Create Control Directory.* Creates a control directory with the name set in Change Control Directory.

Glossary

Access Control List (ACL)   Each LANtastic shared resource has an attached list of users and groups and their associated rights. This allows you to restrict who can do what to what.

access controls   The techniques and methods used to restrict access to files or services. These tools make it possible to build secure systems, ensuring that the effects of accidents, malicious users, computer viruses, and so on are minimized.

access rights   Users can perform various operations on files and directories, such as listing the contents of files, reading from and writing to files, and so on. Access rights define whether a user or a group of users can perform one of these particular operations.

account   The definition of a server user that specifies the user's login name (not necessarily the same as the user's real name), a password, and other control data, such as restrictions on when the user can log in and so forth.

Networking with LANtastic

account privileges Account privileges allow a user management-level access to resources on a server. When you have a *privilege,* you can perform operations on that resource without restriction.

active components In a cabling system, active components amplify and regenerate signals to ensure that they are error free.

adapter cards You can use adapter cards to expand the facilities of a PC. These cards plug into the bus and are available to support different types of displays, networks, and so on. They come in different configurations, depending on the type of machine (ISA, EISA, or MCA) that they will be used with.

ARCnet Attached Resource Computer network. A technology that supports local area networking. One of the most common methods, ARCnet transfers data at 2.5 megabits per second.

audit trail In general, an audit trail is a list of events that allows you to determine what has happened on the network. On a LANtastic server, you can set up an audit trail to log a wide variety of events. An audit trail allows you to monitor activity, error conditions, and other events that affect the performance or correct operation of a server.

backup The process of copying files so that accurate copies of them will exist if the files become lost or corrupt. You usually do backups by copying data from a hard disk or floppy disk to another storage medium (such as another disk, a tape drive, a WORM drive, and so on).

BNC connectors A particular type of connector used in coaxial cabling.

bridge A bridge is a device used to support communications between different networking technologies. For example, you might use a bridge to connect an ARCNET network to an EtherNet system.

bus The components in a PC (processor, memory, disk controller, and so on) are interconnected through the *bus.* The specific design of the bus defines what types of devices can be included in the system and what levels of performance can be achieved.

client See *workstation*.

concentrator A term for a device that acts as a common point for connecting cabling. Also referred to as a *hub*.

data width   This defines how much data (in bits) can be moved simultaneously from one device to another in the PC. The original IBM PC had an 8-bit bus and the IBM AT had a 16-bit bus. Today, the key standards are ISA, EISA, and MCA.

Direct Memory Access (DMA)   A method of moving data from memory or an input/output device directly to another area of memory or other input/output device.

dongle   A popular name for a hardware-based copy protection system. Dongles are usually devices that plug into a serial or parallel port and, without which, the software can't run.

driver   The software that provides the communication between a program and a specific device. The driver hides the details of controlling and communicating with the device and presents the device's services in the generic form expected by the program.

Dynamic Data Exchange (DDE)   Under Microsoft Windows, programs can communicate with each other using DDE. This allows for structured "conversations," which can be used to pass data on demand from one program to another or initiate a service.

EISA   Extended Industry Standard Architecture. One of the standards for building PCs. It defines the architecture of a 32-bit bus that will accommodate 32-, 16-, and 8-bit adapter cards.

electronic mail   A system that allows you to pass messages to another user on the network. The message is stored in a message database, and is then forwarded to the intended recipient at a later time.

EtherNet   EtherNet is a technology that supports local area networking. One of the most common methods used, EtherNet transfers data at 10 megabits per second.

file server   File servers are PCs that run only software that allows other PCs (the server's clients) to share files, printers, and other resources. They cannot be used to run applications. The term is usually used to distinguish products like Artisoft's LANtastic (a peer-to-peer system) from products such as Novell's NetWare (a file-server system).

flow control   The method by which the transfer of data is controlled to prevent the sending device from transmitting when the receiving device is busy. *Hardware flow control* uses a separate wire to indicate whether the receiver is ready. *Software flow control* uses specific characters that are sent by the receiver to the sender to indicate the same thing.

group account   Group accounts are much like user accounts, but they apply to two or more users. Under LANtastic, group accounts are specified by adding a common prefix to users' server login names. Thus, the group ENG-* would include anyone whose login name started with the same characters, such as ENG-TGIBBS or ENG-PJ.

guest account   A guest account is an account which can be used by anyone to gain access to a server resource. In general, you should strictly limit access to these accounts to ensure that someone with malicious intent or thievery in mind can do little damage.

ISA   Industry Standard Architecture. ISA is one of the standards for building PCs and defines the architecture of a 16-bit bus that will accommodate 16-bit and 8-bit adapter cards.

mask   A template which allows you to search for a specific item or a range of items. It is usually used with wildcard symbols that indicate that any character in one or more positions makes a match. The most commonly used wildcards are ?, which allows a match between any single characters, and *, which allows a match between any number of characters.

MCA   MicroChannel Architecture. One of the standards for building PCs that defines the architecture of a 32-bit bus.

Multistation Access Unit (MAU)   MAUs are wiring concentrators used by the Token Ring networking system.

NETBIOS   Network Basic Input/Output System. The software that provides the basic network services for LANtastic systems. This supports the establishment and maintenance of network connections between PCs.

network adapter   To network PCs, you need to have special add-in adapter boards by means of which the PCs are connected together and transfer data.

network interface card   See *network adapter*.

network manager In every network, it is vital to have someone in charge of the system. This person is often called the *network manager*. His or her job is to ensure that the network's services are efficient and reliable and that changes and repairs are carried out.

network supervisor In larger networks, it may be necessary to have several people manage the running of the system. Network supervisors are, in effect, assistants to the network manager. They should be able to perform routine operations, such as adding users and controlling printers, for the section of the network they are responsible for.

passive components Units in a cabling system that allow connections to the network cabling to ensure electrical compatibility but don't amplify or condition the signals. Passive components usually degrade the signal to some degree, which is why most network technologies that use them allow a limited number of passive components.

peer-to-peer networking Instead of using one central PC to supply services for clients (as in the file server systems), peer-to-peer networks allow any PC to be a client, a server, or both client and server at the same time. The distinction between the two systems becomes blurred when you're talking about real products. For example, LANtastic, when you run the ALONE utility, is in principle a file server.

recovery Consists of restoring files from the backup data.

redirector One of the components that connects applications with the LANtastic network software. It must be running on all networked PCs whether they are workstations (clients), servers (server/clients), or server-only (running the ALONE utility).

remote booting If you have a PC that has no floppy or hard disk drives, you can load all of the necessary DOS and other software required for a fully functional PC on a network.

remote execution With LANtastic, it is possible to initiate the running of a program on a remote PC.

repeater A signal regenerator whose function is to recondition and relay signals from one piece of cable to another.

Networking with LANtastic

router A device that connects two segments of a network together and passes network signals from one segment to the other only when the sender and receiver are on different segments. When the sender and receiver are on the same segment, the router doesn't copy the signals to the other segment. In heavily loaded networks, this reduces traffic and therefore increases performance.

server A PC that allows its resources (file storage, printers, and so on) to be used by other computers on the network (the clients).

shared resource The facilities that a server makes available to several users at the same time are called *shared resources*. These facilities can include file storage, printers, and so on.

simple name format The simple name format is a way to generate names for network users so that they conform to a common standard. The advantage to using this method is that if you know a user's real name, that user's network name is obvious. This simplifies network management and makes it easier to send someone electronic mail.

spooler system A spooler system is a service that accepts data, stores it, and then outputs the data to a device when that device becomes available. This allows several users to output to the same printer without having to wait for each other to finish printing.

supervisor See *network supervisor*.

system log The system log is a collection of all of the design, implementation, and ongoing operation notes, and descriptions and paperwork for the network.

thick EtherNet One of the options for cabling of an EtherNet system. It uses a thick coaxial cable that requires extra equipment to support PC connections. It is typically 60%–70% more expensive, will cover greater distances and support more users and traffic than thin EtherNet. In general, it is less suitable for do-it-yourself installation than thin EtherNet.

thin EtherNet One of the options for cabling of an EtherNet system. Thin EtherNet (sometimes called "CheaperNet"), uses a lightweight coaxial cable. It is less expensive than thick EtherNet systems and much easier to work with for do-it-yourself installations. It supports fewer users and will not cover as much distance as thick EtherNet.

Token Ring   Token Ring is a technology that supports local area networking. Popularized by IBM, Token Ring transfers data at either 4 or 16 megabits per second.

TSR   Terminate-and-Stay-Resident. Software that runs and stays resident in memory. This technique is used for software that supplies a service to, or alongside, other software. All of the basic LANtastic networking software (Artisoft's drivers, NETBIOS, redirector, and server) and the pop-up network interface utility LANPUP are TSRs.

Unshielded Twisted Pair (UTP)   UTP is another cabling type that supports EtherNet. The cabling is the same type used in telephone systems, and existing telephone circuits can be reused to support network connections if the cable is the proper grade. Like thick EtherNet, UTP requires extra equipment and is more expensive than thin EtherNet.

wiring hub   See *concentrator*.

workstation   A machine on a network that uses the resources of a remote computer (usually the *server*).

Index

Symbols

! (exclamation point) in strings, 435
%PATH% command, 145
" (quotation marks) in strings, 435
* (asterisk), 178
/ (slash), 285
/WAIT, 146
: (colon), 285
; (semicolon), 287
= (equal sign), 285, 435
@ (at sign), 286
@MAIL, 166
@MAIL mail queue file, 43
\\ (double backslash), 156
{} (braces), 286
|| (vertical bars), 286

A

AC power, status, 423
access
 account privileges, 190-192
 control, 20-21, 158, 499
 limiting, 39
 multiuser, 29-30
 rights, 20, 183-190, 499
  directories, 184-185
  file operations, 184
  queues, 184
  Read with List files, 187
  special operations, 186
  user types, 186-187
  Write, Read, and Create files, 187
 servers, controlling, 181-182
Access Control Lists (ACLs), 183, 188-190, 399

accessing
 files, restricting, 499
 mail, 167
 resources
  controlling, 20-21
  remote, 34
accounts, 499
 attributes, changing, 390-391
 description, 471
 disabling, 352-353, 461
 displaying
  concurrent logins, 392
  description, 392
  expiration dates, 392
  privileges, 392
 expiration date, 181
 groups, 177, 475-477, 502
  expiration date, 390
  managing, 383
  see also group accounts

507

guest, 182, 502
management, 345
names, 471
privileges, 190-192, 500
    Super ACL, 191
    Super Mail, 191
    Super Queue, 191
    System Manager, 191
    User Audit, 191
setup, 41
status, displaying, 462
users
    adding, 473
    copying, 385, 473
    deleting, 473
    locating, 473
    managing, 383, 460-462
acknowledging transactions, 291
ACL (Access Control List), 183, 188-190, 499
active components, 17, 500
active hubs, 103
adapter cards, 500
Adapter Independent Local Area Network Basic Input/Output System (AILANBIOS), 140
adapters, 15-16
    cabling, 16
    card driver, 30
    cards, 102
        data width, 95-96
        EtherNet, 104
        slots, 118
        Token Ring, 106
    configuration, 16, 94
    coprocessors, 94-95
    drivers, 126
        installing, 126-127
        starting, 145
    installation, 404
    multiple, 245–246, 292
    network adapter card, 502
    network interface cards, 27
    number, 486
    static electricity, 119

statistics, 446, 449-451
Xircom EtherNet, 27
see also boards
add-in boards, 15-16, 26-27
add-in cards, 16
addresses, tables, 108
AILANBIO.EXE utility, 289-305
AILANBIOS (Adapter Independent Local Area Network Basic Input/Output System), 140
AIMOVE.EXE utility, 307
allocating buffers, traffic, 395
ALONE.EXE, 32-33, 37, 70, 307-309
analyzing network performance, 443
applications, 14, 43-44
    configuring/reconfiguring, 148-153
    setting up environment, 148
archiving files, 211-212
    see also backups
ARCnet (Attached Resource Computer network), 15-16, 88, 97-99, 108, 500
    compared to other networks, 109
    design rules, 101-102
    hardware, cabling, 102
    hubs, 101-103
asterisk (*), 178
at sign (@), 286
attributes
    accounts, changing, 390-391
    files, 351
audio warnings, 440-441
audit file, 383
audit trail, 192-193, 493-494, 500
    adding entries, 347
    maintenance, 494-495
AUTOEXEC.BAT file, 143

B

B.E.A.R. problem solving, 218-220
backslash \\ (double), 156
BACKUP command (DOS), 206
backups, 9, 52, 201-212, 384, 500
    configuration, 204
    control directory, restoring, 389
    directories, servers, 383
    father, 210
    grandfather, 210
    logs, 85
    networks, 9
    scheduling, 204-205, 209-211
    servers, devices, 208-209
    son, 210
    tape, 9
    utilities, 207
banner pages, 162-164
batch commands, output, suppressing, 145
batch files, 148-150, 241–242
    building, 377
    logins, 146
    startup, 125-126
    termination, 360
battery power, 424, 430
BBSs (bulletin board systems), 256
beeps (audio warnings), 440-441
blackout (power), 423-424
BNC
    barrel connectors, 500
        ARCnet, 102
        EtherNet, 105
    T-connectors
        ARCnet, 102
        EtherNet, 104
    terminators
        ARCnet, 103
        EtherNet, 105

boards
    add-in, 15-16, 26-27
    configuration, 16
    network adapter card, 119
    see also adapters
boot image, 39, 380, 383, 416, 487, 497
boot server, 39
booting remote, 39, 380, 383, 487, 503
bottleneck, 96
braces ({}), 286
branches, 93
bridges, 107, 500
brouters, see routers
brownouts, 55, 423-426
buffers, 37, 292, 304
    allocating, 401
    keyboard, 369
    printers, 488-494
    request, 414
    size, 410, 485, 490
    space, allocating, 417
    traffic, allocating, 395
Builder, 241-242
building batch files, 377
bulletin board systems (BBSs), 256
buses, 500
    interfaces, 96-97
    mastering, 97
    standards
        EISA (Extended Industry Standard Architecture), 16, 96, 501
        ISA (Industry Standard Architecture), 16, 96, 502
        MCA (MicroChannel Architecture), 16, 96, 502
    topology, 90-92
bytes, I/O, 466

C

cabling, 16-17, 64
    ARCnet, 102
    bridges, 107, 500
    bus topology, 91
    clips, 67
    coaxial, 98
    components
        active, 500
        passive, 503
    connectors, 17
        BNC, 500
        BNC barrel connectors, 102, 105
        BNC T-connectors, 102, 104
    cover strips, 64
    EtherNet, 104
    failures, 172
    fiber-optic, 88
    installation, 110, 117
    junction boxes, 17
    layout, 199
    length, 101
    maintenance guidelines, 101
    passive components, 17
    patch, Token Ring, 105
    repeaters, 105-107, 503
    routers, 107-108, 503
    segments, 103, 503
    services, 109-110
    star topology, 90
    T-connectors, 103
    terminators, 17
        BNC, 103-105
        EtherNet, 103
    thick EtherNet, 504
    thin EtherNet, 504
    ties, 67
    Token Ring, 106
    twisted pair, unshielded (UTP), 98, 505
    wiring hubs, 17
cached resources, 492

caches, 37
    disk, 41
    flushing, 315-320
    resources, 415
    seek, 418, 491
    writing to
        forcing, 355
        timers, 314
caching, 311-323
    disabling, 319
    physical disk drives, 316
    read-ahead buffering, 312
    restarting system, 316, 319
canceling
    despooling, 367
    redirection, printers, 381
    shutdowns, servers, 467
cards
    adapters, 102, 500
        data width, 95-96
        EtherNet, 104
        slots, 118
        Token Ring, 106
    add-in, 16
    drivers
        network adapters, 30
        network interface, 30-31, 42
    EISA, 96
    network adapter card, 502
    network interface cards, 15, 27, 502
carrier-scheme multiple-access with collision-detection, (CSMA/CD), 98
CD-ROM drives, 10
central node, 90
Central Station, 242–244
centralization, 52
changing
    passwords, 348, 461
    user names, 460
chat services, 9
chatting, 348, 458
chips, ROM (read-only memory), 39
circuits, overloading, 67

client/server, 2, 18
clients, 2, 18, 500
clips (cabling), 67
clock, 348
coaxial cable, 16, 98
collisions, 98
colon (:), 285
command line mode, 284, 345, 396
command line, running network software, 143
command lines, 369
  : (colon), 285
  = (equal sign), 285
  { } braces, 286
  || (vertical bars), 286
command or filename not recognized, 147
commands, 464-465
  %PATH%, 145
  batch, suppressing output, 145
  DOS
    BACKUP, 206
    COPY, 205
    RESTORE, 206
    XCOPY, 206
  help, 357
  LANCACHE, 316
  NET, 148, 286
  NET USE, 146
  not recognized, 147
  remote servers, 191
  STARTNET.BAT, 144
comparing networks, 109
compatibility, 62
compiling, 44, 241
components, 14
  active, 17, 500
  cabling, 64
  configuration, loading, 125
  groups, 28
  hardware, 16-17
  passive, 17, 503
  PCs, 33
  physical site, 199
  testing for, 438

compressing files, 207
CompuServe, 256
concentrator, 17, 500
CONFIG.SYS file, 127-128
configuration, 14, 82, 200
  adapters, 16, 94
  backups, 204
  components, loading, 125
  current, system log, 85
  data, displaying, 322
  information, displaying, 305
  naming machines, 70
  PCs, 18, 33, 38
  physical layout, 64
  planning, 64, 67, 71, 76
  pre-configured hardware, 16
  printers, 162-166, 200
  resources, shared, 142
  servers, 142-143, 200, 383
  users, 71
  workstations, 200
configuring
  applications, 148-153
  environment, 148
  printers, servers, 162
  remote booting, 41
  servers, 71, 76
  utilities, 148-153
connecting
  drives, shared resources, 345
  printers, shared resources, 345
  resources, 452
connections
  creating, 452
  hubs, passive, 102
  nodes, displaying information, 370
  removing, 350
  servers
    breaking, 459
    canceling, 359
    terminating, 379

connectors, 17
  BNC, 500
    barrel connectors, 102, 105
    T-connectors, 102-104
  bridges, 107
  repeaters, 503
  Ring In, 106
  Ring Out, 106
  routers, 107-108
contention management, 20
control characters, suppressing, 366
control directory, 137, 383-384
  backups, restoring, 389
  maintenance, 498
  restoring contents, 389
  users, 386-388
control files, 42
controlling
  access
    resources, 20-21
    servers, 181-182
  entries, printer queues, 454
  sessions, 327
  spooler, 360
coprocessors, 94-95
COPY command (DOS), 205
copy switch, 349
copy-protection of software, 152
copying
  accounts
    groups, 477
    users, 385, 473
  files, 349, 384
    to spooler, 366
  mail, to file, 457
  users, 385
cost issues, 49, 88-89
counters, resetting, 320-321
cover strips (cabling), 64
CPU, overlapped functions, 312

creating
  connections, 452
  files, indirect, 358
  groups, 178
  mail, 345
  resources, 484
  users, 386-387
CSMA/CD (carrier-scheme multiple-access with collision-detection), 98

D

daisy-chain topology, 90-92
data
  exchange, 14
  integrity, 3
  overhead, 87
  sharing, *see* data transfer
  surfing, 193
  switches, 6
  width, 95-96, 501
data transfer, 13-14
  cost, 5
  data integrity, 3
  overhead, 87
  parallel ports, 15
  rate, 312
  raw data rate, 61-62
  serial ports, 15
  speed, 4
  spooling, 25
databases, searching, remote execution, 44
dates, 436
  expiration, 392
  resetting, 349
day of the week, 437
DDE (Dynamic Data Exchange), 44, 237-239, 501
dedicated servers, 70, 307
default
  directories, 44, 437
  disk, 437
  logins, setting, 234
  names, login, 439
  parameters, logins, 459
  passwords, 382

resources, 136
  username, 382
definitions, disk resources, 157-158
delayed write, 312
deleting
  accounts
    groups, 477
    users, 473
  files, after printing, 366
  mail, 334, 457
  NETBIOS from memory, 300
  redirector from memory, 400, 413
  resources, 484
  UPS (Uninterrptable Power Supply) utility from memory, 432
  users, control directory, 387-388
despooling, 367, 454, 488
  abandoning job, 367
  disabling, 375
  preventing, 405
Device Control window, 455-456
devices, 19-20, 25-26
  listing, 452
  printers, 129, 152
  routing, remote resources, 130
  serial, 129
diagnostics
  disks, 214-216
  system, 221-226
Direct Memory Access (DMA), 501
directories
  access rights, 184
  control, 137, 383-384
    creating users, 386-387
    deleting users, 387-388
    maintenance, 498
    restoring backups, 389
    restoring contents, 389
  default, 44, 437

displaying, 351
installation, 125, 138, 145
LANTASTI, 42
operations, access rights, 185
root, 156
servers
  backing up, 383
  restoring, 383
subdirectories, 43
disabling
  accounts, 352-353, 461
  caching, 319
  despooling, 375
  logins, 467
  pop-up messages, 368
  streams, 375
disconnecting resources, 452
disk drives, 155
  disconnecting, 381
  installation, 133, 135
Disk Operating System, *see* DOS
disk resources, 156-159
  creating, 484
  definitions, 157-158
  drives, connecting/disconnecting, 330-331
  rights, 158
diskless PCs, 39
disks, 5
  caches, 41
  caching, 311
  default, 437
  diagnostic, 214-216
  expanding space, 252
  floppy, 3, 9
  hard
    failures, 172
    management utilities, 215
    read/write heads, 311
  installation, 121-123
  latency, 311
  performance issues, 311
  remote resources, 133-135
  writing, 312

511

displaying
  accounts
    concurrent logins, 392
    description, 392
    expiration dates, 392
    privileges, 392
  configuration information, 305, 322
  directories, 351
  file names in print queue, 366
  files, 351
  information, nodes, 370
  logged-in users, 463
  passwords, expiration date, 392
  status of accounts, 462
  switches, SERVER, 407
displays
  monochrome, 326, 363
  screen, ALONE utility, 308-309
DMA (Direct Memory Access), 501
documentation, 202-203
dongles, 152, 501
DOS (Disk Operating System), 18
  commands
    COPY, 205
    RESTORE, 206
    XCOPY, 206
  extending, 27
  services, 29, 33
  support, 29
  see also MS-DOS
double backslash (\\), 156
DR DOS, 239–241
Drive Connections window, 233-234
drivers, 30, 501
  adapters, 126-127
  cards, network interface, 30-31
  network adapter, starting, 145
  NIC, 33
  program, testing, 140

drives, 155
  CD-ROM, 10
  disconnecting, 381
  disks
    installation, 133-135
    shared resources, 330-331, 345
  floppy disks, remote user access, 406
  local, connecting, 382
  physical, caching, 316
  redirecting, 148, 151, 330, 380
  shared resources, connecting/disconnecting, 330-331, 345
Dynamic Data Exchange (DDE), 44, 501
dynamic environment, 148

E

Echo switch, 353
echoing prompts, 440
EISA (Extended Industry Standard Architecture), 16, 96, 501
electrical outlets, 55
electronic mail, 9, 249-250
  see also mail
elevator seeking, 312
enabling streams, 375
environment, 13
  applications, setting up, 148
  dynamic, 148
  reconfiguring, 148
  recreating, 370
  saving, 370
  static, 148
equal sign (=), 285, 435
equipment
  layout, 199
  log, 85
error messages, 147, 363
error statistics, 443

EtherNet, 15-16, 88, 98, 108, 501
  adapter cards, 104
  cabling, 104
    repeaters, 105
    terminators, 103
    thick, 504
    thin, 504
  comparing to other networks, 109
  design rules, 103-105
  planning, 40
  segments, 103
exclamation point (!) in strings, 435
execution, remote, 503
expiration dates, 392
Extended Industry Standard Architecture (EISA), 16, 96, 501
extending DOS, 18, 27

F

failures
  cabling, 172
  hard disks, 172
  hardware, 171
  power supply, 423
  software, 174
father backups, 210
  see also backups
FDDI (Fiber Distributed Data Interface), 88
fiber-optic cabling, 88, 100
file servers, see servers
file sharing, 29
filename not recognized, 147
files, 42
  accessing
    multiuser, 29
    restricting, 499
  archiving, 211-212
  attributes, 351
  AUTOEXEC.BAT, running network software, 143
  backups, 384, 500

Index

batch, 148-150, 241–242
   building, 377
   logins, 146
   startup, 125-126
   termination, 360
compressing, 207
CONFIG.SYS, modifying, 127-128
control, 42
copying, 349, 384
   mail, 457
   to spooler, 366
deleting after printing, 366
directories, 42
displaying, 351, 366
help, 42
hidden, 351, 384
indirect, 351, 358
locking, 29
open
   maximum, 489
   simultaneous, 406
operations, access rights, 184
paths, 354
printing, first line, 438
queues, mail, 43
random access, 312
reading, 312
recovering, 503
reports, saving, 446-447
server, audit, 383
sharing, 52
STARTNET.BAT, 144-147
switch, 286-287
   @ (at sign), 286
   comments, 287
   names, 286
fire, 171
fixed environment, *see* static environment
flood, 171
floor plan, 55
Floppy Direct option, 487
floppy disks, 3
   backups, 9
   drives, remote user access, 406

flow control, 166, 501
flushing caches, 315-320
form feed printing, 162-164
forms, 86, 259-276
forums (bulletin boards), 256
forwarding mail, 457
front end (hard disk), 37
functions
   LANPUP.EXE utility, 337
   layering, 14
   NETBIOS, 32
   overlapped CPU and I/O functions, 312
   servers, 71

G

global switches, 357
grandfather backups
   see also backups
green field sites, 61-62
grounding straps (cabling), 17
groups
   accounts, 177-178, 475, 502
      adding, 476
      copying, 477
      deleting, 477
      expiration date, 390
      locating, 477
      passwords, 475
   creating, 178
   managing accounts, 383
   names, 178
guest accounts, 182, 502

H

hackers, 173
halting printing, 367
hard disks
   failures, 172
   front end, 37
   management utilities, 215
   read/write heads, 311
hardware, 24-25
   adapters, 26
   ARCnet, 102-103

boards, add-in, 15, 26-27
cabling, 17
components, 16-17
dongles, 152, 501
EtherNet, 104-105
failures, 171
installation, 82, 117-120
modems, 26
network adapter cards, 102
network interface cards, 15, 27
PCs, 24-25
peripherals, 24-26
preconfigured, 16
purchase considerations, 61-62
testing, 139-142
Token Ring, 106
help
   commands, 357
   files, 42
   switches, 356
   topics, 357
hidden files, 351, 384
hubs, 500
   active, 101-103
   loops, 102
   MAUs, 106
   passive, 102-103
   wiring, 17, 505

I

I/O (input/output)
   overlapped functions, 312
   port, 120
IBM Token Ring, 16
increasing disk space, 252
indirect files, 351, 358
Industry Standard Architecture (ISA), 16, 96, 502
installation, 23, 76, 82-83, 137-139
   adapter drivers, 126-127
   adapters, 404
   cabling, 109-110
   CONFIG.SYS file, 127-128
   confirmation window, 138

513

directory, 125, 138, 145
disk drives, 133-135
green field sites, 61-62
hardware, 82, 117-120
naming machines, 124
preparation, 114-116
printers, 129-133
software, 82, 121-139
installation utilities, 41
interfaces
menus, 441-443
NETBIOS, 27
network interface card, 502
interrupts, 302, 317
IO bytes, 466
IRQ numbers, 317
ISA (Industry Standard Architecture), 16, 96, 502

J–K

jumpers, network adapter card, 119
junction boxes, 17

keyboard buffers, 369

L

LANCACHE command, 316
LANCACHE.EXE, 32-33, 37, 311-323
LANCHECK, 443-451
LANCHECK.EXE, 140-142, 325-326
LANPUP.EXE utility, 327-337
LANTASTI directory, 42
LANtastic, 2
LANtastic Z, 250–252
latency (disks), 311
layout
cabling, 199
equipment, 199
physical, 64, 90
see also topology
line noise, 423

links
daisy-chain topology, 92
DDE (Dynamic Data Exchange), 237–239
fiber-optic, 100
radio, 27
listing
devices, 452
resources, remote, 131
servers available, 420
switches, 293-294, 317, 340
lists, access control, 188-190
loading
components, configuration, 125
software, server, 145
local
drives, connecting, 382
requests, 34
servers, logins, 146
services, 28
locking
files, 29
records, 409, 492
logging out from server, 460
logical layout, 90
see also topology
logical security, 170
logical streams, 374
logins, 345, 499
adding, 146
batch file, 146
changing name, 146
concurrent, 397
concurrent, limiting, 182
defaults, setting, 234
disabling, 467
names
default, 439
security ratings, 179-180
parameters, defaults, 459
security, 175-182
servers, 146, 234, 327, 330, 358-460
simultaneous, 409

users
enabling/disabling, 373
terminating, 379
see also security, logins
logs
backups, 85
problems, 221
site, 198-203
loops, ARCnet hubs, 102

M

machine name, 124
magazines, 257
@MAIL, 166
mail, 41, 166-168, 327, 333-334, 345, 365, 456, 501
copying to file, 457
deleting messages, 334, 457
displaying messages, 368
electronic, 249-250
forwarding, 457
queues, 43
access privileges, 191
access rights, 184
voice, 362
see also chatting; electronic mail
@MAIL mail queue file, 43
mail systems, 155
main screen, 445
maintenance, cabling, 101
management applications utilities, 41
managers, system, 212-214
managing
accounts
groups, 383
user, 460-462
users, 383
audit trail, 494-495
boot image, 497
directories, control, 498
passwords, 201, 496-497
queues, printers, 327, 345, 383, 453-457, 496

resources, shared, 477-484
servers, activity, 462-468
shared resources, 383
streams, print, 455
masks, 177, 502
MAUs (Multistation Access Unit), 94, 106, 502
   distance, 105
   Token Ring, 105
MCA (MicroChannel Architecture), 16, 96, 502
memory, 37-38
   caches, 37
   deleting, UPS utility, 432
   NETBIOS, deleting, 300
   redirector, removing, 400, 413
   specifying type, 322
   usage, 38
menu interface mode, 363
menu interfaces, 441-443
menu-driven mode, 284
menus
   custom, 241
   shutdown, 420
messages, 370
   displaying, 368
   error, *see* error messages
   incoming, storing, 414
   mail, 167
   Out of environment space, 147
   pop-up, 368, 398-400
   shutdowns, 433
   text, exchanging, 348
   see also chatting
messaging, 9, 327
   electronic mail, 9
   real-time, 8
   store-and-forward, 8
MicroChannel Architecture (MCA), 16, 96, 502
Microsoft Windows, *see* Windows
modems, 26
   pooling, 6
   sharing, 248-249

modes
   command line, 284, 345
   menu interface, 363
   menu-driven, 284
   monochrome, 444
   windowed, 345
modifying
   files, CONFIG.SYS, 127-128
   resources, 478-483
monitoring, 246-248
   servers, activity, 462-468
monochrome display, 326, 363
monochrome mode, 444
MS-DOS, 29
   see also DOS
multi-user access, 29-30
Multistation Access Unit (MAU), 94, 106, 502

N

names
   accounts, 471
   files, switch, 286
   groups, 178
   login
      default, 439
      security ratings, 179-180
   nodes, 325
   resources, 156
      printers, 161
      shared, 155
   servers, broadcasting, 420
   users
      changing, 460
      simple name format, 176-177, 504
naming
   machines, 70, 124
   printers, 132
NBSETUP.EXE utility, 339-343
NCBs (Network Control Blocks), 296, 300
needs analysis, 49, 52
NET command, 148, 286
NET USE command, 146

NET.EXE utility, 166, 345-383, 451-461, 464-469
NET_MGR.EXE, 41, 142, 155, 383-392, 469-498
NETBIOS (Network Basic Input/Output System), 30-33, 42, 502
   functions, 32
   interface, 27
   modifying setup, 339
   node number, 438
   program, testing, 140
   removing from memory, 300
   starting, 145
NetWare, 244-245
network adapter card, 502
network adapters, 15-16
   cabling, 16
   configuration, 16
   multiple, 245-246
   see also adapters
Network Control Blocks (NCBs), 296, 300
network interface cards, 15, 27-31, 42, 502
network interface subsystem, 28-33
network operating system (NOS), 32-37
networks, 1, 10
   adapters, card driver, 30
   backups, 9
   file servers, *see* servers
   manager, 502
   path, 354
   peer, *see* peer networks
   supervisor, 503
   wireless, 27
NIC driver, 33
nodes
   central, 90
   connections
      displaying information, 370
      removing, 350
   names, 325
   numbers, 438, 446

setup, displaying information, 370
token passing, 97
nonechoing prompts, 440
nonphysical threats, 172-174
NOS (network operating system), 32-37
notification of job completion, 366

O

open files, maximum, 489
operating systems, networks, 28
operations utilities, 41
Out of environment space message, 147
output
   batch commands, suppressing, 145
   printers
      joining, 360
      redirecting, 331-332
overhead (data), 87
overlapped CPU and I/O functions, 312
overloading circuits, 55, 67

P

paper width, 162
parallel ports, 15, 26
parallel rings, 92
parameters
   AILANBIO.EXE utility, 290-291
   default, logins, 459
   start-up, servers, 142, 484
   utilities, 285-286
   see also switches; variables
passive components, 17, 503
passive hubs
   ARCnet, 103
   connections, 102
passwords, 175-181
   changing, 348, 461
   default, 382

expiration date, 392
group accounts, 475
maintenance, 496-497
managing, 201
protecting, 180-181
security ratings, 179-180
setting, 390, 471
testing, 179
see also security
patch cabling, Token Ring, 105
path, 354, 439
   directories, displaying, 351
   files, displaying, 351
%PATH% command, 145
PATH specification, 145
pausing, 364
pausing printing, 367
PCs, 1, 24-25
   components, 33
   configuration, 18, 33, 38
   diskless, 39
   management, 9-10
   remote boot, 380, 383, 416
   servers
      dedicated, 70
      shutting down, 191
   start-up, 143
peer networks, 2-4, 27, 503
peripherals, 24-26
   sharing, 6-7, 52
personal computers, see PCs
physical
   disk drives, caching, 316
   layout, 90
      see also topology
   path, 354
   security, 169-170
   site, 199
   threats, 171-172
      see also nonphysical threats
plotters, sharing, 7
pooling modems, 6
pop-up messages, 368, 398-400
pop-up utilities, 327

ports
   disconnecting, shared printers, 332
   I/O, 120
   parallel, 15, 26
   printers, 162, 367
   redefining, 331
   redirecting, 331
   serial, 15, 26
posting messages, 8
power, 199
   AC, status, 423
   batteries, 424, 430
   blackout, 423-424
   brownout, 423-424
   electrical, 55, 67
   failures, 423
   normal power, 424
   sags, 423
   spikes, 423-424
   surges, 423-424
   uninterruptable supplies, 256
pre-configured hardware, 16
Printer Connections window, 235
printers, 200
   buffers, 488-494
   configuration, 162-165, 200
   devices, 129, 152
   flow control, 166
   installation, 129-133
   naming, 132
   output, joining, 360
   ports, 162, 367
   queues, 43
      access privilges, 191
      access rights, 184
      adding jobs, 454
      controlling entry status, 454-455
      maintenance, 383
      managing, 41, 327, 345, 453-457
   redirecting, 235, 331-332, 381
   resetting, 162-165

Index

resources, 146
    creating, 484
    names, 161
serial, configuration, 165-166
shared resources, 155, 345
sharing, 6-7, 159-166
specifying, 131
spoolers, 20, 159-160, 335, 504
tasks, 489
printing, 366
    abandoning, 367
    banner pages, 162-164
    control characters, suppressing, 366
    deleting files, 366
    despooling, preventing, 405
    files, first line, 438
    form feeds, 162-164
    halting, 367
    notification of completion, 366
    paper width, 162
    queues, 159
        displaying file names, 366
        window, 454-455
    queuing, 21
    setup string, 482
    spooler, controlling, 360
    starting new jobs, 360
    streams, managing, 455
    tab replacement, 366
    tab width, 162, 165
privileges, 466
problem log, 221
problem solving, 218-220
procedures, 201
programs
    compiling, 44
    driver, 140
    installation, 121
    NETBIOS, 140
    virus-checking, 174-175
prompts, 440
protocols, 18

Q

queues, 21, 159, 332
    mail, 43, 333
        access privileges, 191
        access rights, 184
    managing, 41, 496
    printers, 43
        access privileges, 191
        access rights, 184
        adding jobs, 454
        controlling entry status, 454-455
        displaying file names, 366
        maintenance, 383
        managing, 327, 345, 453-457
    windows, print jobs, 454-455
quotation marks ("), strings, 435

R

radio links, 27
random access files, 312
raw data rate, 61-62
Read with List files access rights, 187
read-ahead buffering, 312
read-only memory, *see* ROM
read/write heads, 311
reading
    files, 312
    mail, 457
real-time messages, 8
receiving mail, 345
records, locking, 409, 492
recoveries, 203-212
recovering files, 503
redefining ports, 331
REDIR.EXE, 33-34, 393-401
redirected path, 354
redirecting
    devices, printers, 152
    drives, 148-151, 330, 380

output, printers, 331-332
ports, 331
printers, 235, 381
redirector, 34-35, 42, 503
    removing from memory, 400, 413
    starting, 145
redundant rings, 92
remote
    access, 18
    booting, 39, 487, 503
        configuring, 41
        PCs, 380, 383, 416
    control, 246-248
    execution, 43-44, 503
    requests, 34, 36
    resources, 20, 34
        devices, routing, 130
        disks, 133-135
        listing, 131
    users, floppy disk drives, 406
REMOVE switch, 287, 300
repeaters, 107, 503
    EtherNet, 105
    fiber-optic, 100
reports, saving, in files, 446-447
request buffers, 414, 490
requests, 466
    local, 34-36
    multiple, 411
    remote, 34-36
rerouting requests, 36
resetting
    counters, 320-321
    date, 349
    printers, 162-165
    time, 349
resources, 4, 19-20
    accessing
        controlling, 20-21
        remote, 34
    adding, 484
    cached, 415, 492
    connecting, 327, 452
    default, 136
    deleting, 484

disconnecting, 452
disk, 156
   connecting/disconnecting drives, 330-331
   creating, 484
   definitions, 157-158
   hiding information, 155
   local specification, 155
   mail, 166-168
   modifying, 478-483
   names, 155-156, 161
   printers, 146, 161
      creating, 484
   remote, 20
      disks, 133-135
      listing, 131
      routing devices, 130
   shared, 155-168, 504
      configuring, 142
      contention managment, 20
      disk drives, 155
      mail system, 155
      managing, 41, 477-484
      names, 155
      printers, 155
      servers, 76, 155
   subdirectories, 43
restarting
   caching system, 316-319
   spooler, 367, 405
RESTORE command (DOS), 206
restoring, 201
   backups, control directory, 389
   directories, servers, 383
retrying operations, 301
rights
   access, 499
   users, 158-159
Ring In connector, 106
Ring Out connector, 106
ring topology, 90-92
ROM (read-only memory)
   chips, 39
root directory, 156
routers, 107-108, 503
routing devices, 130
Run Burst option, 491

S

safe computing, 174-175
sags (power drop), 423
saving reports, in files, 446-447
screens
   display, ALONE utility, 308-309
   main, LANCHECK, 445
searching databases, 44
security, 5, 20, 41-42, 52, 169
   access control lists, 188-189
   access controls, 499
   access rights, 183-190
   account privileges, 190-192
   audit trails, 192-193
   data surfing, 193
   group accounts, 177-178
   guest accounts, 182
   hackers, 173
   hardware, failures, 171
   logical, 170
   login, 175-182
   nonphysical threats, 172-174
   passwords, 175-181
   physical, 169-172
   servers, controlling access, 181-182
   shared devices, 7
   user names, 176-177
   vandals, 173-174
   viruses, 173
seek cache, 418, 491
seek time, 311
segments
   EtherNet, 103
   routers, 503
selecting
   servers, 124
   workstations, 124

semicolon (;), 287
sequential file reading, 312
serial
   devices, 129
   ports, 15, 26
   printers, configuration, 165-166
Server Connections window, 234
SERVER switches, displaying, 407
SERVER.EXE, 33-35, 403-421
servers, 1, 18-19, 27-29, 35-36, 42, 70, 124, 501, 504
   access, controlling, 181-182
   activity, 345
      managing, 462-468
      monitoring, 462-468
   attaching to, 41
   backup devices, 208-209
   boot image, 39, 383
   clients, 500
   configuration, 71, 76, 142-143, 200
      printers, 162
      start-up, 383
   connections, breaking, 359, 379, 459
   dedicated, 70, 307
   directories
      backing up, 383
      restoring, 383
   files
      audit, 383
      copying, 349
   functions, 71
   ID, 487
   listing available, 420
   logging out, 460
   logins, 234, 327-330, 345, 358, 460, 499
      concurrent, controlling, 182
      local, 146
      passwords, 175
      security, 175

Index

management utilities, 233
names, broadcasting, 420
organization, 2
remote, running
    commands, 191
remote requests, 35
resources, shared, 76, 155
shutdown, 372, 433
    brownout, 426
    canceling, 467
    restoring power, 427
    scheduling, 467
shutting down from PC, 191
sname (server name), 347-348
software, loading, 145
start-up parameters, 142, 484
services
    cabling, 109-110
    chatting, 9
    DOS, 29, 33
    file sharing, 29
sessions, 298, 397
    maximum amount, 341
    reporting number, 340
setting
    defaults, logins, 234
    passwords, 390
setup
    accounts, 41
    nodes, displaying information, 370
setup string, 482
SHARE.EXE, 30-33
shared printers, 159-166
shared resources, 504
    configuring, 142
    disk drives, 155
    drives, connecting, 345
    mail system, 155
    managing, 41, 383, 477-484
    printers, 155, 345
    servers, 155
sharing

boot image, 416
data, 3-5
files, 29, 52
modems, 248–249
peripherals, 6-7, 52
plotters, 7
printers, 6-7
resources
    contention management, 20
    servers, 76
security, 7
shutdown menu, 420
shutdowns (servers), 433, 467, 372
    restoring power, 427
    scheduled, 425
signals, repeaters, 107
simple name format (user names), 176-177, 504
site analysis, 55, 58
site log, 198-203
SIZE switch, 304
slash (/), 285
slots, network adapter card, 118
sname (server name), 347-348
soak test, 289
software, 18-21
    compatibility
        LANtastic, 152-153
        network, 151
    copy-protection, 152
    drivers, 30
    failures, 174
    installation, 82, 121-139
    license terms, 151
    running
        from AUTOEXEC.BAT file, 143
        from command line, 143
    server, loading, 145
    Trojan, 173
    see also drivers
son backups, 210

see also backups
specifications, local resources, 155
specifying memory type, 322
speed, data transfer, 4
spikes, 55, 423-424
splitting networks, 92
spooler, 20, 159-160, 335, 496, 504
    controlling, 360
    copying files, 366
    data transfer, 25
    restarting, 367, 405
    see also despooling
stacks, 329
standalone systems, 6
standards
    buses
        EISA (Extended Industry Standard Architecture), 16, 96, 501
        ISA (Industry Standard Architecture), 16, 96, 502
        MCA (MicroChannel Architecture), 16, 96, 502
    NETBIOS, 32
star topology, 90-91
start-up
    batch file, 125-126
    configuration, servers, 383
    parameters, servers, 142, 484
    PCs, 143
starting
    LANCHECK, 443
    NETBIOS, 145
    network, 147-148
    network adapter driver, 145
    redirector, 145
STARTNET.BAT file, 144-147
static environment, 148
stations, Token Ring, 105
status, ports, printers, 367
storage

caches, 37
messages, 8
store-and-forward messaging, 8
stream control table, 374-375, 405
streams, 375
Streams Control window, 455
strings, 377-378, 435-440
   ! (exclamation point), 435
   equal sign (=), 435
   quotation marks ("), 435
   setup, 482
subdirectories, 42-43
Super ACL account privilege, 191
Super Mail account privilege, 191
Super Queue account privilege, 191
supervisors, system, 214
suppressing
   control characters, 366
   error messages, 363
   notification of print completion, 366
   spikes, 423
   surges, 423-424
surges (power), 423-424
switch files, 286-287
   @ (at sign), 286
   comments, ; (semicolon), 287
   names, 286
switches, 285-286
   : (colon), 285
   = (equal sign), 285
   command line, 396
   copy, 349
   Echo, 353
   global, 357
   help, 356
   listing, 293-294, 317, 340
   network adapter card, 119
   REMOVE, 287, 300
   SERVER, displaying, 407
   SIZE, 304
   UNUSE, 286

USE, 286
values, 285
system diagnostics, 221-226
system log, 85-86, 504
System Manager account privilege, 191
system managers, 212-214
system supervisors, 214
system utilities, 284

T

T-connectors, EtherNet, 103
tab replacement, 366
tab width, 162, 165
tables
   addresses, routers, 108
   building entries, 375
   stream control, 374-375, 405
tape backups, 9
tasks
   number, 486
   printers, 489
technical support, 226-227
technologies, 87-88
templates, 177, 502
terminate-and-stay-resident, see TSRs
terminating
   connections, servers, 379
   logins, 379
   users, forcibly, 467
terminators (cabling), 17, 103-105
testing, 82
   for components, 438
   hardware, 139-142
   network performance, 443
   soak test, 289
text, messages, exchanging, 348
theft, see security
thick EtherNet cabling, 504
thin EtherNet cabling, 504
ticks, 290-291
ties (cabling), 67

time, 349, 439
timers, 314
token passing, 97
Token Ring, 88-99, 108, 504
   adapter cards, 106
   cabling, 105-106
   comparing to other networks, 109
   design rules, 105-106
   MAUs (Media Access Units), 94, 105
   stations, 105
topologies
   bus, 90-92
   daisy chain, 90-92
   design rules, 100-106
   mixed, 94
   ring, 90-92
   star, 90-91
   tree, 90-94
traffic, 98
   buffers, allocating, 395
   reducing, 349
training users, 83, 216-218
transferring, data, see data transfer
transparency, 34, 83
tree topology, 90-94
Trojan software, 173
TSRs, 504
   ALONE, 37
   ALONE.EXE, 33, 70
   LANCACHE.EXE, 33, 37
   pop-up utilities, 327
   REDIR.EXE, 33-34
   SERVER.EXE, 33-35
   SHARE.EXE, 30, 33
   utilities, 287
twisted pair cabling, unshielded (UTP), 98, 505

U

Uninterruptable Power Supplies (UPSs), 41, 256, 423-425
   see also power
unshielded twisted pair (UTP)

cabling, 98, 505
UNUSE switch, 286
updating information, 4
UPS.EXE utility, 423-433
UPSs (Uninterruptable Power Supplies), 41
USE switch, 286
User Audit account privilege, 191
username, default, 382
users
   access rights, 499
   adding, 473
   copying, 385, 473
   creating, 386-387
   deleting, 387-388, 473
   identification, 463
   logins
      enabling/disabling, 373
      simultaneous, 409
      terminating, 379
   managing, 383, 460-462
   maximum, setting, 485-488
   names, 176-177
      changing, 460
      simple name format, 176-177, 504
   remote, floppy disk drives, 406
   requests, multiple, 411
   rights, 158-159, 499
   terminating, forcibly, 467
   threats, 173
   training, 216-218
   types, access rights, 186-187
   utilities, 284
utilities, 14, 40, 284-285
   AILANBIO.EXE, 289-305
   AIMOVE.EXE, 307
   ALONE, 37
   ALONE.EXE, 309-310
   backups, 207
   command line mode, 285-286
   configuring/reconfiguring, 148-153
   file compression, 207
   hard disk management, 215
   installation, 41
   LANCACHE.EXE, 37, 311-323
   LANCHECK.EXE, 325-326
   LANPUP.EXE, 327-337
   management applications, 41
   NBSETUP.EXE, 339-343
   NET.EXE, 166, 345-383, 451-469
   NET_MGR.EXE, 41, 155, 383-392, 469-498
   operations, 41
   parameters, 285-286
   REDIR.EXE, 393-401
   restore, 207
   SERVER.EXE, 403-421
   switch files, 286-287
   switches, 287
   system, 284
   terminate-and-stay-resident, 30, 33
   UPS.EXE, 423-433
   user, 284
   Windows, 232-233
   WNET.EXE, 233-236
UTP cabling, 98

V

values, switches, 285
vandals, 173-174
variable delayed writes (to disk), 312
variables, 285
vertical bars (||), 286
virus, 173-174
   see also Trojan software
virus-checking programs, 174-175
Voice Board, 9
voice mail, 249-250, 362

W

/WAIT, 146
warnings, audio, 440-441
wildcards, 502
windowed mode, 345
Windows, 232-239, 323
windows
   Device Control, 455-456
   Drive Connections, 233-234
   installation confirmation, 138
   Printer Connections, 235
   queues, print jobs, 454-455
   Server Connections, 234
   Streams Control, 455
   triangles, 441
wireless networks, 27
wiring
   centers, MAUs (Multistation Access Units), 94, 106
   components, 17
   hubs, 17, 106, 505
   see also cabling
WNET.EXE utility, 233-236
WNET_MGR.EXE, 236
workstations, 70, 124, 200
Write, Read, and Create files access rights, 187
write-behind disk writing technique, 312
writing
   to cache
      forcing, 355
      timers, 314
   to disks
      elevator seeking, 312
      variable delayed writes, 312
      write-behind, 312

X–Y–Z

XCOPY command (DOS), 206
Xircom EtherNet Adapter, 27

Sams—Covering The Latest In Computer And Technical Topics!

Audio

Advanced Digital Audio	$39.95
Audio Systems Design and Installation	$59.95
Compact Disc Troubleshooting and Repair	$24.95
Handbook for Sound Engineers: The New Audio Cyclopedia, 2nd Ed.	$99.95
How to Design & Build Loudspeaker & Listening Enclosures	$39.95
Introduction to Professional Recording Techniques	$29.95
The MIDI Manual	$24.95
Modern Recording Techniques, 3rd Ed.	$29.95
OP-AMP Circuits and Principles	$19.95
Principles of Digital Audio, 2nd Ed.	$29.95
Sound Recording Handbook	$49.95
Sound System Engineering, 2nd Ed.	$49.95

Electricity/Electronics

Active-Filter Cookbook	$24.95
Basic Electricity and DC Circuits	$29.95
CMOS Cookbook, 2nd Ed.	$24.95
Electrical Wiring	$19.95
Electricity 1-7, Revised 2nd Ed.	$49.95
Electronics 1-7, Revised 2nd Ed.	$49.95
How to Read Schematics, 4th Ed.	$19.95
IC Op-Amp Cookbook, 3rd Ed.	$24.95
IC Timer Cookbook, 2nd Ed.	$24.95
RF Circuit Design	$24.95
Transformers and Motors	$29.95
TTL Cookbook	$24.95
Understanding Digital Troubleshooting, 3rd Ed.	$24.95
Understanding Solid State Electronics, 5th Ed.	$24.95

Games

Master SimCity/SimEarth	$19.95
Master Ultima	$16.95

Hardware/Technical

First Book of Modem Communications	$16.95
First Book of PS/1	$16.95
Hard Disk Power with the Jamsa Disk Utilities	$39.95
IBM PC Advanced Troubleshooting & Repair	$24.95
IBM Personal Computer Troubleshooting & Repair	$24.95
Microcomputer Troubleshooting & Repair	$24.95
Understanding Fiber Optics	$24.95

IBM: Business

10 Minute Guide to PC Tools 7	$9.95
10 Minute Guide to Q&A 4	$9.95
First Book of Microsoft Works for the PC	$16.95
First Book of Norton Utilities 6	$16.95
First Book of PC Tools 7	$16.95
First Book of Personal Computing, 2nd Ed.	$16.95

IBM: Database

10 Minute Guide to Harvard Graphics 2.3	$9.95
Best Book of AutoCAD	$34.95
dBASE III Plus Programmer's Reference Guide	$24.95
dBASE IV Version 1.1 for the First-Time User	$24.95
Everyman's Database Primer Featuring dBASE IV Version 1.1	$24.95
First Book of Paradox 3.5	$16.95
First Book of PowerPoint for Windows	$16.95
Harvard Graphics 2.3 In Business	$29.95

IBM: Graphics/Desktop Publishing

10 Minute Guide to Lotus 1-2-3	$9.95
Best Book of Harvard Graphics	$24.95
First Book of Harvard Graphics 2.3	$16.95
First Book of PC Paintbrush	$16.95
First Book of PFS: First Publisher	$16.95

IBM: Spreadsheets/Financial

Best Book of Lotus 1-2-3 Release 3.1	$27.95
First Book of Excel 3 for Windows	$16.95
First Book of Lotus 1-2-3 Release 2.3	$16.95
First Book of Quattro Pro 3	$16.95
First Book of Quicken In Business	$16.95
Lotus 1-2-3 Release 2.3 In Business	$29.95
Lotus 1-2-3: Step-by-Step	$24.95
Quattro Pro In Business	$29.95

IBM: Word Processing

Best Book of Microsoft Word 5	$24.95
Best Book of Microsoft Word for Windows	$24.95
Best Book of WordPerfect 5.1	$26.95
First Book of Microsoft Word 5.5	$16.95
First Book of WordPerfect 5.1	$16.95
WordPerfect 5.1: Step-by-Step	$24.95

Macintosh/Apple

First Book of Excel 3 for the Mac	$16.95
First Book of the Mac	$16.95

Operating Systems/Networking

10 Minute Guide to Windows 3	$9.95
Best Book of DESQview	$24.95
Best Book of Microsoft Windows 3	$24.95
Best Book of MS-DOS 5	$24.95
Business Guide to Local Area Networks	$24.95
DOS Batch File Power with the Jamsa Disk Utilities	$39.95
Exploring the UNIX System, 2nd Ed.	$29.95
First Book of DeskMate	$16.95
First Book of Microsoft Windows 3	$16.95
First Book of MS-DOS 5	$16.95
First Book of UNIX	$16.95
Interfacing to the IBM Personal Computer, 2nd Ed.	$24.95
The Waite Group's Discovering MS-DOS, 2nd Edition	$19.95
The Waite Group's MS-DOS Bible, 4th Ed.	$29.95
The Waite Group's MS-DOS Developer's Guide, 2nd Ed.	$29.95
The Waite Group's Tricks of the UNIX Masters	$29.95
The Waite Group's Understanding MS-DOS, 2nd Ed.	$19.95
The Waite Group's UNIX Primer Plus, 2nd Ed.	$29.95
The Waite Group's UNIX System V Bible	$29.95
Understanding Local Area Networks, 2nd Ed.	$24.95
UNIX Applications Programming: Mastering the Shell	$29.95
UNIX Networking	$29.95
UNIX Shell Programming, Revised Ed.	$29.95
UNIX: Step-by-Step	$29.95
UNIX System Administration	$29.95
UNIX System Security	$34.95
UNIX Text Processing	$29.95

Professional/Reference

Data Communications, Networks, and Systems	$39.95
Handbook of Electronics Tables and Formulas, 6th Ed.	$24.95
ISDN, DECnet, and SNA Communications	$49.95
Modern Dictionary of Electronics, 6th Ed.	$39.95
Reference Data for Engineers: Radio, Electronics, Computer, and Communications, 7th Ed.	$99.95

Programming

Advanced C: Tips and Techniques	$29.95
C Programmer's Guide to NetBIOS	$29.95
C Programmer's Guide to Serial Communications	$29.95
Commodore 64 Programmer's Reference Guide	$24.95
Developing Windows Applications with Microsoft SDK	$29.95
DOS Batch File Power	$39.95
Graphical User Interfaces with Turbo C++	$29.95
Learning C++	$39.95
Mastering Turbo Assembler	$29.95
Mastering Turbo Pascal, 4th Ed.	$29.95
Microsoft Macro Assembly Language Programming	$29.95
Microsoft QuickBASIC Programmer's Reference	$29.95
Programming in ANSI C	$29.95
Programming in C, Revised Ed.	$29.95
The Waite Group's BASIC Programming Primer, 2nd Ed.	$24.95
The Waite Group's C Programming Using Turbo C++	$29.95
The Waite Group's C: Step-by-Step	$29.95
The Waite Group's GW-BASIC Primer Plus	$24.95
The Waite Group's Microsoft C Bible, 2nd Ed.	$29.95
The Waite Group's Microsoft C Programming for the PC, 2nd Ed.	$29.95
The Waite Group's New C Primer Plus	$29.95
The Waite Group's Turbo Assembler Bible	$29.95
The Waite Group's Turbo C Bible	$29.95
The Waite Group's Turbo C Programming for the PC, Revised Ed.	$29.95
The Waite Group's Turbo C++Bible	$29.95
X Window System Programming	$29.95

Radio/Video

Camcorder Survival Guide	$14.95
Radio Handbook, 23rd Ed.	$39.95
Radio Operator's License Q&A Manual, 11th Ed.	$24.95
Understanding Fiber Optics	$24.95
Understanding Telephone Electronics, 3rd Ed.	$24.95
VCR Troubleshooting & Repair Guide	$19.95
Video Scrambling & Descrambling for Satellite & Cable TV	$24.95

For More Information, See Your Local Retailer Or Call Toll Free
1-800-428-5331

All prices are subject to change without notice. Non-U.S. prices may be higher. Printed in the U.S.A.

Turn to Sams For Complete Hardware and Networking Information

The Business Guide to Local Area Networks
William Stallings
400 pages, 7 3/8 X 9 1/4, $24.95 USA
0-672-22728-2

LAN Desktop Guide to Printing with NetWare
Sams
350 pages, 7 3/8 X 9 1/4, $27.95 USA
0-672-30084-2

More Hardware & Networking Titles

The First Book of Personal Computing Second Edition
W.E. Wang & Joe Kraynak
275 pages, 7 3/8 X 9 1/4, $16.95 USA
0-672-27385-3

The First Book of PS/1
Kate Barnes
300 pages, 7 3/8 X 9 1/4, $16.95 USA
0-672-27346-2

IBM PC Advanced Troublshooting & Repair
Robert C. Brenner
304 pages, 7 3/8 X 9 1/4, $24.95 USA
0-672-22590-5

IBM Personal Computer Troubleshooting & Repair
Robert C. Brenner
400 pages, 7 3/8 X 9 1/4, $24.95 USA
0-672-22662-6

Interfacing to the IBM Personal Computer, Second Edition
Lewis C. Eggebrecht
432 pages, 7 3/8 X 9 1/4, $24.95 USA
0-672-22722-3

LAN Desktop Guide to E-mail with cc:Mail
Bruce Fryer
350 pages, 7 3/8 X 9 1/4, $24.95 USA
0-672-30243-8

Microcomputer Troubleshooting & Repair
John G. Stephenson & Bob Cahill
368 pages, 7 3/8 X 9 1/4, $24.95 USA
0-672-22629-4

Understanding Local Area Networks, Second Edition
Stan Schatt
300 pages, 7 3/8 X 9 1/4, $24.95 USA
0-672-27303-9

SAMS

See your local retailer or call 1-800-428-5331.